the evolution of a **cro-mag**non

PUNKHOuse
A division of The I S Organization

Punkhouse Publishing Company
601 West 26th Street
Suite 1247
New York, New York 10001
mail@punkhouse.org

PRINTED IN THE UNITED STATES OF AMERICA!

Distributed by Punkhouse Publishing Company.

ISBN-13: 978-0-9800657-0-1

the EVOLUTION of
a CRO-MAGNON

john joseph

Dedicated to Srila Prabhupada
and all his sincere followers

"He who wrestles with us strenghtens our nerves and
sharpens our skill. Our antagonist is our helper"

Edmund Burke

contents

foreword

Nineteen seventy-seven was the year that serial killer, "Son of Sam" wreaked havoc in New York City, Elvis died, and the lights went out in New York. Disco battled punk as the Sex Pistols' Never Mind the Bollocks and the Bee Gees disco soundtrack, Saturday Night Fever, dropped simultaneously. It was also my first year on the streets and what I learned that year not only taught me the skills to make money to survive, but how to survive in the face of life and death situations. Call me a freak, but I thrived on it. The danger of who would try to rob you, stab you, shoot you, hustle you; or who you were going to hustle or have to throw down on. All 130 pounds of me thought I was invincible and you had to think like that back then, because New York City was a different place. It was a jungle and just as an animal living in the wild has to fight for its survival, risking life and limb to eat or sleep, the city was no different.

The 42nd Street Disneyland shit you see today didn't exist; it was simply known as, "The Deuce." I spent many cold winter nights there listening to the "oohs" and "ahhs" and, "Yes baby, fuck me harders!" coming from the screen in some 24-hour, buck and a half porno theatre, as I slept with one eye open and a blade in my pocket.

There was no East Village in Manhattan with its trendy little cafes, bars, and shops. It was called Alphabet City, the LES or Loisaida, a drug addict's heaven, filled with junkies, musicians and your hybrid junkie-musicians. Death lurked around the corner with gangs like the Hitmen and the Allen Street Boys who let you know very quickly that if you were an outsider of the Caucasian persuasion you dared not venture down to those parts without an escort, day or night.

Max's Kansas City, The Mudd Club, CBGB's, Studio 54, Hurrah's, Berlin Club, and The Fun House were just a few of the popular clubs back in '77 and to say they were out of control is an understatement. The city's parks were hunting grounds where dead bodies turned up regularly. Places like Union Square Park, Forrest Park, and Grover Cleveland Park (nicknamed "The Carbines") were open-air drug markets where you could get anything you needed to expand your mental horizons.

When most kids my age were just hitting puberty, I was on my own, a seventh grade dropout running wild. I earned my degree from "The University of the Streets," where my teachers were a bizarre cast of characters including the likes of Junior Nuts, "Demented" Dougie, Bobby K., Crazy Dave, Disco, Bobbie Bird, Buckles, Computer, AWOL Airborne Paratrooper J.K. and my favorite, a low-life hustling junkie named Mikey "Debris."

It was a magical time in the city and I wouldn't trade my experiences for all the money in the world. There was never a dull moment and plenty of, "Holy fuckin' shits!" Nowadays people spend big money on extreme sports to get that ultimate adrenaline rush. I didn't need to travel far and wide in search of danger and adventure. All I had to do was step out of the burnt-out building I lived in, or wander into certain neighborhoods, and I had all the danger, adventure and adrenaline I could handle.

I'll get back to describing all the insane shit that went down back then, but first things first. In any story there needs to be an inciting incident; an event that throws the central character's life out of balance, sending him on a quest to restore that balance in some way, as he struggles through life and death decisions which put him at greater and greater amounts of risk.

My writing teacher, Robert McKee, (without whose knowledge and inspiration this book would never have been written) says that to live meaningfully, is to be at perpetual risk.

Well, from the moment of my conception, risk and I were on a first name basis. Shortly after coming into this world, at the age of five, would come my inciting incident. Most of the details about that night I don't remember, so I had to get them from my mom, but it would be the event that would change my flight plan forever and send me on a new course... a course under the radar.

peace and love?

chapter 1

The year was 1967. Vietnam was raging and the hippies were having their love-ins. But my mom (Marie) my two brothers (Eugene and Frank), and I had our own little guerilla war going down right here in the states. See, we were dodging my pops, a southpaw welterweight who was a violent prick to my mom the entire time they were married. He basically used her as a human punching bag. She, in turn, lived as a prisoner of her own fear, flinching every time he lifted his hand, or jumping at the slightest sound in the middle of the night. I remember telling her a while back that I'd picked up boxing as a hobby. She got this spooked look on her face and told me that when I was little, I hugged her and said, "Don't worry Mommy, I'm gonna be a fighter one day and I'm gonna beat him up for all the times he's hit you."

When we were kids, my mom always made us sleep close to her, just in case we had to make a quick getaway, like we had so many times before. Not that it did us any good, because my dad knew everyone in the neighborhood and it was only a matter of time before someone told him where we were hiding. Inevitably he would find us and convince my mom that things were fine using one of his famous cliché lines like, "Things are gonna be different this time baby, I'm a changed man" or "Marie, I'd die if I ever lost you." Sure enough, she would go back to him and within days the beatings would start again. Well, this time things were different. He beat her so badly that she finally wised-up and decided to leave his ass for good.

We were living in a tiny, one-room dump on the ground floor of a building in Queens. It was a rainy night. Mom took a few Valium and a handful of other mysterious narcotics she'd been prescribed for her recent "nervous breakdown." I still remember the thunder, the flashes of lightning and the surreal moment of dead silence just before the front door came crashing in – and my world along with it. I huddled with my two brothers, frozen with fear, staring at my father. He looked like a rabid animal as he stood there soaking wet and sopping drunk. Mom was clearly woozy from the pills, but she managed to scream at us to run away. My pops mumbled something then he charged at her and began beating her around the apartment like a rag doll. I still remember the sound of a lamp being smashed to pieces – a sound that scared the shit out of me because it told me what was happening wasn't a nightmare. It was all too real, and we were helpless to stop him. We watched in horror as he beat her, until a policeman finally burst in and gave my father a shot with his billy club. Luckily, the old landlady upstairs had called the police when she heard the commotion. If she hadn't, I'm sure my father would have killed my mother or come damn close.

The last memory I have of that night is being in the back seat of a police car and looking out the rear window at the flashing lights. There was a very eerie silence that was only broken by the sound of the windshield wipers slapping back and forth and my two brothers sniffling and wiping at their tears. I remember keeping my eyes locked on those bright, pulsing lights, as we were driven away. We were all crying and the cop turned around and said, "Hey little guys, don't worry, everything's gonna be okay." Somehow, I knew better. I knew it was just the beginning of a long, bleak journey. I had no idea when, or if, I would ever see my mother again. I just kept staring out that window until the lights faded and my view was consumed by total darkness.

My father continued his campaign of terror against my mom and she fell deeper and deeper into depression. She began taking more and more medication, until she was barely able to get out of bed. We moved again, the welfare was cut off and we hardly ate. It was around that same time that our new landlady, Mrs. Mc-Something-or-other, discovered my older brother, Eugene, out in the snow, riding his bike around a tree in his underwear, while Mom was passed out from all the pills she took. The landlady called the cops and reported her to social services. She was deemed an unfit mother by the State of New York and we were taken away.

Eugene went to live with my grandparents while my younger brother, Frank, and I were sent to the Angel Guardian Orphanage Home for Children in Rockville Centre, Long Island. The only things I really remember about that place were the red night-lights and the way they lit the large communal sleeping room. The room housed thirty to forty beds, and it echoed with the heart-wrenching sound of kids crying all night long.

Sounds like hell, don't it? Well, it looked like hell too... a glowing red pit of despair! God only knows what the rest of those poor little souls went through, or what their stories were. At that very moment, our pasts didn't matter anymore. What mattered were our futures. The one common bond that we all shared in that cavernous, scarlet-hued room was the terrible fear and ominous uncertainty about what those futures might bring.

We spent several months in the Angel Guardian orphanage, before they finally sent us to a foster family somewhere in Brooklyn. I have just a few memories of that family. They lived in an apartment complex, where there were a lot of black and Spanish people. They smoked all the time. And they used to feed us hash – nasty crap in a can, made from various kinds of non-descript, ground-up meat. Can you say ALPO? For some unexplained reason they gave us up after a few months (thank God). At that point, Eugene rejoined us for our next move. That's when we went to live with the Sheridans' in Brooklyn.

The Sheridans were unlike anyone we had ever known. They were actually a really nice family. Mr. Sheridan was a mailman and his wife was the nicest lady I had ever met. I honestly believe that they loved the three of us, because they treated us like their own kids. They took us everywhere: the zoo, the museums, the beach, and Coney Island. It was wonderful. At school, our teacher made us plant tulips in a decapitated milk carton, because she said spring represented new beginnings. I gave the flower to Mrs. Sheridan as a symbol of our new life with our new family and she cried.

The Sheridans had a son named Tommy. He had long hair, played the guitar, and walked around acting really weird all the time (the acid perhaps?). He only knew one song on that guitar... "Sunshine of Your Love," by Cream, and he played that riff over and over and over. To this day, I still have that fuckin' song stuck in my head!

What I've learned, from talking to shrinks about kids who've witnessed a lot of abuse, or are victims of either sexual or physical abuse, is that they try and bury it deep into their subconscious. Eventually, though, those emotions will surface, sometimes along with violent behavior. After living with the Sheridans for about a year, mine started to surface. The Sheridans bought us an Erector Set, a classic toy made up of a collection of metal rods and a bunch of nuts and bolts. The idea was to build cranes, buildings, or whatever you could think of. I guess they thought it would be a good bonding experience for us to work together as a family and build something in the basement. Now, Frank could give two shits about building anything and Eugene just didn't like to share. Big problem. I already resented him for the fact that he got to live with my grandparents, while Frank and I went to the orphanage and then had to live with the family that fed us ALPO.

One day, shortly after we got the Erector Set, I snuck into the basement and Eugene was at the worktable, building away. His back was turned and he was oblivious to the fact that I was behind him, bent on his destruction. I crept up, picked up a metal rod and smashed him over the head with it. I dropped him to the floor as his head oozed with blood. It took a shit-load of butterfly bandages to close the gash. Even to this day, he gets mileage from it, by telling people, "You wanna know what a prick John was when we were kids? One day he…"

Next it was my little bro's turn. The big toy every kid had to have back then was an airplane that flew around in circles on a three-foot wire and did stunts, which my birth mother got me for Christmas. Of course, I warned both of my brothers not to touch it, but I guess Frank didn't get the memo, because one day, while I was out playing at my mom's on a visit, he broke it. I knew my revenge had to be especially cruel and painful.

I waited until the next day before I struck back, playing it off the entire time like everything was cool. I convinced him that I wasn't mad. But the fact was, things weren't cool. I was mad as hell, and right after lunch I was going to give him a sensation of unbelievable joy. Frank's Christmas present was an electric train set and I convinced the gullible little fucker that to experience that "joyous" sensation all he had to do was put his tongue on the metal train tracks.

I know what you're thinking. As mad as I was, I wasn't quite that cruel! My idea was to just run his tongue over with the train. In my own defense, I wasn't familiar with the laws of electricity or the conductive properties of saliva, at such a young age.

All the same, the minute he put his tongue on the tracks I threw the power switch on. Frank's tongue sizzled and smoked and he went flying backward, screaming in pain. His tongue swelled to three times its normal size and for the next week I laughed myself sick every time he opened his mouth.

To say I had a mean streak was putting it mildly. I was acting out because of the violence I'd witnessed towards my mom. Not being able to do anything to help her made me feel helpless, powerless. As a result, I was out to get anyone who fucked with me. I lashed out at anyone who crossed me in any way. Even worse, as if to complete the perfect circle of violence and irony, my mom would continuously remind me that my temper was just like my dad's. That only made things worse.

As a result of my emerging rage, I even managed to get kicked out of Catholic school at a young age. A sexually frustrated nun decided to teach me not to be the class clown by beating me with a ruler. I turned the tables by grabbing the ruler out of her hands and beating her ass right out of the classroom and down the hall. Her previous victims cheered me on the entire time. That was 1970, just about the same time that we learned that Mr. Sheridan had cancer and that our time with those two loving souls had come to an end.

The next time around we weren't so lucky. Once again the authorities split us up. Eugene went to stay with a foster family on Long Island, N.Y., but the house was later shut down because some weird shit was going on. But for now, let's get to the wonderful foster parents who took me and Frank: the Valentis of Deer Park, Long Island.

the Valentis - round one

chapter 2

Nick and Rose Valenti were Italian immigrants. I don't know what rat-infested, small pox-infected cargo ship these two parasitic pieces of shit came over on, but what I do know is that it should have sunk to the bottom of the ocean before they had their intestines eaten by sharks. They had two, twenty-something-year-old kids by birth, a boy named Vito (who was actually cool) and Fran, who was a greedy, fat bitch. They also had three other foster kids: a teenage girl named Diane and her two teenage brothers, Harold and Tony. The three of them wore plastic safety helmets and rode a big yellow bus to special ed. school. In other words, they had serious issues, many of which were the result of being in some pretty fucked up foster homes prior to the Valentis.

The morning we arrived at the vomit-orange colored house on West 7th Street, they had the entire family standing in the driveway, lined-up along side Mrs. Valenti's perfectly manicured rose bushes. Rose Valenti had a keen sense of style. She thought it was a great idea to announce her presence to the entire neighborhood by having scores of rose bushes all over the front of the property. Presumably, it was a cardinal sin to have any other form of plant life out front. You could forget about trying to tell her that she over did it, because according to her, Italians wrote the book on style.

I still laugh about how tacky the Guidos in New York were back in the day, with their overly sculpted hairdos (we called them hair-don'ts), tight clothes, moronic dialect, gold chains, and especially, their cars. It was a regular occurrence to see them driving around seven deep, hanging out of the windows yelling dumb shit to girls in their oh-so-mookish accents like, "Hey sweetheart, why don't ya take a ride wit us and we'll drink some fuckin' Jacobazzi (cheap Italian wine) under the stars!"

The Irish - or for that matter, just about everyone else in NYC - didn't get along with the Italians. They lived in their neighborhoods, dated their own, partied at their clubs and if you accidentally ventured into their bar, or their park, or hit on one of their girls, out came the Guido sticks and their famous line, "Fuuhhget about it... bats ain't for fuckin' baseball!" (Insert sounds of broken bones here)

We pulled into the Valentis' driveway and got out of the car. It was like a scene from a movie. They even had a welcome banner with our names on it. Our social worker, Bob Hayes, walked us up the driveway and stood us in front of Rose and Nick, introducing them as our new parents. When Mrs. Valenti bent over to give me a kiss hello, all I could do was stare at the big, hairy, black mole under her nose, her mustache and those yellow teeth. Her husband, Nick, was coughing and it wasn't just any old cough, either. This was a deep, brutal, hacking cough that almost made him vomit. He extended his nicotine-stained fingers (heavy with the weight of three massive gold rings) to shake my hand. Between gasps of breath he managed to say, "Welcome, son." I turned to Mr. Hayes, scared shitless and begged him to get us the hell out of there. Call it kid's intuition, but something immediately told me that these people weren't normal. Mr. Hayes assured us that we were going to love it there. Then he quickly turned around, got in his car and drove off. A year would pass before we would see Mr. Hayes again.

The Valentis walked us into their house. To my horror, every fuckin' thing in it was red - thick shag rug, furniture and even the wallpaper. It was just like the orphanage – that place with the red night-lights and the crying kids – only ten times worse. The carpets had plastic runners and God help you if you stepped off them and onto her precious carpet. The furniture was Mediterranean-style: gold with red crushed-velvet cushions, and these, too, were covered in thick plastic. The wallpaper? You guessed it... red roses. We were in hell!

Mr. Valenti said he was going to show us our room. He walked us into a small den area with two beds. I immediately thought, "This is cool," but when I went to put my bags on one of the beds he snapped, "That's for our guests, your room is in here." He opened another door that led to the garage and gestured for us to enter. There were no beds, just U.S. Army-style cots. I looked at him confused before he snatched our bags and threw them on top of the empty cots.

The first lesson we learned from living there came at that moment. It was delivered in two parts, before and after another violent hacking spasm: the only time we were ever to be allowed in the house was to sleep or work, and we were never, ever to question the man with the hacking cough and the heavy gold rings.

The next morning we were introduced to our real home (a screened-in patio in the backyard that was connected to the house) and to the Valentis' dog, Smokey. Smokey was a dirty, white Husky that was never once let off his chain the entire six years I lived there. Instead, he was hooked to a metal stake in the ground, that would only allow him to run in circles all day and all night, dragging around his turds, hairballs and the half-gallon plastic milk jugs that Mrs. Valenti cut down to make his dog bowls. Since he ran on the same patch of land for so long, he eventually wore away the grass and also dug a five-foot circular ditch in the ground. When you entered the backyard and Smokey's domain, you couldn't even see him unless he climbed up on his beat-up doghouse, which was perched on the island in the center of the moat he created. All you'd see was a cloud of dirt and you'd hear the barking and the sound of the milk jugs being dragged around. Then before you knew it, the horrible stench of shit coming from his ditch would linger over the entire backyard. Smokey's ditch was right next to the patio where my brother and I now lived, and all the patio screens had holes in them so it's safe to say there wasn't a motherfucker on all of Long Island who could beat me in a fly swatting contest.

That same morning Rose Valenti hipped us to her idea of "fine cuisine." Our breakfast was a recipe straight outta Satan's cookbook. She had the nerve to actually scrape the white filling off of a dozen or so Oreo cookies with her lovely, yellow teeth (she only liked the cookie and didn't want to waste the filling) and spit it into a bowl. She then smeared the spit-soaked icing on a piece of stale, moldy-green Wonder Bread and served it to us with tea. For nearly six years, our breakfast was either Oreo-spit sandwiches or moldy bread and butter served with a refreshing gallon of tea. Some days we got lucky and were given Cheerios. But milk was too good for us, so she'd either pour tea over our cereal, or give us Carnation powdered milk. It was the exact same food they fed Smokey, and they let us know where we stood in the pecking order by feeding him first.

When it came time to eat, it turned into a competition between us and Smokey. He could feel the tension, because every time we came near his moat, he would growl and guard his plastic bowl. I understand why he did it though you see, on more than one occasion we were so hungry we would sneak into his doghouse, steal his MILK-BONE biscuits and chow down. Actually, when you're starving, they don't taste half-bad.

In retrospect, it's no wonder we were out of our minds… years of confinement, white bread, Oreo-spit and caffeine. Yeah, the caffeine amped us up all right and that was the idea! Right after breakfast it was time to go to work on the rose bushes, as well as the dozens of other flowers out back. Mrs. V. would walk around shouting, "Pick up the leaves! Take off the dead petals! Don't prune that way. Do it this way!"

After a few weeks of living there, I was picking up leaves from under her bushes when I looked through a gap in the fence. The neighbor's kids were playing in their pool. I watched as their mom brought them sandwiches and drinks on a little, sterling silver serving tray. They jumped out of the water, ran over to her and smothered her in kisses. I looked at that family and thought, "Maybe I'm being treated like this because I haven't told my mom and dad that I loved them. Maybe it's my fault." I remembered how happy Mrs. Sheridan had been when I brought her a tulip. So I located the most beautiful, fragrant, red rose I could find on the bush I was tending and plucked it. I walked in through the kitchen door smiling with the rose hidden behind my back. Mrs. V. turned around, surprised to see me in the house. "Mommy," I said, "I love you." I took my arm from behind my back and presented her with the rose. She just stared at it. I waited for a smile that never came. What came instead was a swift and powerful smack across the face, which sent me and the flower sailing across the room. As I tried to get to my feet, she shoved me out the door and began screaming about never touching her roses or entering her house without permission. As punishment for my crimes I was forced to sit on the patio for the rest of the afternoon. I cried as I listened to the neighbor's kids swimming in their pool shouting, "Marco! Polo!" and "You're it!" As they played games I wondered what the hell I'd done to deserve this place.

While we're on the subject of water, I should use this opportunity to describe how bathing worked at the Valentis'. I was there for a week and a half before it was announced that it was finally bath time. I walked into the bathroom, looked down and saw a tub caked with soap scum, human hair, and dirty water. I pulled the plug to drain it and then heard Mr. V.'s cough; something that had become the official warning of an impending ass whipping. He saw me draining the tub and greeted me with a hard punch to the side of my head, made worse with the weight of his heavy gold rings. The punch knocked me into the wall. This was another hard lesson being delivered: we were not worthy to bathe in anything better than wastewater. They sure as shit weren't about to run up their water or electric bill on us!

When it came time for Mrs. V. to clean her beloved carpets there were no vacuum cleaners. Oh hell no! Why should she waste electricity when she had five slaves with new toilet bowl brushes who could clean the carpets three times a week? We were required to clean the entire house, working the toilet brushes in precise circular motions to get her dyed-black hair and lint balls out of the carpet.

As we slaved on our hands and knees, she marched back and forth, yelled orders and farted in our faces. She swore by her cleaning technique, claiming we were "bringing them carpets back to life." She insisted there was no vacuum in the world that could do what we could do with those toilet brushes. Look out Hoover. Anyone know a good patent lawyer?

As for clothes, how do they say it in Italian? Oh yeah, we were given ungots (pronounced oon-gots). You know what ungots means? It means we got shit! In other words, we wore whatever we scavenged by climbing into The Salvation Army donation boxes. The clothes we stole practically stood up by themselves, because we wore them so long. When they finally did fall apart, we just climbed on in again and dug up a new wardrobe. One of the most embarrassing moments I ever experienced as a kid, happened when a kid at school spotted me wearing his old shirt. He told the entire class that I was wearing his throwaway hand-me-downs. That was just one of many in a long series of humiliations.

Not once did we visit the beach, have a picnic, barbecue or go to a single movie that summer. Keep in mind that these fuckers were getting about $200 a month for each of us for clothes, food and whatever else we needed. Multiply that six times and that's about $1,200 a month, which in 1970 was a shitload of money! We watched their kids, Vito and Fran, eating whatever they wanted, getting new clothes, new cars and basically everything and anything they ever desired, with our money! Fran's fat-ass loved to rub it in our faces that we were being treated this way. She had the nerve to eat in front of us, making overly exaggerated yummy noises as she consumed an insane allotment of calories each day. We were paying for their mortgage, their car payments, their clothes, their jewelry, their food and were never even allowed in the house, much less the car or the refrigerator. Time and time again we had to sit on the patio, swatting flies away from our rancid lunchmeats and moldy bread, as they ate barbecue. We could only imagine how delicious the food must have tasted.

On the weekends, no matter what season or weather condition, we woke up (usually with a knuckle sandwich to the head) before we were forced to walk the mile, or so, to the bakery to get Mr. V.'s order. His list always included fresh Italian bread, hard rolls, jelly and cream donuts, Kent cigarettes, milk and a newspaper. I didn't mind going because the guy who owned the bakery always put a little round pie plate on the counter full of cookie samples or other pastries. Since we were always the first customers of the day, it was usually piled to the top. We would place our order and wait for the baker to turn around then quickly stuff as many samples in our mouths and pockets as fast as we possibly could. When the guy returned with Mr. V.'s order, he would inevitably find his dish empty before giving us this raised eyebrow look. After a while, he must have figured out that we were just a couple of starving kids because day after day, we'd show up to find two full sample dishes on the counter. Sometimes the business owner would bring out pastries and rolls and tell us how he "accidentally" made too many and that we'd be helping him out if we'd take the extras. Fucking angel is what he was!

Another of our obligations during our so-called "summer vacations" at the Valentis' was to work on Mr. V.'s Benjamin Moore paint and wallpaper truck making deliveries. Every morning he'd drive us to the Rockville Centre warehouse, before we started work. We never met any of Mr. V.'s co-workers. He always made us wait down the block while he got his truck, because it was against company policy to have anyone besides employees on the truck. It certainly must have been against company policy to have two dirty, half-starved foster children doing all the fucking work! He just sat at the wheel smoking, coughing and screaming at the other drivers in traffic, while we busted our asses arranging the heavy boxes of paint and rolls of wallpaper. We never got paid, but we did get fed. We usually had coffee and buttered rolls in the morning, with a salami sandwich and a can of Coke for lunch. I hated being around him and I hated salami, but still I volunteered to work every day because it gave me an opportunity to get something substantial to eat. But more importantly, it allowed me to get off of Long Island. The job would frequently take us to Rockaway, Brooklyn and all over Manhattan. We even delivered in Flushing, Queens, which was right up the road from my mom's house. I used to fantasize about jumping off the truck and running away, but I never did. I just kept on delivering the wallpaper and paint and taking in the sites of the city, dreaming of the day I'd be free.

I was so glad when that first summer was over because I was desperate to start school. I remember lying on my cot in the garage on the last night of summer vacation, just thinking that if I told someone about what was going on at the Valentis' that they would help us. They would have to!

The first day of school began just like any other. As soon as I woke up I began working on the rosebushes and raking up Smokey's shit and hairballs. Then it was inside to scrub Rose's hairballs and breathe her methane, before some early morning carpet brushing. Work was followed by the usual vomitous breakfast. The thing that was most on my mind that morning was, what the hell was she going to give us for our first school lunch?

At the Sheridans', I had a Superman lunch box, complete with two sandwiches in little clear baggies, an apple or orange and money to buy an extra dessert and a drink. But come on now, this was Mrs. V. We knew her warped mind was going to come up with something really twisted. There were no lunch boxes or brown paper bags with our names written on them. Instead, we got the long, white, wax bags that her Italian bread came in. She also used polka-dotted Wonder Bread bags complete with moldy crumbs at the bottom to put that spoiled deli meat sandwich in.

As I marched off to school with my see-through, white bag I quickly found out what all the neighborhood kids thought about us. They yelled, "Freaks!" and Orphans!" as we walked by. "Holy shit," I thought. "This whole fuckin' town knows my business." Another thing I noticed when I arrived was that everyone at May Moore Elementary School had on brand new clothes except us. When I got to the lunchroom they were all staring at me and pointing. My inadequate meal was surrounded by a lunchroom full of immaculate suburban lunches. There was no way in hell that I was going to break out my two-foot-long bread bag, open it up and retrieve my Wonder Bread bag to woof down a purple and green, moldy sandwich.

I was so hungry and full of shame that I would hide the bag under the table, carefully unroll it and reach inside to pull out the second bag when…..SHIT! The little jerk sitting across from me reached under the table and quickly snatched it. He screamed for everyone to look, as he stood up and swung the bag around over his head like a helicopter's rotor blade. The entire lunchroom erupted in laughter at my misfortune. I was so pissed and embarrassed that I jumped up and socked the instigator dead in his mouth, before the room fell silent. I might have been a "freak" and an "orphan," but I was a freak and an orphan who'd fuck you up in a New York minute if you tried to diss me.

As the adult lunchroom monitor dragged me off to the principal's office by my ear, I thought, "Here's my chance to tell someone about what's going on at the Valentis'." I still remember the look of total disbelief on the principal's face when I told him the intimate details of life in that house. I described the beatings, the slave labor, the Oreo-spit... everything. He was stunned. The first thing he did was call the Valentis and make Mr. V. come and get me. Man, was Mr. V. pissed! He talked to the principal and convinced him that I was lying. According to him, I'd been traumatized by the violence I saw in my household, so I made up all the stories to gain sympathy and attention. He also claimed that I made up stories, so my mother would feel bad and would take me back. The principal fell for the Valenti bullshit - hook, line and sinker. He was convinced that no adult could ever do the things I was saying, especially to defenseless children.

The car ride home from school that day forever silenced my attempts to call for help from the outside world. As Mr. V. drove I didn't know what to expect as he traveled through unknown parts of Long Island. There was dead silence in the car only broken by Mr. V.'s coughing. I jumped every time I heard it. I had no idea where we were going. He just kept driving and coughing. Eventually, we drove down a road with a high fence. About 100 yards beyond the fence was a scary-looking, dark building. There were people behind the fence talking to themselves and other people in uniforms just standing around. What kind of place was this and why did he bring me here? As we drove by the main gate we passed a sign that stated Pilgrim State Mental Hospital. At that point the coughing stopped completely and it really freaked me out. Mr. V. drove around to the other side and pulled along the fence next to where a few extremely weird looking people congregated. He threw the car in park, came around to my side and opened my door, before yanking me out by the arm. He dragged me over to the fence and as I screamed bloody murder he yelled, "You don't like it where you're at mister?" He smashed my face against the fence and held it there as the mental patients shouted and stuck their fingers through the fence, grabbing at my eyes, ears, and nose. I was repeatedly punched in the head, as he shouted about how I needed to keep my big mouth shut and how he was going to show me what happened to snitches. I was terrified as Mr. V. pulled me by my hair and got in my face. "Take a good look, Garibaldi," he shouted. "'Cause this is your next stop. I'll have you locked up in here in a minute if you ever open your mouth to anyone again, you got me?" I nodded in agreement before he gave me another punch to the top of the head, "You got me?" I whimpered, "Yes."

I was only eight at the time and I honestly believed that he could put me in a place like that and no one would ever know I was there. I never told anyone anything again. Each day, I ate my lunch on the way to school, in order to avoid another humiliating lunchroom incident. I also took the beatings at home and I kept my mouth shut.

Mr. V. was a strict and crafty disciplinarian who knew not to punch us in the face, because that would leave visual marks and raise obvious suspicion at school. Instead he would punch us on the side or the top of the head with those heavy, motherfucking rings! Another one of his favorite forms of punishment was to whip us on the back of the legs with his belt. He also loved to pull our hair or yank on our ears as hard as he could. The sickest thing was, the more you screamed, the longer you were tortured, because that twisted fuck really got off on hurting us.

They say if you constantly beat a dog that it will eventually turn out to be one mean son of a bitch and it will turn on you. You might forget all the fucked up shit you did to it, but the dog doesn't forget. Just like that abused dog, I remembered every sick and demented thing the Valentis did to me during my stay there.

They once made me suffer in agony for more than a week with an abscessed tooth that caused me so much pain I began to vomit and hallucinate. They refused to take me to the free dentist at the Angel Guardian Home, because it was in Mineola, almost thirty minutes away, which was obviously a major inconvenience for them. Despite the pain and dangerously high fever from my infected gums, Mrs. V. just threw me out of the house every morning, while I begged her with tears in my eyes to be taken to a dentist. She denied me medical attention and I suffered through the most severe pain I had ever experienced in my life. Finally, after my jaw swelled to nearly the size of a baseball and puss oozed from my inflamed gums, I was taken to the dentist.

When I sat in the chair and the dentist examined me, he couldn't believe my condition. He performed emergency extraction surgery to remove the abscessed tooth.

He also asked how long I'd been in this condition, but before I could say anything, Mrs. Valenti quickly interjected, "Two days, but he only told us this morning." I spent the next two weeks on antibiotics fighting the infection.

After the Pilgrim State incident there was only one other minor outburst from me. One day after school, I went to a friend's house to flip baseball cards, which was all the rage in early-'70s. When I saw how amazing his house and family were I announced that I was running away from home. I climbed into a huge tree in my classmate's backyard and refused to come down. I told them I wanted to live up there and I really meant it! It was pretty funny to see my friend, and his entire family all standing below me at 9 p.m. trying unsuccessfully to coax me to come down. I was up there for more than an hour before they brought out their secret weapon.... Food! In exchange for coming out of the tree they would give me peanut butter and jelly sandwiches, coconut layer-cake smothered in shredded coconut, and milk with Bosco syrup. Before they could blink, I was on the ground stuffing the bait in my mouth. I ate everything, chugged the chocolate milk and ran home without ever telling my friend or his folks why I wanted to run away in the first place. For the next two years, I put up with everything the Valentis did to my little brother and me. I continued in silence and grew angrier as the days passed. Then one day everything changed. My big brother arrived and it was time to flip the script on these fuckers.

Eugene or, "E," as he was known in those days, was a cunning, little bastard. He would act like little Mr. Goodie Two Shoes to your face, but behind your back he'd be plotting to scam you out of your last quarter, or in our case, the last slice of moldy bread. It's no coincidence that this devious individual eventually found his way to Wall Street. Wall Street was built by hustlers and to put it simply, E put the capital "H" in hustle.

I'll give you a quick example of just how slick this motherfucker was in every aspect of the word, including the romance department. After hustling five or ten G's in some stock that according to E was a "sure-fire hit," (and weren't they all?) he'd go out on this party yacht that sailed around Manhattan to celebrate and play it off like he was a high roller. On the yacht there were always a bunch of gold-digging bitches. Their primary business was to scam the scammers out of the money they had scammed, by any means necessary. Of course, those means typically involved sex, but it didn't end there. Let me tell you folks, scamming is just like the food chain. The boyfriends of the gold-diggers, the guys that the gold-diggers actually loved, would just scam the gold-diggers out of the cash they had scammed. The bottom dwellers: the extra girlfriends of the gold-diggers' boyfriends, would then hustle a few dollars for themselves. They, in turn, would be fucking somebody else, too, and no doubt that person would be getting a little, until finally there was nothing left.

In any case, E was working it hard, handing out business cards and trying to pick up a few of these broads. One of the waitresses on the boat (call her Miranda) catches his eye (yeah, they get in on it too). Miranda was a Puerto Rican cutie from the Manhattanville Project Houses on the West Side of Harlem. She was looking for a rich, white boy to get her the fuck up out the PJs (the projects). So, E takes her out, wines and dines her and shows her the office - complete with his nameplate on the door. Miranda was like, "Ka-ching, ka-ching... jackpot!" She was seeing nothing but dollar signs and even had her bags packed and ready to go. Six months later, Miranda rolls over in her same old bed in the PJs and guess whose ass is sleeping right next to her, living rent free, farting away, telling her to turn up the air-conditioning before she headed off to work? El Gringo, easy mother fuckin' E, that's who! Miranda sat there scratching her head thinking, "Mira... how the fuck did this shit happen, yo?" Miranda, you were dealin' with a pro, that's how!

E was all business and to him, the Valenti household was no exception. As soon as he arrived, he immediately took charge of the food situation. From now on, we ditched our lunches on the way to school - tossing our bread bags down an open sewer a few blocks from the house. As the months passed, we would literally throw hundreds of lunches down there. E had a plan and according to him, from that day forward we were gonna, "eat like kings."

His gig went like this: we would wait until all the other kids left homeroom, then we would sneak into the closet where they stored their lunch boxes and nice brown baggies, close the door, and munch the fuck out. We had a smorgasbord going on! I'd take one kid's sandwich, another's cookies and some other kid's apple. You should have seen the look on their faces when they opened their lunch boxes and bags in the lunchroom. "Hey, where's my sandwich and Ring Dings?" "Who took my Yodels?" "My Funny Bones (my personal favorites) are missing!" I'd just burp loudly and think some smart-ass shit to myself like, "Yeah, and uh, kid, tell your mom to use a little less mustard tomorrow, okay?" I'd smile, feeling a little bit of satisfaction knowing that I got back at those little pricks in some small way for fucking with me.

E was also the mastermind behind stealing several UNICEF "Feed The Needy Children" donation boxes from the classrooms. With the proceeds from the scores, the three of us would stuff our faces with dinner and ice cream at Friendly's, before E would clown on the UNICEF kids by saying, "Shiiiit... fuck that! We needy too!"

On the nights when we went to bed hungry, E would organize the late night 'fridge raids that usually went down after midnight. He was the only one who had the balls to do it properly, because Frank and I were just too damn scared to step up. If we got caught we knew it was gonna mean the beating of our lives. But E was always out to prove just how easy getting over on these fuckers really was.

With his arrival, the Valentis were forced to move us out of the garage and into a little den, and that was cool. The three of us always stayed up late making plans and imagining what life would be like when we got outta there. We talked a lot about buying a customized van, which in the '70s was all the rage.

It would be just the three brothers, driving all over the country before moving to California. I would even steal magazines that had pictures of vans and together we customized the imaginary ride of our dreams. "Yeah man, I'm puttin' in that crushed-velvet interior and shag carpet. It's gotta have those wheels and I'm gonna finish it off with crazy air-brushed paintings of half-naked chicks in bikinis all over the outside."

Anyway, all those plans were for the future and we still had to survive the present situation, which naturally brought us back to the most basic necessity - food. We knew the Valentis kept the freshest bread in a big bread drawer in the kitchen. We thought E would just sneak in under the cover of darkness, grab some bread and bologna, or whatever was available in the 'fridge, sneak back into the den and we'd devour it, right? Wrong. We're talking about E here, people. You give this son of a bitch an inch and he'll not only take the yard, but he's coming back for the whole damn football field! His ass was in there toasting bread, making triple-decker sandwiches, cutting up friggin' tomatoes, lettuce, adding a little mayo, and opening cans of soup. Talk about balls; E had King Kong's nuts hanging.

When my number came up to do a raid I was scared shitless. I quietly snuck out of the den, up the small flight of stairs, crawled on all fours through the dining room and entered the kitchen. The second my hand touched the bread drawer, Mr. V. started coughing from his bedroom. That noise scared me shitless. I feared what might happen if he caught me red-handed, so I broke the world record for the 10-yard dash on the way back to our room! Once again, E had to save us by proving just how fearless he really was.

On Saturday night Mrs. V. always made her "world famous" marinara sauce for the following evening's family dinner. She would leave it on top of the stove to cool over night and let the bajouls (a hard-boiled egg wrapped in a flank steak) soak up the sauce. We knew those were off-limits, because she counted them. But they sure did look good. And believe me, we fantasized, sometimes drooling into the pot, just wishing we could sink our teeth into one. E was always the first to step up. Once the coast was clear, he'd dash off and steal some bread before giving us the signal to join him. The three of us would then stand around that huge pot of sauce before dunking the bread and munching the fuck out. I have to say, as rotten a human being as Mrs. V. was, she really knew how to make sauce.

Another weekend scam that we perfected was to go up and down the aisles of the local supermarket and just eat our way through the place. We'd munch on whatever we could get our hands on - chips, candy, bread, and donuts. The three of us would go to the register with our faces and clothes covered in crumbs and pay for a two-cent-piece of Bazooka. The girl at the register was obviously onto us, but I always made sure to flirt with her, so we always got away with it.

Another one of our scams was to stand outside the same supermarket and tell people that our mom forgot to pick us up and that we needed money to call her. People found the three of us irresistible – with our blonde hair and blue eyes – and the dimes piled up. Fuck dimes, they gave us dollars! They'd even treat us to donuts and hot chocolate from Dunkin' Donuts, while we were waiting for her to come pick us up. Hey, I had no problem with their generosity and the distinct smell of Dunkin' Donuts still sends my mind racing back to our time with the Valentis.

The three of us hustled 24/7 – even on the Lord's Day. Every Sunday the Valentis would drop us off at church, but instead of sitting through a boring-ass sermon, we'd go in the front door and scoot right out the back for an afternoon of panhandling. I truly believe that thieves and scammers aren't born, they're created. Survival is the primary human instinct, plain and simple. If you take any rich boy or Harvard-educated yuppie and drop his ass in some fucked up shit like we were dealing with, I guarantee he'd learn the fine art of the hustle just like we did. The funny shit was that the Valentis couldn't figure out how the hell we were gaining so much weight, with what little they were feeding us. As a matter of fact, Mr. Hayes even commented about how much we'd grown, when he made his bi-annual check-up. Of course, Mrs. V. took all the credit for it, explaining that it was due to her good old-fashioned, home-cooked Italian meals.

The second order of business that E took on after his arrival was hygiene. With his help we developed a trick for bathing on the way to school. We would usually stop at a local gas station, go into the bathroom, lock the door and strip down naked. We would then dump water over our heads from a little bucket and lather up with a green, greasy bar of Irish Spring. After rinsing off, we'd dry ourselves with the hand dryer and paper towels, before getting dressed. We'd then head to school, leaving a big mess behind.

One day we forgot to lock the door and a woman walked in on us in the middle of our "shower." The three of us turned around stunned, butt-naked and covered in green lather from head to toe. She screamed in shock and ran off. Jesus lady! You acted like you never saw three little naked kids with green soap suds all over them in a filthy gas station bathroom. That was the end of that gas station. But no worries, there were plenty of other stations in town to use as our private bathroom.

Even climbing in The Salvation Army box for clothes turned into fun, when E was around. We would always perform little skits with the clothes that we found. E would put on some woman's clothes. I'd dress up like Mr. V. and cough and Frank would put on five layers of clothes and pretend to be fat-ass Fran. "My carpets, get the specks!" E would mimic, adding the sound of her farting. I would cough, "Where the hell's my Kent's?" Frank would waddle around and whine, imitating Fran's horrible voice, "I'm starving. Make me something to eat!" We were learning one of life's most powerful lessons - how to laugh off the misery. I think even now, that's why the three of us have such an overly developed sense of humor. Laughter has always been our Prozac and either we took our meds or we'd go crazy.

Another thing that E did was keep a daily journal. For the next four years, we kept detailed records of everything that went down at the Valentis' house: the threats, the beatings, the shit they fed us, the work they forced us to do - everything. Well, almost everything - minus the most painful memories of all. Everything except the stuff that we couldn't even admit to ourselves was actually happening. That stuff we left out of our journal. And even now, up until this very point, for very personal reasons, I was considering leaving it out of this book. If I did leave it out though, that would deny a critical part of the story - a critical element that helped shape the characters.

In 2001, I took Robert McKee's world famous story seminar held in Manhattan's FIT school auditorium. He'd be up on stage and in the groove and if a cellphone or pager went off, or if someone interrupted his flow - look the fuck out! So, rule numero uno was, no questions, until the break. When the break came, I waited until the last person had asked their question and walked off. It was just me and Bobby McKee. I took a deep breath. "Mr. McKee," I said. "In terms of the unconscious desire of a protagonist who was abused as a kid…" He cut me off immediately. "Child abuse is the fuckin' cliché of the day. Simply bad writers trying to raise sympathy for a character we would otherwise not give two shits about. It's not the child abuse… it's about what they do as a result of it. That's what makes a great story."

No one had ever said anything like that to me before and it was true in more ways than one. If you crumbled, if you let your life fall to pieces as a result of what some scumbag did, then they'd won. I had never told anyone about the sexual abuse I suffered at the hands of Diane's two, helmet-wearing brothers, Harold and Tony. It had been eating at me for years, but I hadn't done anything about it.

The sexual abuse started, pretty much, as soon as I arrived at the Valentis'. It went on for years, although I can't specifically recall when it started or ended. They told me that if I said anything to anyone, I would never see my brothers again. They also told me that if I divulged that deep, dark secret that the state would shut the house down and my brothers and I would be separated forever. I knew what had taken place was wrong, but I believed their threats. So, I remained silent.

The process of writing this book is a form of therapy for me and if I don't spill my guts… all my guts… my healing won't be complete. I found ways to work out a lot of the other fucked up shit that happened to me, to some degree, but this plague was deeper and darker. This was the secret I kept from the world. And as I said, it truly was a cancer eating me alive. One thing's for sure though, I'll never forget the moment that I, Johnny fuckin' Cro-Mag, the tattooed street-surviving motherfucker, came clean.

A few years ago, I was writing a screenplay with my then girlfriend and writing partner, Priscilla Sommer. I used a lot of the stuff that happened at the Valentis' in the script. As I started digging into the past, all the shit that I had buried in my subconscious started to slowly surface. I began remembering the most minute details of my life. She couldn't believe what I was telling her about my childhood, but she also knew there was a lot more that I wasn't telling her. She never hinted or pried in any way, and because of that I trusted her immensely. She was, and still is, one of my best friends. We developed a really close relationship, because of that, confiding in each other about our childhoods.

All this shit was really opening old wounds, wounds that had never really healed in the first place. When we went to sleep one night I had a dream that brought me back to the Valenti house. All I remember was that it was winter and E, Frank and I, were freezing in the garage as we slept on our cots. Harold and Tony came over to my cot and angrily looked down at me. One snatched my pillow and the other took my blanket. Then they went back to their beds and went to sleep. I just lay there naked and shivering. I'm no dream analyst, but I'm willing to guess the dream had everything to do with the two of them stealing a part of my childhood. I woke up and started crying uncontrollably. She asked me what was wrong, but all I could say was, "Why did they do that to me?" She knew exactly what I was talking about. She held me all night as I cried and told her about the awful things they did.

I've met a lot of people who use their unhappy, abusive childhood as an excuse to be an abuser, a drug addict, an alcoholic or a con artist. But there comes a point in life when you can't use that excuse anymore. It's a crutch for weakness if you don't deal with it, because you never grow as a human being. My spiritual practice taught me an important principle in life - perhaps the most important - forgiveness. Not the corny "turn the other cheek" Bible-thumper sort of forgiveness. Fuck that! You swing on me and I will try and fuck your ass up, by any means necessary. No, this was deep forgiveness. This was the kind of shit you just have to do, because the power is not in your hands in the first place and you need to throw up those hands asking God for help. I've been around some of the toughest, scariest people you would ever want to meet and all of them, in some weird way or another, acknowledged God for his blessing. I was so angry into my early twenties for what was done to me as a kid, that I just wanted to hurt, maim or kill. I did whatever it took to let people know not to fuck with me. I had no desire to sit in therapy, because my therapy sessions consisted of causing pain to others.

Ultimately, I had to dig deeper and I had to seek change. I chanted and I set up a vegetarian food relief program to help the homeless on the streets of NYC. I kicked ass on stage, all over the world, with the Cro-Mags. But more importantly, I started writing down my thoughts and documenting the events of my life.

After years of working on myself (and believe me it's been a steep uphill battle), I've come to the point where my advice to anyone who has lived through negativity is to get it out some way. Express it. You can't just keep it bound up inside and let it eat at you, because it won't stop. And in the end it'll swallow you whole.

These days my brothers and I laugh about sweeping the carpets with toilet brushes, Smokey the dog, stealing food, and the rest of the crap at the Valentis', but the sexual abuse is still off limits. We just pretend it never happened.

I'm convinced that the collective denial has been terribly destructive, especially for my brothers who, as far as I know, have never acknowledged it. As a result, my younger brother's an alcoholic and a constantly relapsing drug addict, who also continued the cycle of bad parenting by pretty much abandoning his own two sons. He was also locked in an abusive relationship and thinks that all the drama with his psycho bitch means she loves him. E, on the other hand, never really shows his true emotions to anyone, but my mom and his son. So, E and Frank: You guys got my number. Maybe it's finally time to slay those demons and move on.

Despite the abuse we suffered at the hands of the Valentis, we always schemed on how we could get over on them. From the moment E arrived, his underhanded tactic was to kiss a whole lot of ass. Mr. V. could always be heard saying, "Why can't you just be like Eugene?" or "Because Eugene did so well this week with his chores he gets to pick a box of cereal." That was the big pay-off bribe. Whoever did the most work that week got to pick whatever breakfast cereal they wanted, Cap 'N Crunch, Count Chocula or Boo Berry. He'd get to eat the entire box in front of the losers, while we had butter and Oreo-spit sandwiches topped off with Mrs. V.'s black hair. What that fucker, Mr. V., didn't know was that innocent, little Eugene was just trying to find out where they kept the stash of cash. In the last home he stayed in, E had uncovered that those people were getting a substantial amount of money each month for clothes, food and all kinds of other stuff. Since the Valentis barely spent a dime on us and couldn't put the state issued funds in a legitimate bank account, he knew there had to be a bankroll hidden somewhere in the house. Oddly enough, I felt hurt when I found out about the money. It really drove home the sense of being unwanted. I then realized that there wasn't even the slightest chance that these people actually loved us, because it was all about the money. I had to let go of that hope because of what they had done. But I still had to call them Mom and Dad, and that pissed me off. As a result, I wanted swift revenge on the Valentis.

Every day while E was bringing those carpets to life or polishing their bedroom furniture, he searched for the hidden scratch. He rifled through everything, until he eventually hit pay dirt. Bingo! They kept hundreds and hundreds of dollars stashed in a metal security box in fat-ass Fran's bedroom closet. Although the box was well hidden and took a while to find, they also keep a change jar that was sitting out in plain view. During our housecleaning sessions we developed a signal where, when the coast was clear, to run downstairs and help ourselves to the money. I would punch my palm with a closed fist and say, "Fran," which translated as, "Hit Fran."

At first we never took a lot of money. We took $5 one day, and $10 a couple of days later. Basically, just enough to get some food, so that we didn't have to go to bed hungry. I did spend $3 of the pilfered cash on one luxury item for myself - a small, black transistor radio. I would retreat with it under my blanket and enter my own little world: a world where Mr. V.'s beatings couldn't get to me; a world where I was the boss.

Immersed in the music or the banter of the D.J., I would forget about the growling in my empty stomach or the mean kids in the neighborhood who called me an orphan or a freak. Having the radio up to my ear was my nightly ritual and my solace. Harry Harrison was the D.J. on WABC-AM and the songs he played literally saved my life. Most of my favorite feel-good anthems were what I guess you would call '70's "black" music: Sly and the Family Stone's "Stand," Kool and the Gang's "Jungle Boogie," and Stevie Wonder's "Superstitions," just to name a few.

Those uplifting songs made me feel like I could survive anything, no matter how bad it was in that house. They helped me keep my chin up high and fight on for another day. Only E and Frank knew I had the radio. So, I had to hide it because, if Mr. V. caught me, a shattered radio and another ass-kicking was sure to follow.

Of course, I liked other genres of music, too, and a lot of those songs were featured in the Channel 11 TV show, The Now Explosion. Strangely, when I think about those songs, they bring back memories of certain foods. I suppose it's not too surprising. When you're starving, every single thought or memory, good or bad, can be related to food. For instance ever since the Sheridans, fish sticks remind me of the theme song from The Howdy Doody Show. The Sheridans were Catholic and never ate meat on Friday during Lent, and every time we watched that show we ironically had fish sticks for dinner. Olive loaf makes me think of Don McLean's song, "American Pie." Why? Because the first time it ever showed up in Mrs. V.'s sick lunch program, I threw it out and stole two Hostess fruit pies from a supermarket. Oatmeal? That equates to Rod Stewart's, "Maggie May." I still remember stealing a package of uncooked Quaker Oatmeal from the Valentis' closet late one night and devouring it, under my blanket, as that song played on my radio. Bill Withers' "Lean On Me" takes me back to stuffing my face with ice cream at Friendly's. It also makes me think of how strong E was for swiping money from Fran's room to feed his two little brothers.

In addition to my blanket and radio there was another musical ritual for me: Soul Train. Vito gave us a little, round TV, which everyone had in the '70s and because the antenna was broken, we stuck a metal hanger in the back of it and fucked with it, until we eventually managed to get a fuzzy reception. I remember watching Soul Train in the den every Saturday afternoon. Those brothers and sisters danced their asses off, and they had some sick moves, too! The original host, Don Cornelius, was the coolest, flyest motherfucker ever! He would sign off every show with his famous "Peace and Soul" outro, before he would flash a peace sign and a cartoon train would boogie down the tracks and the words "The Soooooooooooul Train" would later blast across the screen.

I was so envious of those brothers and sisters on Soul Train. I used to wish I was black because, in my opinion, they were just so much cooler than any white people I had ever met. Back then, the brothers and sisters had it rough in this country. But you couldn't tell that by looking at them. Oh, hell no! What you saw was the joy. They just danced the pain and frustration away. Their happiness was contagious and I know, because I caught it. With all that I was going through, just watching those beautiful people having so much fun had me dancing around and imitating them. When I danced, my own pain didn't seem like such a big deal. Music was medicine to me back then, and to this day it's what keeps me positive. It keeps me keepin' on. Thanks, Don. "Peace and soul" to you brother, wherever you are!

Months passed and we started to save a little bit of the money we were taking from the Valentis. We dreamed about saving enough to buy that customized van and start our journey around the country. One day when we got home from school, Mr. V. was standing there in the yard waiting for us. He looked really pissed and ordered the three of us into the house. "Holy fuckin' shit," I thought. "Did he know what we were doing? Had he noticed the missing money?" We had some money and a few candy bars in our pockets and there was no time to hide it. If he searched us, we were dead meat. We marched into the house, ready to receive the beating of our lives. He stood beside the kitchen table smoking a cigarette and looking down at us menacingly. I braced for impact, but instead of blasting us with a closed fist he said, "Your mother wants to take you this weekend for a visit. Mr. Hayes is going to be here in an hour to take you to the city."

Was this a cruel joke? I wouldn't have put it past a fuckin' low-life like him to say, "Ah, just kidding." We stood there completely stunned as he bent over and got in our faces. "So what are you going to tell her?" he asked in a firm tone. "That we love you and love it here," I said quickly. He smiled and patted my head. Then Mrs. V. entered with three new outfits that included shoes. She told us all about trips to IHOP we were going to make, summer pool passes and the new outfits we were going to get as soon as we got back on Monday - if we were good and kept our mouths shut. Mr. V. had been given a raise, she claimed, and now they could afford to give us all this really nice stuff. Yeah, right bitch!

People wonder how all this crazy shit can go on in these foster homes and no one ever finds out about it. In my case, the Valentis threatened and beat the hell out of us to keep us quiet. Second, the social workers rarely ever showed up and when they did it was always announced, "I'll be there next Tuesday, Nick." Brilliant asshole, you just let Nick know he's got five days to put the fear of God into us and get everything in order. Not once did Mr. Hayes make a surprise visit. If he did, we would have been pulled out of that house much sooner.

On the way to my mom's place in Jackson Heights, Queens, Mr. Hayes explained to us, how she really loved us and one day wanted to have us back. He also said that she was still too sick, and if we brought it up, it would just upset her. When he asked about how the Valentis were treating us, we lied. E said we'd better not rock the boat with the Valentis just yet. We had the diary as our secret weapon and that was the torpedo that was going to sink them to Davy Jones's fuckin' locker once and for all.

We pulled up to an apartment building on 85th Street, a block from the No. 7 train, and there she was. She was so pretty just standing there with her straight, fine blonde hair, and a big smile on her face. We ran out of the van, raced up to her and started crying. Even Mr. Hayes was moved. "I love you guys," she kept saying over and over and we knew she meant it. She would have done anything for us. Now that I know the details of how fucked up her life had been, I wish I hadn't held so much of what happened to us, against her. As a kid, I always thought she didn't take us back because her boyfriend, Carl, didn't like us being around. I now realize that she was scared to death of failure, because she had previously failed in so many ways, especially in her choices of mates. If she failed at parenthood, I know it would have killed her. At that moment, I didn't want to think about any of that shit. No way, because we had a lot of catching up to do. Besides, Saturday meant Soul Train and that was the perfect opportunity to show off my dance moves.

That Friday night we literally ate her out of house and home. We started with pizza and ice cream, which I ate until my stomach nearly burst. Then I ate some more. My mom was a great cook. She made mashed potatoes, mac and cheese, burgers, and chicken cutlets. I'm a vegetarian now and would never eat any of that shit, but hey, back then it was dope. She noticed that we ate like we'd never seen food before and the fact is we hadn't seen much of it in a long, long time. I just kept eating and eating and looking for flies to swat, but there were none. That night we stayed up really late watching Creature Feature, a horror show on Channel 11. We watched a scary movie called, The Crawling Eye, before we fell asleep on the floor.

The next morning we all watched Soul Train together and bugged out. She did the robot (like a white person of course) and I busted my patented move: dropping down to a semi-split, flailing my arms around then popping back up to my feet. Eat your heart out Soul Train Gang! My two brothers joined in, with some moves of their own, as well. All I got to say is fuck those Brooklyn disco boys with their Saturday Night Fever shit. John Travolta may have been their idol, but I learned my moves from the greatest dancers in the world!

After breakfast she took us to her beauty salon for haircuts. She said she wanted to get a perm and add a little curl to her shit. A little curl? The chick that was doing her hair somehow fucked up and Mom walked out with a full on Afro. It was hysterical - her pale, white ass, freckles and all, and a big, bleached-blonde Afro. I jokingly tried to buy her one of those black fisted Afro-picks that were all the rage with the brothers in the '70s, but she didn't appreciate my sense of humor. Somehow, I still think she did that to her hair on purpose. I think Soul Train got her, too.

Next, E and I were off to get our ears pierced. E got his left ear pierced and, since I didn't want to have the same thing, I told the guy to pierce my right ear. Nowadays, a lot of people have both ears pierced. But back in the '70s, the rule was set in stone: if you were straight you had your left ear pierced and if you were gay, you pierced the right. Of course, nobody ever told me that shit and the entire day I walked around getting smiles from weird dudes, while other guys yelled, "Fag" in my direction. Luckily we ran into someone and they hipped me to the deal. When I found out what was up, let's just say, I couldn't have taken that stud out of my ear any quicker.

We had a blast that weekend and we never mentioned anything to our mother about the shit that was going on at the Valentis'. Sunday came too quickly, and Carl couldn't have been happier to drive us back to Long Island. We could tell he was obviously pissed that we came home. In his eyes, we were "cock-blocking" and he didn't want us around, because he wanted my mother all to himself. I was so sad during that car ride back out to the Island, but I knew I had to be tough. Carl was the last person on Earth I wanted to see me cry. That was the life I wanted back there, with my mom, and now I was leaving it all behind. How was I supposed to go back to that nuthouse and pretend to like it, after we had such a great time with our mom? The entire way back we were silent. All three of us wanted to cry but we had to be strong. Although we were going back to the Valenti nuthouse, we were now armed with our mother's phone number, which would be our lifeline when things got thick.

The minute Carl left, Mr. and Mrs. V. drilled us with questions about what we told Mr. Hayes and our mom. We swore up and down that as promised we said we loved it there and that they were really nice. As a payback for keeping our mouths shut, they sent us to bed hungry.

Over the next few months our attitudes changed. We played lots of sports, especially basketball, and didn't let any of their shit get to us. We wrote in E's diary each day, stole money and did our new favorite thing - called our mom. Having those moments on the phone with her, made life at the Valenti house a little more bearable. I still remember the little drug store on Deer Park Avenue that we called her from. We couldn't just call her from any pay phone. These calls meant everything to us and we needed a special, private phone with a booth.

The booth in the drugstore was made out of aged wood and it smelled great. It had this noisy, little fan in its ceiling that kicked on when you closed the door. It was so noisy you had to talk over it loudly. But that didn't matter, because we had privacy - something we never had at the Valentis'. Three times a week, we would go down to the drugstore, located in a strip-mall, to place our calls. We would go in one at a time, close the door and have a few minutes of talk time. E was always first, before Frank and I would take our turns. We were there so often, we befriended the old man who owned the drugstore. He really liked us and would always give us free candy when we arrived.

Between begging from our supermarket scams and stealing money from the Valentis, we had saved almost a $100. With the cash, we decided we wanted to buy our mom a present, to show her just how much we loved her. In the strip-mall near the drugstore was a jewelry store. It was there that we picked out a 14k gold, Christ-head necklace with the words "To Mom" engraved on the back. We mailed it to her and she absolutely loved it, because she had a strong Catholic faith and really appreciated the gesture. More gifts eventually followed, including rings, money, framed oil paintings, and radios. Those gifts were small potatoes in comparison, because the biggest gift, and my boldest heist to date, was yet to come.

During one of our phone calls, she casually mentioned that she was thinking about getting a fish tank. Her friend had one and she said it was relaxing to just sit and watch the fish swim around. As soon as we hung up the phone, we immediately went to the local pet store and saw a fish tank they had on display. It was a 25-gallon tank complete with everything, except the fish and the water. There was a skeleton, that would sit up and then lay back down, an underwater filtration system, lots of cool-looking, multi-colored gravel, and this little house for the fish to hide in. All for $75. We counted our money, but realized buying this gift was going to nearly deplete our pilfered funds. We were fully prepared to use all of our money, because we knew my mother would really love and appreciate the gift. But instead of that, I came up with a scheme that would get her the fish tank and still allow us to eat like kings.

The fish tank was on display right near the front door of the shop. So, we waited until the time was right to move in for the kill. I stood outside the front door, while E hammered the guy with all sorts of dumb-ass questions about tropical fish, which the salesman didn't have a fuckin' clue about. When our other accomplice, Frank went to the register to ask for change for $1, I sprung into action. I opened the front door, grabbed the tank and ran down the street, laughing the entire way home.

The next day, I went back to the shop we previously hit to buy some fish for the new tank. Ironically, the same salesman E had talked to the previous day, waited on me. Since E and I looked alike, the salesman just kept staring at me suspiciously, before finally asking, "So... exactly what kind of tank and set up do you have?"

Sensing he was onto our scam, I cut him off saying, "Look guy, I'm in a hurry, shut up and sell me some fuckin' fish already." I guess E's ballsy attitude was finally starting to rub off on me.

Mom appreciated the gifts, but she also encouraged us to stop buying stuff for her. We didn't listen, because it was our only form of escape. It was something we could do. Hitting Fran and the Valentis in their wallets, then making plans for all the cool stuff we'd buy my mom, was exciting, but, most of all, it connected us to her. It was a connection we really needed.

My mother asked us where we were getting the money for all the presents and we told her we all had jobs. We never told her where it really came from and we never bought anything for ourselves except food. Everything was for her. Looking back, I think we were trying to buy her love with the gifts. We were hoping she would be happy with us; hoping there would be the one gift that would make her say, "That's it, you guys are coming home for good." Sadly, it never happened.

Over time, our visits with her began to lose their magic. The fish died and we seemed like a big inconvenience to her and her relationship with Carl. It hurt me more knowing that my mother was fifty miles away in NYC and not taking us, than it did before she took us for that first home visit. Toward the end of our six-year stay at the Valentis', we really wanted to go home for good. We slowly started to tell our mother about all the things they were doing to us. We thought she would take us out of there if she knew. But she didn't. Instead, she had one of her nervous breakdowns screaming, "I can't listen to this shit. My nerves can't take it. If yous leave there yous ain't coming here!" She was right. Her nerves couldn't take it and she sure as hell couldn't handle taking care of the three of us. I started to realize that I was never going to be with her. But this isn't a story about caving in. It's a story of survival. I pulled myself up by the proverbial bootstraps and buckled in for the long and bumpy ride.

I turned thirteen in 1975 and was quite an athlete for my age. The Valentis' whole trip, at this point, was that once the house and garden work was done, they wanted us out of their faces. So, we took shelter in sports. They sent us to the park to play and play we did, for hours on end. On some weekends we would spend eight-to-ten hours playing sports. We played football, basketball, baseball, stickball, catches flies up (a self-hit baseball game), HORSE, and kill the carrier. There wasn't a motherfucker in Deer Park my age that could school me on a basketball court, except one: a three-letter, black athlete named Kevin Baugh (RIP). He went on to play football for Penn State, but was shot and killed in a crack deal some years ago. What a fucking waste.

When we played sports, we always fantasized about being O.J. Simpson, Julius "Dr. J" Erving, or Vida Blue, the Oakland A's ace pitcher. One day I was Hank Aaron and the next day I was Reggie Jackson. If we slap-boxed I was Muhammad Ali and the other poor chump, usually my little brother, was Chuck Wepner, a white boy who was nicknamed "The Bayonne Bleeder." The reason was plain and simple - we didn't idolize white athletes. Oh, hell no! Our heroes were all black. You would never catch me calling out, "Dave DeBusschere, from downtown!" It was always, "Dr. J dribbles to the basket with that big-ass 'fro!" or, "Julius, the patented reverse lay-up. In your face, honky!" We had to be O.J. cutting through the line, dancing away from the defense, or Hank Aaron hitting his record-breaking 715th home run over the left center field wall.

On the playing field it didn't matter what color they were or where they came from, they got respect and so did I. I was always picked first and I always gave it my all. I had to win, because losing wasn't an option. You could make fun of my clothes or my shitty lunch, or the fact that I was a foster kid, but you had to respect the mother fuckin' finger roll, the hard-ass tackling, the fact I could hit a line-drive down your throat or punch you dead in your face. I drew blood every time I played and not just my opponent's, but my own, as well. I loved competition! My competitive nature and athletic ability soon came to the attention of the John F. Kennedy Junior High School Athletic Department.

One afternoon, we were playing a three-on-three half-court game on the schoolyard court. It was E and me, and another older guy, against some older Italian dude and two other kids my own age. These kids couldn't hold me on defense and I was scoring all the points and talking trash, of course. I loved letting people know what shot was coming next as I dribbled, "Jump shot!" "Reverse finger roll!" "Hook!"

Yeah, I loved to talk trash all right, but I could back it up. The Italian guy on the other team was in his late-20s or early-30s and I guess he wasn't feeling all the shit talking. He figured he'd check me on 'D' and teach me a lesson in humility by shutting my game down. Wrong. I scored the next three points, including a game-winning luck shot, which was a hook from the top of the key. It was straight-up garbage, but hey, it went in, right? He may have been bigger and stronger, but I out-hustled him and that, my friends, is the name of the game, not only in sports, but in life, as well.

Who's going to hustle harder? Who wants it more than the next guy? It turns out the guy was the coach at our junior high. He respected my game so much, that he invited me to try out for the team. As he walked away semi-pissed he said, "Leave the big mouth at home."

Wow, I'd been personally invited by the coach to try out for the team! I couldn't believe it. There was only one problem - there was no way the Valentis would let me be on that team. It would mean long practices and that would cut into my house, or should I say, slave work. All the same, this was my chance to make a name for myself in town. From that moment on, I was on a mission. This was the first time I really wanted something for myself. I desperately wanted to be in that JFK Eagles uniform and have those cute cheerleaders jumping up, giving me shout-outs every time I scored a basket, "John! John! He's our man! If he can't do it, no one can!" The solution to get what I wanted was simple - don't tell the Valentis.

I attended every tryout under the guise of an "after school study group." Every day, when the three o'clock bell rang, I ran up to the wall outside the gym to check the list to see who had been cut. If you got cut your name wasn't on the list. But if you made it to the next round it was there. Every day my name was up and when the final cut list was posted, sure enough John McGowan was number five on the roster. I was on cloud nine and my brothers (who had been covering for me) were pretty stoked, as well. We celebrated that Friday night by sneaking a whole bag of Dunkin' Donuts back to the Valentis' and chowing down after everyone was asleep. My mother also took the last of their money and chipped in to buy me a pair of white Converse All-Stars (Chuck Taylor's), because you couldn't play ball in Skips.

Skips were cheap sneakers that usually fell apart as you ran up and down the gym floor. If you tried to stop quickly and do a lay-up, you usually kept right on going, right into a wall. The $1.99 Skips, that the Valentis bought us from the big basket of sneakers at the King Kullen supermarket, were definitely a fashion faux pas, both on and off the court.

Monday finally rolled around and there was just one more list to go: the final cuts that would determine the starting five. I was so nervous with anticipation, I couldn't eat anything the entire day. I just kept looking at the clock... twelve, one, two... then the bell. I ran at warp speed to the gym and was first to the list. I scrolled down it with my finger and... what? Wait a minute, something was wrong. My name didn't appear on the starting five or on the team list. I raced frantically to the coach's office and burst in. "Mr. P. how come I got cut?" He informed me that it was because I hadn't come up with the $100 for uniforms and team expenses. In my excitement, I forgot to read the fine print at the bottom of the cut list that stated the required money was due by the final tryout. I assured him I'd have it tomorrow and he said that as long as I had it by then it'd be okay.

The only problem was the McGowan brothers were comin' Straight Outta Locash. We were spending a lot of our loot we pinched from the Valentis on food and gifts for Mom and as a result, didn't have much saved. Later that day, the hand signal went out to bank up some cash. I snuck into Fran's closet, opened it and to my horror, the cash box was gone. Holy shit! They'd moved the stash and I had less than twelve hours to come up with $100 or my dream of making the team would be a thing of the past. Plan B, which was really dangerous, now went into effect. I had no other choice but to search the entire house after everyone was asleep in order to scrape up enough cash. Keep in mind, up until that point, we had never taken that much money at one clip. I didn't know if they would notice, or if we could even find it, but I had to try. That night, I searched everywhere and came up empty - virtually crushing my hoop dreams.

The next day the school bell rang and I had a lump in my throat the size of a grapefruit. I had to go to the coach's office and tell him I couldn't make the team because I didn't have the money for the uniform and team expenses. I was fighting back tears the entire way to the gym, but there was no way I was going to let the little bastards in school see me cry. I walked past all the kids in the hall and entered the gym. The walk from the gym entrance to the coach's office had to be the most difficult fifty feet I'd ever walked. I thought, "So this is what it's like heading to the gas chamber."

I reached his door and it was open. The coach was talking on the phone and waved me in with a smile. "Yeah Bob, talk is cheap." He listened for a moment. "Oh you'll get to see him don't worry. Listen I gotta go." He hung up the phone. "I was just telling the coach from North Babylon about our new point guard. Congrats McGowan, you got the spot. You bring me a check?" I lost it right there. I started sobbing which freaked him out. He knew my tears weren't tears of joy. "What the heck is wrong?" he asked. I broke down and then the dam burst wide open. I told him everything... about my life and about the Valentis.

I told him what Mr. V. had done to me years ago when I tried to tell some of the school administration about the abuse I endured. I told him how much it meant to me to be on this team, because I'd been the outsider my entire life and this was the first chance I had to be part of something real. He was moved to tears by my story and he hugged me. He said that anyone who was willing to go through this much shit and still come to practice every day was good enough for his team. He said he would pay for my uniform and team expenses out of his own pocket. He swore it would be our secret and that everything I told him would never leave that room. Mr. P. was a man of his word. Not only did he never utter a word to anyone at the school, he also called the Valentis and pretended to be my English teacher. He covered for me with some bullshit story about making up credits after school, so I could practice and make the games.

He jumped up from his desk as if nothing had happened and asked me if I was hungry. Of course I was. That afternoon he took the entire team out for pizza. When we got to the pizza parlor, the coach stood in front of the team and performed the yearly ritual of announcing the team captains, and I was selected as one. Mr. P. was the first person to show me that it's okay to trust people. If you're out there somewhere, I want to thank you Mr. P. You rock!

I was a little bummed that our first game was on the road, because that meant no cheerleaders. We were going to play North Babylon and on the bus ride over I was so nervous I almost puked. When it was game time, I'll never forget the feeling of euphoria I had running out of the locker room with my teammates for the first time. From the opening tip off, our team was all business. I was so amped up, I scored close to 15 points and grabbed a dozen rebounds in our exciting debut victory.

The bus ride back to Deer Park was no less amazing. There I was in the thick of things, just one of the guys laughing it up, banging on the seats, the walls and ceiling of the team bus, chanting, "Undefeated! Undefeated!" I looked over at Mr. P., he smiled and gave me the thumbs up. I wished that moment could have lasted all night, but it couldn't. It was already 8 p.m. and I had to get my ass home quick fast.

We pulled into the school parking lot in a heavy rain and right under the John F. Kennedy marquee were our cheerleaders standing there with pom-poms in their hands. The bus made the final turn in the circular driveway and pulled up to where they stood. The brakes screeched and we came to a stop. I was the first one at the door ready to jump off. I was smiling from ear to ear looking at the girls. They saw me, smiled and waved. The bus driver prepared to open the door and I got ready to hear these cute girls give me a victory cheer. As the door opened, Mr. V. appeared with an umbrella in his hand. He was standing in the driving rain, coughing and was clearly very pissed. Not a word was spoken as I stepped off the bus, because I knew what was going to happen next. He grabbed me by the ear in front of the cheerleaders and my teammates and dragged me off to his car.

When Mr. P. saw what was going down, he raced off the bus and pushed him screaming, "Why don't you try doing that to me you coward?"

Mr. Valenti ordered me to get in the car and I did as I was told. I watched as they got into a shouting match, before Mr. Valenti walked over and got in the car in a blind rage.

I was scared shitless. He raced out of the parking lot yelling at me like a maniac about how I was a lying little piece of shit, and that me and my brothers didn't appreciate anything they did for us. That was followed by a few smacks as we drove down the road. He suddenly slammed on the brakes and yelled, "Get the fuck out!"

I did just that and when I did, he hit his high beams and illuminated the woods near where we had been throwing our lunches for the past few years. The trees were covered with hundreds of multi-colored bread bags. They were everywhere: in the trees, on the ground, stuck to the fences and all over this bulldozer that was parked on the property. E was up in a tree collecting bags and throwing them down to Frank who was stuffing them into garbage bags.

A construction company started clearing the woods to build a house and as the bulldozer loosened the soil, the heavy rain from the storm washed the mud into the sewer and clogged it up. It was Harold or Tony who saw it and ran home to tell Mr. V. That's when he came to JFK to pull me out of my supposed "after school study class." I stood there for a moment and watched as dozens of bags bubbled from the sewer and danced around in the wind. For the next three hours, I joined my brothers collecting bags in the driving rain and hurricane-force winds.

The bottom line was, things would never be the same at the Valentis' from that moment on. There were no more late night raids on the bread drawer or the 'fridge and no more hits on Fran. Sadly, I never got to hear my personal shout-out by those cute cheerleaders when I scored a basket or made a great play.

Carl was also sick of us being around and his negativity eventually rubbed off on my mother. There was so much tension, it seemed like she just yelled at us the entire time we went to visit her. From that point on, things just went from bad to worse. The visits had given us something to look forward to, something to hope for, and now we had nothing. Nothing but the Valentis.

Mrs. Valenti loved to rub in our face the fact that our visits had come to an abrupt end. Over and over, we heard, "Even your own mother don't want yous around. Yous are damn lucky to have us."

The Valentis weren't only fucked up to us though; Diane, Harold and Tony were also equally abused. They were there a few years longer than the three of us and they were smacked, starved and beaten just the same. Harold and Tony were fucked in the head, but Diane was just a vulnerable and shy teenager who was actually pretty cute. She worked at a plastic factory in Deer Park that was run by this wealthy German family. The owner's twenty-something-year-old son, Ludi, fell head over heels for her and they started a secret romance. Diane was so happy to be in love and it showed. She was like a giddy little girl around the house and you could just see that for the first time in her life, someone finally loved her unconditionally. A few weeks later she found out that she was pregnant with Ludi's child.

Ludi came over and declared his love for Diane saying he wanted to marry her, have this child and move in together as a family. Now you'd think any normal foster family would be happy that their foster daughter had found someone who loved her and was willing to take care of her. I mean, at that point, their job was done. Mission accomplished, right? Wrong. The Valentis were pissed. They screamed about how she had violated their trust by sneaking around and all this other shit, but the real reason was much more sinister. They were taking Diane's entire paycheck every week. If she left, that extra income and all her hours of housework were going to be a thing of the past. No slave owner wants to lose a slave. On top of that they saw another opportunity. Diane was a minor and Ludi was an adult. That meant that he could be in pretty big trouble with the cops if the Valentis chose to have him arrested for having sex with a minor. They figured they would keep Diane at the house and extort the German family for money in exchange for keeping things quiet.

As a result, Diane was depressed and cried all the time. She never saw a dime of the hush money, nor any of the money that later came for child support and other so-called expenses. It was money the Valentis would add to the small fortune they had amassed over the years.

Mrs. V. even brainwashed Diane, making her hate Ludi for taking advantage of her at such a young age. She made up a little jingle for Ludi, which she made Diane and the rest of us sing, "Ludi Gestapo, Ludi Gestapo wanted Diane, but he's a big floppo." Mrs. V., if you're still alive, you are one sick bitch! And just as a footnote to this story, you'll never guess what Diane named her little boy - Nick Jr., as in Nick Valenti. What else?

Shortly after the post-game shouting match between Mr. P. and Mr. Valenti, Mr. P. convinced E and me to call Mr. Hayes and show him the diary. We were in the principal's office with Mr. P and Mr. Hayes. After Mr. Hayes read the diary entries and heard all the stories he said he was shutting down their house immediately and removing all the foster children. We wanted to leave with him that day and never step foot in that house again, but he said he'd have to find a new home for us first. He'd also have to confront the Valentis about our allegations. We were terrified of having to face and confront them about the horrible shit they did to us. When that day came E and his big balls seized the moment, once again. Frank and I just looked at the floor, answering "Yes" or "No," to Mr. Hayes' questions. Not E. He stared the bastards down and spoke his mind. I couldn't believe he knew so many curse words at fourteen. Then Mr. Hayes did the unthinkable: he left without us. That night the Valentis took us to eat at IHOP and tried to convince us to tell Mr. Hayes that we'd lied. I could see that Mr. V. just wanted to slug us, but he knew better.

For the next two weeks we made them buy us all the things we never had: clothes, food, toys, and anything and everything our little hearts desired. If I passed a shop and saw a toy I'd say, "I want that," and Mr. V. would jump out and buy it for me. They were waiting on us hand and foot, and I have to tell you, it felt damn good. Now we had the power. Mr. Hayes was coming to get us later that week. We told the Valentis that we would tell him we lied as long as all this cool treatment continued. With that Mr. V. pulled out three, small yellow envelopes and said, "Guess what's in here you guys?" He handed one envelope to each of us. "Pool passes. This is going to be the best summer you guys ever had."

Finally, the day of reckoning came. Mr. Hayes showed up and Mr. V. said, "Bob, the boys have something to tell you." Mr. Hayes waited, as E elbowed me as a sign to drop the bomb on the entire Valenti clan.

I finally stepped up, as Mr. V. smiled at me and nodded his head. "Mr. Hayes," I said. There was dead silence. "Everything we told you is true and we want to leave here right now!"

The Valentis were shocked and Mr. Hayes waited while we packed our stuff. As I carried my few possessions to the door, I turned to Mr. V. and said, "You scared me by taking me to that nuthouse, but you're far worse than any of the people on the other side of that fence!" As we walked out, E flipped them off and Frank shouted that he hated them. When all was said and done with that insane asylum, E wasn't the only one who'd developed King Kong-sized nuts. The shit I endured in the Valenti house gave me thick skin and it would come in handy later on in life.

That was the last time we would ever see the Valentis, but I heard a few things about them through the grapevine. That cough of Mr. V.'s? Lung cancer. He died soon after we left, along with all his wife's rose bushes. Mrs. V. went crazy, or should I say crazier. Fran bought a house with her husband and it burned to the ground. I never heard about Vito, but I kind of hope he's okay. Diane took care of Mrs. V. in that house at 246 West 7th Street between Oakland and Central while raising her son, Nick Jr., and last but not least, Tony and Harold were placed somewhere else and later became drug addicts. Karma.

the funkiest little white boy of the year

chapter 3

It was the spring of '75 and Mr. Hayes put us in a temporary foster home in Massapequa, Long Island, until he found us a permanent place to live. The news came that he had a family that was willing to take the three of us together. As fate would have it, their last name was McGowan. That's right, McGowan. He found us a foster family with the same last name. Our cover story would be that our parents had died and they were our aunt and uncle. This was going to be a whole new ball game. No more snotty little kids reading my foster parents' signatures on report cards and saying, "How come your last name is McGowan and theirs is Valenti?" Nope, they were our "aunt" and "uncle." The best part was that they were rich! Mr. McGowan was a bank president and we were going to live in a huge house on North Poplar Street in Garden City. My only question for Mr. Hayes was, "Do they have rose bushes?" He laughed and assured me that even if they did all the work was done by the hired help. I heaved a sigh of relief and Mr. Hayes repeatedly apologized for not checking up on the Valentis. He promised that it would never happen again.

The day finally arrived when we were to meet Uncle Jim and Aunt Susan, our long lost relatives. I remember driving through their neighborhood, looking at the pricey homes and asking, "Is it this block, is it that block?" Mr. Hayes answered over and over, "No, but we're close." We came to North Poplar, made a left and there it was on the corner, Number 41. The place was huge! When we pulled in, the first thing I noticed was a basketball court in the driveway. I looked at my brothers and we all smiled because that was a good sign. There was no welcome banners or weird entourage. This place felt right.

We got out of the van and Mrs. McGowan came out to meet us. She was a pretty woman who was elegantly dressed and smelled great. When I scanned her upper lip for any sign of facial hair or moles there were none. Cool. She said everyone was dying to meet us and she led us into the house through a side door, with Mr. Hayes following behind.

I still remember the distinct smell when I first walked in the door at the McGowan house. It was a good, fresh smell. It was an aroma I never smelled at the Valentis' - soap powder, fabric softener, and the smell of clean laundry. As we walked through the laundry room Mrs. Mac said, "This is where you can wash your clothes." I stared at her like she was speaking fuckin' Swahili and said, "We can wash our clothes?" She looked at me so sweetly with a warm smile and said, "I know you may have had people do it for you in the last home you were in, but we believe in teaching our kids responsibilities." Shit, if she'd only known.

She opened a door and I saw the most amazing sight. It was a huge modern kitchen. The kind you see in House & Garden magazine. She pointed at the huge double-door 'fridge and told us we could go in and make sandwiches, or help ourselves to anything we wanted. These words were so foreign to us; we acted as if she was speaking in tongues again. "Are you telling me we can go into that refrigerator anytime we want and take anything we want?" I challenged her. Her reply, "Of course." I continued the drilling, thinking, there had to be a catch. "So..." I said, "...if it's two o'clock... no, no even better... three in the morning and I'm hungry, I can just stroll on down to the kitchen, go in the 'fridge and make anything I want?" I thought I had her for sure this time. She leaned over, pinched my cheek and said, "As long as you clean up after yourself." The three McGowan brothers looked at each other stunned. I'm sure Mrs. Mac found my line of questioning a little odd.

She changed the subject and led us into the living room saying everyone was waiting for our arrival. Mr. Hayes nudged me and told me to stop asking so many questions. I realized then that Mr. Hayes hadn't exactly been straight up with these people about everything we'd been through up until that point. His reason was simple

- we'd be considered damaged goods. No family, especially these well to do folks, wanted to take kids with emotional problems.

To the McGowans of Garden City, we looked like three sweet, little blonde-haired, blue-eyed Irish boys, but underneath we had some serious shit going on and some major demons to exorcise.

The McGowans had two daughters by birth, Maureen and Cathy. They also had a son who was away at college whom we only met once. Maureen and Cathy were our age and we all attended Stratford Avenue Junior High School together. They were good-looking, popular and embarrassed by us. All of their friends were a bunch of preppies and after they met us, concluded that we must be McGowans from the other side of the tracks.

The first thing the McGowans noticed was how light our bags were. We didn't have shit besides the clothes on our back, a couple of clean pairs of underwear, and some socks stuffed in a few plastic bags. The check that the Angel Guardian Home cut them for clothes wasn't going to cover everything we needed, but that was okay. They were rich and I still chuckle every time I think about my first shopping spree courtesy of Aunt Sue.

Mrs. Mac was anal about everything: her house, her car and her clothes. Shopping for us was no different. "First," she said, "We'll get you guys some pants, shoes, shirts and other accessories, like socks, belts, underwear, and whatever else you need." She would hand pick the clothes to make sure everything was perfect. The problem was that she tried to take me over to the - dare I say it - white people's section. It was full of stale-ass slacks, penny-loafers, and Izod shirts with the little alligator insignia that the preppies wore. In my head I was seeing myself out on that Soul Train dance floor and not in the wack stuff she was picking out. If my Soul Train brothers and sisters ever saw me in that gear, I would have been laughed right off the dance floor. So I let E and Frank get that crap and after some heavy nagging on my part she caved in and took me to the 'black' neighborhood. Mrs. Mac pulled her Mercedes-Benz into the parking lot of Yoshanda's (I can't remember the actual name) Soul Boutique and you had to see the look of terror on her face. I don't think she ever went to that neighborhood, much less interacted with the people there. I told her not to worry because everything was going to be cool - these were my people.

We made our way inside and the sweet sound of soul music was playing. I immediately felt right at home, but I have to tell you, I knew what black people felt like when they entered a store and got eyeballed by uppity, white folk who thought they didn't belong there. Everybody in Yoshanda's stopped what they were doing and fell silent. They were staring at me like, "I know you's lost little white man." But I wasn't. I knew exactly where I was. They had an endless supply of the gear I desired and I had to have it, plain and simple. I picked out the most essential stuff first: the outfit for my first day of school. As I shopped Mrs. Mac stood close to the front door trying to look comfortable, but I could sense she was out of her lily-white element. She smiled nervously and constantly glanced out the window to make sure her Mercedes wasn't up on blocks.

Up and down the aisles I went, carefully glancing over the merchandise. Money was no object, I assured the saleswoman. It wasn't, 'cause I wasn't paying. Just then I saw a sight that made me stop dead in my tracks. I stared in awe: a pair of shiny, bell-bottomed metallic pants, the kind worn in blacksploitation films by the coolest motherfucker you've ever seen on camera. The kind that were so tight you could tell the person's religion, if you know what I mean. The crowd leaned forward in anticipation. I knew exactly what they were thinking, "Does this little honky got the flava?" They gasped collectively as I pulled them off the rack and then they smiled. Yes! Little white man got game!

The shirt would have to be something equally loud. Green polyester. Then came the crowning glory... the biggest pair of, 'as-brother-as-you-can-get,' Harlem-ass platform shoes you have ever seen! At this point people were pulling out their flasks of booze. Most of the customers were shocked by what was going on, they needed a drink. This was just pure entertainment, so why not get your swerve on and kick back a couple. The saleswoman bent over and whispered in my ear, "Even my 'regular' customers get stares with these shoes." "All the better," I proclaimed.

I made my way to the dressing room, gear in hand, and got dressed. Carefully. See, if you were white back then, you didn't wear shit like that. And if you did, you had best get it right. Now came the moment of truth, judgment by my peers. I took a deep breath, pulled open the curtain and made my entrance into the Soul Train hall of fame. All the brothers and sisters in the joint exploded. They cheered me on with whoops and applause and of course I had to drop one of my moves on them. Some of you old-school dogs might remember this one - look left, look right, flail your arms in circles pointing left, then right, spin 360 degrees and stop, pointing at whoever it was you were trying to impress. In this case it was the saleswoman and she loved it.

So did the rest of the gang at Yoshanda's. They were so proud of me that they inducted me into their crew. My honorary title: "The Funkiest Little White Boy of the Year." Mrs. Mac was frozen in a state of shock. She barely managed to squeeze out the words, "Are you actually going to wear that?" Hell yeah I was! I bought five more outfits just like it before saying goodbye to my new crew and strutting out the door.

All that was left to do now was to get a haircut. David Bowie was making noise back then and I thought he was a total freak with his Ziggy Stardust look. I decided to get that exact haircut. A head of spiky, punk rock hair would definitely complete my new look. I was finally ready for my first day at Stratford Avenue Junior High School. I was out to meet me the finest African-American princess in the whole place and make her mine.

I barely slept the night before in anticipation of my big day. I had my gear laid out on a chair and I just kept staring at it. The platforms, the shirt and those pants all had the nightlight reflecting off them. I was hypnotized and at that moment I thought, "For the first time in a long time I actually feel really good. I mean, here I am with a foster family who has the same last name, they're cool and they have money, I'm in my room, in my bed, looking at my new clothes." It was too good to be true. Talk about opposite ends of the spectrum - from the Valentis to this. Was I dreaming? I pinched myself just to make sure.

Morning finally arrived and I made my way down to the breakfast table to debut my new threads. You know how when you enter a room and everyone stops talking because you know they were talking about you? Well, that's exactly what happened when I entered the kitchen. It was like, "But Mom he's..." Maureen and Cathy fell silent. Then they mysteriously got sick after breakfast and stayed home from school. Eugene didn't have to worry about me embarrassing him, because he went to Garden City High School. Frank also steered clear of me and opted to take the bus to school instead of going with me. Mrs. Mac had no other choice but to drive me to school.

She pulled the Mercedes into the driveway and parked. I surveyed the area as the kids hurried to make it to homeroom. I hesitated for a minute because something was obviously wrong. I scanned the entire grounds, what the hell... what was this? My heart rate jumped to 250 beats per minute as I continued to search frantically. It was no use. I couldn't spot one single person of color! Not one. Zip, zero, zilch. I turned to Mrs. Mac in a state of panic and asked, "Where's all the black people?" She replied with a chuckle, "Black people? We don't have any black people in Garden City, silly." Holy shit, this was going to be interesting. No, buying the clothes at the soul boutique was interesting, wearing them around these people, this was going to be epic! I turned to Mrs. Mac, smiled and thought, "Well... you do now."

Let me give you some background on Garden City. Back in the day, it was a very affluent section of Nassau County, Long Island, made up of mostly upper-middle-class and upper class, as-white-as-you-can-get families. All the dudes were preppy and the girls were even more sterile with their non-revealing dresses and prissy, little attitudes. Garden City was the epitome of soft pastel colors, Captain & Tennille, the Beach Boys and country club culture.

I was all about clothes so loud you needed earplugs. I was P-Funk and '70's b-ball Dr. J style all rolled into one. I looked like David Bowie meets George Clinton and believe me, "I had a whole lotta' rhythm goin' down."

When we arrived at school, Mrs. Mac signed me in at the office and left very quickly. The office administration gave me a sheet of paper with my schedule on it. Class was already in session, so I had to get to steppin'. I exited the office feeling every eyeball in the place burning holes in the back of my head.

Now you know I ain't about to wear some fly-ass shit like that and not bring it to these preppy chumps. I didn't just walk down the hall. Oh, hell no y'all! I strutted down the empty halls like a proud brother with my big, funky-ass platforms echoing every time my heel hit the ground. Clonk! Clonk! Clonk! Every classroom I passed emptied and the kids, even the teachers, filled the halls and stared in amazement. They looked at me like I was from another planet because "I Just Got Back" to Long Island courtesy of Parliament's Mothership Connection. There was probably ten seconds of dead silence and then the halls erupted in laughter and a flurry of pointed fingers, but I didn't care. They weren't laughing because I had Wonder Bread lunch bags, or I was wearing pants their moms threw in The Salvation Army poor box. They were laughing 'cause they were herbs, squares.

See, if I had strutted down 125th Street in my new shit, them Harlem brothers woulda been noddin' and sayin', "Shit, you one fly-ass motherfuckin' white boy." So, laugh y'all. Laugh all y'all want. 'Cause your girls ain't laughin'. They think I'm cute and more importantly they know I'm different, and pretty soon I was going to have my pick. From that day forward my nickname in Garden City became "Bowie."

Back then if you made it with a girl it was measured in terms synonymous with the bases on a baseball field. First base was kissing and second equaled grabbing a little tittie. Third base meant you and your boys got to smell your fingers and home plate meant you were the hometown hero. I'd never had a girlfriend while I was at the Valentis' and at this point I was raring to go. It was late spring and everyone was trying to hook up with the girl they were going to spend the summer with. The fourteen-year-old girl I stepped to (whose name I still can't remember) was one of the hottest girls in the entire school. Although she was well developed for her age, she was no sister, but still cute as hell for a white girl. When the jocks and preppies saw us together they yelled stuff in the halls like, "Good luck, Bowie." They snickered and said something about blue something or others.

After a week of talking and holding hands I was ready to take it to the next level with my new girl. We went out to the school bleachers one day and started kissing. An hour later we were still kissing. You remember what it was like when you were a teenager and had the hots for someone right? We kissed and kissed, then kissed some more. Two hours had gone by and we were still kissing. That's when I had my first major erection in the close proximity of a girl. Not that I really knew what to do, but in my mind at least we "were going all the way," whatever that meant. I moved around first and headed toward second, sliding my hand up and under the front of her blouse. I was about to grab my first handful of the firmest, juiciest breasts when she stopped me. She removed my hand and whispered, "Not yet, okay?"

I thought, maybe she needed some more kissing to loosen her up. So there I was again, rounding first and heading to second. This time I tried to go in and cop a side feel and again she stopped me. Back to some more kissing. On the third try, I went for it all - the two handed grab. This time she got angry and stated that she wasn't that kind of girl. My reply was something to the effect of, "Well, could you please assist me in finding someone who is." With that, she stormed off and cried, before calling me a pervert.

I was thrown out at second and as I got up and tried to figure out where I went wrong, it hit me. It felt like someone had kicked me in the groin and fellas, I know you know what I'm talking about. That's right, I was introduced to the dreaded world of blue balls. Now green kryptonite might be Superman's downfall, but the tiniest woman could easily bring the biggest fucker to his knees by the simple technique known as, "The Tease." I found out later that she loved to do that to guys, and this no doubt had influenced the thinking behind her public nickname, "The Tease." Now I knew why the preppies had all wished me luck.

Later that night my groin was still throbbing. For some strange reason as I passed Maureen on the way to the shower, she looked especially hot. As I stood under the piping-hot shower stream, I discovered a certain measure of release. I walked out of the bathroom smiling and my skin was so wrinkled I looked like a shriveled up prune. E was waiting patiently outside the bathroom door in a towel. He was fully aware of the first rule in the "Masturbator's Handbook Code of Ethics," you never knock! I winked at him and he nodded back in approval. His look said, "It's about time, little brother." I passed Maureen on the way back to my room and turned beet-red. Then I thought, what the hell, she ain't my real cousin. And that throbbing pain in my groin, gone.

The rest of the school year flew by and I don't remember much academically. What I do remember was that by the time it was over, Maureen and Cathy seemed to hate E and I with a passion. Frank, on the other hand, had turned into a little brownnoser, so I guess they could tolerate him. To be honest, we didn't care if Maureen and Cathy hated us, because the feelings were mutual. We constantly fought with them and called them stuck-up preppy bitches, or any other expletives that fit. I would say shit like, "I ain't gonna have no problem making the basketball team next year." And they'd say in their little snobby way, "Don't be so sure, we have some great athletes in this town." Anything E and I said, they had a smart-ass comeback.

It would piss me off, but E took a different stance. E had a girlfriend (we'll call her Rebecca) who absolutely hated the McGowan sisters. She made it known throughout Garden City that one day, when the right opportunity presented itself, she was going to kick their asses. E just waited and bit his tongue, because he knew it was just a matter of time before his girl would do all the dirty work. Once again folks, it was E who put the 'H' (hustler) factor into effect.

E swiped some of the two sisters' jewelry for Rebecca. I guess he figured, "What better way to get revenge than to have those two see Rebecca wearing their shit?" He was right and things really started to heat up at that point. They really despised us because money went missing from their rooms, they disapproved of our friends (the Garden City degenerates) and that we smoked weed. I swear we didn't inhale but that's only because we didn't know how. We were basically wilding-out, and we became the talk of the town very quickly. E was hanging around with the local burnouts who nicknamed him "Huey," because to them, the name Eugene was kinda nerdy.

E and one of his friends named Arthur, the son of the famous boxing referee Arthur Macante Sr., were raising hell all over Garden City High. One day, they let a bunch of wild geese into the school causing a huge commotion and that forced the school to shut down for the afternoon. While the faculty chased the birds up and down the halls, E and his boy had the perfect cover to smoke weed throughout the school.

The only cool people I met in school were the "Rockers" and since I wasn't about to hang with any preppies I thought the pairing was perfect. They were your typical rock-n-roll, burnout types, and most of them were older, but despite the age difference, I fit right in with these misfits. E's "high" school classmates were guys who smoked a lot of pot, listened to very loud rock music and didn't mind me dressing like a freak. Although they liked me, the one concession I did have to make while hanging out with them was over my musical tastes. I was told point blank, "No fuckin' black music, Bowie." I didn't mind it entirely because I also liked rock and they turned me on to Black Sabbath, fronted by this crazy-ass lead singer, Ozzy Osbourne. "Fuck," I thought, after hearing about Black Sabbath's music and dark message, "These are some people I can relate to." I ran to the local record store to try and find anything by Black Sabbath. I walked in and there it was: this weird looking album cover, mostly black, with this multi-colored figure swinging a sword. I picked it up and studied it intensely before I read the title, Paranoid. It was like I could feel the power and electricity of what was inside. A few skipped heartbeats later, I had purchased my first album - oddly enough, it was by a group of white guys from Birmingham, England.

I ran home in excitement, ripped off the plastic wrapper and slapped the album on the record player. As soon as I dropped the needle into the first groove, I was hooked from the opening note of "War Pigs." I blasted it as loud as the stereo would go and the two McGowan girls ran in screaming and complaining about how awful it sounded. I couldn't hear a word they said because I just sat there in a musical trance. I was mesmerized and I played it over and over again. I played it twenty times… thirty times…I learned every word and sang along as I stared into space and punched my fist into the couch. I felt it. I was it. I was fuckin' indestructible and just like Ozzy, I was transformed into "Iron Man!"

At the same time I got into Black Sabbath I also started to smoke pot more often. I didn't just inhale, I made sure I held it in until my eyeballs were ready to pop. I still played ball, but I was definitely known as a "head" which meant, of course, that I liked to get stoned as frequently as possible. Mr. and Mrs. McGowan had started to realize that there was definitely something fucked up about us. They told Mr. Hayes that he had better come clean about what exactly went down in the last home we were in. After Mr. Hayes told them they began to lock their bedroom doors at night, never again left money lying around and Maureen and Cathy eyeballed us like we were axe murderers.

In regard to the stealing, I think that, more than anything else, it was the excitement of taking things that didn't belong to us. Honestly, if we needed anything the McGowans would have gladly bought it for us, no questions asked. I think we missed the whole "Hit Fran" scam that we perfected at the Valentis' and sneaking around the McGowans' house at night gave us that same rush of adrenaline.

As the last day of school came, I thought to myself, "This is going to be one wild summer, dude." It was America's bicentennial, 1976, and it was one hell of a party. I looked fly and I was finally going to make that turn around third and cross home plate with some girl, somewhere and somehow.

Mr. and Mrs. Mac were about to take their annual weeklong summer vacation. They almost postponed it that year because of the stuff with us, but Maureen and Cathy convinced them it would be fine. Just to make sure we didn't get into any trouble, Maureen and Cathy said they'd also keep an eye on us, and call if anything went wrong. So, off they went. It was a good thing they left town, because as it turned out, their two little holier-than-thou daughters were planning a big party for the first weekend without parental supervision. The Little Miss Goodie Two Shoes sisters were actually doing something bad!

They packed the house to the gills with alcohol and we received strict instructions, "This is our party for our friends and we don't want your derelict friends ruining it!" We were allowed only two friends each and E's girlfriend Rebecca was definitely not invited. Friday night came. The house was ready and the two sisters waited anxiously for their houseguests to arrive. The doorbell rang and Cathy and Maureen raced to the front door. In their minds, this was to be the event that would carve their place in Garden City folklore. This was the party their friends would talk about into their adult lives, saying shit like, "Remember that time in '76 when the McGowan sisters' parents went out of town and we..." They stood there for a moment and smiled at each other. Cathy took a deep breath and opened the front door. To their surprise, the first to arrive was a very stoned teenager with long hair and an Aerosmith concert T-shirt. He took a break from swapping spit with his girlfriend before he yelled, "What's up! We're here for Huey and Bowie's party."

Before you knew it, a group of stoned teenagers pushed their way past the sisters and made a beeline for the alcohol. The next dozen or so times that the doorbell rang it was our friends. "Hey dudes, we're here for Huey and Bowie's party." Our party crew raided the alcohol, destroyed the neat, little snack table and was straight-up fuckin' obnoxious.

Maureen and Cathy were both fuming mad. Their douchebag friends started showing up just as the party started to rage out of control. We were smoking pot, trashing the house, and getting in their faces. The wimpy sounds of Chicago and Seals & Crofts were replaced with heavy thunder of Deep Purple, Led Zeppelin and Black Sabbath.

One of their friends made the crucial mistake of taking off Aerosmith's "Back in the Saddle" mid-song and in retaliation, one our cronies punched him square in the face. We continued getting really drunk and stupid and just when the party had a slight lull, Rebecca crashed it with her girlfriends. I think it took fifteen minutes before she was beating the living-day-lights out of Cathy, while her friends threw Maureen and their guests around the house like dolls. Eventually the party got so crazy the cops came and kicked everyone out. The McGowans were called and were forced to cut their vacation short by returning to Long Island the following morning. That party was the final straw that ultimately sealed our fate with the McGowans. Their decision was made. Frank could stay, but E and I... we were outta there.

They packed up my silver pants, platform shoes, and the rest of my funky shit and gave us our walking papers. Frank was asked if he wanted to stay and naturally, he did. A couple of days later, Mr. Hayes came to pick us up in the Angel Guardian van. I had no idea what would happen, but I remember E and I were trying to make light of the entire situation. "Guess we blew that one bro, huh?" I said. E piped in, "Yeah, do me a favor Mr. Hayes, leave out the bitchy cousins next time." Mr. Hayes looked at the two of us like we were clueless. He was pissed. "I got news for you two," he said. "There aren't too many families in the market for two little wise-asses." He told us that the Angel Guardian Home was done with us and the only other alternative was to turn us back over to the state. We were now on our way to a little boardwalk villa on "The Irish Riviera," known as "St. John's Home for Boys."

rock, rock, rock, rockaway beach

chapter 4

Not much was said between Mr. Hayes, E and I on the way out of the McGowan home. I was definitely starting to feel like we'd fucked up and bit off more than we could chew. I was too tough to beg for another chance, so I put on my best everybody-fuck-off-and-die face and kept quiet. As we approached the beach it was so foggy you could barely see fifty feet in front of our faces. We drove over the Cross Bay Bridge toward Rockaway and I can remember seeing the silhouette of the Rockaway Playland roller coaster on 98th Street. I thought, " Shit, we got the beach and an amusement park! How bad could this place be?" When we finally made the left onto Beach and 110th Street, the outline of a large beige brick building came clearly into view. It looked ominous and eerie and there was a dead calm about it - as if it were haunted. We then turned into the parking lot and figures slowly became more defined in the fog. Upon closer inspection, we noticed the figures were a group of black and Spanish teenagers who were hanging out of open windows. I quickly realized they were checking out the "New Jacks" who were about to call St. John's home.

The majority of the Catholic brothers who ran St. John's were really weird and I believe, gay. I recall some of the brothers took some of the younger residents off the property on several occasions. Who knows what the hell went on but, in light of the current sexual abuse within the Catholic church involving priests and minors, it's not too much of a stretch to imagine that whatever was going down wasn't legal. The brother who was assigned to me, Brother Mark, was such a herb it killed me. He looked like a character straight out of a Norman Rockwell painting, complete with tight-legged, polyester pants, a heavily starched, white-collared, button down shirt, and corny-ass, brown wingtips. He wore his hair parted on the side and had those nerdy, black Coke-bottle glasses. His attitude matched his wardrobe - stale and very white. The funny thing is that Brother Mark actually thought he was tough. As you probably guessed, he would become my archnemesis in the months to come.

E and I got out of the van and watched the young thugs glaring down from above. They looked really fuckin' mean and I nodded, as if to say, "What's up?" They made snarling faces that answered, "Who the fuck does this white boy think he is?" I brushed off their menacing looks, convinced that once they got to know me it was going to be a whole different story. I scanned the property and saw a dark, red building across the street. Mr. Hayes informed us that the red building was the school and the beige building near it was the residence. Both buildings had a creepy vibe to them. There were basketball courts in the schoolyard, but no kids were playing ball, which was rather odd. I later found out that the St. John's residents' stayed off the courts for safety reasons. Mr. Hayes then walked us into the reception area where the first thing I noticed was the smell. They use the same industrial cleaning fluid in every group home and correctional institution, which has this very distinct piney, chemical smell. Anyone who has ever done time, or has been institutionalized, knows what I'm talking about. It was something I'd never smelled before and the odor was straight-up nauseating. Over the years, I got to know that scent very well and it still turns my stomach to think about it.

I was assigned to the third-floor residence, 3B, while E went to 2D. Mr. Hayes said goodbye and wished us good luck, before taking off. It was the last time I ever saw him.

A staff member escorted me through the halls and up the stairs. Along the way we passed a few of the residents and all of them shot evil eyes in my direction. Couldn't these people see I had flavor? Couldn't they see past the color of my skin? Couldn't they see that I was one of them? Not a chance in hell! On my way up the stairs the staffer informed me that my brother and I were the only white people in the entire facility. In terms of demographics, this place was on the complete opposite end of the spectrum from Garden City. Once again I was the outsider.

The staffer brought me to my wing and I stepped into the hallway. He knocked on the counselor's door and a voice from behind it said to enter. The staff member signaled for me to enter then he split. I pushed open the door and the room was dark except for the light illuminating from a few candles. The air was thick with incense. In the dark haze I spotted a man sitting in front of a Chinese Buddhist altar in a lotus position. He appeared to be meditating. I scoped out the room and saw several Bruce Lee posters along with a bunch of crushed-velvet black light posters that were very popular in the '70s. Most of the posters depicted sexy black women with big Afros. The man bowed his head and in one single motion popped to his feet. His name was Ray Madrazo, a Puerto Rican badass, who was in his late-twenties. Ray earned a black belt in karate and was also a cool-as-shit motherfucker. He wore these wooden Japanese clogs and if you fucked up or acted like a wise-ass he would give you a three-second head start before he would snap out one of his lightning fast kicks and nail you with a clog.

We sat and talked for a while as he tried to gauge how I was feeling. I could tell by his questions that he probably knew more about me than I did. Ray was no dummy and, as far as I knew, he went to college for psychiatry or some shit. He knew about people, especially kids. He told me what he expected; I had chores and if I pulled my weight I could earn an allowance. I had a strict curfew and by moving up in the ranks of " The Groupie's" (group home residents) from D group to A, I could earn the right to stay out longer, earn more money, and have more privileges.

I asked Ray why the kids had ice-grilled me on the way in and that's when he explained the day-to-day realities of life at St. John's. Rockaway Beach, it turns out, was the poor Irishman's resort town. It was nicknamed The Irish Riviera and the last thing the Irish wanted to see in their town were blacks and Puerto Ricans. As a result, every time one of the kids from St. John's stepped off the property they usually caught a major beat-down by people who looked just like me. They had beer bottles heaved over the fences at them by the same Irish-lookin' fuckers who hung out on the boardwalk. "Well shit!" I thought, "That kind of puts a different spin on things around here now doesn't it?"

I was raised around a lot of black and Spanish kids and I always had to go overboard to prove I wasn't like other white people. Time and time again, I had to prove I wasn't prejudiced and I was cool with people of any race or religion, as long as they were cool with me. I can't blame people assuming otherwise because, as American history proved, whites were pretty fucked up to people of color on more than one occasion. I saw it firsthand in the environments where I continuously found myself. St. John's was no exception.

During my first few weeks as a St. John's resident I tried really hard to get along with everyone. I assured them that I was on their side and God help any motherfucker who messed with any one of us. At the same time I had a free pass through white man's land, which meant I could get weed at the local weed spot, make deli runs for cigarettes, porno mags, soda, chips, beer, and whatever else they needed. After a while my endeavors paid off and the kids started to take a liking to me. I felt bad for them being out there in that neighborhood knowing the crazy shit some of them had been through.

They were physically, sexually, and mentally abused. Some turned to drugs and alcohol to escape, while others carried the emotional scars of witnessing the murder of their parents. Collectively, these kids experienced it all - most of which was shit ten times worse than anything I'd been through, up until my thirteenth-birthday.

If these assholes from Rockaway had just given them a chance they might have actually gotten along with them, because they were cool.

What sucks is that this one-eighth of an inch thick covering known as skin has so may stigmas attached to it. People build walls of fear between themselves and won't even talk to each other. Truth is, if you catch the "skin disease" you lose out. As for me, I'll roll through any neighborhood, anywhere, anytime and I'll talk to anyone who's interested. No matter what their backgrounds, people almost always have something interesting to share. Some folks say race relations are better these days compared to the '70s or '80s, but I live in New York – one of the most liberal and diverse cities in the world – and I'm not convinced.

If a black man rolls into an affluent white neighborhood at night, just watch how long it takes the cops to show up. The reverse was in effect when I recently went up to Harlem and had people tell me to get my white ass out of their 'hood. The bottom line is, people are still getting beat up for the color of their skin. It's so bad that even immigrants who come here to pursue the American Dream have already been schooled on the perverse rules of racism. It's like they get trained up in their native countries on how to play the race card. Unfortunately, most of it is directed at black people. If you're Chinese they tell you, "Ah, Confucius say you go to 'hood and open fried chicken stand with bulletproof glass for lazy blacks and you be rich!" I saw one of these places up on 127th and Broadway in Harlem. You walk in and it's just a bunch of huge vats of chicken parts, deep fryers, and bulletproof glass. When the brothers walk in, the Chinese are really rude. They're basically like, "What kinda wing you want nigga?" Skin disease.

I remember an incident that took place in the little Indian cigarette stand downstairs from my old apartment on Second Avenue. It was one of those "What the fuck?" moments that you don't easily forget. I knew the middle-aged Indian man who owned the establishment. I would stop in to get the newspaper and talk to him. He would greet me with a huge smile and a thick Indian accent, "So nice to see you. How you are doing? How is your wife?" I explained on more than one occasion that she was only my girlfriend and not my wife, but it didn't matter because apparently in India if you're knockin' the boots, she's your wife, whether you acknowledge it or not. He was always very friendly to me and the other white yuppie-types who came in, but one day while I was there making small talk, a well-dressed black man entered the store. At first the Indian shopkeeper was unaware he was there and was still smiling as he looked down at some papers. He looked up and said, "So, how is your…" when he saw the black brother. The smile instantly dropped from his face, replaced by a look of sheer terror. He screamed at the top of his lungs, "Hoopti, Hoopti!" and out runs this twenty-something-year-old, 4'9," Indian dude from the back of the store. He stood right behind the brother, who upon seeing this dude behind him says, "Yeah, yeah. Hoopti, Hoopti. The niggas is here." If the brother stepped left to look at a magazine the little Indian dude was right there behind him. If he stepped right, there he was again. The brother bought a copy of Vibe and the entire time they watched him like a hawk. Little Hoopti had the "eyes on" and the shopkeeper (who was so proud of the video surveillance camera he had recently installed in his 15-foot by 3-foot shit-hole of a store) stayed glued to the video monitor the entire time. The brother paid with a hundred dollar bill, walked out of that store and got into his brand new Mercedes. Skin disease!

Let's not forget black-on-black racism either. If you're a black man in Manhattan who's dealt with trying to hail a cab, you know what I'm talking about. The disease is so bad even black cab drivers won't pick up black people! My brother E's boy, Jay is black. He was recently trying to get a cab with his girl and not one of those pricks would stop. Talk about fucked up. Then E stuck his white hand up in the air and no fewer than five cabs raced over, cutting each other off to get the fare. The cabbie that was first in line was from Africa and when he turned and saw Jay get into the cab and not E, he said in a pissed off tone, "Where you go?" Jay replied, "Brooklyn." The cabbie went ballistic shouting, "No take black to Brooklyn! No take black to Brooklyn!" Jay was like, "Nigga you blacker than the motherfuckin' ace of spades and you talkin' about 'No take black to Brooklyn?'" But it was no use. Montombu was not having it. Jay got out and left a few extra dents in the side of his cab free of charge, because of that African brother's skin disease.

The bottom line is that assumptions of character based on race alone are bullshit of the highest order. The first teaching of any real spiritual practice is: "Aham Brahmasmi," which in Sanskrit means, "I am spirit." You are not the material body, but the spiritual spark within. People who think they are white are trapped in a cage of illusion. People who think they are black are trapped in the same cage. The soul has no material designation or color.

Anyway, all the effort I was putting towards being accepted by the kids at St. John's was paying off. They no longer referred to me as white boy or honky. I was their boy, crazy-ass Little J., and they were going to do something they'd never done before - bring a white person 'round their way.

There was an upcoming Fourth of July dance being held at the school and they invited a crew of fine-ass sisters from a Queens group home. Since I was going to be the only white boy there, (E hated disco) I had to be the flyest motherfucker there, which required me to step up my fashion game. The St. John's homies let me into their inner circle by hipping me to 70's greatest trade secret of inner city fashion. There was a new king of black fashion, a king I was completely ignorant of. It was something no pair of shiny metallic, or funky bell-bottom pants could even come close to fuckin' with: Gabardines. We went to the Mecca of fashion that had every style, color and size imaginable - Nostrand Avenue in Brooklyn.

For those who don't know what gabardines are, let me drop some old-school science on you. Gabardines are pants made out of a polyester blend, nothing-special right? But what made them the shit was that they had a double-stitched seam that ran down the side of the pant leg. You would pull the seam apart and in between was a thin strip of black material. If the pants were orange, green, blue, or whatever, you would go to the tailor, (in our case the little, gay Spanish kid on our wing) pay him with cigarettes and he would remove the black strip and sew a different color strip inside. If you had orange pants, you would rock a blue strip of material. If you had green pants, you would rock a light yellow strip inside, etc. These joints were hot and every kid in St. John's had a pair.

Of course, I also had to make a footwear change to go with my new pants. My platform shoes were now extinct like the dinosaurs. The latest flavor were suede Pro-Keds. The 3B kids took me to their Brooklyn neighborhood where I met the rest of their crew. We copped weed at their local weed spot, drank Mad Dog 20/20, vomited and spent every penny we had saved on Gabardines and Pro-Keds. We had a great time. We all got along really well, so well in fact that one of the kids took us to his mom's house for lunch. She actually told me if I didn't have a place to go for visits I could come stay with them. I was appreciative as hell, despite the negative vibes I was catching from the kid's drunken uncle. He just kept staring at me, muttering shit like, "I never thought I'd see the day… a cracker-ass, honky in my motherfuckin' house." But I didn't let it bother me. He was the one with the skin disease, not me. I just tore into those two fried bologna and ketchup sandwiches, washed them down with red Kool-Aid and flashed a big smile, because I was in. I was now the token white boy of the posse.

Before I knew it the Fourth of July arrived and the big dance would be upon us in a matter of hours. Some of the kids went home to their families, but most of us had nowhere else to go. The staff really went out of their way to make this dance special, especially since many of us didn't have a lot. Our housemother, Margie, also went all out. The psychiatrists felt it was important to have a mother figure in each wing so the kids had some sense of parental love. The counselors were like our fathers and Margie was definitely our mom. She loved every one of us unconditionally. Most of the other housemoms were black, but Margie was a middle-aged, Irish woman from the neighborhood. As Irish as the day was long, with freckles and red hair. God help you if you were from Rockaway and messed with any of her kids. Margie knew everyone out on The Riviera. She also had two, twenty-something-year-old, crazier than shit sons. They were well respected and the last thing you wanted was Margie and those two lunatics showing up at your front door, because you'd have hell to pay.

Margie made sure our clothes were pressed, that we were clean and most importantly, respectful of the young ladies who were arriving that evening. The clothing and the hygiene stuff we were cool with, but the respect - shit! We were out to get some ass! Even though most of us were still virgins, we swore up and down that we'd already conquered many a booty and were masters of the bedroom arts. Plain and simple, we were going to bring it to these females. Margie helped everyone get ready and we looked good. I had on my new, tangerine gabardines with a chiffon-yellow stripe running down both sides, baby blue Pro-Keds with thick, red laces and a tight, pullover, black-knit shirt. Damn!

We made our way across the street and waited in the schoolyard with the rest of the kids for the vanloads of girls to arrive. The tension was so thick you could cut it with a knife, especially with all those teenage hormones raging out of control. There was so much testosterone in the air that if a girl had walked within 100 yards of that schoolyard she would have definitely gotten pregnant! We were like starving, caged lions waiting for the lambs to be led to the slaughter. And they were almost an hour late!

Then, like something out of a movie, one van after another made the turn onto 110th Street. Someone shouted, "Ahh, yeah. These bitches is in for some shit now!" We all looked at each other confidently and nodded. We closely eyeballed those vans like vultures watch a carcass about to keel over, before swooping in to take their prey. We were mesmerized as the five vans lined up in a caravan, pulled into the parking lot and came to a complete stop. Time stood still momentarily before the doors opened. Then like the roar of the No. 2 express train speeding past a local stop, dozens and dozens of girls exploded out of the vans in a complete frenzy. They were loud and obnoxious as hell. Margie had wasted her breath telling us to be respectful. We were scared shitless of these girls. They were our age, but way more physically developed. They were tough as shit and their mouths were worse than any truck driver on the BQE during rush hour traffic. They marched across the street and totally flipped the script on us. We were the lambs and they, the lions. They did the choosing and we became the chosen. At that moment, all our macho bullshit and braggadocio went right out the window. What replaced it was fear and we all know what fear can do to a man's prowess. So much for big impressions, eh?

One after another these females picked the guys around me as they dropped racist comments about white people and looked in my general direction. These girls definitely did not like Caucasians and a four-hour dance wouldn't give me enough time to convince them otherwise. Dusk was upon us, thank God, and the fireworks on the beach provided enough cover for me to sneak away. I was so crushed by what went down. I went back to the residence, got out of my new clothes, put on jeans and an old T-shirt and made my way down to the boardwalk.

I walked down the beach to 98th Street where Rockaway's Playland stood and watched the fireworks finale. I rode the roller coaster a few times, then I went to a grease-pit burger joint called Martin's Corner and woofed down some food. After my experiences with the Valentis, food (like laughter) also became my Prozac. I mean, I can be having the worst day possible, but a good meal with good conversation can instantly change everything. The problem was, that evening I was alone and it sucked. I walked around watching parents taking pictures of their kids as they played arcade games and laughed it up. I watched the young couples in love, holding hands, and kissing. It was a beautiful summer night with a warm breeze coming off the ocean and at that moment, I desperately wished that I had a family, or better yet, a girl to enjoy it with. Instead, I stuffed myself with junk food and went to Pinky's Fascination to play skee ball - a skill game where you roll a ball up a ramp and into a series of holes shaped like targets in order to win cheap prizes.

Pinky's was bugged out and the only reason I ever went in there (the prizes always sucked) was because of the lighting. It reminded me of Christmas as thousands of red, green and white lights flashed constantly. Not that Christmas was such a cheerful thing to be reminded of. It was always the hardest time of the year for me as a kid. Christmas was supposed to mean family, eggnog, singing carols and staying up all night on Christmas Eve in anticipation of Santa. Not in my world. For my brothers and me it meant starving and being alone in the cold on the screened-in patio. It meant listening to the Valentis and their relatives laughing it up, while we suffered. Christmas meant dreaming extra hard about how we were gonna get that customized van and be on our own. We didn't have a clue as to how in the hell that was going to happen, but we needed at least some sense of hope for the future. For us it was that van; that beautifully upholstered, airbrushed dream of escape.

Christmas Eve for us meant staying awake 'til 2 a.m., not to see Santa, but for a late night bread drawer raid, because Mrs. V. let her Christmas Day pasta sauce cool down in a big pot on the stove. There were no presents because Santa never showed up at that house. Christmas was supposed to be the holiday to watch classic movies like Miracle on 34th Street, The Bells of St. Mary's, March of the Wooden Soldiers, or those cartoons with their happy voices, Frosty the Snowman, and How the Grinch Stole Christmas! It was everything that the day was supposed to stand for that really got to me. We wanted to be with people whom we loved and who loved us, but that never happened. My mom would take us sometimes, but I had so much anger toward her that it never really worked out. I felt like it was her fault that I was molested, beaten and starved. I would have gotten out of her life in a second to go with the first family that wholeheartedly accepted me. But for Christ's sakes, it was only the Fourth of July! Christmas was still five-and-a-half months away and I was already depressed just thinking about it. I suppose the loneliness and Pinky's Fascination had lured me in. There I was, dreaming about the day when I'd be grown up and have my own family... and by God, when that happened I was going to show the world how to celebrate a fuckin' Christmas! So for now, Pinky's lights would have to do.

I stayed at the arcade for a few hours and before I knew it, it was almost 11 p.m., which meant curfew. At St. John's there were two ways of dealing with curfew. The first was to get an apartment in A-Level, where there was no curfew. But since you had to be at least seventeen that was out of the question for a young buck like me. Those of us too young for A-Level living opted for mode two - doing it on the sneak tip. At 11 p.m., the majority of the staff went home and that meant we were on our own. You would show up for the mandatory bed check and, once the staff completed their rounds, split too. Leaving wasn't the problem; getting back in was. There was a night watchman on duty near the front entrance, so you had to use the back staircase and exit from the south side of the complex. You'd stuff the lock on your floor with toilet paper so you could get back in. For this escape tactic to work properly, you had to be on good terms with the other kids, because if they took the paper out of the lock, you were fucked. This would allow you to run out the back door, hop the tall fence and disappear into the night.

Getting back in was a lot more difficult than going out, because the guard always checked the ground level rear door to make sure it was locked. We had to find another way to make it up to the third floor. St. John's had windows in the rear of the building that ran the height of the building. On each side were cement structures that stuck out and created a channel about three-feet wide. You could put your feet against one side and your back against the other and shimmy your way up the channel to your floor. Once you climbed in the window, you just had to get to the door you had stuffed and you were home free. After a while I was deemed cool enough and the other kids would come down and let me in the door, so I didn't have to fuck around and shimmy up the walls anymore.

Since I was put in charge of the late night supply runs, they knew that if they wanted their shit, they'd better be letting my ass back in. Since E and I were the only white kids at St. John's, we were earning a little extra cash and smokes by running a small-time trafficking operation.

Kids also earned extra loot and smokes by charging the residents a toll if you wanted to move freely through the building after hours. For example, if someone wanted to get from 2D to 3B you had to cut through 2A, and 2A wanted their toll: a joint, a pack of smokes, a six-pack of beer or whatever else was agreed upon. You couldn't get through any of the wings unless you paid tolls or had carte blanche, which E and I both had, so we moved freely around the complex.

Fourth of July 1976 marked America's 200th-year anniversary and people were out to celebrate. As I walked down the boardwalk toward St. John's, there were bonfires on the beach as far as the eye could see, and groups of loud people circulating around each of them. The scene was way out of control and, for some reason, I decided to walk along the beach instead of taking the boardwalk. There were people partying everywhere, having sex in public, drinking and smoking weed. As I passed this one campfire on the sand, I was invited by a few girls and their boyfriends to come hang out. They were really stoned, but this was a different kind of stoned, a stoned I had never seen before. It was like they were zombified. I was curious about what was up, so I sat on their sandy blanket and tried to talk to them, but everything they said didn't make sense. Then one of the guys pulled out a stalk of weed and a bottle of gooey liquid. He told me it was Thai-stick and hash oil. He broke up the weed, and then smeared the oil all over the rolling paper.

A few moments later, this weird, spearmint-smelling joint came around, but before I could grab it, this dude snatched it and told me he didn't think I should smoke it. He said it was angel dust and that I wasn't ready for it. I figured what the hell, who am I to complain? I was freeloading and I had already stolen all their roaches, conveniently tucking them into my pocket so I could go smoke them with my boys back at St. John's. Actually, it was funny as shit, because they would pass a joint and as soon as it got to me I would take a hit, clip it, and steal it. They were so stoned they couldn't figure out what was really happening. They'd just scratch their heads in bewilderment. The looks on their faces asked, "Dudes, didn't we just light a joint?"

I smoked the rest of the Thai-stick and by the time they finished the last of their dust joints they weren't even able to talk. They just stared out at the ocean in a daze. Seizing the opportunity to boost my ass off, I stuffed the last roach in my pocket along with the others, grabbed a pack of cigarettes and a few beers off their blanket and walked off without saying goodbye. As I did, I laughed at how easy a vic (heist) it was and thought to myself, "Angel dust... what a stupid fuckin' drug."

I was psyched to get back to the 3B crew and share the pilfered spoils from my night at the beach. I had about eight-to-ten roaches, which definitely contained enough herb to roll up a nice fat joint. Hell, the night was young enough that I could even sneak out after curfew to find a few more of those beach parties and boost some more shit.

As I approached St. John's I saw red and blue emergency lights bouncing off the buildings and grounds. I ran up and asked a counselor what had happened and he told me that a few of the kids walked out onto the boardwalk with their dates and got jumped by a gang of whites. Even the girls got beaten to a pulp. One kid, who fought back, was knocked unconscious with a bat and was in bad shape. I was pissed and I suggested we rally up thirty or forty of us – including the seniors from the first floor wings – and go up to 116th Street, "The Circle" as it was called, and retaliate.

The Circle was just a circular concrete formation on the boardwalk, but it was sacred ground to the locals. The last stop on the C train is 116th Street. I remember one summer afternoon, a bunch of black kids got off the train two blocks down, walked up to The Circle and all the bikers and locals put their arms together making a human wall across the entrance to keep them off the beach. The Circle was definitely where the guys who beat up my friends were and I was ready to go serve the fuckers notice. The problem was the St. John's kids in my wing were looking at me with really pissed-off expressions. Their reply to my request was, "Fuck off, honky." A little later the gay tailor kid told me he'd heard some of them talking, saying that they were going to jump me that night. Now for the first time at St. John's, I was actually scared.

That night, I remember hearing Ray Madrazo leave at 11 p.m. I was in my room, lying in my bed and listening to every noise including my heart beating out of my chest. I was without any protection and I decided I was gonna have to leave quickly that night and come back in the morning when things had cooled off. I waited about an hour, got up and put my ear to the door. It sounded quiet, so I unlocked my door. Opening it slowly, I stepped into the desolate hallway.

I made my way to the back door and, just as I reached for the doorknob to make my escape, I got jumped. Figures leapt out of the darkness and snatched me up.

I got punched and kicked, before being dragged to the living room. I tried to fight them off, but I was severely outnumbered. When I went to look at the faces of my attackers, the perpetrators were all my St. John's homies - including the kids I had gone to Brooklyn with! I yelled for help but that only produced more kids... running out of their rooms to get their licks in. The gay Spanish tailor kid ran out screaming for them to stop, shouting that I was one of them, but it was no use. They pushed him away and dragged me off to the bathroom, still kicking and punching me in the face. They threw me in the shower, turned on the cold water and just kept beating me. One kid yoked me (put me in a choke hold) and they began yelling, "Put his ass to sleep!" Just as I was about to pass out, I heard the apartment door crash open and a voice call my name. It was E and he brought back up. During my ass kicking, my tailor friend had run over to E's apartment and told him what was going on. E came to the rescue with Bobby K., a total animal who put the fear of God into everyone at St. John's, including the staff.

Bobby K. looked like that Marvel Comics' character from The Fantastic Four... you know, the one that was made out of stone and called The Thing. He was 5'8" and a solid 200 pounds with fists the size of your head and as hard as granite. He was half-Puerto Rican, half-Irish and he had this wild, kinky, Afro-like brown hair. His eyes said, "I'll rip your fuckin' heart out and eat it in front of you while it's still beating."

Bobby K. spent his entire childhood being beaten and abused by his alcoholic father and I don't mean hit in the head with rings, or starved like we were. I'm talking severely abused.

Sometime shortly after his eighth birthday his father gave him a present that he would carry with him for the rest of his life. Dear old Dad was sleeping and hung-over after a hard night of drinking and little Bobby K. was running around the house playing. Unfortunately, he made the mistake of waking his father from his drunken stupor. He grabbed Bobby K. and dragged him to the bathroom, threw him in the bathtub, and dowsed him with lighter fluid. The whole time Bobby K. was screaming, "Please Daddy I'm sorry, I'll be good." But his pleas for mercy were blatantly ignored. His father threw a lit match into the tub, forever scarring his son for life, both physically and mentally.

Little Bobby K. lay in the burn unit for months fighting for his life. From the neck down he was nothing but scar tissue. To add insult to injury, his mom sided with his dad. They testified that Bobby K. was playing with the fluid and matches, and burned himself accidentally. They never came to pick him up from the hospital and he never saw them again. After he was released from the hospital, he was put into foster care where the cycle of abuse continued. Now, you can understand why this kid would snap. Later in life, Bobby K. ended up serving some pretty heavy prison sentences, but as I was getting the shit beaten out of me, he proved to be my St. John's savior.

The bathroom door crashed open and E, Bobby K. and Wolfie (a crazy Spanish kid, who had the facial features that resembled a wolf) rushed in and just started teeing-off on these kids. Bobby K. did the most damage, but E was really pissed and was wildly swinging away. A few seconds later, the melee was all over and they carried my beaten body to my room. Bobby K. was screaming the entire time how he was going to kill any motherfucker who ever put his hands on me again. He must have done a damn good job convincing them because I never had another problem with anyone in St. John's after that incident. I never ratted on the kids in 3B for beating me up, but from that moment on we never spoke. One funny thing that followed was that I had a new "theme song" courtesy of E and Bobby K. It was Frank Sinatra's "Strangers in the Night." They would constantly sing the lyrics just to fuck with me about my late-night beating, because that's how they were. They'd go to war to save your ass and the next minute they'd turn around and have a laugh at your expense.

Bobby K. only identified with his Caucasian persuasion and I guess that's because his dad was Spanish. He was a rocker and the first thing he made me do after the incident was to take all my "nigger clothes," as he called them, and burn them in a big bonfire on the beach. It was hard for me to watch my shit go up in flames, but it was symbolic because it represented a new beginning.

The rest of the summer was spent smoking weed, listening to rock music, writing graffiti, and huffing. Most people huffed glue, but glue was expensive, so we had to steal shit to maintain our high. We'd use graffiti-cleaning chemicals, Carbona, Vandalex or anything else we could get our hands on. We would raid the janitorial locker, spray the solution on a rag and then put it in a paper bag. We'd sit under the boardwalk, on garbage cans and huff for three, four, sometimes five hours at a pop. I remember the sound that would immediately hit you after putting that bag over your nose and mouth and inhaling the toxic vapors. It was a low, vibrating hum that caused you to simply lose track of time and space. E and I always knew to be careful when Bobby K. huffed. That's when he was the most dangerous and unpredictable. He had a crazed look in his eyes, masking a darker evil that we never wanted to see. Huffing sessions typically ended with Bobby K. walking up to the biggest dude, or dudes, he could find and knocking them out cold. He was a ferocious fighter who held the St. John's record with four consecutive knockouts in one night.

Bobby K. got away with stuff no one else could, while living at St. John's. He openly smoked weed in his room and he never had to lock his door. Everyone knew to stay clear and never to complain about the loud rock music coming from behind the door with the Black Sabbath poster. His room was bugged-out. As I said, black light posters were big in the '70s and Bobby K. had a shitload of them. We would smoke weed, listen to music, talk about all kinds of shit and draw our "tags" on paper, which in the world of graffiti was your nom de plume.

While living in New York City, I got to know a handful of the world's most well-respected graf artists. Although I rolled with many legends like Futura 2000, Dondi White (RIP), Dr. Revolt, Hyper (Mackie of the Cro-Mags), Zephyr, Team, even meeting Lee a few times, I was what they would call a "toy". In other words… I sucked. I sucked at everything related to graffiti.

Bobby K. adopted the tag "Sen 1" and mine would become, "Nate 1." Don't ask me why, I still can't figure out why I chose it. All right, all right. So, maybe I do know why. I saw it on a train and I liked it. Unfortunately, in the world of graffiti, copying someone else's tag and just adding a number to it was like raping their wife and burning their house down with their kids inside. You just didn't do it. But things being what they were, needing a tag quick and having no idea what the hell to write, Nate now had a cousin - Nate 1. I wrote the shit everywhere: the walls of my school (P.S. 180 in Rockaway which I barely attended), the 116th Street train station and the walls of St. John's. The common denominator between all my tags was that they were horrible. It was frustrating to be a shitty graf artist because I would throw up my tag and come back two days, or a week later, to find it crossed out with the word 'toy' written over it. I blatantly stole my tag off the CC train (which later became the C train) and when I got crossed-out, there was also a threatening message - "Nate 1 you's a dead motherfucker," signed Nate. I found it funny that I got under this dude's skin so much that he threatened me on the walls of the train. E told me I had better come up with my own tag soon, but I wasn't worried. I was rolling with the sickest motherfucker out there and he had my back if anything went down.

After a few weeks Bobby K. informed me I was ready for the big time - a late night graf-bombing trip to the lay-ups in East New York, Brooklyn. To graffiti artists, the lay-ups were considered the Holy Land. These yards were like Mecca to a Muslim, the Ganges River to a Hindu, the Wailing Wall to a Jew or Bethlehem to a Christian. Dozens and dozens of unattended trains sat on the tracks and were out of service for the evening just begging artists to tag them.

If you got up in the yards, the next day your tag would be seen all over the city, according to what train you hit. If you tagged the A or F trains your shit would be seen over three boroughs: Queens, Brooklyn and Manhattan. The D got you fame in different parts of Brooklyn and Manhattan. Back in the day, the American Indians used to send smoke signals to get their messages out. Graffiti artists used trains to communicate. They knew the neighborhoods where the trains traveled and if they wanted to show off their work, or diss another artist, all one had to do was cross out their tag and sign it.

Bobby K. told me stories about the lay-ups and about the cops who patrolled them. At that time, New York City had transit cops who were real pricks. Most of them were fat and out of shape and that's why a lot of them were sent to the transit in the first place: they couldn't make it on the streets. In the lay-ups some of them patrolled with dogs and if they caught you they would give you a choice - jail, a beating or emptying your spray cans in your mouth or all over your face and clothes. Bobby K. said that if you ran they would send the K-9's after you and then shit really got hairy. He told me that during one night of bombing he got chased and had to run along the top of the trains in order to escape the K-9 posse. "Holy shit." I thought to myself, "This is going to be interesting."

The big night at the yard finally arrived. We waited until 1 a.m. before Bobby K. and I met on the boardwalk. He stole two cans of Vandalex because, according to him, we had to be high as shit to really get in a flow in the lay-ups. We walked down to the train, smoked a big joint, then climbed onto the roof of the staircase that led from the street to the token booth. We called it "The Red Carpet," because the roof-tiles were red. We ran along the roof of the train platform to the end, hung off and dropped down onto the platform. It didn't end there. Bobby K., maniac that he was, first had a little game of chicken to play with the train. We would get on the tracks and wait until we could see the lights of the "Double C" pulling out of 116th Street station. The challenge was to try to out run it from 105th to 98th Streets. There was no room for error, because if you didn't make it you had to jump over to the other side. If there was a train heading the other way to 116th Street, you were fucked. We obviously made it and got up onto the platform, before nonchalantly waiting for our train like law-abiding citizens.

All you old-school heads out there will attest to the fact that, back in the '70s, the New York City Transit subway system was out of control. It was basically a fuckin' free-for-all where any crazy motherfucker who wanted to smoke weed, rob people, drink or, in our case, huff, would go to the last car of the train to carry out their mischief. On the CC, you did your shit when you hit the last stop in Rockaway en route to Broad Channel. At Broad Channel you would get on the A train, check for cops, and if it was cool, get busy again from Broad Channel to Howard Beach. Bobby K. and I huffed all the way to Brooklyn, passed a few joints, threw up a couple of tags and got extremely high.

Eventually, we arrived in East New York. We stood near the doors and I still remember the look on all the black guys' faces that said, "I know you white boys ain't gettin' off here." One of them even gave us the sign of the cross, blessing us as we exited. I looked out from the elevated train platform and all I could see was destruction. The entire neighborhood was filled with run-down tenements and burned-out buildings. I looked at Bobby K., unsure if we had made the right decision. He punched me in the arm and pointed to my right. I looked over and saw dozens and dozens of idle trains. We smiled at each other and calmly walked out of the station.

When we hit the street in the wee hours the scene was surreal as hell. Shadowy figures lurked in some of the doorways, checking us out. A prostitute asked us if we were lost and a couple of 70's pimp mobiles slowly lurched past us with their music blasting. We ignored all of it and kept walking at a swift pace en route to the lay-ups. We got in and Bobby K. surveyed the area. He assured me there were no cops around, so we huffed some more before we broke out our spray cans. Before I could finish the 'N' in Nate, we saw a group of guys with big Afros approaching in the distance. The sight of them produced an "Oh shit!" from Bobby K. When I hear somebody like crazy-ass Bobby K. say, "Oh shit!" it doesn't make me feel too good. I was high as shit and looking at him like, "What now?" Well, our approaching friends quickly answered that. "White boys! Get those motherfuckers!" I was so wasted that my legs felt like rubber, but we still managed to run out of there like two bats outta hell. We safely made it back to the Rockaway train where we both agreed that our time could be better spent doing other shit, like getting high. My short-lived graffiti career, then came to an end. I never ran into the real Nate and I often wondered who he was, or what he looked like. I even thought about going back on those trains and throwing up a few tags just to see if I'd get a response by signing them, "Nate 1... Return of The Notorious!!!!" Somehow, I never quite got around to it.

Later that summer my mom came back into the picture. She was going to a resort up in the Catskill Mountains called Ingleside Farms. She wanted to take the three of us up there for a week. We had been up there one previous summer and everything was cool. That may have sounded like a good idea, but what she didn't know was that E and I had gone through some major changes in the last year. Gone were her two, sweet, little, shorthaired blonde sons. They'd been transformed into a couple of longhaired badasses who loved to get high and get into trouble. She had Carl pick us up at St. John's and then we went to get Frank who was by then in another foster home in Lawrence, Long Island. We spent the night at her house and in the morning, a limo picked us up and drove us three hours north to Greenville, New York. It was a long ride upstate, but I wasn't thinking about nature, trees and that kind of shit. My mind was back in Rockaway, huffing under the boardwalk, smoking weed and listening to Black Sabbath in Bobby K.'s room. Plain and simple... trees fuckin' bored me. I craved the excitement of the dirty concrete.

We pulled into Ingleside Farms and there were even more trees than I imagined. At that point I was really starting to wish I hadn't come. Then I saw something that changed my mind completely, something I didn't pay too much attention to on my last trip there - girls. Hot girls! Dozens of them, walking around in skimpy little '70's outfits looking like Daisy Duke from The Dukes of Hazzard. E and I looked at each other and immediately knew what the other was thinking: "We're either going to get some ass and lose our virginity up here, or take some really long hot showers."

After about an hour we finished checking in, then made our way down to the dining hall for lunch. The dining hall was huge and a lot more civilized than the one I was used to. At St. John's you had dinner in your wing, but breakfast and lunch were served at the dining hall across the street. Those meals usually went like this: we walked over in a very loud group, entered the hall and immediately started yelling and complaining about the food. Then we sat down and did some more yelling and talked shit about the other fuckers who were in there. Basically, you could be up on the boardwalk two blocks away and you knew when it was time to eat at St. John's. That's how loud it was in there. Not so at the Ingleside Farms' dining hall. Families walked in quietly and sat and ate in silence. No one complained and no one yelled, except for us. We were just loud. By now we were programmed to act a certain way and my mom was obviously embarrassed by our obnoxious behavior. We were products of our environment and all eyes in that dining hall were on us, especially the girls.

The first few days up there we tried to behave. We were involved in various activities, including softball games, hayrides and the square dance. But eventually E and I decided it was time to liven shit up and the first thing on the agenda was to find out who had the smoke. We located this older chick, who lived somewhere near the Queens/Nassau County border, and man, was she fine. She was seventeen or eighteen, with big boobs and a skinny waist, but more importantly, in possession of several grams of black hash. She turned out to have the brains to match her body. She constructed a pipe out of a plastic tampon applicator (unused of course) and the group of us snuck off and smoked on this grassy knoll.

E and I got fucked up and started telling stories about where we came from and the shit we'd been through. These kids were in awe. They came from nice suburban families and the closest they had ever been to people like us was reading about us in the police blotter. The other dudes had nothing interesting to offer and the girls really liked hearing our stories about hustling and everything else. It was obvious, the competition was getting jealous. This one dude was eighteen and the boyfriend of the girl who provided the hash and the tampon. I took a fancy to her and I could tell she was feeling me, as well. The next couple of days she came by and picked me up to go smoke and was constantly saying shit to him like, "John this and John that," and "Isn't John so cute" and "Tell us some more stories about that foster home, John." I could see it was pissing the guy off, and that was fine by me. He was one of those Garden City-types anyway. I knew if it caused them to fight that she'd probably get drunk and need a friend to talk to. And what better time to take advantage of a woman, than when she's drunk and vulnerable? Um, that's a joke, girls.

During our time at Ingleside we turned each day into one big party. And on the fifth day, God created gin. The parents were off drinking and acting really stupid at the bar so, E and I decided to find out where they kept all the alcohol. We found it in an old barn where they stored all of the kitchen supplies. We stole two half-gallons of gin and some orange juice, and headed out to the knoll to get all lit up. A short time later I was absolutely fuckin' trashed. I was so polluted that I was literally stumbling around the property and talking shit to everyone and challenging people to fight, including the owner! I yelled and screamed and was eventually confined to my room under threat of the police being called. Once there, I vomited all over everything and passed out on the floor in the middle of it.

The next day I had a hangover from hell and the McGowan brothers were the talk of the whole place. It soon went from bad to worse. Apparently in my drunken stupor, I made out with tampon girl. I don't even remember the shit happening, but with the headache I had the last thing I wanted was her asshole boyfriend in my face. There he was screaming at me. I'd told him more or less to shut the fuck up and get out of my face or I was going to kick his ass. He actually laughed and I believe the phrase he used was, "He'd whip my little ass in a minute." I even gave him a second chance, but he ignored my request and put his hands in my face. I slugged the fucker right in front of everyone. One shot and it was all over. I dropped him with a quick left hand. Naturally, just like a bitch, the girl who instigated the whole shit felt sorry for him and ran to his side, cursing me out. The place was in an uproar and everyone was pissed at me. Everyone, that is, except for this middle-aged guy who walked up to my mom while she was yelling at me. He introduced himself as a boxing trainer who represented a few fighters in the city. He shoved his business card into her hand and told her he was so impressed with my skills that he'd offer to train me for free.

Mom tore up his card and said that after what she went through with my dad, she was never going to let me box.

Well, that was the end of our vacation at Ingleside. They asked us to leave and to never come back. Mom was really mad, especially at me, and she drove us back to St. John's to "be with our own kind," before she split. I still think about what might have happened if I had taken that guy's card and gone down the same career path as my dad. The thought is kind of freaky and I guess that's why my mom quickly snatched that card away and immediately tore it up.

The rest of the summer was spent in Rockaway getting high and hanging out with the locals. I would go to The Circle at 116th Street not giving two shits that most of them didn't like me because I was from St. John's. I'd lived my whole life as an outsider and just as I had so many times in the past, I got those people to realize I was cool. There were a few locals, in particular, who really didn't like me. One was this kid, Phillip, and the other was his crazy-ass older cousin, Danny. Phillip was a bully who constantly fucked with me. I put up with his antagonistic shit, but I also warned him that one day he was going to get it and he just laughed in my face. Danny, he was a complete psycho who had been arrested numerous times for assault, burglary, and other shit. The word on the street was that the cops in the 100th Precinct just needed one more conviction on him and his ass was getting sent away to serve a long stretch.

Although a few of the locals couldn't stand me, I did make a few friends who hung in the neighborhood. Connie Crowley and her brother, Kevin (RIP) were cool and I often hung out at their house during the summer months. Connie would always feed me and Kevin (who became a pretty good boxer before he died of alcohol poisoning) would listen to Beatles records, get drunk and smoke. His favorite song was "Back in the USSR" and I still think about him whenever I hear it. He played it over and over on his little, beat-up record player. My closest friends in the 'hood though, were the drunken bums out on The Irish Riviera. There was a bunch, whose names I can't remember, like the Vietnam veteran who lost his legs and lived under the abandoned theatre marquee on 116 in his wheelchair, always smelling like piss. There was one guy who lived out there who I'll never forget, Paulie. He was in his late-30s, maybe early-40s, and had thick blonde hair with highlights from endless hours passed out in the sun. Like the veteran with no legs, Paulie also smelled like hell, but he reminded me of a character from one of Shakespeare's plays. He always had a story to tell and spoke in rhymes and riddles, the subtext of which usually came down to the fact that he had the shakes and needed some money for a bottle. Paulie was a gifted storyteller because he knew the golden rule: always save the best for last. He kept the audience hanging on to every word of every beat, every scene, every sequence, every act. By the time he got to his climactic episode, you were on the edge of your dirty cardboard box. He'd look at you with those big, blue eyes, summon up his finest deadpan punch line and deliver the perfect ending to his story. Then he'd hit you up for a buck or two.

I liked running into Paulie at The Circle, when the sun came up. That was his reflective time, when he would open up and speak from the heart. At that time there was no booze and no jokes, just 100 percent real fuckin' Paulie. He was also a Vietnam veteran, who had lost a lot of friends in the war. When he got home, as so many other veterans will attest, this country turned its back on him.

Regardless of whatever bullshit politics (and to me they're all bullshit) you adhere to, we owe the veterans a huge debt. They had a job to do and they did it, no questions asked. Personally, I don't agree with invading other countries, but guys like Paulie were one in a million and we wasted them. I knew his pain, and the jokes and booze were just a mask he wore to hide. But, for a brief moment each day, Paulie took off that mask and let you see what was underneath: a caring, very intelligent and brave-as-all-hell man. Rest in Peace, Paulie.

On 115th Street stood the Holland House, an old abandoned five-story hotel that was booming back in the 1950s. In the '70s, it was a haven for the homeless and for teenage runaways. I spent countless hours there just hanging out, talking shit with the squatters. It was wild to hear everyone's life story and the circumstances that had led them to this place.

The Holland House smelled like death and some say it was haunted. At night I heard all kinds of creepy shit going on and it was kind of scary. The funny thing is, just like that chemical cleaner they use in institutions always smells the same, every single squat I ever stayed in also had a similar odor: human waste mixed with mold, mildew, booze and pulverized plaster dust.

Although the Holland House was a total flophouse, it did have a working telephone, which was the weirdest thing ever. As a bug-out we prank called people all over the world on that fuckin' thing! We ordered fortune cookies from China, geishas from Japan and asked to speak to Hitler in Germany, which produced some choice words from the dude on the other end of the line. I don't speak German, but I can pretty much guess the gist of what he was saying. We even ordered a dozen pizzas from Italy and when the guy who barely spoke English asked for our address and we told him New York City, his reply was a straight up "Fongul," which in Italian means, fuck you.

As dirty as that place was, there was a certain mystique about it. I hung out there on rainy nights. We smoked weed, shot the shit and drank Carstair's (a cheap Irish whiskey), and Miller nips all night, until I had to run back to St. John's to make curfew. I always went to the Holland House alone because Bobby K. wasn't welcome around the locals since he'd started fooling around with a local Irish girl. That was a first for anyone living at St. John's, but if anyone was going to make history it was going to be Bobby K.

Although the locals disapproved of his romance to one of The Irish Rivera homegirls, they never thought about jumping him, because even if ten dudes tried to roll him they knew they were all getting hurt. They didn't want to lose face though, so they constantly reminded me that when they caught "Torch Boy" as they referred to him, they were going to cut his burnt nuts off. I just nodded in agreement to keep cool with them, but I knew if shit actually went down that Bobby K. would go through these guys like wet rice paper.

September rolled around and right after Labor Day weekend Rockaway Beach turned into a ghost town. There were no more all night parties on the beach and Playland Amusement Park shut down. The weather also changed as the warm air was replaced with a brisk wind that whipped off the ocean. I also started school at P.S. 180 in Rockaway Beach and I hated it. The only cool thing about that school was that a lot of really cute black girls from Far Rockaway went there. They added a little flavor to an otherwise stale-ass, white-bread school full of local trash from Rockaway and Water Rats (people from Broad Channel who we believed were all inbreeds). E went to Beach Channel High and we barely hung out anymore. He had a new group of friends, the primary one being Tommy the Beast, leader of the Water Rats.

A month into the new school year, I began cutting classes and hooking up with Bobby K. on a daily basis. We spent a lot of time together, exploring the burned-out bungalows on 101st Street and smoking weed. If it was really cold we'd take the train to Manhattan and head up to The Deuce to catch a few flicks at one of those cheap multiplex theatres.

The great thing about seeing movies on 42nd Street wasn't the movie itself, but experiencing the audience and witnessing all the wild shit that went down in the theatre. There were families with strollers in the aisles and their babies crying, people smoking dust and weed, drinking, fighting, and having sex. You name it, it happened. The brothers always yelled at the screen and their comments were always hysterical. No matter what kind of movie was playing, people said shit about every scene in every movie and it always turned it into comedy. It didn't matter. Rocky, a comedy. Star Wars, a comedy. The Exorcist, serious comedy. Butch Cassidy and the Sundance Kid, pure, fuckin' stand-up. Besides, the added commentary was usually a lot more entertaining then the original scripted dialogue. In all the years I went to movies on The Deuce, I don't think I ever heard anyone say, "Shhhh."

The Deuce itself, that piece of New York real estate on 42nd Street from Broadway to Eighth Avenue, was crawling with hookers, dealers and street urchins looking for an easy victim. Even me and Bobby K. got caught out there on one occasion. We had gone up to The Deuce, walked past a bunch of fly-ass, pimp-looking brothers hustling their illegal shit. One of them started his sales pitch, "Acid, acid. Good blotters, y'all." Bobby K. thought it would be fun to see a movie and trip. As for me, I had never dropped before, but if Bobby K. said it was cool, it was cool. We scored two hits for five bucks each and bought two tickets for a movie playing an hour-and-a-half later. We wanted to be high when the movie started. So, to kill time we went to play video games at an arcade on Broadway and wait for the acid to kick in. Once we started tripping, we would go see our movie and bug the fuck out.

We waited patiently for the acid to kick in, but nothing happened. More time had passed and the acid still didn't hit us. Before we knew it, an hour had passed, but we were still stone cold sober. We decided to go back to our dealer friend and tell him that we thought the stuff he gave us wasn't strong enough. Maybe out of sympathy he'd give us another hit to split. We walked back over to The Deuce and found him. He was with his crew and when we voiced our complaint, instead of a refund or another hit on the house, he convinced us to each buy another hit. He justified the weak hits by telling us, "See you brothers gotta high tolerance to my shit. Whatcha' need to do is drop another one each. And to get it into your bloodstreams quicker, ya'll need to run around the block." Shit, was that all? No problem there. Taking the dealer's advice, we each took another hit before we sprinted down the block. The dealers stared at us in total disbelief, trying to hold back from cracking up in our faces.

We ran from 42nd Street and 8th Avenue to 9th Avenue, up to 43rd, over to Broadway and back to The Deuce, stopping out of breath in front of our guy who was like, "What's up?" We said in unison, "Still nothin', man." He gave us the signal to loop around again and off we went, coming back and stopping again, still without the slightest buzz. At this point he and his boys were barely able to contain their laughter. He assured us that if we took one more lap it would definitely kick in so off we went. When we came back running at full blast he put his hands up as if to say, "What's up?" We shook our heads and with that he pointed toward 9th Avenue. This time, we didn't even bother stopping, we just kept on going. Well, by this point I guess Bobby K. started to put two and two together. When we finally stopped back on The Deuce, we were so exhausted that we almost puked. As for the dude and his boys, well, let's just say they were having a real good laugh at our expense. They were slapping each other five and calling us jive-ass turkeys. The dealer then said with tears in his eyes, "I think one more lap'll do it," which put them all in stitches. As for me, I was ready to take one more lap, but that's when Bobby K. slapped me on the back and told me the bad news. "Dude, we got beat." With that, the brother who sold us the beat acid told us to get our dumb, honky asses off The Deuce. We took his advice. After a night of blowing our money and missing the flick, we decided to cut our losses and jump the subway turnstile in order to get back home.

I have to admit, I really miss The Deuce with its seedy-ass vibe and crazy characters filling the streets. I recently saw an interview with the singer, Alicia Keys, who grew up in that part of Manhattan. During the interview she explained that the thing she loved about The Deuce was, it was so real, so New York. There was so much hustling and jostling going on by brothers trying to control their little, ten-foot piece of real estate. The crazy shit was, if you just walked a couple of blocks north, you hit the theatre district and it was this whole other world, this whole other vibe. That's what was so cool about New York. You had these distinct universes coexisting right next to each other. If you didn't want to deal with the shit in any particular universe, you just stayed out of it. Personally, I think what former Mayor Rudy Giuliani turned The Deuce into really sucks. If you want Disneyworld go to fuckin' Florida. I believe a lot of tourists back in the day actually went up to The Deuce to get a real taste of New York's seedy side.

As a native New Yorker, I can honestly say that it's something that's getting harder and harder to find these days. So I say fuck Giuliani, fuck Mickey and fuck Disney's Lion King! I say bring back the pimps, ho's, derelicts and con artists. Shit, you could even charge admission to walk down the strip, because I bet the tourists would pay it. I mean, it's gotta be more entertaining then the crappy shows they got goin' on up there now, right?

The other place Bobby K. and I would hang in Rockaway was a secret dungeon-like room under the Cross Bay Bridge that connected Rockaway to Broad Channel. The door to the dungeon was made out of metal and weighed about 200 pounds. We would push it open and light some candles to see. We'd then close the door and Bobby K. would pull out his converted gas mask/bong contraption, fill it with weed and start smoking. The funny shit about Bobby K. and smoking always involved him taking the biggest hit humanly possible. Once he inhaled, his eyes would get really wide and crazy looking like they were ready to pop, along with all the blood vessels in his head. Then, once the sweat started pouring off his face, he would exhale and pass the pipe. On one particular day, after we'd been sitting around bullshitting for a while, he told me he had a surprise. I knew from experience that when Bobby K.'s face lit up like a little kid, illegal drugs were usually involved. He reached into his coat pocket and produced two hits of blotter acid that had little pictures of Star Trek's USS Enterprise stamped on them. He informed me that tonight, we were going to trip our balls off, unlike our previous mishap on The Deuce. He said he copped the acid from a local dude and they were 100 percent guaranteed, which I wholeheartedly believed.

In the '70s, there was still some good acid floating around Rockaway, especially if you knew where to look. Besides, if anyone knew where to find quality trips, it was Bobby K. He hated the speedy stuff and favored the clean acid where you really hallucinated and saw crazy shit. He handed me one of the hits and told me that at exactly 10 p.m. I was to take mine. Then, after the counselors left an hour later, I was to make my way to his wing so we could hang out in his room all night and trip our faces off. I put the hit of acid away for safe keeping, before we finished up our smoking session and went to Martin's Corner for some munchies.

I cut school for the rest of the day and showed up at St. John's for dinner. The kids in 3B weren't talking to me, but I didn't give a shit, because I was still keeping my silence after being jumped. We just ate our food and watched TV before I ducked out to study the hit of acid in my room. I was amazed that something so tiny was going to be able to get me so high. As I lay in bed watching the minutes and hours tick away, the moment of truth arrived. The clock struck 10 p.m. I looked at the hit one last time, put it in my mouth and said, "Beam me up, Scotty!"

I waited twenty minutes and nothing happened. Thirty minutes had passed and still nothing. Forty-five minutes later I still didn't even have a buzz. Before I realized it, the 11 p.m. curfew came. I heard a counselor turn out the lights and leave. At this point, I was still sober and I started to think Bobby K. got beat once again. As I jumped up out of bed to make my way over to his wing to tell him the bad news... BAM! It hit me!

Colors melted, lights flashed and shit started to rearrange itself on the top of my shelf as millions of little black spots raced around on my walls. Holy shit, this was sick! I fell back onto my bed and was momentarily paralyzed. I lay there for a moment while staring at all the movement. I was bugging-out, but it was a positive bug-out. I had heard about so-called 'bad trips,' where everything sucked for a 24-hour period, but this wasn't one of those. I felt amazing and I knew I had to get to Bobby K.'s room ASAP or I would never make it, because the acid was hitting me hard.

I got off the bed and made it to the door. I opened the self-made lock, entered the hall and strolled to the back door hoping I wouldn't see anybody. One of the Spanish kids who helped kick my ass came out of his room to smoke a cigarette. When I looked in his direction, he was transformed into a big mouse. I laughed hysterically in his face and pointed at him. He looked at me like I was crazy and at that moment I felt like I was super-human. I ran out the back door and slammed it, never even considering for a moment how I was going to get back in. I ran down the stairs laughing my ass off. Out behind the building I whistled and called Bobby K.'s name. He ran down the stairs and opened the back door. When we just looked at each other, both of us had the same shit-eating grin on our faces.

Bobby K.'s room was amazing with the black lights and posters. I could feel what it was like to be in each one. The fine-ass, crushed-velvet sister with the beautiful Afro, riding a jaguar through the jungle… I was there. I could feel the heat of the flames coming from the fire-breathing dragon's mouth. On the "I get High With a Little Help from my Friends" poster, which had these little elves getting this giant high with a big old joint, I could hear the elves chatter. We settled into two chairs and Bobby K. coached me on how to control the high. He told me to think positive thoughts and don't start laughing, 'cause you won't be able to stop. He said that one of his boys laughed so hard on one trip, that he got a hernia. He told me to breath deep and (he handed me a bong) smoke lots of weed. I lit the bong and watched the smoke fill the lower chamber, while the water bubbled away. It flew up the glass tube and into my lungs. As I took my finger off the carburetor hole, I don't think a hit of weed ever tasted so good.

I was so high colors were flying. Bobby K. looked so fuckin' cool and in command of his high. I felt at ease tripping with him. Oddly enough, my mind flashed back to the Sheridans' and that goddamn guitar riff from Cream's "Sunshine of Your Love." Right on Tommy. Now I know what you were experiencing. At that moment I wished I had a guitar in my hands because I was sure I could play the notes. Bobby K. put on Pink Floyd's "Speak To Me/Breathe" off The Dark Side of the Moon and when that heart started beating louder and louder it was like Edgar Allen Poe's "The Tell Tale Heart". Then a cash register sounded off, while someone chanted, "I know I've been mad. I've always been mad." Followed by laughing, screams, someone running in the airport to catch a plane, the plane flying around, then crashing and exploding. When the next song kicked-in, I felt it vibrate through my entire body. It came over me like a rush of the purest energy in the world and my God those lyrics, "Breathe. Breathe in the air. Don't be afraid to care." I took a deep breath and let it out slowly. I was high as shit. We listened to the entire album, talked, smoked and drank some Jack Daniel's. He turned on a strobe light and put on the ultimate song of all time to trip to - Pink Floyd's classic, "Several Species of Small Furry Animals Gathered Together in a Cave and Grooving With a Pict," from Ummagumma. To really get the feeling on how this shit went down, I think you need to find that album, put on that song and imagine experiencing this entire thing while you're trippin' your fuckin' nuts off.

The smoke rose and flickered in the strobe light. The sounds of these little creatures, running around this cave waking up the evil giant who yelled at them in a Scottish-type brogue, was scarier than shit. It was even scarier because Bobby K. was sweating profusely and getting that look in his eyes I only saw when he huffed and was about to lose control. He told me about how the original singer from Pink Floyd, Syd Barrett, went crazy and was locked in a nuthouse. He looked at me strangely and said, "You know, they locked me up in one, too." This was new info for me, info that I really didn't need to know at this point in time. I brushed it off with a quick, "That's fucked up, man." And quickly followed it with, "Hey, let's smoke some more weed." But Bobby K. wasn't letting it go. He reiterated, "Did you hear what the fuck I said, asshole? I said they locked me in a nuthouse with these people screaming all day and all fuckin' night, while the staff beat your ass, and all you can say is, "Let's smoke some fuckin' weed!" He looked really pissed and the energy in the room quickly went from white light to a very dark vibe. He was hyperventilating and sweating, and that scared the shit out of me. My acid guru, my guide, was flipping on me. I was downright fuckin' terrified, because it was Bobby K. and that meant anything could happen.

He then stood up and ripped off his shirt like The Incredible Hulk. "Look what the fuck he did to me!" I gasped in complete disbelief and horror. When I saw his bare chest for the first time, he was covered in thick scar tissue traveling from his Adam's apple to his navel and continuing below his belt line. How the fuck could anybody do that to a child? Tears rolled down his face. "She didn't even stop him… she was my mother!" he said, sobbing. I was hallucinating so heavily by that point that I saw the dragon from the poster breath fire onto Bobby K. and his skin started to bubble. Things got worse as his wild eyes met mine in an intense stare down. "Who are you?" he demanded. He grabbed me and shook me like a puppet, "You're with them aren't you?" I pleaded for him to chill-out, but it was no use. "You're not takin' me back to that place motherfucker!" he yelled. He punched me dead in the face and I saw stars. He screamed and paced around smashing his furniture before reaching behind his bed and pulling out a very large kitchen knife. He turned to me with this insane look in his eyes and right fuckin' then and there, I knew it was time to make a quick exit. I'd seen that look before and I knew what it meant… run!

I stood up and he lunged with the knife, trying to stab me. I just barely got out of the way as he fell onto the bed and I ran out of his room. He chased me down the hallway yelling that he was going to kill me. Again he made a stabbing motion, and missed. The gods were definitely looking out for me and my athleticism was paying big dividends as he chased me around the furniture in his wing. I ran down the stairs with him in hot pursuit, but he wasn't letting up. I yelled for help as I ran to an apartment door and banged on it frantically. It was opened by a very tired brother with a nappy 'fro. I'll never forget the look on his face when he first saw me, with a scarred-up, butcher knife-wielding Bobby K. a few paces behind. We went in the back door and ran around some more furniture. I threw a chair in his way and he tripped over it. Then I ran out the front door and down the stairs with him in pursuit. I sprinted across the front lawn and thank God he finally ran out of gas. He collapsed on the grass, rolled around and screamed at the top of his lungs like a madman. I ran off the property and up onto the boardwalk. I looked back and saw that the windows were full of St. John's residents who were watching the action unfold. They were yelling and cheering Bobby K. on as he paced back across the front lawn with the night watchmen walking behind him and demanding he drop the knife.

That was my first trip, and one I would never forget, but the night wasn't over yet boys and girls. It was just getting started. I ran up to the Holland House, because I knew it was one place that Bobby K. would never go. I was still high on acid wanting the trip and the night to end. As I entered the Holland House, I found Paulie sprawled out across the hallway floor obviously too drunk to make it to one of the rooms. I stepped over him and noticed he was cradling a half-full bottle of whiskey. It was at that moment I committed the biggest sin you could ever commit to an alcoholic, I took his morning drink, the one that stopped him from shaking and got him, "right". Under the present circumstances I thought Paulie would understand, so I grabbed it and made my way up the stairs looking for an empty room to crash. I pushed a door open and found one with an old bed and smelly blanket that only God knew who, or what, had previously been sleeping on it. I closed the door, stretched out and drank that cheap whiskey. It was horrible, but it was made even worse because Paulie's breath could literally knock a maggot off a shit pile. I started to get tired before the whiskey kicked in and knocked me out. I pulled the blanket over my head and passed out.

Shortly after I blacked out I heard the door open and a female giggling. She came over to the bed and got under the blanket with me. Was this a dream? Was I still tripping? I reached over and touched her and I knew at that moment, it wasn't a dream. She was warm and soothing to the touch. She was also drunk and had I known what to do, believe me, I would have done it. I was still a virgin and just to have my arm around this girl and have her whisper, "That feels nice," softly in my ear was all I needed. We went to sleep, cuddling each other.

The only thing I remember, about the events that followed, was hearing someone shouting in the hallway. The sun was just coming up and as I lay there face down, still wasted and groggy from my big acid and booze-fueled adventure the night before, I shook it off thinking it was probably just Paulie complaining about me stealing his morning drink. Then the door to my room came crashing open and Danny (Phillip's cousin) barged in wielding a two-foot metal pipe. He rushed over, called the girl a slut and threw her on the floor. Then as I lay there face down, he smashed me in the back of the head without warning and everything went black.

I woke up some time later with my head throbbing and a huge gash, which was bleeding profusely. I made my way back to St. John's and stumbled into the infirmary to seek medical attention. My injuries were so severe that I was rushed to Peninsula Hospital in Far Rockaway. I had a slight fracture at the base of my skull and I had a very serious concussion. They kept me there for two days for observation, just to make sure my brain didn't swell. Two detectives from the 100th Precinct paid me a visit while I was laid up. Apparently, someone at St. John's called the cops about the incident and they wanted me to press charges against Danny for assault with a deadly weapon, which was a felony. They said this could be the final incident to put Danny away for a long stretch. Someone had witnessed him run into the building with the pipe and that obviously placed him at the scene, but they needed my testimony to prove he assaulted me. They told me he beat his girlfriend pretty badly, too, but she wouldn't press charges. "We need your help, John." they said. "Sign a statement and we'll lock his ass up for what he did to you." I looked up at the two cops and studied their faces. It was obvious they didn't give a fuck about me, because this was a personal vendetta against Danny. That's how it is with some cops. They take shit personally, especially if you beat them at their own game and get over on the system. Danny had beaten the system up until this point, and there was no doubt that fucker was a sick son of a bitch. But to put him in jail for doing what any male would have done, if he thought someone was boning his girl?

I looked up at the two cops and they smiled at me, pen and pad in hand, ready to take down my statement. The statement I made, "I don't know who hit me, I was sleeping." When they heard this, their smiles fell from their faces. They later said it didn't matter, all I had to do was just say I saw him with the pipe coming at me and that's the last thing I remember. I told them several more times that I didn't know who hit me and I wasn't signing anything. Well, they cared so much they walked out without even so much as goodbye or get-well soon. Go figure.

I checked out of the hospital later that day. When I got back to St. John's the staff put me in a room with a team of counselors and my caseworker, Brother Mark. They wanted me to press charges, because they were convinced it would teach the neighborhood thugs a lesson about what could happen to them if they continued to assault kids at St. John's. They all got the same response I gave the cops. "No dice, yo. I ain't no fuckin' rat."

Meanwhile, Danny's Rockaway clan was shitting bricks. Fuck bricks. They were shitting cinderblocks! I could seal Danny's fate with my testimony and his crew didn't know what I had told the cops. Danny was a lunatic who knew everyone in the neighborhood. He was the one guy even Margie's two sons wouldn't dare fuck with. As far as retribution was concerned, I was on my own. It became the talk of the town. "Did you hear the latest? Danny's crazy ass is in deep shit. They might finally get him for beating up that kid from St. John's." Although I didn't want to help out the cops, what they said to me at the hospital was true. Danny was a low-life scumbag who had robbed and beaten people beyond recognition, and done a slew of other shit they could never nail him for because everyone was scared to press charges. The law of the street back in the day said, and I quote, "Payback's a bitch, but revenge, that's a motherfucker." In other words, if someone does some shit to you, either get paybacks, or you get punked out. But never, ever, do you go to the cops and rat someone out, because they will live 'till their last dying breath waiting for their revenge. These days, especially in New York, things are much different. These chumps will talk shit, even pick a fight and after you try to convince these assholes nine ways to Sunday to chill out, they don't listen. Then they have to get what's coming to them. And would you believe it? Afterward, they actually call the cops on you. Back in the day, if you had beef, you fought it out. If you got your ass kicked fair and square, you shook hands and squashed it. That was old-school New York City.

Later that night, with bandages and all (for effect), I went down to one of the Irish bars near 116th where Danny hung out. When I walked in I could see he was nervous as shit. He had a drink in one hand and a crowd surrounding him. The bar went silent. His girl was sporting a nice shiner and she tapped him on the shoulder, pointing at me. The entire bar, including Danny, turned and looked at me. "Did anybody see these two, black fuckers who beat me up the other day?" I said. They all rushed at me cheering and hugging in approval.

See, I looked at it this way - I was a little light in the ass at a buck thirty to seek revenge on Danny. Besides, now I was on the inside of the Rockaway crew and for someone who lived his whole life as an outsider, the most important thing for me was to be part of something. Nevertheless, from that moment on, no matter how big, or how crazy they were, no one ever got away with any shit like that again. Even if I knew I was going to get my ass kicked, it didn't matter. If you fucked with me, I would fight you, take the beating, come back with an equalizer and hit a homerun upside your skull, because if you fucked me over, you had better watch your back 24/7.

The rest of that evening was spent getting free drinks. Danny repeatedly thanked me for not ratting to the cops and further assured me that I was his bro for life. He announced loudly to everyone in the bar that no one in Rockaway had better ever fuck with his little brother. At that moment, I had a good buzz going, but the best part about that entire night was yet to come. I was playing pool when out of the corner of my eye, I saw this really pretty girl looking at me. She was a local girl I'd seen around (who's name I don't remember), but never gave me the time of day. Making the most of my newfound neighborhood fame, I guess being the man for the moment had its benefits. She was about eighteen, with big breasts, and curly strawberry blonde hair. I was kind of drunk when she walked over and took the mug of beer out of my hand and informed me that if I drank anymore I'd be of no use to her. With that, she grabbed my hand and led me out of the bar. I passed Danny on the way out. He winked and gave me the thumbs up knowing what was coming next.

She took me to her mother's house in Rockaway Park - somewhere in the 120's. When we got there, she snuck me upstairs to her bedroom in the attic, where we smoked weed, listened to music and chatted. I was chatting nervously to break the tension, because I didn't know what the hell I was supposed to be doing up there. Sensing my nervousness, she told me to be quiet and took off all of her clothes except for her panties. She was so beautiful and way more physically developed than I was. When she reached down and took off her panties my eyes nearly popped out of my head. She had the biggest, hairiest, scariest, strawberry blonde bush I ever saw in my life. Not that I'd ever seen one in person before, but holy shit! There was more hair there than anything I had ever seen in my stacks of pornos, and that heap a' strawberry bush was making me feel inadequate compared to the small patch of fuzz I was sporting. I could literally get lost in that jungle. I just sat on the edge of her bed with my clothes on, staring at it in amazement. It was like she had Robert Plant in a leg lock. I mean shit, with a little braiding she could have given her shit the Bo Derek cornrow look from the movie, 10, complete with multi-colored beads.

She finally snapped me out of my trance by asking if I was going to take my clothes off. I was like, "Huh? Oh, yeah." I tried to play it off by giving her some line I read in a Sidney Sheldon novel like, "I was just taking in the awe and beauty of your nakedness" or some dumb shit, but she wasn't buying it. Then she said the five words no teenage male ever wants to hear, "You're a virgin, aren't you?" I nodded. She smiled and said it was obvious. She came toward me, unzipped my pants, got on her knees and started to give me head. My whole body felt flush. The blood was running out of my head and down to my lower extremity. She told me not to cum, but it was too late.

The rest of the night was a disappointment for her in terms of her own orgasms, but hey, I was a fourteen-year-old virgin. This was about me right? I didn't know shit about a G-spot, clitoral stimulation, sexual positions, or the fact that it takes a woman three times longer than a man to climax. I just let the sperm fly, even when her pleas turned into Linda Blair, Exorcist-type sounding demands as we had sex. Just replace, "Your mother sucks cocks in hell!" with, "I'm almost there! Don't cum this time or I'll fuckin' kill you and you'll burn in hell eternally," and you'll get the idea. I was waiting for her head to start spinning as she vomited split pea soup. In my naïveté I questioned, "What the hell are you waiting for, I came five times already?

Geeze-Louise." I know. I was a jerk. I tried to call her a couple of days later and she basically told me to call her after I'd had sex a few dozen times and had acquired some skills. As it turned out, it had nothing to do with my animal magnetism or my momentary celebrity; Danny had asked her to take me home. When I got back to St. John's three days later, they put me on restrictions for a week. I couldn't leave the wing except for school, which I cut anyway, so I didn't give a shit. Bobby K. was sent to a stricter place, since he broke wild on staff. In his maniacal rage he fucked a few of them up really badly. I hadn't heard anything from E, but I had heard the cops were looking for him for running away from St. John's.

A week after I was off restriction, I heard through the grapevine that a huge concert was happening at Madison Square Garden. On the bill were AC/DC, Ted Nugent and the headliner, the gods of rock themselves, Black Sabbath. I was amped and immediately began organizing my stash for the event. I had some weed, hash and money for tickets, liquor and other concert essentials. There was only one thing I still didn't have and that was a date. Having a date at a concert back then was crucial, because if you took a girl to a show she was yours forever, or for at least a week afterward. I knew super-bush wasn't going to go with me, but just to make sure I had to get a date, I bought two tickets. It would be the hottest concert of the year and all I had to do was find a girl to take with me.

I couldn't ask any of the locals, because all the good-looking ones already had boyfriends. I didn't like any of the white girls at P.S. 180 and the sisters didn't go for that type of heavy, rock music. At that point, landing a date for the show was looking grim. The concert was fast approaching and I still didn't have a girl to go with me. I walked around with the tickets in my pocket as a potential bargaining chip, just in case I met that special someone.

One day, after hanging out in The Circle drinking, I was walking down 116th Street and as I passed the Baskin-Robbins and looked inside, working behind the counter was the owner's daughter, Nadine. She was the prettiest girl I'd ever seen. She was a thin, seventeen-year-old with beautiful, long, wavy brown hair and an amazing smile.

At first, I just stood outside and watched her, thinking of what to say. I waited for all the customers to leave before I made my entrance. I ordered ice cream and had a whole line of bullshit prepared, but as soon as she said hello, it all went out the window. I was like Jackie Gleason's character, Ralph Cramden, on that episode of The Honeymooners, when he made it onto the $60,000 Question TV show. The first music trivia question they asked Ralph was to name the composer of a song that Norton was warming up with the whole time he and Ralph were practicing. Well, unfortunately he kept telling Norton to stop playing it and never bothered to find out who the composer was. So Ralph's reaction when he heard it on that show.... "Hummin-a, hummin-a, hummin-a... Ed Norton." My rap went something like that, except I finished it off with me holding up my Black Sabbath tickets and choking on the words, "You... like... uhh... I mean... wanna go with me?" She nodded yes. "What?" I asked. She said she'd love to go and her response blew me away. We made plans to meet and then as I turned to walk out she yelled, "Hey, what about your ice cream?" I said, "What ice cream?" She just laughed as I walked outside and waved goodbye, then she smiled and waved back at me.

The day of the show finally arrived and I was psyched. I had all the concert essentials - money, weed and a pint of Southern Comfort. We drank and smoked with the other concertgoers on the train to Manhattan. I was so proud that, once again, I was going to potentially score with an older chick. This time I swore I was not going to fuck it up. I really did my best to act cool and mature. By the time we got off at 34th Street I had the munchies bad. We stopped at one of the nasty pizza places they have near the Garden. She warned me not to eat too much with all the alcohol I had consumed, but I was hungry and assured her very confidently that I could handle my liquor. I bragged about my ability to drink people under the table. When we arrived at the pizza spot, I ordered three slices, an eggplant-parm hero, half a meatball sub, and a jumbo Coke. She had a slice but didn't finish it, and not wanting to waste food, I finished it for her.

When we got into the Garden and up to our seats (the key word here is, "up"), the tickets turned out to be severe nose-bleeders. It was funny seeing the look of disgust on her face as the ushers looked at our tickets and kept pointing towards the upper levels. By the time we finally sat down all you could basically see of the stage was a little speck. She was definitely not too happy about it, but I assured her the sound would be great (like I really knew what the fuck I was talking about). AC/DC opened up and they were cool, but I was more interested in getting something going with my date. I tried to kiss her, but she kept pushing me away saying that she wanted to watch the show. I was like, "Get with it here. I didn't spend $12.50 on your ticket for you to watch the opening fuckin' act." It's like this comedian said on BET's Comic View,

"Oh, when I take a bitch out to dinner I let her know right away, there's two sides to this menu. This side here, with the filet mignon, lobster and champagne, that's the 'A' side, the pussy side. Now the other side, the $3.99 dinner specials, complete with an eight-ounce, non-alcoholic beverage of your choice and greasy fries, that's the 'B' side, the no pussy side. Now, you tell me baby, which side we gonna be eatin' from?"

Right now, my date was strictly the 'B' side and I was pissed. I just played it off and put my arm around her, which she let me get away with. I was happy enough with that for the time being. I figured once Black Sabbath came out she would lose it and I would at least make my way to second base. In the '70s, part of the whole concert experience was when the headliner hit the stage, the crowd went crazy and the girls tongued down their boyfriends in appreciation. The other show ritual was that people used to pass joints, drinks and all kinds of shit around to the people sitting in their section. That night was no exception. I was passed blackberry brandy, dozens of joints, Southern Comfort, more joints, hash and now a familiar smell: dust. I smoked three, dust-laced joints and I was completely zooted. Nadine didn't take a single toke and, at this point, there was zero conversation between us. The room was spinning, I was higher than I had ever been in my entire life and that's when the house lights went out and everyone cheered and held up their lighters. Holy shit! Black Sabbath was taking the stage. I heard Geezer Butler's bass thump, Bill Ward's snare crack and Tony Iommi's Les Paul guitar wail, then Ozzy screamed, "Hello, New York!" I couldn't even begin to tell you what song they opened up with, but I remember the music was so fuckin' loud I felt it in my bone marrow. The explosion of white stage light flashed brighter than the sun, illuminating the entire arena. I also distinctly remember that I never got my kiss.

I was in my own world, but I still managed to drink and smoke some more during the first few songs. After about the third song everyone was sitting down and Ozzy was talking shit on stage. My head was spinning and I was starting to feel the pizza, meatball and eggplant parm subs and Coca-Cola, mixed with eight different types of alcohol and smoke-ables, all talking back to me. Loudly! Screaming, as a matter of fact. Now, to puke at a concert was the greatest mortal sin imaginable. Only chumps did it, so there was no way I was getting put into that category. Nadine looked over at me and asked if I was okay, because she said I looked green. Green? Shit, I felt like hell as the contents of my stomach were doing continuous loops. I told her I was fine and even managed to sneak in a quick peck on her cheek. Then I heard it, that unmistakable bass drum kick and heavy guitar intro before Ozzy screamed, "I am Iron Man."

I immediately jumped up and shouted "Ozz..." and before I got to the, "zeeee" out came the biggest flood of projectile vomit you have ever seen in your life! Since, I was way up in the blue section at the Garden, it sprayed out and covered every single person within a twenty-foot radius. I mean, you actually heard the "Uhhhhhs" over the thunderous music. This was proceeded by a loud chorus of people calling me a fuckin' douche-bag, asshole and scumbag motherfucker. Yes boys and girls, I chumped-out and it smelled like shit up there. Thanks to me, the people around me who were so cool before would now have to sit through the entire concert covered in my stomach regurgitation and they were pissed. Nadine was totally embarrassed and she moved two seats away from me in disgust. I looked up at her with mozzarella and Parmesan cheese dangling off my chin, my breath smelling like shit and I still had the balls to blurt out, "Can I have that kiss now?" She flipped me off. I attempted to speak again, but before I could get the words out I again covered my peers with cheap Italian food. Now I had people seriously wanting to kick my ass. They were like, "Puke on the floor, asshole!" Puke on the floor? How the hell was I going to see Ozzy if I puked on the floor? I let out another raging flood of undigested 34th Street specials and that was that. I slouched in my seat, hunched over and don't even remember the rest of the concert. What I do remember is that Nadine woke me up when the show was over. The house lights were on and the place was basically empty except for the Garden employees cleaning up and a few of the other fuckers who were in a similar state of consciousness.

I spent the entire two-hour train ride puking my brains out between subway cars. Nadine was so pissed off that she wouldn't even talk to me. She became strike number two on my list of dating experiences and, at that point, I promised myself there wouldn't be a third.

That Christmas I spent a few days at my mom's. When it was over I took the cash the family gave me and ran to the Q-53 bus stop. Right underneath it, in the subway station at 74th and Roosevelt Avenue, was the city's coolest headshop. It was tucked away in the back behind a barbershop. The guy who ran it always played loud, rock music and burned massive amounts of incense. That sound and scent is what first lured me down to "The Dungeon," as I referred to it. It was dark inside, illuminated with black lights and the slickest selection of black light posters money could buy. They had all the pipes, bongs, gas masks, papers, poppers (amyl-nitrate), roach clips, and anything else you needed to get lifted. I think they also sold weed, but the guy working there would act like I was crazy whenever I brought it up. Every time I went there, I saw people come in, slap him five with a bill in their hand and pick up a brown paper bag. They'd look around at the pipes without ever buying anything and leave thirty seconds later. You do the math.

I always bought something and this trip was no different. My latest purchase was a multi-colored gas mask with a huge bowl attached and shotgun tube for joints. It came complete with an elastic band to go around your head, so you didn't even have to hold it while you got high. I got on the Q-53, went to the back of the bus, filled up my bowl, and smoked a couple on my way back to St. John's. Man, you had to love the city back then.

By mid-January of '77, I was barely at St. John's, because I was getting pretty tight with the Rockaway locals. I made friends with the Otts, the Pullises and most of the 116 crew. I think they liked me, because in my quest to fit in, I always went overboard to prove my loyalty to whatever crew I rolled with. They were my makeshift family and I was always the first to fight for their cause, even if it meant beating someone up for calling Tommy Pullise's brother a dick under their breath, more than seven months ago.

During that time, I was also hanging with the local dealers. Guys like Wally C., Silah and a cat named, Jimbo, became my "go to guys". They always had the best shit: wacky weed, Panama red, Acapulco gold, Thai-stick, microdots (LSD), or whatever else was around. They were older guys, in their late-twenties and they all had crazy stories to tell about hanging out in Manhattan, getting into trouble. Their stories fascinated me and I was hooked. They made Manhattan sound like such a far off and different place, almost foreign. They talked about the downtown scene and this new music called punk rock. They talked about how the people who were into punk dressed like freaks and were crazy as shit. Up until that point, all I'd ever been exposed to in Manhattan was The Deuce, and I promised myself that at the first opportunity I was going downtown to check it out.

welcome to the LES - the ABCD's of survival

chapter 5

During the last week of January '77, I ran away from St. John's. As a fourteen-year-old runaway, the first thing I realized was that I needed to find shelter on the frozen wasteland known as Rockaway Beach. Brother Mark had convinced the cops to put a warrant out for my arrest, so I had to keep a low profile. Seeking refuge at the Holland House was out of the question. It had pretty much burned to the ground because some drunk fell asleep with a lit cigarette. Instead, my first two nights on the street were spent under an abandoned movie theatre marquee on 116th Street. I huddled together with several other people, whom I guess you'd call bums. To keep warm, someone lit a fire in a garbage can filled with planks of wood from the boardwalk. I have to give major props to the city for giving us an endless supply. It was funny as shit, too, because every winter huge sections of the boardwalk were removed and we would crack up when they sent workers out there in the freezing cold to fix it. Sure as shit, a day later they'd be somewhere else replacing another section, we'd ripped out the night before. After two nights of that I smelled like a smoked piece of meat. Everything I owned smelled like wood smoke, which didn't amount to much more than the clothes on my back.

On the third day the wind picked up and the temperature substantially dropped. According to Paulie, a winter storm was headed right for us and we desperately needed a place to stay. The marquee was out, (it had huge holes in the roof) so my third night on the street was spent under the boardwalk with Paulie and two other guys. We strung ropes across the beams and hung two large pieces of plastic on either side of us to act as wind barriers from the frigid air. The wind whipped about 40 mph off the water and dropped the temperature into the teens. That night, I spent a considerable amount of time on the frozen sand looking out at the cargo ships' lights flickering in the distance. It began to snow and despite the frigid weather, I felt a warm sense of peace come over me.

As far as I was concerned the New York State Foster Care and Group Home Systems had failed me. For the most part, state agencies didn't really try to help kids who had problems as a result of the abuse they had suffered. Even to this day, they try to remedy the situation by putting these kids on heavy meds to shut them up and calm them down. They receive more money from the government for every kid they medicate. I was glad that I was finally on my own. Even though my living conditions were horrible, I was content and convinced I could do better on my own.

The following morning, I woke up at dawn, soaking wet and freezing. My alcoholic compadres and I forgot to take into consideration that the snow would eventually make its way through the cracks in the boardwalk. Being the half-assed Boy Scouts we were, we didn't think to hang something above us. I crawled out to the edge of the boardwalk. To my delight, I found a huge snowdrift blocking the exit. I pushed my way through it and stood out on the desolate beach for a moment. It had snowed all night and there was at least two feet on the sand. At that point, I started to think that maybe I had made a mistake by leaving St. John's. I could have gone back at that moment and my punishment would have been more restriction time. But my sense of adventure got the better of me. I had lived that life, thus far, and now it was time for a change. I didn't know where this road was going to take me, but at that moment I had just three things on my mind - dry clothes, a warm place to crash, and some hot food. I had $20 to my name, so shopping at Macy's and eating at Tavern on the Green were both out of the question. Instead, I settled for stealing someone's clothes out of a dryer at the Laundromat and a trip to my favorite greasy spoon.

It was business as usual at Martin's Corner. The rude, obese, balding manager was running around barking orders at everyone. The stench from the smoked meat filled the air along with the smell of French fries, coffee, eggs and cigarettes. Anyone who lives near a beach town knows that once winter hits it's locals only. The local population of Rockaway consisted of mostly derelicts, drunks, drug addicts and insane old people who were dumped in the nursing homes that lined the boardwalk. It was about 11 a.m. and I had just made the cut off point for M.C.'s breakfast special: two eggs, home fries, toast and juice, for a $1.99. I kicked up the cash then counted my life savings - $18.01 left.

I sat down in the back next to this crazy, old guy who had a big, wet pee stain on his crotch. He stunk like shit. He was puffing his cigarette like it was his first in years and washing it down with Martin's Corner's finest coffee. His fingers were stained yellow and his nails were very long and dirty - outdone only by his filthy hair and clothes. I sat next to him and wondered, "Who loves this person? What's his story? Does he have any kids? If so, how could they just forget about him?" I looked around Martin's Corner at the rest of the crazy old people. Most of them were talking to themselves and the thought entered my mind that even though my mom wasn't there for me as a kid, I would never dump her in an old age home. I would never let her become like the forgotten old people of Rockaway Beach.

I took my time with breakfast. I warmed up and contemplated my next move, which came to me a short time later. It was about noon and a lot of the kids from P.S. 180 had come in to eat lunch and play pinball. The first thing that changes in a human being, when he or she goes into survival mode, is their perspective. When I had three hots and a cot at St. John's, I took things for granted. I didn't appreciate every bite of food and I never worried about my next meal. I never thought about finding a warm place to spend the night and I never paid attention to the kids playing pinball. But things were different now. I was like a tiger lurking in the jungle that never takes for granted a potential passing meal. I watched kid after kid pumping quarters into those machines and I'm thinking, "There's four machines back there. There's got to be at least fifty bucks in each of them."

I looked around to figure what my odds were. The manager couldn't see me from behind the counter, which was a plus. I didn't have anything to pry the front door of the machines open, but there was a hardware store down the block. If I went that route, it would mean spending money on a scheme that might not even come off. I scanned the rest of the room and noticed someone staring at me. It was this weird looking dude with long, straight brown hair, a droopy mouth and eyes, and lots of track marks running up and down his arms. He went by the name of Mikey Debris. Mikey was always either high, or on a mission to get high. The one thing that really got under my skin about him was that he always had this nasty, white foam caked on the corners of his mouth and when he talked, you had to dodge the shit. I was always saying, "Fuck Mikey! Say it, don't spray it!"

Mikey consistently read the newspaper every single day, so he could keep up with the latest music and entertainment news. Actually, the motherfucker was kind of intelligent and he knew something about everything. He was definitely crazy and not just your dictionary definition of crazy. He was crazy in a Nietzsche-syphilis kind of way. That's one thing a lot of people who read Nietzsche's shit don't know about him. When he was coming up with all that speculative philosophy, he was going mad from advanced syphilis. Mikey was definitely the Nietzsche-type. He was a junkie/philosopher who could philosophically scam any fucker out of their last ten bucks, just so he could get high. In the process, he actually made you feel good that you gave it to him. When I saw him for the first time at Martin's Corner, I realized something else too: I wasn't the only one keeping track of the money being pumped into the pinball machines. He nodded at me, as if to say, "Get a late pass kid, I'm way ahead of ya on this one." He reached under his coat and produced a huge screwdriver that he had hidden in his folded-up newspaper. My burnt-out new friend and I were on the same wavelength.

I learned one thing very quickly about life on the streets and it's this: if you need to make money, hang out with junkies. Reason being, they never take a day off! There's no, "I think I'll take a couple of weeks off and gather my thoughts. You know, come up with a new life plan." Fuck no, those bastards have a habit to support and they work seven days a week, 365 days a year. There is no calling in sick. When a junkie gets sick, it means they really have to get off their ass and get moving. Now, you ask any business owner if they'd like to have a work force of motivated individuals like that and see what they say. Mikey used to make the classic junkie joke, that if he put the same effort into a legit career, he would be a wealthy retiree. I didn't doubt his hustle, because simply put, he was the best I'd ever seen. Compared to what I had done in the past, he made our Valenti capers look like the fuckin' Cub Scouts.

Mikey waved me over and I went and sat with him. He explained that he would watch out for the manager and since I was a strapping, young lad with lots of energy, I would be the one doing all the work. That's how it was with him. He wanted you to do the work and he would collect at the end. His reasoning was, that he was the mastermind and that 50 percent of the effort was coming up with the shit in the first place. I had to agree because he had the screwdriver and a pillowcase to carry the loot. I grabbed both, and with that our business venture was now up and running.

I stepped up and moved the kids out of the way. I told them to be quiet and pointed at Mikey, who looked at them menacingly and intimidated them with a large knife. He then made a slicing motion across his neck and the kids were frozen with fear. I popped one machine after another. The metal boxes inside were filled to the top with coins and I emptied them all into the pillowcase. When I got to the fourth and final machine, a shitload of them fell on the floor making a loud noise. The manager heard the commotion and came around the corner. He looked at his machines and the chase was on. I never saw that fat bastard move so quickly. He called Mikey and me every curse word under the sun, as he grabbed a baseball bat from behind the counter and chased us out the back door. We barely escaped a Louisville Slugger homerun attempt at our heads. We ran down the street laughing before the manager finally gave up a half-block later. He collapsed on the sidewalk, not even able to finish his, "If you pricks ever come back I'll..." declaration. I turned to Mikey and said, "The food sucked ass, anyway." He laughed and slapped me five, as we headed over to his place to split up the cash.

We walked a few blocks and came upon a run-down bungalow surrounded by a dilapidated fence. It looked abandoned but Mikey pushed open the swinging gate. He told me his roommate was a crazy motherfucker and was most likely asleep. He said the last thing we wanted to do was wake his ass up. I nodded and we went inside. The first thing I was hit with when he opened the front door was the stench. I'm not just talking a little foul odor here, folks. I'm talking rotting corpses. When he saw the look on my face, Mikey said, "Sorry, the maid comes on Wednesdays." We stepped over somebody who was passed out in the hallway and walked toward the living room. I heard a record player with its needle stuck in a groove. Yes' "Roundabout" endlessly repeated, "I'll be a... I'll be a..."

It was the filthiest place I had ever seen. Empty Chef Boyardee ravioli cans (a junkies' favorite, eaten cold from the can) littered the room, along with beer bottles, Cap 'N Crunch cereal boxes, milk containers and enough trash to fill a 25-cubic-yard-dumpster. This dump made the Holland House look like the Ritz-Carlton. And where there's trash and old food, there are always roaches. Here, there were hundreds of them running around.

The room was dark except for the light coming from a little lamp. They'd hung thick blankets over the windows to block out the sunlight. When I scanned the room further, I saw someone passed out in an old, cushioned chair. Upon further examination, I noticed he had a syringe sticking out of his hand and a belt wrapped around his wrist. This fine upstanding citizen of the Rockaway community was Buckles. Buckles was in his late-20s, maybe even early-30s. He had long, thick, bushy black hair and a goatee and looked exactly like Jesus Christ, if Jesus had a $100-a-day heroin habit. As legend had it in Rockaway, Buckles got his name from beating several individuals close to death with his belt and buckle, which he wrapped around his fist like brass knuckles.

Mikey walked over and slapped the table, which skipped the record forward. The song kicked in, "…Roundabout. The words will make you out and out. You spend the day your way…" He walked over to Buckles and tenderly, as only a loving, junkie brother could, pulled the needle out of Buckles' hand. Buckles woke up singing (it was more like moaning) right on fuckin' cue, "In and around the lake, mountains come out of the sky and they stand there." He wiped his mouth, rolled his eyes and nodded at Mikey. He looked at me and said, "Who the fuck are you?" Before I could speak Mikey interrupted. He held up the pillowcase full of coins, "That's John. We just hit the machines at Martin's Corner." I think the word Buckles mumbled was, "Cool," or something like it. Mikey asked Buckles if he'd saved him a taste. He pointed to the kitchen and nodded back out. Mikey headed off with the coins and I followed him thinking that it might have been some cue for him to run out the back door.

In the kitchen I noticed baking pans, blotter paper, and empty gelatin capsules, next to bottles of vitamins. I'm thinking either Betty fuckin' Crocker's been over, or these fuckers are up to something. Mikey noticed my interest in the stuff and said he'd tell me all about it later. Right now, he had a more pressing issue to deal with. He put the bag of coins on the table, reached above the sink and pulled down a coffee can. He opened it, reached in and pulled out a small wax baggie. Mikey said he needed to get "right" and I was pretty sure I knew what that meant.

I'd never seen anyone do heroin before. So, I watched anxiously as he removed his works from a cereal box, before gathering the rest of his tools. He sat down in a chair, cooked the dope on a spoon and pulled it up into the syringe through a piece of cotton. He lightly tapped on the syringe, checking for air bubbles and squirted out the smallest drop. He looked at me and said, "If you're scared of needles don't watch." I wasn't. I watched him try to find a vein by tapping on his arm. He explained how most of his veins had collapsed from years of heroin abuse and he often had trouble finding an undamaged one. Finally, he injected himself and pulled the needle out before dropping it on the table. His eyes rolled back and a warm smile came over his face as he nodded out for a second. I looked at him and the pillowcase of coins and thought about just taking it and cutting out. He looked up at me and said, "Don't even think about it." I tried to play dumb, but Mikey wasn't buying it. He clutched the pillowcase with one hand and mumbled, "Never try this shit kid. You might like it," before he passed out. I looked around at his living conditions and I noticed his swollen vein. He had blood oozing from it, and a foot-and-a-half long river of drool, dangling from his mouth. "No worries there, Mikey." I said.

He woke up about a half-hour later and we got down to the business of counting coins. When we finished, his face lit up, because the final tally was close to $250. The split according to Mikey was $110 for him and $110 for me. Hearing that, I gave him a look and said, "I guess math wasn't your best subject, huh?" He went on to explain that, since it was Buckles' place, we had to give him a small cut, which was cool with me. I wanted to get on Buckle's good side, since I was also looking for a place to crash for the night.

I hung out with Buckles and Mikey, and they both wanted to know my story. I told them about my mom and Dad, the Valentis, Garden City and St. John's. I think they were blown away with what I had told them, even though I left out some of the most fucked up details. Buckles was a really cool dude and he knew a lot about life and music. Mikey told me his own life was a series of tragedies. As a kid, his father repeatedly beat him and I believe it damaged his brain, because his speech and motor functions were slow, even when he wasn't high. Mikey said he'd started doing heroin at sixteen and a year later it had progressed into a $100-a-day habit. He told me he was locked up and from what I could gather, most of it was hard time. Since he was a frail junkie, he wasn't a good fighter and when he talked about jail, I saw something in his eyes that told me he probably ended up as somebody's bitch.

Buckles said that if I needed to crash at his place for a little while it was cool with him. We shook hands and he split to take care of some business. Mikey immediately hipped me to the fact that Buckles must have thought I was cool, because he gave me the nod to crash at his place. If he thought otherwise, he would have smacked the shit out of me, taken my money and thrown me the fuck out. Then, he informed me that I had to earn my keep and he had a job for me. When I asked what kind of job, he just smiled and said, "Something in the transportation field."

Later that night I found out what he meant by 'transportation field.' Mikey had a little business on the beach, which explained why sketchy motherfuckers constantly knocked on the door, day and night, looking for him. His scheme worked like this: he would take orders from the junkies in Rockaway and Far Rockaway, then travel to Manhattan, which he called "First & First. " Once he got to Manhattan, he would regularly cop upwards of ten bundles of dope, which consisted of ten bags for $100. He would take the bundles back to Rockaway, tap a little bit from each bag and sell it to the junkies who had ordered it. Not only did he steal their shit, they each had to give him a bag for every bundle they bought from him. His business prowess allowed him to have his habit paid for and he even made a few bucks on top of it. As a side note, Mikey never did give Buckles his $30 cut from the pinball machine caper.

Now, here's where I fit into the transportation equation. In the past, Mikey got snatched up on the LES by two DT's (narcotics detectives) who were on to his little dope-peddling operation. These guys were getting pay-offs from the local, and the out-of-town, dealers. Back in the '70s, there was a history of corruption in the 9th Precinct (the location of TV show, Barney Miller). It was so bad at one point that they had to transfer half the cops to other precincts.

Mikey refused to pay these cops off, citing economic reasons. The two cops put the word out that, if he came down there, he was definitely going to jail. With Mikey's previous record, another arrest translated into more time upstate. So, we agreed that I would be Mikey's drug mule to smuggle the dope back to Rockaway. Mikey would ride the train with me to the LES. There we'd get off and he'd tell me the dealer's name, what he looked like and what building he set up shop in front of. I'd pick up the dope and meet him back at the train station. We'd ride the train back to Rockaway and he'd sit at the opposite end of the subway car, while I carried all the shit. He thought the cops wouldn't even look twice at some little fourteen-year-old Irish kid with blonde hair and blue eyes. Since he looked like a junkie, he got tossed just about every time he traveled the LES to score dope.

The train ride was long as shit and it carried us through some of the worst neighborhoods in the city. If you want an experience you'll never forget, ride the A train from Queens through Brooklyn and up to 207th Street in Manhattan. Right behind me on a wall of the CC train was one of my wack Nate 1 tags, crossed out with toy scrawled over it. I laughed to myself and wondered what the fuck was up with that crazy son of a bitch Bobby K. Two hours later, we arrived at our stop, Second Avenue. Before I even got out of the train station I heard, "C and D, C and D. What you need white boys?" Mikey and I turned around. A black junkie was pissing on a subway girder with one hand and scratching his face with the other. He looked up and said, "Oh shit, what up Mikey?" Turned out Mikey knew the guy. His gig was to hang out in the train station and wait for white people who were too terrified, about being down on the LES, to venture any further. He'd get their money to go cop for them and rip them off. If he did honest business with anyone, he would cop, then escort them to one of the many shooting galleries in Alphabet City. Now, you may be thinking, why didn't they just cop and go home to get high? Junkies... you can answer that one for me. When you're fiending and you have a couple of bags of dope burning a hole in your pocket, the last thing you're going to do is wait 'til you get home. Most seasoned veterans would usually cop a couple of bags first, test it to see if it's good, then go back and cop another bundle or two. Over the years, I noticed that as soon as word got out that people were overdosing – even dying – because of the potency of a certain brand of heroin, there would be a mad rush of junkies showing up looking for that specific brand. It got to the point that whenever we saw a sudden influx of junkies invading our neighborhood (like zombies from the Night of the Living Dead) we'd just assume that some junkies had recently O.D.'d.

Mikey waved off the street-urchin junkie on the platform and we went upstairs. I exited the train station alone and looked around. I was completely blown away. I'd never seen anything like it in my life – the derelicts, the addicts, the fucked up buildings and the brazen attitude of the dealers who lined the street. The dealers announced their shit like it was some kind of Middle-Eastern flea market. They each had a name for their particular brand of dope - poison, mad dog, express and the list went on and on. I couldn't help but wonder how the fuck they came up with those names. I imagined a bunch of whacked out, junkie-ass dealers sitting around a corporate boardroom all dressed in suits, notepads in hand, having a marketing conference on dope names. "I say, Roger. I shot up a few cc's of the new product – purely for research you understand – and I saw Satan. How 'bout we call it, red devil? All those in favor..." I think there could be a funny skit or two in it for Saturday Night Live. In fact, I've seen a lot of shit down there back in the day that would make great material. I remember one time seeing something so out of place, I thought I was in a fuckin' Twilight Zone episode. It was the dead of winter and freezing, but parked on a street corner was an ice cream truck. The name on the side, "Cool Man." Can you believe it? Cool Man fuckin' ice cream! But there were no children lining up to purchase a double scoop of vanilla-chocolate with sprinkles on top. Hell, no. There was a line of junkies halfway down the block. There were dozens and dozens of them, all high as hell and on the nod, ice cream cones melting all over them. Then they would do that weird thing junkies do (perhaps you've witnessed it for yourself); like some ritual dance, they move in ultra-slow, Matrix-type speed, bend over until they practically have their heads on the ground and just when you think they're going to fall over, they pop back up. In my day, I've seen some pretty fuckin' acrobatic junkies and if I was a betting man, I'd put my money on any one of them in a limbo contest. Just give them a couple of bags of dope, or their methadone fixes, and let the games begin.

Anyhow, Mikey told me how to find the dealer, then he split. Just as he did, a cop car made a show of patrolling (they never actually get out). The dealers' mantra resounded loudly, "Bahando! Bahando!" they shouted. It means, "duck," in Spanish and that's exactly what they would do, scattering like roaches. Once the cops passed, they would re-emerge and handle their business without missing a beat.

After about ten minutes had passed (and of course he wasn't where Mikey said he was) I finally found his dealer, a Puerto Rican named, Poppo. Poppo had really bad acne, lots of horrible, jailhouse tattoos, and track marks running up and down his arms. We exchanged pleasantries and then made the transaction in an alleyway. He then told me, in barely comprehensible English, that he was going to have some banging shit the following week. I nodded in approval and paid him. We shook hands and made plans to meet at the same time and place a week later. I stuffed the ten bundles in my underwear and before I split, he told me to watch my back. I took a deep breath and walked out of that alley with a whole new sense of importance.

A few weeks later, we went to the LES to cop, when Mikey ran into another one of his old Puerto Rican homies, Canito, his former "cellie" (cellmate) upstate. Canito was one scary lookin', muscle-bound motherfucker, who was just released after serving a three-year bid. See, in most cases, when you're locked up, you aren't getting high every day, you're eating three squares and passing the time by banging weights to put on size, what's referred to as "getting your weight up." For the first few months after they get out, most junkie-convicts have a clear head and are still pretty diesel, which makes them extremely dangerous.

Canito told Mikey about their homies upstate and they also reminisced about the time spent locked up. He knew exactly what Mikey was doing down on the LES. They talked privately for a few minutes then Mikey looked at me and said, "Change of plans." We walked out of the train station and headed up First Avenue, where Canito was showered with praise from his homies who lived on the block. He knew everyone and with all the handshakes, hugs and "Good to see you, yo. When you get out's?" it took us a half-hour just to make it to Twelfth Street. As we crossed First Avenue, Canito stopped and looked me dead in the eyes with this crazed look. Even though I was nervous as shit, I played it cool. He pointed up at the First Avenue street sign and with this wild-eyed stare, he explained that "The Guardians of the Threshold" (the sick motherfuckers who hung out east of First Avenue in Alphabet City) had a saying about crossing this avenue and leaving the demilitarized zone. If you came to 'A' you was adventurous, 'B' you was bold, 'C' you was crazy and 'D,' you was a dead, maricón." I smiled and dropped one of my St. John's homeboy lines on him, "Damn! You's a poet and you know it." Canito smiled, realizing I'd had a little contact with the brothers. He told Mikey that he liked my little motherfuckin' white ass and with that, we headed east.

I didn't dare ask where we were going. I just played it cool. I tagged along and kept my mouth shut, trying to take in as much scenery as possible without obviously staring. It was even wilder than Eldridge Street complete, with bodegas, loud Spanish music, even more decrepit looking junkies and a serious element of danger I'd never felt before. To be honest with you, I liked everything about the place. Our Latino friend walked into a bodega and walked out with two needles in his hand, before he tucked them in his pocket and we continued on. At that point I figured out what was going on. Mikey was paranoid and kept looking around for his two undercover buddies in their unmarked, dark blue Plymouth Fury III. Canito told him to relax, because they weren't on duty that day. Mikey let out a sigh of relief and smiled with his broke, greenish-black teeth, before the three of us walked down Avenue C to an abandoned building.

When we got to the building, we walked around to the back and headed down a set of stairs. Canito pushed open a door and we entered the basement. Inside there were a lot of dirty chairs and mattresses, and when we proceeded to the back room, I saw dozens of used needles littering the floor. I now understood that we were in a shooting gallery. Mikey looked at me and said, "Gimme the package." I pulled it out of my pants and gave it to him figuring his buddy was going to buy a couple of bags. Wrong. The greed and bad habits of Mikey Debris were about to get the best of him.

He completely ripped off the dudes he was copping for, and when one of them caught up with Mikey a week later, he threw him a serious beating. When word got around Rockaway that everyone was looking for Mikey, Buckles had to throw Mikey and me out. Since people knew Buckles and Mikey lived together, Buckles feared someone would burn his bungalow down as payback for Mikey's stupidity. It was freezing out and we were broke, but according to Mikey, not for long. I was about to find out what all those kitchen supplies were for, and what his obsession with knowing about every concert in the area was all about.

One great thing about Rockaway in the wintertime was that most people never came out there to check on their summer rentals. You could basically live in one all winter, if you could deal with the cold. We broke into an abandoned bungalow, somewhere near Playland. Then we went to a drug store. The first thing on the list was Vicks Formula 44 cough syrup, then a pack of cigarettes. Then it was off to a stationary store for blotter paper. Mikey always loved to keep you in suspense and he was doing a damn good job so far. We sat in the freezing cold bungalow. Our breath was visible in the sunlight that crept through the broken boards covering the windows. "Alright Mikey," I said, "what the fuck is up?" He pulled out a torn newspaper ad announcing the band, Yes, was playing at the Garden the next two nights. I still didn't get it. He looked at me like I was a lost case and then he went to work like a surgeon.

He put some newspaper down, pulled out the blotter paper and set it on top. He opened the bottle of cough syrup, poured some into the cap and opened the pack of cigarettes. He took one out, snapped off the filter and tore the paper away so the only thing left was the cotton. He carefully dipped the cotton filter into the cough syrup and pressed it onto the blotter paper, making perfect little circles. He counted, "Five, ten, fifteen, twenty… you catchin' on yet, slow-poke?" I sure-as-shit was! This fucker was going to have us selling this stuff as tabs of acid at the next two Yes shows. When I expressed some doubt, Mikey looked at me and said, "Let me give you a quote from a notorious scammer and one of my heroes, P.T. Barnum. 'There's a sucker born every minute, and two to take him.' We are the two." Mikey kept working away and

I realized he was right. I mean, Bobby K. and I fell for the acid scam up on The Deuce, right? Although there was no way in hell I would ever tell Mikey, because I knew I'd never hear the end of it.

According to our sales pitch this wasn't just any acid, this was brown blotter (Vicks being brown) and it was the most potent, mind-altering, knock-your-dick-in-the-dirt shit around. If they said they never heard of it, our rebuttal was perfect, "That's because we got an inside guy who steals it from a government testing facility in D.C. You know those pricks keep the best drugs for themselves." That would usually seal the deal. In reality, the bottom line was that at best, the most our shit would do for them was relieve their coughs and scratchy throats.

Mikey was aware of several important facts when it came to this scam. Just as Sir Isaac Newton had his laws of physics – what goes up must come down and all that bullshit – Sir Mikey Debris, the self-declared "King of all Street Hustling Scumbags," had his laws of the hustle. He knew that there were thousands of people at these concerts all running around trying to find that last little piece of get-high, so their concert went down perfectly. That brings us to Mikey's First Law: "It's All a Numbers Game." For every person that suspects you might be beating them, there are twenty people who don't. With that ratio, never waste your time on some lone asshole who doubts your shit and asks a million questions.

It was all about supply and demand. Anywhere Mikey dealt, he always had an unlimited supply, and not just acid. He could make hash (he baked himself and it smelled exactly like the real thing), weed, speed, coke, dope, you name it. If it was a drug, this junkie fucker could create its pseudo-counterpart. One day, I remember his ass needed to get high so badly that he bought a bottle of vitamin B-12. He dumped those fuckers in a plastic baggie, ran into Forrest Park in Queens and a half-hour later, had sold forty of them as pink 697's for $3 each. Talk about productivity in the work force.

We finished the rest of the bogus brown blotter hits in the freezing bungalow and cut them into perfect little squares. Since Mikey was a stickler for detail, he went so far as to wrap them up in individual little pieces of aluminum foil. Then it was finally time to head into the city for the most important ingredient of our sales pitch - real acid. Mikey had a real dose and we each took half, so that when people asked, "Dude, how do we know this shit is good?" We'd be like, "Shmedrick, take a look at me. I'm tripping my fuckin' nuts off on half a hit. We dropped and then hopped the train to the city, which was packed with concert goin' folk. Mikey said he could feel it in his bones, it was going to be a big night, but I was nervous. I kept asking him questions concerning my sales pitch. I could tell it was starting to annoy him because, when you annoyed Mikey, he would just ignore you and act like you didn't exist. The A train pulled into the 34th Street station and came to a stop. The doors opened and we jumped out. That's when the acid hit me and I got a solid head-rush. It was only a microdot and it wasn't really spacey, but I was definitely high.

The trick was not to start selling your shit, until an hour before the concert started. If someone bought your acid and it didn't get them high, there wasn't enough time for them to look for you, because they wouldn't want to miss the show. Instead, they cursed you and your first born, and went inside. We walked back and forth between 33rd and 35th Streets. Within forty minutes I moved about thirty hits of that crap and it was great! We traded our stuff for some seconals (a barbiturate) for Mikey. We swapped for bootleg T-shirts and tickets, so after we handled our business we could check out the show. This shit was better than having an American Express Gold Card with an unlimited line of credit. Eventually we took our operation inside and sold fake trips in the hallways, the bathrooms, and up and down the aisles before the show started. Then, like the faithful fans we were, we walked over to our section and watched the show.

You wanna know what's hilarious about people who buy acid? They all want a step-by-step breakdown of the fuckin' high. "Alright, asshole. First you're gonna see fuckin' trails, lotsa fuckin' trails. Then, shit's gonna melt in front of your fuckin' face and before the end of the night, you'll see God and he'll tell you what an amazing fuckin' human being you are. How's that?" Bottom line, no acid ever affects people in exactly the same way and we knew that. We just told them what they wanted to hear. I've seen two people take a hit of the exact same shit and one have a beautiful trip and the other freak the fuck out. Perfect example - me and Bobby K. I understood their concerns though. No one wants a bad trip, especially at a concert and I constantly assured them, "Dude, believe me, with our shit – and you have my word on this – you got absolutely nothing to worry about."

We sold out that first night, before we went inside. Not a problem for Mikey. I shit you not. We went into a bathroom stall inside the Garden and pressed up more bogus hits. We were actually selling shit that still had wet cough syrup on it. The vics would even comment that it tasted sweet as they put it on their tongues. Mikey and me would elbow each other and try to hold back from cracking the fuck up in their faces. It was hard, too, because one of the side effects of microdot is laughing your ass off.

Although I was initially nervous about selling the fake trips, Mikey watched me close a few sales and he said I was a natural. He said he'd never seen anyone like me, operating with such sheer balls on the first time out. I can't take all the credit on that though. I have to give props to E for inspiring me to hustle. I was just as, if not more, convincing than Mikey and he assured me I had a definite future in the beat drug market, because I understood Mikey's Second Law: "You Have to Believe your own Bullshit."

The reason was simple. If you didn't convince yourself, how could you convince anyone else? When we sold our shit, we never, not even for a second, let the thought enter our minds that we were scamming people. It's like this cosmic vibe of conviction in your product. Any good salesperson has to have that, no matter what they're selling, or the customer will pick up on it and you'll lose the sale. When we went out to meet the buying public, no matter what the location or the product, we had the best shit and the fuckers would be lucky to get some of it. I even saw Mikey turn people down and walk away from anyone who ever questioned his integrity in the slightest way. For his sheer prowess and determination I named Mikey Chairman of the Board of our street pharmaceutical corporation, PPI - Pseudo Products, Inc.

I made more than $300 that first night at the Garden, and back then that was a shit load of money, especially for a fourteen-year-old kid. Mikey jokingly told me not to spend it all on candy. I didn't know what the hell to spend it on other than food. I had all the drugs I needed, just from bartering at the concert. I felt pretty damn good about my skills and I remember thinking that E would be proud of my hustle. Even in the face of adversity, with one highly skeptical customer, I stuck to my guns and got through it. I was outside the Garden that first night, near 33rd Street and 7th Avenue, and I was in the 'flow' as we called it. The bullshit was pouring out of me and I had an amazing 100 percent success rate with my last twenty, consecutive customers. The flow only came after you made a few sales and had your rebuttals firing off left, right and fuckin' center, like a sixth sense. We knew exactly what they were going to say and had a quick comeback everytime.

Mikey was working up and down 7th Avenue, across from the Garden. We never worked the same spot for two main reasons. First, it upped the chances of cops spotting us because crowds would gather when we were wheeling and dealing as a team. And second, recognition. When it's only one person it's harder to remember. But when they're like, "Yeah, it's this little kid and this junkie-looking motherfucker with white foam all over his mouth," you're a dead mark. Prior to show time we'd meet at this dingy Irish bar on 32nd and 8th Avenue to have a brew before going in.

I was just about to head over and meet Mikey when this big motherfucker with red hair walked over and said that he heard I had trips and that he needed two hits. He put up the usual argument, "Brown blotter? I never heard of the shit... blah, blah, blah," and he's holding it up, looking at it suspiciously. For a beat artist, (and we were artists, trust me) when people start examining your shit closely you have to react. I immediately pushed his hands down and said, "Dude, what are you trying to do, get me busted?" Notice the psychology. Immediately he thinks, "Busted? Hmmm, he wouldn't be worried about getting busted if his shit was fake, right?" I took a defensive stance telling him to give me my shit back and that I didn't have time to sit there convincing someone my shit was good. I already sold forty hits and even showed him my wad of cash to prove business was booming. I continued saying that several motherfuckers already returned for two and three more hits and I was extremely wasted on half a hit. He looked in my eyes and I stared right back, of course, making sure he bought my sales pitch. He was on the hook and bought two for himself and two for his boy. Before we parted ways, he said this junkie fucker had once ripped him off for $50 on some beat hash. When I asked what he looked like he said, "Droopy face, long hair, foam on his mouth, and a fucked up set of teeth." He went on to say that if he ever saw him again he was gonna fuckin' kill the guy. I put my arm around him and said, "I'll tell you what 'Big Red,'" he smiled. (Using a nickname puts people at ease). "I'll even help you kick the fuck outta that scumbag!" I continued. "It's fuckers like him who ruin business for the honest salespeople like me." He nodded in approval before we shook hands, did the deal and went our separate ways.

About an hour later I'm in the Garden hallway and it's packed with wasted burnouts who can barely read their ticket stubs, let alone find their seats. I'm walking around selling my shit, when who do I see down the hall pointing at me with a whole posse of other, bigger dudes? You guessed it, Big Red. I took off running with him yelling, "Yo, that's him!" He ran after me screaming for me to hold up. Yeah right! The problem was I couldn't shake this motherfucker and he was clearly in hot pursuit. I was pushing stoned people out of the way, but he just kept charging. I ducked into the arena and ran through some rows and he just kept coming. I thought I lost him at one point but as I turned around, there he was gaining ground. He was screaming some shit I couldn't clearly make out because the music was so loud. Doesn't it seem like I'm always running, for some reason, when acid is involved? First The Deuce, then Bobby K. and now this fucker. Once again, I'm barreling down the hall doing my best O.J. moves, jumping over people passed out and lying on the ground. When I turned around to see where he was, I smashed into this group of people and fell to the ground. That gave Big Red enough time to catch me. I was still lying on the floor when he stood over me. I covered up anticipating one severe beating, but he pulled my hands away from my face, leaned over and said with a big smile, "Dude, that shit is fuckin' balls, gimme five more, man!" I practically shit myself, before I remembered Mikey's Second Law. I smiled and said confidently, "I told you, bro." Lucky for me I wasn't his only supplier that night.

Yes was great during their Garden run and by doing that beat acid gig I got to see some of the best rock bands of the era. We usually went to the Garden, but if there was a good show and we could make money, we would travel out to Nassau Coliseum on the Island. I never once caught any beef. For all you folks who had high hopes, but could only afford one hit and had the great misfortune of buying it from us, I apologize. No, really. I am truly sorry. But hey, you fucked up, you trusted us.

There was one post show incident that really scared the shit out of me and brought me back down to earth. It reminded me of the dangers a kid could face on the streets of New York City. Mikey didn't work that particular show, because he had some shit to take care of, which usually meant he was getting high with some bitch. I decided to work by myself and, although I quickly sold most of my stuff, things just didn't seem right. See, believe it or not, as stoned and out of his mind as Mikey was, he had a third sense that told him, "Look out, Mikey." On a number of occasions, Mikey told me not to let greed get the better of me. When that voice warned him of shit, he listened, and for that reason he lasted so many years doing the concert hustle. Mikey strictly followed his third and final law, what he called his "Spiritual Law." Law Number Three: "Always trust your vibe. If something feels weird, it usually is. Split."

I walked over to the Irish pub on 32nd Street to grab a bite to eat, count my dough, play pinball and do the rest of the usual shit we did after each show. It was one of those old-school NYC bars. It was dark, dingy and designed specifically for alcoholics who could go in there in the middle of the day, block out the sun and order a few fifty-cent-mugs of beer. There was never any socializing going on - just a bunch of drunks minding their alcohol intake and pretending to be watching some sporting event or movie on the cheap black-and-white set that hung above the bar. These guys didn't initiate any conversation about the movie, or game, and I didn't make any conversation either. The people in there were so sad looking and depressed, but Mikey knew them all by name. When they saw him they would smile and shake his hand because Mikey usually bought a round for the bar with his concert earnings. Although Mikey was a junkie and a scam artist, he wasn't all that bad.

The bar smelled like shit and was smoky as hell. It had the most disgusting buffet set-up and grill I ever saw. Only a severely drunk person would even attempt to eat that shit, but for someone who ate Oreo-spit sandwiches, dog biscuits, and ALPO-hash in the past, who the fuck was I to complain? I told the bartender/chef to make me a burger and fries and went to the back to sit at a table. I had done okay that night - about a buck fifty. When I finished counting my loot, I went to take a piss. I entered the bathroom at the back of the bar, walked up to the urinal and waited. When you're on acid it takes forever for that first drop to come, but once you start it seems like you could piss forever. Before that first drop hit the urinal, I heard someone taking a shit in one of the stalls. I tried to make a joke about the gourmet food in the joint not agreeing with him, but there was no response from my smelly friend with the Hershey-squirts.

The bathroom door opened and in walked this scary-looking Spanish dude with an ill look on his face. Ill, being evil. He came up behind me while I was pissing. As I turned around about to say something, he pulled out a large knife and held it up to my face. Was this to be my fate? Stabbed to death and robbed in the nastiest bathroom bar in Manhattan? Not even a decent last meal? He held his finger up to his mouth signaling me to be quiet. I couldn't make a sound even if I wanted to. He walked over to the stall door where the dude was shitting and just stood in front of it. Without saying a word, he kicked it open, surprising the sketchy-looking black dude who was sitting on the bowl. My amigo with the knife grabbed him by the hair and slit his throat right in front of my eyes. He repeatedly stabbed him before giving him a few slashes to the face, which just tore away the skin and covered his face with blood. The flesh on his face was just hanging off and it looked like cold cuts getting sliced by an electric meat slicer. Blood squirted from his neck and I was certain he was dying right in front of my eyes. I barely managed to put my privates away, when the dude's lifeless body slouched over, still on the bowl, coming to rest against the stall wall.

Then the dude with the knife turned around. I was so terrified I stood there frozen, literally pissing my pants. He had blood all over him and it was dripping off the knife. We stared at each other. I knew exactly what was going through his head: "This motherfucker's a witness, I gotta kill his ass." Time stood still. I watched his chest inhale and exhale, his heart raced, and his breath was deep. As I stood there paralyzed with fear, he studied my face trying to figure me out. This guy had just killed someone right in front of me without any hesitation and I was certain I was next. After a good thirty seconds, he walked up and got right in my face. I was trembling with fear and, at that very moment, all my tough guy shit went right out the window. This guy was bigger, stronger and totally capable of ending my life right then and there. He looked me dead in the eyes. His were cold and bore the scars of a troubled life, while mine begged for mercy. He put his finger up to his lip again and I trembled and nodded in agreement. Then he simply put the knife under his jacket and walked out as if nothing ever happened. I took a deep breath and almost fell over as I exhaled the biggest sigh of relief. I thanked God and snuck one last look at the poor unfortunate fucker who took his last breath in that bathroom. The strangest thing was, that not a single word was spoken by any one of us during the entire murder. I walked out without eating my burger and fries and never went back to that bar, ever again.

That was one of the times in my life when death stared me in the face and I lived through it. When I saw the Quentin Tarantino film, Pulp Fiction and Samuel L. Jackson's character, Jules, talked about divine intervention after all the bullets miraculously missed him, I could relate because it hit home. Why didn't that dude kill me? I could have totally identified him and put his ass away. I truly believe God was with me in that smelly, dirty little bathroom.

Some years ago, I knew a man in his late-sixties, who practiced Bhakti-Yoga, like me. He told me something that I'll always remember. "I was in the trenches of some of the bloodiest battles of World War II. I had friends – good friends – die in my arms and speak their last words to me, and let me tell you something - there are no atheists on the battlefield."

Most people I know who've been through crazy shit in their lives have a belief in God and I'm no exception. When I was in that bathroom and staring down death, what did I do? Pray, and very hard I might add. I remember reading about a famous atheist in the '80s who was a famous author and well known for his works denying the existence of God and crap like that. He was kidnapped and held for ransom. His captors tied him up, gagged him and kept him locked in the trunk of a car for days. When he was released, he told the media he prayed to God the entire time he was in that dark trunk and told people to burn every book he'd ever written.

I always wondered why God put me through so much insanity and misery in my life. It wasn't until my mid-20s that I finally accepted it as a blessing. God was laying the groundwork for what would be my lifelong quest for truth. A famous Chinese philosopher once said, "Discontent is the first step in the progress of a man or a nation." If we think this material world is our home and a great place to live, with its miseries of the body and mind, miseries caused by other living entities, miseries caused by natural disturbances: birth, death, disease, and old age; we are in Maya (illusion). It's like that song by the band the Police, "Spirits in the Material World." This material world is designed as a place of suffering so that, eventually, when we come to our senses, we'll want to get out. It's a nuthouse, and when you start your path it's like the outpatient program; your journey back home, back to the spiritual world has begun.

It was early March, and Mikey had problems with his teeth, so he did what any junkie does when they need medical attention, he checked himself into a rehab. It's an old trick junkies used when they had a condition, or when the weather got too cold for them to be on the street. They got methadone in "The Program," as they called it, and if they could get their hands on some Valium, it's a combination that's close to a heroin high. When they're feeling better, or when spring rolls around, they're back out on the streets with new clothes and 10-pounds heavier from all the government cheese and Fink bread they ate while inside. All of my institutionalized brothers in New York remember Fink's famous slogan. "Fink Means Good Bread." My slogan: "No it don't motherfucker. The shit tastes nasty."

I was now on my own, but thanks to Mikey, I had skills to pay the bills. I'd make money if there was a concert, or occasionally buy a bunch of nickel bags to turn over from a dealer named Jimbo, in Rockaway. Back then a nickel bag was 3.5 grams for $5 and I would break it up and make loose joints. My joints consisted of one-part seeds (which always exploded), one part sticks and stems and one part real weed. I sold them around Martin's Corner to the lunch crowd from P.S. 180, or stood at The Circle and hustled to the few stragglers who passed by. It was still winter and Rockaway was freezing. It was getting harder to find a place to crash, but I got by crashing here and there. My social worker from St. John's, Brother Mark, was out, along with the cops from the 100th Precinct, showing people my picture and asking if they had seen me around, or had any other information about me. With that, I decided it was time break out and I headed inland to Forrest Park.

Forrest Park was a great place to set up shop. We called it "The Dome," because there was a white-domed band shell where horrible bands played for free during the summer months. It was pretty funny because most of the bands sucked and were so loud they pissed off the dealers. They were bad for business and we would throw bottles at them until they stopped playing. The Dome had the three essential qualities in New York real estate - location, location, location. The Dome was in the center of everything and if I needed to go back to Rockaway, I just hitched, or hopped on the Q-53 bus. If I wanted to hang out in the city, go work a concert, or just get into trouble, no problem; the trains were right there. If I needed to go to The Carbines in Ridgewood (angel dust central), pick something up and go hang out on 63rd Drive in Rego Park, Queens, with its crazy dust heads, it was only a stone's throw away.

Business at The Dome went like this: cars entered at the back of this huge parking lot and drove slowly along the tree line. We (the dealers) stood on the stairs about 75-yards in front of the band shell. The potential customers would drive up to the stairs and yell their order out the window. "Tooeys (Tuinals, a powerful barbiturate), who got tooeys?" "Ludes!" "Dust!" Whatever the fuck they needed, we were guaranteed to have it. They would park, before the dealers would walk over and show his goods. The dealers at The Dome definitely didn't like people selling fake shit, because it was bad for biz. So, I mainly sold weed and at times would pass off a few bad hits of acid, or a beat pink 697 or two, here and there.

The sleeping arrangements at that time were plentiful, due to a low-life Forrest Park beat artist named Bobbie Bird who showed me the ropes. They called him Bobbie Bird because he was homeless and only took birdbaths in the park bathroom sink. Man, did he stink like shit. He was one of those short, really fast-talking, cliché New York Italian-types, but by no means a Guido, because Guidos usually doused themselves in cologne. He thought he could con anyone and always bragged about it. I learned one thing from Mikey early in the game - loose lips sink ships. Ordinarily

I wouldn't be caught dead with a big mouth, asshole like Bobbie Bird. But when you're on the streets, you deal with a lot of undesirables because they have the ways and means… and it's all about ways and means. That dude might not have had the shower thing down, but when it came to finding a warm place to sleep, he was the man. If we were in Manhattan working or partying, we would pay $1.50 to sleep in a warm chair in one of the 24-hour porno theatres on The Deuce. One night, I remember him punching the shit out of a deviant motherfucker, who was jerking off a little too close to him. I gotta tell you, it was weird as shit falling asleep to porno soundtracks and the sounds of an entire theatre shuffling their meat, but hey, it was warm.

We would also go to the top of some apartment building staircases in Queens to stay warm. Since most of them had radiators up there we would climb to the top and crawl up next to them to crash. If the spot was cool we would stash our plastic bags and belongings in the hatchway of the elevator shaft. Occasionally we woke up to an unsuspecting and screaming superintendent who came up there to sweep and mop and found us in his building. Another warm place we used to sleep was the A train. It took nearly three hours to go from Rockaway to 207th Street in Manhattan, and if you did that twice, you had six hours of sleep, before you were woken up by the morning commuters jockeying for your seat. One thing I learned the hard way about the train gig was keeping my money safely hidden in my draws. One morning I woke up after a night of drinking and my front pocket was sliced open and its contents - almost $300 - was gone.

I had my suspicions about the perpetrator who robbed me while I was passed out in a drunken haze. One night, after we finished work at The Dome, Bobbie Bird took me over to The Carbines to cop a couple of bags of dust. We smoked both bags and got high as shit. The Carbines were spooky at night because you had zombified dust fiends roaming the parks, woods, and graveyards all night long. To make matters worse, crazy-ass paranoid dust dealers who packed guns controlled The Carbines. If you thought coke dealers are sketched-out, just try dealing with a dust dealer who's smokin' his own shit. After we came down from the stratosphere we headed into Manhattan to hang out. Bobbie took me to 14th Street's Union Square Park to cop Tuinals. Back in the day, Union Square Park didn't have the farmer's market like they have these days. It was an open-air drug supermarket filled with dealers pushing every illegal drug imaginable. We picked up two Tuinals and Bobbie told me to take two, because according to him, they weren't that strong. Later we hung out and drank in a few bars on the LES. At this point, I was completely fucked up, and since I couldn't stand up straight, I got tossed out of the bar.

Bobbie, on the other hand, was still sober. We decided to take a cab back out to Forrest Park and I passed out as soon as we climbed in. A short time later, we pulled up to The Dome where Bobbie opened the door and threw my ass out as the cab peeled off. I stumbled up the stairs, fell flat on my face and smashed my nose. Before I passed out, alone, in the cold, it occurred to me to check my pockets - I had $300 on me and it was all gone. Six months had passed before I saw Bobbie, again. When I did, he was getting his karmic payback.

I survived the next couple of months by hustling my ass off. When spring rolled around, it started to warm up and I was back out at The Irish Riviera. Not much had changed, as I quickly re-immersed myself in local culture. I frequently hung out at The Playroom, a local bar on 98th Street across from Playland. The local band, Small Axe, played there almost every night. They did all covers except for one original called "Rapid Succession." The only reason I still remember it is because they played it four times a fuckin' night. It didn't matter what time you walked in - chances were pretty good that you were going to hear that song. Guys, if you're still a band, I hope you've learned some new shit.

When the cold weather broke, Playland Amusement Park opened up for the season. They had a pay-one-price deal, which allowed you to ride the rides all day for $5. If there was nothing else to do we'd get high, scrounge up the money and ride the roller coaster ten times in a row. My other favorite ride was "The Whip," that spun you around so fast you got whiplash as you were pinned against the side of the ride. Then it would go in reverse to make sure the other side of your neck hurt just as badly. Now, I know most of you have probably been to one of the many fine amusement parks across the country, like Six Flags or Disneyland. No doubt you've seen some of the clean cut and wholesome people who are gainfully employed at these amusement parks. Well, Playland was the exact opposite. The Playland employees, especially the ones operating the rides, were the craziest cast of brothers from the five boroughs ever assembled at any amusement park. While on the job they got high, drank, smoked and were rude as shit to everyone. They even cursed over the P.A. system. If one of their homeboys walked by, they would give 'em a shout-out like, "Ah nigga, what up motherfucker?" It was definitely not family day at the beach.

The brother that ran The Whip was hysterical and he's the reason it was my favorite ride. He had this big-ass 'fro and would always come to work all pimped-out. I asked him why he was all dressed up to work at an amusement park and he said, "Man, is you crazy? The job's just a cover. You see all this fine young sugar walkin' around in here? I'm tryin' ta put some a' that out on the corner with my other ho's. Shit, I still gots five bitches workin' from last summer." I think he was full of shit, but he was bugged out and he made us laugh, so we let him ramble on. He was always weeded and usually had a bottle of brew in close proximity. He also pushed the limits of the rides to dangerously high speeds. When he did, people screamed to get off, but he'd just ignore them and chant his mantra into the mic, "Ah you punk-ass pussy motherfuckers, screamin' like a bunch of little bitches. It's time to speed this motherfucker up. You gonna remember The Whip!" Then he'd put the music up loud as shit and sing along out of key. Some people were so dizzy that they'd vomit and get off the ride pissed. Others, like me, thought his comedy routine was great.

"The Haunted House" was another Playland favorite. We floated through in little boats, smoked joints and bugged out. We would jump out in the middle of the ride and stand on the landing with our shirts over our faces trying to scare the shit out of people by lunging at them with a hunting knife, a billy club or a broken bottle. When we were done, we would run out through the emergency exit. We did this so frequently, we befriended one of the homeboys in a green ghoul costume. Since he was cool, we helped the dude get high by blowing shotguns of weed smoke into the small air hole of his costume. He told me that he loved our scare tactics and that Playland even received a few complaints from some concerned parents about the "serial killers" scaring the living shit out of their kids. The management could only say, "serial killers? We don't have any serial killers in The Haunted House."

The sweltering summer of '77 was upon us, but NYC was in a serious recession and everybody was freaking out about the murders carried out by David "Son of Sam" Berkowitz. People stayed off the streets at night and away from the parks. It also put a real dent in the whole disco scene because Berkowitz shot Sal Lupo and Judy Placido outside the Elephas discotheque in Bayside, Queens. Punk was also exploding at this point, but I think Berkowitz knew better than to fuck with punk rockers. I remember hanging out and smoking dust in Bayside a few days prior to the shootings. I was wearing the hot-ticket item of the day - a shirt with a target on it that read, "Come on... take your best shot." I think that if Berkowitz ran into some of us dust-heads at The Carbines he would have been the victim of some swift street justice.

School let out for the summer and Rockaway was really hoppin'. The Ramones had a song about hitching a ride to Rockaway Beach and I could relate, because I did it almost every day. If I slept in Forrest Park or on a bench in the city, I'd make my way to Woodhaven Boulevard, stick out my thumb and get my ass to Rockaway. Simply put, in the summer of '77, Rockaway was the shit. Constant parties, no hassle from the cops, and lots of girls. A year before I was the outsider. Now, everyone knew me as the crazy little kid who ran away from St. John's. The older guys and girls would take me under their wings and look out for me. My daily routine consisted of chatting up the girls, drinking, fighting, playing Frisbee, and selling drugs on the beach. I always came up with the money for the next case of beer, so I became a hero in Paulie's eyes. As soon as I'd get some money I'd spend it just as fast. No matter how much I made, within a day, it was gone because I always bought everyone food, drinks, and drugs.

I ran into E at The Circle and he looked pretty worn down from all the drugs and late-night hangout sessions with Tommy the Beast. Their new moneymaking scam was to steal meat from the local supermarkets and sell it elsewhere for a profit. E told me that Frank was living with my mom and Carl, and well, we were both dirty (mom had showers), we were both hungry (she always kept a stocked 'fridge), and we were both almost broke (by-golly she owed us). So, E and I scrounged up money for the Q-53 bus and off we went to Jackson Heights.

We knew my mother and Carl both worked at Con Ed during the day. We also knew Frank had strict orders not to let E and me in the house while they were at work. My mom knew that we were "raising fuckin' hell" on the streets and there was just no telling what we were capable of, especially at an unsupervised house. We showed up at her door anyway and put our plan into action. We rang the bell and Frank stuck his head out from the second floor window to see who was at the door. Once he saw us, he immediately ducked back inside. When we screamed, "We saw you Frank," he stuck his head back out again. He looked down at us and informed us that there was no way he was letting us in the house. We told him we were just hungry and wanted to eat. We went on, "Frank, you're our brother. Have a heart, man." He disappeared inside only to return several minutes later. He used a piece of rope to lower down a basket with a gallon of milk, a box of cereal, two spoons, and two bowls - smart-ass little fucker.

We sat there and finished the whole box of cereal before E yelled up and once again, Frank stuck his head out the window. E said, "Open the door, so we can give mom back her bowl and spoons." No dice. He ordered us to put everything back into the basket. He lowered down another rope, which we tied around the basket so he could hoist it back up. We were thoroughly pissed at him. We asked him to let us take showers. No dice. Brush our teeth. Nope. E, being the quick thinker, thought of the one thing Frank couldn't lower down on a rope or refuse us - a toilet. E said we both had to take dumps and if Frank refused we were going to shit right on the doorstep and he would have to clean it up before the landlady saw it. She already wanted to kick my mom out and that would surely be the incident that would seal her fate. That would mean back to another foster family for the little brownnoser. Realizing he was had, he made us promise that we would just shit and leave. We looked up at him with the most honest, sincere looks we could summon up and said, "Frank, we love you, we would never do anything to get you in trouble. We promise."

We stood in front of the door and heard his footsteps coming down the stairs. One, two, three locks unlocked, before he opened the door. E and I smiled and then I knocked him out. We went raging through the apartment. We took her Valium, her bottles of alcohol, her change jars, TV's, and radio. We even took her telephone, so my brother couldn't call the cops. Frank was crying the entire time and tried to run downstairs to call my mother from a nearby payphone, but after I threatened to beat his ass again, he calmed down. We showered, ate everything in sight and yes, finally did take those shits. Then we headed out to Rockaway and partied all night with my mom's money, alcohol and pills. Carl was so pissed that he came out there with the cops and looked for us. Frank was sent to live with a foster family in Lawrence, Long Island, which made E and me laugh. It was nice hanging out with E, but after a couple of days, he was back over in Broad Channel. E's the type of older brother who somehow always managed to show up at the right time and save the day, even if it wasn't by the most legitimate and honest means.

One hot afternoon I was hanging out on the boardwalk, sweating my ass off and decided to head over to Pinky's Fascination where I knew the air-conditioning was pumping. After playing a few games with no luck, I got bored. I walked out and saw my weed guy, Jimbo, and his girlfriend loading shit into a hamburger stand. Apparently they were going to run a summer business that sold hot dogs, burgers, fries and, oh yeah, weed. I was hired on the spot. The cool thing about working for

Jimbo (beyond the free weed) was that he let me crash on his couch, so I'd be on time for work every day. Business was booming, the weed biz that is. Jimbo wasn't exactly a five-star celebrity chef like Bobby Flay. To put it bluntly, his food sucked. That part of the business only lasted about a week and then it was all weed. Since the stand was right next to the 98th Street Playland train station, we had the busiest stand on the beach. People would get off the train, come over to the stand and get their bag tucked in a hamburger or hot dog bun. As a cover, we always kept a few items on the grill just in case the cops rolled by, or someone who didn't know our deal wanted some food.

Buckles came by one day and we hung out and rapped a bit. He asked where Mikey was and I told him that I hadn't seen him in awhile. The last thing I heard, he was in rehab. He told me to stay away from Mikey and his scams because one day, sooner or later, beating people for drugs eventually catches up to you. He was preaching to the choir, because I really enjoyed the new gig selling quality pot. We always had Panama red, Acapulco gold or some really kick-ass Colombian, which kept happy customers coming back day after day. Besides, this gig was unlike the concert hustle because I didn't have to look over my shoulder, wondering if I was going to get my ass kicked for selling bogus shit. This job was less stressful, and it also provided me with a lot of far-out customers. One couple in particular was really cool - a guy, who looked like Gregg Allman from the Allman Brothers Band, and his girl, who was a really pretty hippie-looking chick with long, dark brown hair. From a business stand point, Jimbo and his girl were loving them too, because they usually stopped by three or four times a week and bought at least half-an-ounce each time. They said they were going to hip all their friends to the spot and that sound was music to Jimbo's ears. This guy's girl was a real flirt though. Every time her man wasn't looking, she was smiling at me, and not the "trying to be polite" sort of smile either. This was one of those "I wanna fuck you, little man" smiles. I told Jimbo and he said he noticed it, too. He told me to slip her my number, which was actually Jimbo's, since I was crashing with him. One day Jimbo acted as a decoy by showing the dude his whole grill set up and I stood there like an awkward teenager with a folded napkin in my hand. I said, "Uhh, I think you might want this" (great line asshole). She took it, looked at it, smiled and asked, "What took you so long?" She whispered in my ear that hooking up with teenagers was her fantasy and I shouldn't worry about her boyfriend, because he was cool with it. When I heard that, I had an insta-boner. She said she would definitely be in touch and kissed me on the cheek, before they copped their pot and split.

I couldn't get her out of my mind and I waited patiently for her to call. Two days had passed and I didn't hear from her. One morning, I slept in after a hard night of drinking, so Jimbo and his girl opened the stand without me. I told them I'd be over there in a bit and fell back asleep. An hour later the phone rang and lo-and-behold, she called. She said she was at the stand and wanted to hang out. I got the hell off that couch, got dressed, and raced right down. When I arrived, she waved me over. I immediately noticed her boyfriend was standing behind the counter with Jimbo and his girl. Jimbo was looking at me really strangely giving me the eye and shook his head ever so slightly from side to side. I also noticed Jimbo and his girl's hands were behind their backs. When I walked up the hippie chick went to hug me and Jimbo turned slightly, showing me he was in handcuffs and apparently under arrest. I looked at the girl in disbelief. She went to grab me and I took off before undercover cops converged on the area from every direction. I took off and raced up to the subway platform, but they caught me, effortlessly. When I was on the ground and under arrest, the cops smacked me around to teach me the biggest lesson you learn after a hot pursuit: never run, asshole.

Those two fuckers were the best undercover narcs I ever saw. When we arrived at the 100th Precinct and the interrogation started, she turned into a total bitch. I knew I was in trouble, but I never lost my sense of humor. She was coming down on me threatening me with lock-up if I didn't tell her the numbers of Jimbo's dealers. They wanted to work their way up the food chain and pinch the bigger dealers and they were going to put pressure on us, until we helped them. When I told her I didn't know where Jimbo got his weed, she got really nasty and cursed me out. I replied, "Does this mean we're not gonna have sex?" According to her, the only contact she was going to have with my privates was when she threatened to kick me in the nuts, while I sat there handcuffed to the radiator. They had the weed on Jimbo, but they also knew that he knew all the local dealers who pushed weight. They figured if they pressed him hard enough he'd flip and they could build a bigger case. But that, my friends, was just not going to happen with Jimbo. He was no fuckin' rat.

Several hours of interrogation passed before Brother Mark, my St. John's archnemesis, walked into the room. The look of satisfaction on his face, seeing me handcuffed and at a low point, made me want to slap the livin' shit out of him. Before the police released me into his custody, Brother Mark made me sign a waiver that said I'd either go back to St. John's and follow the program with full restrictions until my court date, or he'd leave me in jail - which meant I was going to Spofford.

Spofford Juvenile Detention Center, in The Bronx, was like Rikers Island for people under 21. It was the most feared place for juvenile offenders, because it was full of young punks who wanted to make a name for themselves. If you were white, you'd better know how to throw down or you were fucked. I definitely didn't want to go there and swore up and down on ten stacks of Bibles that I would turn over a new leaf. Brother Mark took me back to St. John's to wait for my day in court.

That day never came, because a week later I went back out on the streets. Since I skipped my court date, the cops put out a bench warrant for my arrest, which put Brother Mark on the warpath. Armed with a photo, he helped the cops search all over Rockaway. Everywhere I hung out, they looked. With all the heat from the cops, no one would even come near me, especially the dealers. The exception to that rule was this one dealer, Wally, who was this tall, burnout with stringy, blonde hair. He was the type of guy who, if you told him something, the shit usually took an hour to register. I'm sure he had heard the cops were after me, but just forgot, because his short-term memory was shot from all the drugs he'd done.

One warm summer night, Wally and I were selling nickel bags down at the card tables on 98th Street near the beach. Biz was good and we quickly sold out, so Wally went back to his house and brought back a quarter-pound of Acapulco. He put a newspaper down on the card table and emptied the entire bag, so we could break it into nickel sacks. We were smoking and laughing when we noticed a car pull up next to the curb. As the front passenger door opened, I looked down and saw a sight that made my heart sink. It was Brother Mark's dreaded brown wingtips. I got up and immediately made a run for it, but he chased me. Wally was in shock. Even more so, when the two cops didn't bust him for the weed, deciding to chase after me, instead.

I ran down 98th Street toward The Playroom with Brother Mark and the two cops in hot pursuit. I ran through the front door and guess who's playing? Small Axe. And the song? What else: "Rapid Succession." The band saw me run in and waved. When I blew past them with my entourage in tow they all did a double take. I ran out the back, up the rear staircase, and up to the roof. I ran along the bungalows, jumping from roof to roof. I was about to jump across one roof when I heard, "Freeze!" I looked down and saw a cop fumbling around in the alley. He was tripping over the garbage, while aiming his gun up at me. I don't know if he intentionally fired that shot, but I heard the fuckin' thing whiz right by my head. I was scared shitless and I ran down the entire block by way of those rooftops. When I got to that last roof, I jumped down and hid under a parked car for nearly three hours while the cops looked for me.

After that close call I stayed away from my usual hangouts for a few weeks to let things cool down. With all the heat, nobody wanted me around fearing the cops would show up at their door. Since I had nowhere to sleep, I sought refuge under the boardwalk and in a burned-out bungalow on 116th Street.

I went the entire time without showering. The predominant memory of those weeks was the horrid smell of my feet and beat-up sneakers. I didn't wear socks, so the sand, mixed with the sweat, created this caked-on, funkier-than-shit, black sand in my sneakers and on my feet. E will tell you about the time he woke me up in that bungalow and nearly vomited because my feet stunk like shit. I believe his exact words were, "Holy shit! (gag, gag, gag) What the fuck is that?" He had to use his T-shirt to cover his nose and mouth. That afternoon he took me to a shoe store and bought me a new pair of sneakers and some socks. You should have seen the look on the guy's face who measured my foot - it was priceless.

One dude I was hanging around with a lot at the beach was Crazy Dave. He got his nickname because he was a crazy motherfucker. Crazy Dave was from 63rd Drive in Rego Park and was my dust-smoking partner. We would hang out at the beach, then hitch out to Forrest Park, or to The Carbines, and cop sherm. Another thing I liked about Crazy Dave was that he knew the best clubs in the city. We always managed to get into trouble when we went out. We smoked a lot of dust and enjoyed our favorite NYC pastime, getting into fights, most of which we instigated. One night we fucked with one of the guys at Mamoun's Falafel on MacDougal Street and the guy tried to attack us with this huge machete. He was looking to decapitate the fuck out of one of us and, I swear, if I hadn't broken a chair over his head I probably wouldn't be sitting here telling you about it.

Another night we crashed a party in Queens and this guy, Little Paulie, was there from Spaghetti Park, which (in case you didn't figure out from the name) was a big Italian hang out. He was a stocky eighteen-year-old who was supposedly a Golden Gloves boxer. He always sported a thick, gold rope chain with a boxing glove pendant, Jordache jeans and slicked-back hair, and drank from his very own bottle of Jacobazzi. Little Paulie was there hanging out and Crazy Dave was wasted, as usual. One thing about Crazy Dave was, no matter how fucked up he got, he always tried to get laid. He would say anything to any girl in order to hit skins. On this particular night, he was flirting with Little Paulie's girl, singing her a little tune called "My Dick is Big as a Monster" every time Paulie walked away from her.

I went downstairs to get some air and no more than five minutes later Crazy Dave followed me all beaten up. I asked what happened and he said Little Paulie fucked him up. I was pissed that he beat up my boy, but also that his coward-ass would start a fight with someone who could barely stand up. Just then the elevator door opened and out walked Little Paulie and his girl. We exchanged words and immediately went with the hands, as they say. I gave him a boxing lesson in the lobby of the building. After a few really big haymakers, he ran out fearing for his life. Crazy Dave congratulated me and we went back upstairs to do some celebratory drinking.

An hour passed and Dave split, but I decided to hang out a little longer because I had my eye on this hot, little, guidette chick. Unfortunately, I told her that I hated disco people, to which she replied, "Fuck you. I'm a disco person, asshole." She walked off before I could explain that I only meant the dudes. The guys were definitely assholes, but there was no denying that the disco chicks were the hottest girls in the city, especially the Italian ones. That ruined the party for me, so I left. When I split out of the building I saw three Cadillacs' pull up. A few Guido's jumped out of each one and they ran to the trunks and grabbed baseball bats. I remembered saying to someone from the party, "Shit, somebody's about to get fucked up." Just then Little Paulie jumped out of one of the cars, pointed at me and yelled, "That's him right there!" I was so wasted, I didn't immediately put two and two together, until they walked toward me with their Louisville Sluggers raised. Then I bolted, but they caught me in an alleyway behind some row houses. They cornered me and began swinging big homerun shots to my legs, back and arms, while one of them kept yelling, "Hit 'em in the fuckin' head!" Luckily for me, there were so many of them they couldn't get clean shots in.

Spaghetti Park was famous for exactly this reason. These Guidos had beaten a few people to death with bats and everyone in Queens knew it. I knew I had to fight back, but if I went to grab one of the bats I'd get hit with another.

I saw a neighbor's light go on, so I yelled for someone to call the police. At that moment, I turned to see a bat coming toward my face. I grabbed it before he connected and the struggle to control the weapon was on. I then looked at the back of one of the houses and saw a large sliding glass door. Making a quick move, I shoved the bat under this dude's chin and pushed as hard as I could driving the both of us right through the glass. We both crashed down hard on the inside of the house in a pile of shattered glass. With all the commotion, I heard a man shouting that he was calling the police. Little Paulie and the Guidos took off and left me lying there bloody and with a pain in my back. I was barely able to walk, but I managed to elude the cops and slowly make my way to Elmhurst General Hospital. When I walked into the emergency room to seek medical attention, they wouldn't treat me because I was still considered a minor and I didn't have a parent or legal guardian with me. I hadn't spoken to my mother since I robbed her house, but I decided to call her anyway, because I had no one else to turn to. I called her crying because I was in such severe pain. I begged her to come to the hospital, but her exact words were, "To hell with you. You made your bed now you can lie in it." I stumbled out of the emergency room in pain and eventually got on the train. I rode it out to Rockaway and collapsed on a bench on the boardwalk.

The other ass-whipping I got courtesy of Crazy Dave was actually pretty funny. He told me about this punk club in the city called, Max's Kansas City, where the girls were easy. Dave didn't know shit about punk, but according to him any girl who dressed like that was out for one thing - to get fucked. So, off we went.

Max's was across the street from Union Square Park where we copped four Placidyls, giant green gelatin capsules that were used to tranquilize horses. They were called green jellybeans on the street. To wash those down we got a few beers at the deli. The next thing I knew I was wasted. We walked, or should I say, stumbled over to Max's and went inside. On the ground floor was a bar, the next floor up was where the bands played and the third floor was where the VIP rooms were. The New York City chapter of the Hells Angels frequently did security at the club and they were notorious for fuckin' people up before tossing them down the really steep flight of stairs.

I don't remember who was playing upstairs that night, but people were jumping around doing the pogo. The shit was making me dizzy, so I told Crazy Dave that I was going outside to get some fresh air and chill out for a second. He walked down to the bar on the first floor and I went outside and sat in a doorway next to the club. I was pretty much nodded out, when I heard the door of the bar crash open and people yelling. I was barely able to lift my head, but I noticed that a group of punk rockers were kicking the living shit out of someone who was crawling on all fours. Nowadays most people think punk rockers are these posers you see on MTV with their tattoos, piercings, slick fashion sense, and wimpy lyrics about relationships.

These fuckers today are nothin' but a bunch of pussies. The original punks were badass motherfuckers who would just as soon stab you in your face with a broken bottle, than look at you. And God help you if you started some shit with them. They were kicking this guy in the face, ribs and the head. It was bad. The dude crawled over to me and I managed to lift up my head. He looked up at me and his face was a bloody mess. "John," he said. "Help." It was Crazy Dave! He had stolen someone's money off the bar and took their drink while they went to the bathroom, which was a big mistake at Max's. The punks looked down at me and said, "Oh, so you're his fuckin' mate are ya?" and proceeded to kick the living shit out of me, as well. We had black eyes, fat lips and our heads were so swollen they resembled basketballs. Dave even lost a tooth. That was my first experience at a real punk club, with real punks, and it was one I'll never forget.

Nevertheless, the summer of '77 was in full swing and I was having a blast. I usually slept at Forrest Park, but if there was a party out at the beach I'd wake up somewhere in Rockaway. I'd hang out there until around 5 p.m., then head back to The Dome, where I'd sell some more shit. If there was a concert I'd end up in the city with a pocket full of cash. If I wasn't crashing parties with Crazy Dave at the NYU dorm on West 3rd in the Village, I was at some club drinking. The NYU parties were hysterical because you had a majority of yuppie-ass fuckers and me and my crew, Crazy Dave and sometimes E, all getting loose. Every week they'd ask the same question after seeing us stash their bottles of whiskey, vodka, or wine under our shirts, and harassing their women, "Umm... excuse me... who invited you guys?" We'd always give them the same answer, "Sue." Then they'd look at each other confused and say, "Who the hell is Sue?"

That summer I had no place to live, no real family and no future, but I was living every kid's dream. I was fourteen, on my own, with a pocket full of dough, and calling all the shots. I really didn't have your typical teen problems, either, because those elements were taken out of the equation. I didn't have any parental supervision, but that was just fine by me. There was no sibling rivalry between my brothers and I, because we helped one another get through some real shit. I didn't have to worry about those annoying fuckers at school anymore, because I dropped out in the seventh grade. My pass/fail wasn't on a report card, but measured in terms of whether or not I made it through another day. If my eyes opened the next morning, I passed. I was way ahead of the pack in terms of my survival and social skills (most of my crew were in their twenties), but there was one skill I still needed to work on.

One morning, I was lying on the sand near The Circle. My jacket was still damp from the ocean mist and the previous evening's beer-soaked festivities, when I was startled by an ear-piercing scream coming from the boardwalk. I stood up, brushed off the sand and made my way over to see what was up. That's when I first saw Nancy. She was cute as a button with her spiky blonde hair and punk gear. She was pogo-ing around and singing the lyrics to a Sex Pistols song. I watched her dance and her energy just made me smile. Every now and then in life you run into certain people and you just know there's something special about them. It's like they're not from this planet, but you feel this gravitational pull toward them and their world. Well, Nancy was one of those people.

I watched her for a few minutes and tried to think of some way to talk to her. Finally, I decided to ask her for a cigarette, even though I really didn't smoke unless I was drunk, or in this case, horny. She gave me this really pissed-off punk look, then reached in her leather jacket and pulled out a pack of smokes. I told her my name. She said she didn't ask. I studied her features and the closer I did, the more I realized that under all the spikes, chains and make-up, was a really pretty girl. I had to think quickly. "Didn't I see you at Max's Kansas City a little while back?" I asked. She replied in an obviously fake English accent, "What the fuck do you know about Max's, wanka?" Now, I didn't know what a wanka was, but I knew it didn't sound too cool. I had to break the tension. "Well, I know me and my friend got the shit kicked out of us there last Friday by some guys with really pointy shoes." I rubbed my head and she laughed. "Was that you? You guys stole money from one of Johnny Thunder's friends, you stupid fucks." We spent the rest of the day smoking weed, drinking, talking and laughing.

Nancy was so cool and we bonded on so many levels that we were both able to drop our facades: my tough, street kid and her mean punker. We were just teenagers and we knew right away that we could trust each other. She told me about her life and when she did, I realized her story wasn't any better than mine. She was eighteen and living on the street for two years. Her dad was an abusive, alcoholic, who beat her and her mom while she was growing up. She was molested at eleven by one of her dad's drinking buddies who used to come over at night when her mom was working and her dad was passed-out drunk. The scumbag threatened to kill her if she ever said anything. I could relate to her story because, just as I believed Mr. V. could put me in that nuthouse, Nancy believed she would be killed when that knife-wielding guy threatened her. She could sense the pain I had suffered and when I looked into her eyes I saw a beautiful person who was handed a raw deal. Like me, Nancy also had the courage to pick up the pieces and try to salvage something. Despite the pain and sadness, her laugh was infectious and it lit up her whole face. I just wanted to make her laugh forever because when she laughed I forgot all my worries and laughed as well.

We talked for hours and before we knew it the sun was setting. That's when mischievous, little girl Nancy snuck down on the beach and stole a blanket from someone who had gone for a swim. She led me by the hand to the alleyway adjacent to the Holland House on 115th Street. When we got there, she spread out the blanket, took off her clothes and laid down. She was so beautiful. She told me to lie down next to her, so I did. She laughed and said, "I meant naked." I laughed, too, and took off my clothes. Just lying there, next to her, having my body touching hers, felt so amazing. She was so caring when we made love - the complete opposite of her tough-girl, punk rock front. Her true character was a warm, loving person who just needed to be loved in return. She had so much love to give to the world and if you got to see that side of Nancy you were one lucky son of a bitch. Unfortunately, not many people saw that side of her. We may have been in a piss-soaked alleyway, littered with beer bottles and trash, on a blanket that smelled like some stranger's sweat and suntan lotion, but as far as I was concerned it was as classy as the Ritz-Carlton. The moments spent with her were so amazing that I lost track of time and space. That's when I feel I truly lost my virginity. The sex I experienced with the girl from the bar wasn't making love, but this was. I honestly think that until you experience sex with someone where there are real emotions and feelings involved, in a way, you are still a virgin.

After we slept together, we were inseparable. I even introduced her to my beach crew. She liked Paulie best and he was smitten with her. They even did one of New York's first poetry slams together, kicking poems back and forth. She was a regular at a number of now-defunct Manhattan clubs that catered to punk rock and introduced me to her friends at Max's Kansas City, CBGB's, The Mudd Club, Fun House, Hurrah's, and an after-hours place called, Stickballs, where I saw people having sex on couches in the middle of the club. She would always make out with me in public, grabbing my crotch while telling me I was a sexual animal. Although I really didn't know what the hell I was doing on the sexual tip, she sure seemed to like it.

One night we went to Max's and it was packed. We were watching some band whose members were done up in make-up and women's clothes. When they were done she said she'd be right back and went upstairs to the third floor. I waited for her for nearly an hour before I finally went upstairs to find her. There were all kinds of freaky motherfuckers hanging out and they were all really high. I asked someone if they'd seen Nancy and they pointed towards the back of the room. When I went through a curtain I saw her high as shit and making out with some older guy. I was shocked. I yelled her name and she looked up at me, smiled and said, "Hey baby." I knew that look, because I'd seen it before. She had pinned-out eyes, a droopy face and slurred speech. I scanned her arms and my suspicions about her were correct. My little punk rock girlfriend used heroin. I was so fucking pissed. I tried to get her out of there, but she wouldn't leave. So I did - without her. I went back out to Rockaway, got totally shit-faced and woke up down by the water's edge.

I didn't see her for three days and when she finally showed up she apologized a million times. I was on her case about her heroin and told her about Mikey and Buckles and all the circumstances surrounding their fucked up junkie lifestyles. She swore she didn't have a habit and just used recreationally. She said that if it upset me, she wouldn't use anymore. I made her promise and when she saw how much I genuinely cared about her, she started to cry. She hugged me and we put it behind us, or least that's what I thought.

It was right around the Fourth of July when Mikey showed up at The Circle looking pretty healthy. He looked like he had gained ten pounds during his stay, had new clothes, a couple of new teeth and a bag of some damn good weed. The three of us hung out and smoked and he told us about what he referred to as his "Country Club Adventure." They had sent him upstate to Ellenville, New York, where he stayed for several months to clean out. He said it was hysterical because you ran into the same "members" each year, just like a country club. And just like your finer clubs, they offered a number of recreational activities. Not because they wanted to, but because they had to. They would try to get your brain to release some endorphins by playing sports, while pumping you full of Nutrament energy shakes to replace all the depleted vitamins. He said you'd never seen anything until you saw a full court basketball game, with the players high on methadone and on the nod.

Mikey wasn't such a bad guy when he wasn't strung-out. We sat and listened to him ramble for hours. He bragged about how he was able to get someone to sneak in some dope and how good it felt when he got high for the first time after being sober for a few weeks. He had Nancy's ear and I started to realize that, as they talked about "the dope high," fucking on dope and all this other bullshit, that she liked the crap a little more than she had let on. I tried to change the subject by telling Nancy about how Mikey and I made money at the concerts and she just laughed. Mikey explained that he had to make that much money, because at that point he had a $200-a-day habit. No matter what I talked about, the conversation always went back to dope. I wanted Mikey to step the fuck off, because I was getting jealous and my girl thought he was "pretty cool", as she put it.

I've seen a lot of junkie dudes get some really nice girls strung out on that shit over the years. It's pretty fucked up. A lot of them have the gift of the gab and girls who like the heroin high are allured by someone who'd take care of them, get them their drug money, make love to them all night and promise to give his life for hers, if it came to that. I guess there's a certain fucked up romanticism involved in the beginning. But have you ever seen a junkie couple that's been together for years? You'd be hard-pressed to find a more wretched, miserable pair of fuckers walking the face of the Earth. They both look like shit, hardly ever shower and they argue over every little fuckin' thing, like it's the end of the world. One time, while I was on the train, I saw one dude slap the shit out of his woman because she folded his newspaper the wrong way after she had finished reading it. And as far as the female getting high first, you can forget that shit. From what I've witnessed, the male in the relationship will always make sure he gets his first, even if his woman is sick, lying on a subway bench, breaking out in a cold sweat and crying, while she begs, "Just a taste baby, just a little taste."

In the early-'90s, I dated a model who had a contract with Elite Modeling Agency in New York City. She would fly back to Paris once a month to model underwear and would get paid a shit-load of money. Well, as the cliché goes, she started using drugs to stay thin, or so she said. The thing I hated most about dating an addict was all the lying and deception. She would constantly be stoned out of her fuckin' mind and tell me she was just tired, not knowing I had been around the shit longer than she could even imagine. Finally, I got sick of the bullshit and left her ass. Sure enough, she hooked up with one of those romantic junkie-types and that was the last I saw of her. Five years later, I was getting on the F train at Second Avenue and there she was, right next to the token booth begging for change, wearing dirty clothes and sporting open sores all over her face and arms.

She was scratching like crazy and in obvious pain, crying and asking commuters for spare change. When I heard her voice, I immediately knew it was her. I didn't want to believe that she had lost everything - her beauty, her vibe and her soul. When I looked over, her knight in shining armor was high as a kite and smiling, sitting on the floor next to the wall. I was so fucked up over it that I walked through the turnstile and never even said hello to her. I should have beaten her boyfriend's ass, but that wouldn't have changed a thing. The truth was, she got what she wanted and died a few years later from an overdose. I have a thousand stories like hers from growing up in New York City and I thank God every day that the one time I did try heroin as a kid, I got so sick I threw up for an hour straight. I swore I'd never do the shit again and kept that promise to this day.

Nancy, on the other hand, didn't keep the promise she made to me. She disappeared for several days and oddly enough so did Mikey. I didn't want to assume the worst, but I heard through the grapevine that they were seen together. I looked everywhere and couldn't find them. I had so many mixed emotions: anger, fear, sorrow, and the one I hated the most after falling in love and losing it, loneliness. To never have, is one thing. But to have, and to lose - it's the worst. The hopeless romantic I am, I slept in the alleyway where we first made love. I was so upset, I barely nodded off a wink most nights.

One morning I cut through the alley in the rain and jumped the fence onto 116th Street. I found Paulie under the movie theatre marquee with his wheelchair-bound veteran buddy. I could tell, for some reason, that Paulie was really upset. I tried to joke with him, hoping in return that maybe he could cheer me up, but he was dead serious. He said, "I just left the bungalow. There's a dead girl in there." I got this really weird vibe, like I already knew what was up, but I felt the need to ask anyway. "What girl?" I said nervously, with this sick feeling in my stomach. He didn't answer. He just looked at me with those sunrise serious eyes. I ran up the street and into the abandoned bungalow. I found Nancy on the second floor lying slumped over a pissy mattress. Her skin was bluish-grey and a needle was beside her. I fell to my knees and hugged her, but her body was as cold as ice. I sat there in that damp, dirty fucking shit-hole bungalow holding her body close for what seemed like hours. I cried like I never had before, even in all the years of pain and bullshit. I wailed because she was the most beautiful soul I had ever known and the only person I had ever truly loved.

I loved her so much and the loss was compounded because I never got the chance to tell her how I really felt about her. It was over and there was nothing more for me to do. I took my T-shirt off and covered her beautiful face. I walked out of the bungalow and found a beat cop. I told him where she was and cursed myself, because the thought of having carried heroin back to Rockaway in the past might have in some strange way contributed to destroying someone else's life like this. My tears immediately turned to guilt and rage minutes later when I saw Paulie. He told me that Mikey had gone in there with her the night before. I couldn't believe he would just cut out and leave her there alone, to die. She died right around the corner from where I was sleeping in that alley, just around the corner from the sacred place where I had first made love to her. In a blind rage, I looked everywhere for Mikey but never found him.

Something snapped in me after Nancy died. I would hurt people who even looked at me wrong and being the runt that I was, I always carried a weapon. I often fought dudes bigger and I'd hit them with whatever I could get my hands on - a 2x4 from the boardwalk, a pipe, a bottle, a brick or a rock. I'm not bragging about it, or proud of my actions in any way, but the sick thing was that it made me feel good to hurt people. It was like therapy and a twisted way of working out my anger. I never picked fights and I justified my actions by telling myself, "Hey, they started the shit, they deserve whatever they get." As I said before, back then you fought with your hands and my philosophy was since most of them were older, bigger and stronger, I was allowed an equalizer to make it a fair fight. "You may be six-one motherfucker, but this here metal pipe, this makes me your size." Looking back at my state of mind in those days, I thank God for the three things that eventually saved my life. Without yoga, vegetarianism and music, I might have written this book from inside a prison cell, or maybe not all. Someone would have definitely killed my ass by now.

Some years later, someone approached me in Washington Square Park. "Hey dude," he said, "I got acid and hash what do you need?" We just looked at each other for a long time. It was Mikey and he looked like death. We sat and talked about old times. According to him, he warned Nancy not to do so much dope that day, but she wouldn't listen. He said he couldn't stick around because of his previous arrest record. He justified his actions, saying that if the cops had found him with heroin and a dead girl at the bungalow, he would have been locked up. Now, I don't know if I believed him or not, but at that point, it didn't matter anymore. The anger I felt towards him was now replaced with pity. He told me he had this new disease called AIDS and wasn't expected to live much longer. For all the bullshit stories and cons Mikey Debris ran in his life, when I looked in his eyes and saw the fear of death, I knew he was telling the truth. Some of the junkies in the park confirmed later on that Mikey had died a year later from complications associated with AIDS. I guess it was ironic that he went the same way Nancy did that day in that bungalow, alone.

Soon after finding Nancy, on a sweltering July evening in the summer of '77, I was back in Forrest Park pushing a batch of Qualudes for a local dealer. That was one of the things I loved about that park - freelancing. You could get there in the late afternoon and, as long as you were cool and never ripped-off any of the dealers, they would give you shit to sell for them. If I took thirty seconals off Brooklyn Pete for $2 each and marked 'em up a buck, I'd make $30. If you do that with three or four dealers, you can walk out of there with a pocket full of cash for a few hours work. The dealers were happy because they made money without taking any risk, and I was happy because I made money and met a lot of girls in the process. It was like clockwork, people got off work, headed straight over to us and we'd sell them something to help them temporarily forget about their quiet lives of desperation.

I paid off the guy who gave me the 'ludes and a couple of us headed over to the deli on Woodhaven Boulevard to get a few cold beers and some rolling papers. On an average night we'd drink Miller, Bud, or Michelob, but this was a great night, so we decided to celebrate with Heineken. We each grabbed a six-pack and walked up to the counter to pay. I also asked the fat, deli owner to get me a pack of E-Z Wider rolling papers from behind the counter and this prick said, "What are you like twelve, kid?" I think I told him to fuck off and lick my nuts or something to that effect. He didn't like any of us and made his opinion known often by saying, "All you fuckin' drug dealers should be shot." My reply, "Oh yeah you fat fuckin' piece of shit, then who the fuck is gonna keep your nasty-ass store in business?" The fact was the dealers in the park did keep this prick in business. We were the ones who got the people so high they weren't able to recognize that the sandwiches, macaroni salad and other horrible shit he had in his deli case wasn't fit for human consumption. We were the ones who spent hundreds every night just on beer. So, fuck 'em. He deserved to get told off. With that he gave me a dirty look, turned around to get my rolling papers and that's when the lights went out. Not just the lights in his store, all the lights! The Woodhaven Boulevard streetlights, the traffic lights, the lights in apartment buildings - everything went dark. The Blackout of '77 was now in full effect.

A few seconds later, I heard a shotgun being cocked before a flashlight blasted in our in our faces. It was the deli owner. He screamed, "All you scumbags get the fuck out or I'll blow your fuckin' heads off!" We knew he meant business and we weren't going to give him a reason to fulfill his vigilante fantasies. As we turned to walk out, he added with a smile, "And leave the beer, assholes." We stepped out into the darkness as people were running around the streets like maniacs yelling, "The whole fuckin' city lost power!" We had to see it for ourselves. We got a ride from one of the dealers near the mall on Queens Boulevard. From that spot you could look toward the 59th Street Bridge and see the entire Manhattan skyline. We got out of the car and just stood there gawking at the entire city which was in total darkness.

A few moments later, the chaos erupted as alarms sounded and windows were being smashed along the boulevard. Everyone got in on the action, as tow-truck drivers hooked up chains to store security gates and ripped them clean off their hinges, so that looters could enter. People set fires and I even saw looters beat the shit out of other looters to steal the shit they had just looted. People were walking down the street pushing refrigerators and carrying TV's. I even saw a group of looters trying to carry off an entire living room set. The scenario was completely insane.

We knew Manhattan was where the real bucks were, so we got back into the car and raced down Queens Boulevard toward the 59th Street Bridge. Queens Boulevard had earned the nickname, "The Boulevard of Death". Even when the traffic lights were working, it's dangerous as hell, because people drive recklessly down that patch of roadway. You can just imagine the number of accidents that happened that day. En route to the 59th Street Bridge, we weaved in and out of the traffic and around cars that were involved in accidents. When we finally got there, no dice. The police had it completely blocked off and were stopping anyone who tried to drive into Manhattan. We drove around the side of the bridge and went down by the water to look at the island. It was so strange to see Manhattan blacked-out and quiet. It was like a scene from Escape from New York. We knew there was all kinds of crazy shit going on right across the East River, but we weren't going to get a chance to partake in any of it that night. When we heard gunshots ring out from the Queensbridge Housing Projects, we knew we had better get our white asses the fuck out of there as soon as possible.

We never looted that night, because we decided to gamble on Manhattan and missed out. By the time we got back near the mall on Queens Boulevard, storeowners were guarding their property with guns and there were cops everywhere. I did some research to find out the exact statistics from that night - 3,776 arrests and the precincts were so full they had to re-open "The Tombs" in Lower Manhattan to deal with the scores of arrests. There were 1,037 fires set and the largest costs associated with the '77 Blackout were for looting and arson. I guess it was a good thing I didn't do any looting that night. I still had a bench warrant for my arrest and the last thing I needed to do was get popped over some dumb shit, like stealing a radio or TV and ending up as number 3,777. Besides, there were other ways to make a living.

Toward the end of July, I ran into E, again. He was hanging out with Tommy the Beast. After meeting Tommy, I understood how he got the nickname - he was one ugly-ass motherfucker. Tommy's older brother, Joey was also with them. Joey told me he'd just gone AWOL from the U.S. Army Airborne Division and, plain and simple, he was a sick bastard. He stood about 5'9", always had a constant evil look in his eyes, was solid as shit and fearless. If you didn't know he was from Broad Channel, Queens, you'd swear he was a redneck from the Deep South. Joey and Tommy looked nothing alike and for some reason they had a deep hatred for each other. They used to get in these knockdown, drag-out fistfights, which Joey usually won. The first time I saw this I couldn't believe it, because they went at it like two pit bulls. I mean, E and I had our spats as kids, but it was nothing like that.

Joey and me started hanging out a lot and we distanced ourselves from E and Tommy. We played doubles handball by day, (gambling and winning money at the Rockaway Beach handball courts on 101st Street) and at night Joey turned into Spiderman. He had no fear of heights and his hands were incredibly strong - so strong in fact, that if you gave the son of a bitch a brick building with as little as one inch sticking out, he was able to hold on. He'd effortlessly climb up in a flash and enter a fourth - or fifth-story window in order to relieve some poor fucker of their property. Only on one occasion did I see him fall. He crashed to the concrete from three stories above and broke his ankle, but only because we were both shit-faced and he did it on a dare.

Joey abstained from drugs, but loved to drink lots of beer. I've never seen anyone kill a six-pack quicker than this guy. He may have gotten shit-face drunk at night, but he did his push-ups, sit-ups, jogged or played handball, just about every day.

He said drugs were for faggots and weak-minded people, and I think that's one of the reasons he hated Tommy so much.

As time went on, Joey and I became a couple of night crawlers. Together, we robbed stores and houses, and even a bar down by 90th Street that belonged to his uncle. We started drinking as we robbed the pool table, the pinball machines and change jars. By the time we walked out of there, we were piss-drunk. Joey bet me that he could finish off two six-packs before we hit the beach, which was only a block away. He won the bet, of course. To find out who robbed him, all his uncle had to do the next morning was follow the trail of crushed beer cans down to the beach where he found us crashed out. We woke up with him screaming and cursing at us, but thankfully he wasn't stupid enough to call the cops. After a couple of weeks worth of small-time hustles had passed, Joey told me about a big score he had set up. Since I was interested in making a few bucks on the side, I listened carefully to his potential business proposition.

According to Joey, there was a supermarket on 115th Street and Beach Channel Drive that had a weak access point in the roof. Inside was a safe that Joey said he could easily get into because the manager was going to give him the combo. For a cut, of course. According to the manager, on this specific night there would be upwards of 5 Gs inside. All we had to do was cut the steel security bars that went across the skylight then rappel down to the supermarket floor. Easy enough, right? Wrong. I'd never even heard of rappelling much less done it. Joey assured me that I'd quickly get the hang of it, especially if I wanted my cut. We got our ropes, hacksaws, ski masks and other essentials and waited for our day to get busy.

When our day finally came, we couldn't have picked a worse night to try to pull off our caper. The moon was full and we discovered that the roof had no sidewall around it, which meant we couldn't stand up without being seen. We climbed up a drainage pipe around the back, made it to the roof and crawled over to the skylight. Joey broke the glass and it went crashing down onto the supermarket floor. We both went to work on the steel bars with our hacksaws, cutting through one bar, before starting on the next. Since the bars were pretty close together, we were gonna have to remove at least four of them before we could squeeze our bodies through the opening. Despite the obstacle, we made quick progress, cutting through the metal like a hot knife through butter. Before we knew it, bar number three hit the supermarket floor below. At that very same moment a bright spotlight lit up the roof. We dropped down onto our stomachs and laid there in total shock as the flashing lights of police cars suddenly converged on our location. A few seconds later, their guns were aimed up at us and they began issuing demands from their loudspeakers. In plain and simple terms, they told us to get down off the fucking roof.

Joey looked at me and said, "That scumbag prick, shit-for-brains, faggot motherfucker set me up!" I was in handcuffs and on my way to the 100th Precinct when I finally learned that Joey had messed around with the supermarket manager's wife while he was on leave some time ago. Somehow, he'd forgotten to tell me about that little part of the equation when he asked me to get involved in his moneymaking scheme.

The two detectives assigned to our case were De Leon and Moran, Rockaway's finest crime-fighters, who were respectively nicknamed "Starsky" and "Hutch" because they looked like the characters from the '70's cop show of the same name. As I waited in the stationhouse, Joey was picked up by the military police for desertion, while I waited patiently for those brown wing tips to show up, once again. When Brother Mark arrived he was insistent on sending my ass to Spofford and making me sit it out until my weed (and now pending breaking and entering and burglary charges) case came up. As a way to avoid being sent to Spofford, I put on an Academy Award-winning performance that included begging, pleading and crying. I hammed it up by telling him about being jumped by the brothers one night at St. John's and that I didn't feel safe there. I even gave him the "I've had a hard life" speech, telling him about some of the Valenti stuff. I completed this dramatic act with the climactic "Now I'm ready to change" ending. It worked and Brother Mark caved in. After my court appearance in Kew Gardens he took me back to St. John's while I waited for my day in court.

On the car ride back out to the beach, Brother Mark informed me of a grim statistic. "John," he said, "the sad fact is 85 percent of the kids in St. John's will spend their entire lives going in and out of prison. You have a chance to be in the 15 percent who make something out of their life. Don't blow it." I thought Brother Mark was an herb, but the simple fact was, that shit got me thinking. He told me that my behavior at the boys' home in the next few weeks was crucial and would determine the outcome of these cases. If I stayed at St. John's and followed the regs, I had a good chance of getting off with probation. If I left again, he guaranteed me that I was going to Spofford, before I would be headed upstate. "Brother Mark," I said, "I meant everything I said back at the precinct. I would never do such a thing after you went out of your way for me." That night, an hour after lights out, I walked out of the back door of 3B and never returned.

I missed my court dates that fall and now had two bench warrants for my arrest. I did the usual Garden concert hustles and a little dealing at The Dome before winter set in. It was brutal that year and there were no customers at the park or concerts. I was homeless, hungry and alone. That's when I did the only honorable thing left to do, I checked into Samaritan Village Rehab Center in Queens. Since I had those warrants, I became Bobby Johnson, a seventeen-year-old from Ridgewood, whose parents had recently died in a plane crash overseas. Their tragic deaths left me alone in the world, so I escaped the pain through painkillers and alcohol.

The thing I hated most about that place was putting up with what they referred to as "Daily Group." These were meetings we were required to attend with the staff and residents. I'm not just talking one or two, I'm talking eight, nine, twelve fuckin' meetings a day! You had your 7 and 9:30 a.m., which got you ready for the meeting at 11 a.m. with your appointed psychologist, only to be followed by the pre-lunch meeting. Great for your appetite, right? Everyone sitting around, talking about the most horrible shit they'd suffered in their lives. These people needed drugs, and after a couple of days of listening to their gut-wrenching testimonies, so did I. I'm proud of myself though for the constant flow of bullshit that came out of my mouth at that place. You had to be smart about it because too much and they'd send you to a more difficult place. Too little and they'd say, "You're cured, see you later." It was all about yin and yang, and I had the perfect balance of the ever-flowing stream of bullshit routine down pat. I have to hand it to you, Mikey Debris, because you were no dummy and I want to thank you for showing me the ropes.

On New Year's Eve, '77 a few guys and I decided to go into town and have some fun getting fucked up while ringing in '78. We split and came back three days later, which was what was known in the program as a "Split-Tee."

Split-Tees had two choices if they came back - leave or go with the guys who set up tables at the local supermarket and handed-out the anti-drug pamphlets, raised donations and looked for new recruits. The downside was Split-Tees had to wear huge signs front and back that said stuff like: "I'm a drug addict and a loser because God has given me a chance at Samaritan Village and I'm screwing it up," before taking a shift in the doghouse. That's right, the doghouse! They brought an actual doghouse and you had to lay in it with your head sticking out with a humiliating sign hanging above you that said, "Please don't pet the idiot." I was so happy when April rolled around and it was warm because I Split-Teed for good right out of that fuckin' whacked out place with its whacked out counselors. They were more fucked up than the addicts they were supposedly helping.

While I was there I had gained some weight on the steady diet of government cheese and Nutraments. I had a bag of new clothes and $75 worth of Samaritan Village donations that I'd collected on the street that last week and never turned in. I made my way straight to Forrest Park and it was like I'd never left. I immediately picked up where I'd left off, hustling black beauties, 697's, Tuinals and Mandrax, which were pharmaceutical Quaaludes that came from Mexico and were sealed in aluminum foil. This dude, Sticky-Fingers Richie, who would steal the dirty drawers off your grandma's ass if you didn't watch him, had robbed a local drug store and made off with bags of them. Everyone in the park was high on those fuckin' things for weeks and I sold practically every one for him.

I worked a Who concert at the Garden with my famous brown blotters and sold close to thirty hits in record time. As a goof I threw a bunch of beat hits wrapped in aluminum foil on the ground and yelled, "Free trips!" just to watch people go nuts. It was funny as shit watching the mob of burnouts scrambling and diving for that crap.

The show was sold out, but I managed to trade this dude a few 'ludes for what he assured me were great seats. At that point, a really sketched-out guy comes up to me and says he's been up for three days straight on red gels (windowpane) and needed a couple of 'ludes to come down. Red gels were the strongest acid you could buy, and also the hardest to find. For an acidhead it would be the equivalent of a baseball card collector finding Hank Aaron's rookie card at a flea market in 2007. Rumor had it that a bunch of religious hippies made the shit and were adamant about keeping it clean and in limited quantities. They didn't cut their doses with speed, and instead made sure it was 100 percent LSD, so that you'd trip your fuckin' balls off. The dude offered to trade his two little pieces of what looked like red plastic with a bubble of liquid in the center for the 'ludes. Now either this fucker was an amazing actor, or he was telling me the truth, because he looked torn-up. Those Forty-Deuce days of me getting hustled for beat hits were long gone. I basically told him that if he was ripping me off I was going to find him and cut his fuckin' nuts off. This guy was a solid 200 pounds, but I had my equalizer. I lifted my shirt and displayed a very large military-style knife.

He assured me the acid was real, and that he would stay with me until I got high. That was good enough for me and we made the deal. I took one hit, stashed the other in my pocket and went inside.

The seats I got for those four hits of Vicks Form... I mean, brown blotters, were great. They were first level, off to the right of the stage. After forty-five minutes, I started to get really, really high. After an hour, I was zooted beyond belief. It was the cleanest and strongest shit I ever had. There was no speed, just colors, lights and an over-all sense of well being. The house lights inside the Garden went down and the crowd went nuts. The Who played their biggest hits during their phenomenal set including, "5:15", "Won't Get Fooled Again", "My Generation" and "Pinball Wizard." During my high, I watched the band members melt into blobs of flesh at least eight times before the night was over. I was really bugging out on their horn section because they looked like little trolls and their moves were totally synchronized. Without a doubt, it was the best acid I have ever done, and after trippin' like that, I honestly had to wonder how the hell the hippies ever made it out of the '60's alive.

By the time summer rolled around I was back in Rockaway. I saw one of the St. John's kids on the boardwalk and he told me that Brother Mark had been transferred to another boys' home. That was music to my ears. I still had two bench warrants out on me, but now only Starksy and Hutch were actually looking for me. Not much had changed at the beach other than the fact that everybody knew the cops were after me, so they avoided me like the plague. I spent most of my days at The Circle on 116th. Most of the people there came from Queens and Brooklyn and either just didn't give a fuck, or didn't know that I was wanted. Demented Dougie and Junior Nuts, both from Greenpoint, Brooklyn, were two such individuals and they took an instant liking to me.

Dougie was a big dude and a serious drinker. He always read the morning paper while having a beer. He thought of himself as a real thinker and always had something to say about everything. Dougie could fight his ass off too and said he'd boxed as a teenager in the PAL (Police Athletic League), which I totally believed. There was no doubt in my mind he could handle himself in any street fight. I never saw him back down from anyone and if he punched you with one of those big fists, as he used to say, it was, "Lights out, sissy scout." With Dougie you were either "In like Flynn," which meant you were cool, or you were "Out like a sissy scout," which meant you were an asshole and going to catch a beating. He was the brains of the operation and what I refer to as a "next guy." He always made sure there was a next hustle going down, a next bottle to drink, a next group of girls to bang and a next bag of weed to smoke.

Junior Nuts, now he was a piece of work. The first night I saw him at the boardwalk Junior broke a bottle and was slicing his arms and chest to pieces laughing the entire time. He was the Polish-American answer to Sid Vicious. He was punk-as-shit and didn't even know it. His catch phrase was "Yo, rectum breath," which he called everyone regardless of how good your breath smelled or what your real name was and God help you if you argued with him about it. Junior Nuts had blonde, spiked hair and a perpetual stare that never let you know what he would do next. He loved to fight, not that he was any good at it. But what made him deadly was he wouldn't think twice about stabbing you, shooting you or doing whatever it took to cause you bodily harm.

I've been around crazy people and people who thought they were crazy, but Junior was the real deal. He was always down for anything and was basically an attack pit bull that Doggie would yell commands at. "Sick 'em, Junior! Bite 'em, Junior!" Everyone in Rockaway knew not to fuck with these two and it was cool to hang out with them for that particular reason. I was like their little brother and on several occasions was pressured into hurting some people pretty badly while they cheered me on.

What I truly loved about the dynamic duo was that they partied hard. Piel's was their beer, Aerosmith's "Toys in the Attic" and "Rocks" were their anthems and Belle Harbor, well that was their goldmine and the real reason they chose Rockaway over Coney Island Beach, which was much closer to their Brooklyn neighborhood.

Belle Harbor was an affluent neighborhood just north of Rockaway Beach, complete with tree-lined streets, million-dollar, beachfront homes and that kind of affluent shit. You might not remember this, but in the '70s there was a cleaning product called Tidy Bowl and its TV commercial featured its nautical spokesperson, the Tidy Bowl Man. He wore a captain's hat, a blazer and turtleneck, and floated around the toilet in a boat. I guess the idea was that as he circled around your bowl, he also removed the shit stains in the process. Not a very glamorous job, but hey, what the fuck? He became a '70's pop culture icon, as did a bunch of other weird fuckers like the Jolly Green Giant and Mr. Clean.

Anyway, the guy who played the Tidy Bowl Man was just one of the wealthy people who lived in Belle Harbor and I'm sure you're wondering what that has to do with the three of us.

Each night at around 1 a.m., we would walk along the beach north up to 130th Street (I believe Belle Harbor starts at around 125th), where the really nice houses started. Belle Harbor's residents watched their neighborhood at night and if they saw anything out of the ordinary they would instantly call the police. We had to be careful, so the first thing we would do after arriving was a little clothesline shopping. We grabbed anything - pants, underwear, socks and shirts, and we usually left them the stuff we had on. We were living on the beach and anything they had was better than the shit we were wearing for the last three or four days. The best part was Junior had some kind of intestinal disorder from drinking and was always shittin' his draws when he was drunk. He'd leave his draws on the line in such a way that when the unsuspecting fucks came out in the morning to get their nice, clean laundry, the first thing that greeted them was his skid-marked draws.

After we got our clothes it was on to bigger and better things - garages. We never robbed houses because that was too risky. What they would do was lift up the garage door ever so slightly, and I would crawl under. That's why they liked my smaller frame. Once inside, I would flick my Bic lighter or turn on my flashlight and look around. What was I looking for? Anything that Pops, our fence in Greenpoint, wanted. Dougie called him every day for the evening's shopping list and every night we filled the order. When we got everything on the list it was then time to look for the Tidy Bowl Man's house. See, Junior Nuts just had to have the captain's hat that fucker wore in those commercials and was even willing to risk going into the guy's house if he ever found out where he lived.

Pops was a tough, old Polish fucker who stood about 5'5" and had these fat fingers that looked like little Polish sausages. He had a raspy voice and was always smoking a big, nasty cigar, referred to back then as Guinea stinkers because all the Italian guys smoked them. When we showed up with the merchandise every morning at five, Pops would always answer the door the same way - wearing a wife-beater and boxers, while chomping on a cigar. He would take one look at us standing on his stoop, laugh and say, "Get in here ya crazy bastards." Then we'd haggle on a price for all our shit, while we kicked back a few beers and Junior told stories. Afterwards he'd treat us all to breakfast at the diner up the block. The first time I went in his house I couldn't believe all the stolen shit this guy had. If you needed a toaster, Pops had it. A gun, TV's, stereos, toilets, plumbing supplies, stoves, pots and pans. Pops had it all and he knew exactly where everything was in that cluttered house. I even saw three of those big hair-dryer units you sit under in a beauty salon. Everybody in Brooklyn who was a thief knew Pops, but he never dealt with blacks or Spanish people, because he bought some shit from them once and they beat him up and robbed him.

That night, we finished getting everything on Pops' list and I questioned my two partners in crime as to how the fuck we were going to get all of our shit from Belle Harbor to Pop's house in Greenpoint? The answer was one of the many reasons why I loved NYC back then - there wasn't a whole lot of eye contact going on. People minded their own fuckin' business. New York was one of the most violent cities in the country and if you didn't mind your P's and Q's, you were going to have problems. It wasn't like it is nowadays with police tip-lines, rewards and 800 numbers to call and rat people out. People feared retaliation from the thugs who were paying off the cops for info on who dropped dimes on them. Back then, plain and simple, most motherfuckers who did commit crimes got away with it.

That first night we hit a few garages and afterwards had two bicycles, a gas-powered lawnmower, a chainsaw, hedge clippers and some really nice tennis rackets. Walking on the street was out of the question for obvious reasons, so we made our way down to the beach and headed for the water. The sand was hard down there and that made it easy to transport our stuff. Lucky for us, there was a sand dune and we walked behind it, concealing our illegal activity from the police cars patrolling the boardwalk. We would walk down to 116th Street on the beach and then wheel our shit up the street to the CC train two blocks away. On this particular night there was an older guy walking his dog near where we had to pick up the train. He definitely looked like a nosy concerned citizen who was out to single-handedly put a stop to all crime in the neighborhood. We were staring him down to see if he was paying attention to us, or even if he occasionally glanced at us for a description. As he passed us, he looked down at the ground and Junior Nuts immediately got in his face. He said something to the effect of he knew where the guy lived and would eat his dog alive if he opened his mouth to the cops. I believed Junior would do it too and so did this guy, because we crossed paths with him on several other occasions, he never ratted on us.

We entered the train station and rolled through the gate with our merchandise. The dude inside the token booth was in shock, but he minded his own business. He knew he had to work that booth every day and obviously didn't want any trouble. Actually, he turned out to be cool and after a while wouldn't even make us pay. Dougie even managed to fill a few orders for the guy including an electric hedge clipper and some bikes for his kids. When we got on the CC, the A, or GG trains to Greenpoint it was the same thing. Nobody looked, nobody asked questions and nobody cared.

We did that shit for almost a month and never got caught. We hit about thirty garages that summer and made some really good money fencing the stolen stuff. It wasn't the money or the nice clothes that got me hooked. Shit, I could have made more money in less time with half the risk at Forrest Park. It was the thrill. Dougie and Junior were a fuckin' pisser to hang out with and I wouldn't have traded it for all the money in Forrest Park. Unfortunately, you know the saying, "All good things must come to an end" and two incidents brought our lucrative operation to a screeching halt. The first was an article in the local paper detailing the Belle Harbor robberies. The other was a serious car accident where the local police got a pretty good description of us as we fled the scene.

That particular night started off the same; we had our list of shit from Pops and we killed time by smoking weed and drinking up on the boardwalk. Believe it or not, Dougie was going out with Nadine, the same Nadine who was my date to the Black Sabbath concert. When she was closing the Baskin-Robbins where she worked, we showed up and got some munchies. Her parents had an apartment on the boardwalk and they always went away for the summer. Dougie would go up and fuck Nadine, come out on the balcony in her dad's robe and then call Junior and me up for showers. We'd hang out and smoke some more, eat their food and then jet up to Belle Harbor for work.

As we were heading up we passed this old, drunk Irishman who occasionally knocked back a few with Junior. He was sprawled out on a bench drunk as shit with his car in park. The driver's-side door was wide open, the engine was running and he was blaring oldies on the radio. The joke the kids in Rockaway played on him almost every night when he got wasted was to steal his car, park it somewhere out of the way and see how many days it would take him to find it. At that point Junior decided we were going to take the drunk's car to work in Belle Harbor instead of walking on the beach.

There were two problems with that particular scenario. First, Junior was a lousy driver and second, there was an unopened quart of Jack Daniel's on the front seat. We finished it off in record time and were totally shit-faced as we cruised around Rockaway doing 60 mph down side streets. Dougie was in the back seat and I was in the front as Junior sped north on Beach Channel Drive. I turned the FM radio dial to 102.7 WNEW and Aerosmith's "Rats in the Cellar" was playing, so I cranked it. Big mistake. Junior was already driving like a fucking maniac and he didn't need any more encouragement. We were now doing close to 90 mph, screaming along with Steven Tyler's lyrics and then instead of taking the road to Belle Harbor Junior yells, "Greenpoint!" and drives over the Marine Parkway Bridge. Seems we were now going to their Brooklyn neighborhood to raise hell. As we approached the tollbooth on the opposite side at speeds in excess of 75 mph, we realized that none of us had money for the toll. Junior then threw the car in a spin doing 45 mph right in front of the tollbooths and on-coming traffic. The car spun out and fishtailed all over the road, narrowly missing a few cars. Then he punched the gas pedal and headed over the bridge back toward Rockaway with a police car in hot pursuit.

We got back on Beach Channel Drive with Junior and Dougie laughing their asses off, but I was starting to get a little nervous, since I had two warrants and we were now engaged in a high-speed chase with the cops. I started yelling at Junior to pull over so we could make a run for it, but that just wasn't going to happen. He hung a right and drove onto Rockaway Beach Boulevard figuring he could get the cop off our tail by driving on the wrong side of traffic. Well, he was right, because the cop didn't follow us. He drove neck and neck on the other side, screaming and waving at us to pull over. I was pretty shit-faced, but I could clearly see those headlights coming at us. I pulled the steering wheel really hard to the right, narrowly avoiding a head on collision. We jumped over the divider and cut off the cop who slammed on his brakes. His car skidded sideways into the divider and blew out his tires. When we hit the curb, we were sent airborne right through someone's garage.

When we crashed my nose was split open along with my head, but surprisingly we were all alive. We climbed out of the demolished car and pushed our way through the debris to get out of the garage. When we walked outside, standing on the front lawn in their pajamas were a husband and wife in complete shock. The air was filled with smoke and there was broken shit everywhere. Junior looks at the couple and asks, "Yo... you motherfuckers know where the Tidy Bowl Man lives?" The cop was also pretty shaken up, but as he stumbled out of his car, we grabbed Junior and took off laughing with our T-shirts covering our bloodied faces. At that point, the neighbors were coming out of their houses to see what the commotion was all about, so we figured it was best to hide our identities. As we ran down to the beach I joked that at least the old drunken fucker would be able to find his car when he woke up in the morning. Junior then held up the car keys and said, "Maybe we should go give him these," which had us cracking up all the way back to The Circle at 116.

We didn't get away from the crash free and clear though, because someone apparently saw us take the old guy's car earlier that night and gave the cops our descriptions. They were looking all over Rockaway for us, so we decided to stay the hell out of the area and pulled the plug on our late-night Belle Harbor escapades. Our only real regret was that we never found the Tidy Bowl Man's house and his captain's hat for Junior. Lord knows we looked for it that summer.

That's how it was back then and that's what I miss about the old-school New York City. It was a town of outlaws and growing up back then taught me some valuable lessons - lessons that helped me survive in any situation, anywhere in the world. I had an education from the "University of the Streets" and that's something you can't find in any college curriculum. I don't endorse crime, but it was time and circumstance; I was a kid who was homeless and I hustled and did whatever I had to do, to stay alive and see another day. I never robbed old ladies or poor people and all the danger and unpredictability of the lifestyle I once lived was a rush. I was a Robin Hood who bought Paulie and the bums at The Circle a hot meal and a case or two of Piel's after every job. Those times are long gone and now New York City is a sterile, safe version of what once was. I have to say, I'm glad I was there and in some ways maybe it's cool the city has changed. At least my mom can walk down the street without looking over her shoulder and the residents of Belle Harbor could leave their garage doors unlocked and not worry about people like us.

A few days after our accident we were on the boardwalk at The Circle partying and drinking when this really pretty local girl walked over and asked Junior for a light. Well, he took it as a sign that she was coming on to him and responded by groping her. When she told him to fuck off he smashed his whiskey bottle across her face. She was bleeding profusely and grabbing for the boardwalk railing. He then punched her in the face several times before he called her a stuck-up cunt. Junior was covered in her blood and was laughing like a maniac. The bad news for him was she was friendly with the Rockaway locals and it caused some major shit. Dougie and Junior got on the first CC train out of Rockaway and were never seen or heard from again.

The girl needed a lot of stitches to close the wound on her face and everyone at the beach was pissed at me because I was with those guys when the shit went down.

It was during this time that I found out E got busted while breaking into a liquor store in Rockaway. When the cops nabbed him, they beat him up pretty badly, breaking his nose and all kinds of other shit. He was arrested prior to the liquor store break-in and did some time in Spofford, which scared the shit outta me. Thinking I could be next, I moved out of The Irish Riviera and headed back to my old stomping grounds, before September rolled around.

I ran into a few of the local dealers at The Dome and they told me the undercovers were making a lot of arrests, which wasn't good news or particularly good for biz. That first night I got there, I didn't work, but hung out with the local dealers. When the last dealer left the park, so did I, in search of a place to crash. It was chilly that night, so I went to a building seeking shelter, but a tenant caught me going into the stairwell and threatened to call the cops if I didn't leave. Not wanting to bring any heat to the situation, I went back to the park, lay down on a bench, pulled my jacket over my head and crashed out.

That night this guy sleeping one bench over from me was making these gurgling sounds, which kept disrupting my sleep. I yelled at him a few times to find somewhere else to sleep and each time I yelled, he would momentarily stop making noises. Every time I was about to fall back asleep the gurgling continued. At this point, I was convinced the guy was fucking with me and at dawn I got up and went over to confront him. He was now passed out cold and that pissed me off because he slept like a baby, while I was up all night. I shook him to wake him up and as I did, this nasty looking orange foam began oozing out of his mouth. A voice behind me said, "Don't waste your time, he's been dead for hours." It was Computer and his armed bodyguard, Disco who informed me that the dude was just a local junkie who must have overdosed during the night. The orange foamy shit coming out of his mouth was methadone and I remember getting a weird feeling thinking about a person dying only a few feet away from where I was sleeping.

Computer looked like a normal dude, but in all actuality he was anything but normal. He was a reclusive guy who only came out on special occasions. Rumor had it he earned his nickname because he held a degree in chemical engineering that he didn't exactly use to find a cure for cancer. Computer used his know-how to invent what was called "Black Zombie Dust" or "Computer Dust." His patented brand of dust was so potent, he had people coming from all over New York to sample his shit, and for good reason: one hit was guaranteed to send you to the moon.

For some strange reason when Computer would finish a new batch of his dust, he loved to test it out on some guinea pig to see how potent it really was. There was never a shortage of willing participants at Forrest Park who would sample his shit for free.

Computer's partner, Disco, was a huge, 6'3" disco-looking motherfucker, who had slicked-back hair and always sported disco pants, a silk disco shirt, platform shoes, an assortment of gold chains, and Elton John-style diamond-encrusted Cazal sunglasses. Disco was a body-builder and a known steroid user who provided the muscle to the local dealers, aided by a nickel-plated .45-caliber automatic. If you could picture John Travolta's character Tony Manero from Saturday Night Fever jacked on 'roids, that was Disco in a nutshell. He always carried a vast assortment of pills and usually had younger kids hanging around him.

When Computer made his brand of dust he perfected a technique he called "whipping up," which involved mixing embalming fluid, ether, PCP and a bunch of other toxic chemicals. The process of whipping up the volatile chemicals was very dangerous and there was always a risk of explosion, so Computer never mixed indoors. One night, I helped Computer whip up and I got the worst headache after breathing all that shit in. But that dude, he just worked like some kind of mad scientist totally unaffected by the hazards of the job. Did I mention that Computer usually whipped up at the Machpelah Cemetery on top of Harry Houdini's gravestone? Don't ask me why, but for some reason Computer was obsessed with the guy and I remember reading the grave's inscription: "Harry Houdini Legendary Magician and Escape Artist."

Anyway, guess who the guinea pig was going to be for Computer's new batch? That's right... moi. He told Disco to pack me a bowl and he followed his instructions. Disco handed me the pipe and just as I was about to light it up he says, "You're the kid that sold beat shit out here with that prick Bobbie Bird, right?" I was like, "Nah dude... I uhh..." He opened his jacket and lifted up his silk shirt revealing his .45-caliber automatic. "He's lucky he split, because when I catch him I'm gonna blow that scumbag's knee-caps off for rippin' off a friend of mine." I told him that Bobbie ripped me off, too, and deserved whatever he's got coming to him.

Disco and I talked about The Dome, the dealers, the cops, the drugs and the whole time Computer just stared out into Never Never Land and didn't say shit. He wouldn't answer my questions, laugh at my jokes, or even acknowledge me. Disco said not to take it personally, that the years of inhaling the chemicals made him a little bugged-out. Shit, Computer was beyond bugged out. He was the weirdest fucker I had ever met. He had conversations with himself, he laughed out of nowhere and he would turn to you out of the blue with some out of context statement like you had talked about it for hours. I must have won Computer over, because he told Disco to give me Scotty's job.

Scotty was a kid who dealt for Computer and had split with more than fifty of his bags, which frequently happened to dust dealers. After smoking a few bags they'd usually wake-up three days later and realize they either smoked all their shit, or somebody ripped them off when they passed out. So, to save face and their asses, they just never bothered showing up again. I guess the old saying, "Good help is hard to find," also applies to selling zombie dust.

Disco lit my bowl and the next thing I knew I was in the parking lot laying on the trunk of a car, staring up at the sky. When I did, this huge demon's claw came out of the clouds and swiped at me. It was the strangest shit I ever smoked and it allowed me to glimpse into a very demonic world. To be honest, it scared the shit of me. In the Vedas from India, it says that there are many planes of existence, different levels of consciousness if you will, and according to what we do in life we associate with beings on those planes. Yoga and meditation bring positive beings and auras of light and positivity around you. Drugs and alcohol bring beings of negativity, destruction and darkness to your life. If you think that alcoholic, homeless dude on the train platform is just crazy and yelling at himself, think again. Drugs artificially open your third eye and allow you to be haunted by ghosts, because you lack the control to stop them. Ghosts are living entities that misused their bodies in the previous life either from suicide, drug overdoses, or dying while intoxicated. As a result, they're forced to exist in subtle bodies. They still have desires, but they just lack the body to fulfill them. When they do find a very intoxicated person they enter through their third eye and carry out their dark desires. How many people have we seen get fucked up, go out and do some crazy shit that was way out of character for them? When they end up sitting in that prison cell, doing a ten-to-fifteen-year bid, they scratch their heads and say, "I don't know what got into me. I just snapped." Well now, you not only know what got into them, but whom, why and how. Did you see The Sixth Sense? Check it out.

M. Night Shyamalan, who wrote and directed the film, definitely did his research on ghosts and spirits - believe me.

After about an hour, I finally came down from my high. Disco gave me fifty bags to sell at $10-a-piece and I sold out within an hour. My take was $1 for each bag I sold, plus a freebie. Disco made sure I only got my free bag at the end of the day and for good reasons. Now a $1-a-bag might not seem like a lot, but Computer couldn't keep up with the demand. I was selling anywhere from 150 to 200 bags in a four-hour shift and my take wasn't exactly chicken feed, especially in the '70s. The main thing I enjoyed about working for Computer was the sense of importance it gave me. Everyone came to me, everyone liked me and everyone respected me, because not only did I have the best dust in the city, I also had Disco with that .45 on his side. Disco was a valued asset, because he knew exactly when the undercover cops were coming to sweep The Dome (he had a cop on the inside he sold steroids to). When the shakedown was coming, we'd just head over to The Carbines in Queens to hustle.

Selling at The Carbines was weird, because the dealers were either disco boys or burnt-out Rockers. I think at that point, with the war between the two in the city, The Carbines was the only place the two factions got along. That's because they shared one common desire: to keep the peace. They all got along so they could all make big money - bigger money than they made at Forrest Park.

I'd easily sell a hundred bags within an hour then we'd have to split because The Carbines was crawling with cops. We got in fast, sold our shit and bounced. That was the routine and in that first week I made about $800, smoked some great dust and had achieved near celebrity status.

I was the man with Computer's shit and the dust-heads always greeted me warmly, like I was a long-lost relative. They brought me beer, weed, jewelry to trade (which Disco always took) and if I'd asked, they would've let me fuck their girls as long as I traded them for the fattest bags. Computer's batches were getting stronger and stronger and we always sold out. Whether we sold in Forrest Park or The Carbines it didn't matter, everyone wanted Computer Dust. It got to the point where some assholes looking for some quick cash were falsely claiming they had the bomb Computer shit. When Disco found the two perpetrating salesmen at The Dome he pistol-whipped the shit out of them in front of everyone to send a message that you don't fuck with their moneymaking operation. Up until that point, everything was running like a well-oiled machine. But then, as it always goes down in the drug business, things took a turn for the worst.

One night in September, word got out to the dealers at The Dome that this crazy motherfucker, Irish Tony from Woodside's sister had copped some dust in the park a few days earlier. While she was dusted, she thought she could fly and jumped out of a third-story window. She ended up in intensive care at the hospital and that wasn't good, because Irish Tony was now looking for the dealer who sold to his sister. Irish Tony was one tough son of a bitch and he was one of the only dudes ever crazy enough to go into Spaghetti Park on a Friday night and fight all those Guido fuckers without any back up.

He called himself Irish Tony even though his mom was Irish and his father, who named him Tony, was Italian. From what I heard, his dad beat on his mom all the time when he was a kid and for that sole reason, he despised Italians. Tony had mostly Italian features, except for his red hair. He insisted to the local Irish hooligans in Woodside, who would never have hung out with a Guido, that he was only one-third Italian and the other two-thirds Irish. And if Irish Tony says there's very little Sicilian blood running in his veins and you had any scruples, you didn't question his genetic make-up, trust me. Besides, the Irish and Italians are notorious for their hot-blooded tempers, so whatever his exact ethnic breakdown was, Irish Tony was nobody to fuck with.

Since Irish Tony was on the warpath, I thought we should have laid low for a few days until things blew over, but Disco thought otherwise. He said point blank, "No fuckin' way! Fuck him. This is my fuckin' park and I got a forty-five-automatic that says so. What kind of mixed-up, fuckin' asshole goes around calling themselves Irish Tony, anyway?" A few days went by and nothing happened. Disco began bragging that his reputation as a badass must have gotten back to Woodside, because Irish Tony had bitched up. I made a conscious effort to keep my distance from Disco, because I didn't feel right about the entire situation. Everyone knew he sold Computer's shit and in a park full of derelict looking, rock-n-roll fuckers, a big-as-shit disco dude was hard to miss.

It was about 9 p.m., our supplies were running low and I was ready to call it a night. Disco had this fifteen or sixteen-year-old-kid in matching Saturday Night Fever clothes who looked like a mini version of himself hanging around. I thought the kid was annoying and should get lost, but Disco said they had business to attend to later in the evening, so I didn't pay much attention to him. At this point, a lot of the dealers had returned to the drug spot, because nothing ever happened with Irish Tony. We also got word that his sister was going to pull through with a few broken bones and that was good news.

We were standing at the top of the stairs in front of the parking lot, when a caravan of cars and vans came rolling through. One of the vans was a custom joint and the other was a black cargo van. They drove along the tree line as protocol required and slowly crept in front of the stairs. The cars wanted Tuinals, Quaaludes, and weed. The guy in the front passenger seat of the cargo van stuck his head out the window and asked if any had dust and Disco yelled, "Right here!" I took one step down the stairs when the side door of the cargo van popped open and this red haired Italian guy pulled out a burner and started blasting wildly in our direction. Everyone scattered like cockroaches as bullets began to ricochet off the stairs and railings. As I ran up the stairs toward The Dome, I heard him pop off several more rounds, before I felt a burning sensation in the back of my left calf. I heard Disco yell in a terrified voice, "This way" and I ran toward the woods where he was hiding with his disco protégé.

It turned out that when shit got thick with Irish Tony, big-ass, tougher-than-shit, trash-talking Disco lost his nerve and was shook. He never even got off a single round from his gun, or even pulled it out of his shirt for that matter. His chump-ass was shaking like a leaf. Apparently that was the first time anyone ever shot at him and he didn't like it. I can't explain how those first rounds missed me other than to say that Irish Tony was a lousy shot and the good Lord, once again, intervened on behalf of my dumb ass. I found out later that besides the ricochet th at hit me, only one of Irish Tony's bullets found its mark, causing a slight flesh wound to someone's arm. Disco looked at my leg and said he could see the bullet sitting slightly under my skin. I couldn't go to a hospital with a gunshot wound, because that would obviously raise suspicion, so Disco assured me he could pull the slug out at his house. I agreed and we took off in his car.

Disco's house looked like a '70's nightclub, complete with tacky furniture, lots of mirrors and lights. He also had the essential "Enjoy Coke" Coca-Cola mirror that every disco dude in the '70's used for sniffing coke. He made us drinks before he got to work and rinsed a pair of tweezers in rubbing alcohol. I quickly downed my drink and for some reason soon afterward, I was really high. In fact, I was so high I was on the verge of passing out that I barely even noticed him pulling the 22 caliber slug out of my leg. I crashed out on his couch and woke up some time later to the sound of someone screaming bloody murder from a back room. My leg was bandaged and I was still fucked up as I followed the sound of the screams. I got closer to the room the screams were coming from and as I did, I heard these animal-type grunts coming from behind the door. I opened it slightly and peaked in and there was Disco on the bed pumping his little protégé from behind. The kid was barely conscious and pleading for him to stop. Disco kept trying to cover the kid's mouth with one hand as he held him down with the other. I stood there momentarily in shock, but when I realized what was going on I got really pissed. I looked around for the first thing I could use to hit that oversized, fag fucker with, when I spotted a baseball bat near his closet. While Disco kept fucking this kid, I snuck in, picked up the bat and blasted that motherfucker across his back. He screamed in agony and flopped off the bed. The kid collapsed and I went into a rage, beating Disco in the legs, arms and head.

I made him beg for mercy and when he did, I hit him some more. That day, he was on the receiving end of the worst beating of his life and who better to give a pedophile his karma than me? I mean my writing teacher, Mr. McKee, did say it's what you do as a result of the abuse, right? Well, I chose to beat this fucker senseless and trash his entire apartment.

I spread the word all over Forrest Park that Disco was a fag rapist, and as a result he never showed his face in the park again. It seems that the kid he messed with that day wasn't an isolated incident. Word on the street was he'd done it to some other kids, as well, and his modus operandi was always the same. He invited one, two, sometimes three kids over to smoke weed or do blow and listen to music. Then he'd put very strong barbiturates in their drinks and have his way with them when they passed out. None of his victims ever said anything because they feared being called fags and homos. When I found out what really went down with Disco and those teenagers, my only thought was, "Holy shit, that coulda been me that night." If that actually happened, I woulda gotten locked up for murder, because I definitely would have killed that steroid-taking, disco-faggot motherfucker. End of story.

As a result of the gunshot, my leg got seriously infected. It took two weeks to heal after I started changing the bandages and using anti-bacterial ointment on a daily basis. It was now late September and I was still selling for Computer. As the temperature in the city started to drop, The Dome was still really hot following the Irish Tony shoot-out. Business dropped considerably, because even the regular customers feared getting busted by cops who were now posing as dealers. Computer would only give me twenty-five bags at a time fearing I would get busted and lose his shit. To be honest, it was a real pain in the ass selling-out and then having to go wait for that burnt-out fucker or his friend to show, before I could re-up. Things were hot at The Dome and business at The Carbines was no better. People who were using dust were committing some pretty horrific crimes in the city and I guess the cops decided it was time to crack down on the known drug spots.

It got really tough on the streets at that point. It was tough to make money, tough to find a place to sleep and tough to eat. Then, on a cold night during the last week of September '78, my worst nightmare came true. I sold a bag of dust to an undercover cop and was arrested.

Have you ever been in a situation where you knew your life was never going to be the same? Well, that's how I felt as I sat in the prisoner interrogation room at Central Booking in Kew Gardens. The cops knew I had two outstanding warrants and St. John's didn't want anything to do with me. As I sat there alone, I had two detectives pulling the old good cop/bad cop routine on me. The good cop sat across from me and calmly said he really cared about me and knew I had a rough life, but was willing to give me another chance. Here was his offer - rat out who I got the dust from and he would see about getting me six months in a drug program, followed by a halfway-house group home. The bad cop stomped around the room, kicked the chair I was sitting on and said shit like, "Fuck this little prick, Jim. Send him to Spofford and let him go upstate. Them niggas'll love his little, lily-white ass." The good cop's rebuttal: "Those places just turn people into animals, Mike. I still think there's hope for John, here. John, tell me where I can find this guy you're selling for. He's a piece of shit, you know what angel dust has been doing to people in this city. You help me out and I'll help you out."

I stuck to my story, "I'm a freelancer. Guys come in, give me stuff to sell and they come back at the end of the night to collect their money. That's all I know about them." Bad cop screamed, "We got fuckin' photos of you selling dust on several occasions and even got a tip that you were working directly for the manufacturer. We can get you on making the shit, too, and that's federal tough guy. You link that with your two other cases for B and E (breaking and entering) and marijuana sales, and you won't see the streets for at least five years. I can fuckin' guarantee you that!" Good cop... "Give us a name John, that's all we need just one name?" Bad cop... "He's got one fuckin' minute to decide, then he's mine." Good cop... "John this one's for all the marbles. You could fuck up your whole life here. Once you enter the system it's virtually impossible to stop the downward spiral. What do you wanna do?"

I sat there nervous as fuck, because I knew he was right. The odds were against me and the statistics proved this to be true. Most teenagers who entered the prison system spent their lives going around that revolving door of the penal system, before they're back on the streets. Those cops wanted Computer, not me. I knew where he worked, where he lived, ate, shat, fucked... shit, I even knew where he bought his fuckin' toilet paper. I literally had the whole nine on his ass and all I had to do was give him up and I could have pretty much walked away from my three pending cases with little more than a slap on the wrist.

Decisions under pressure are the hardest to make and that's why it's the only way to ever know anything about a person's true character. Anybody can put on a big show of being a tough guy, just look at Disco. He was all mouth, until the bullets started flying. You want to see what somebody's really made of, tighten the screws and put the pressure on. You might see the skinny, little nerdy guy with glasses rise to the occasion and the tattooed, muscle guy crumble. I've seen it time and time, again. As for me, the code of the street clearly says, "You Never Rat" plain and fuckin' simple. I stuck to it and now I was on my way to the Spofford Juvenile Detention Center in the Boogie Down Bronx.

As I sat handcuffed in the back of the police car, I was scared shitless. My chauffeurs were two Irish cops, one of whom didn't make the ride any easier by telling me that they didn't take a lot of white kids up there. Then the other cop in the front passenger seat asked me if I smoked and I said, "I do now." He lit up a cigarette, held it up and let me take a drag. He saw the fear in my eyes and said, "Listen McGowan, I'm gonna give you a little piece of advice and it's only because you're Irish. You better beat the shit out of the first nigger or spic that fucks with you or you're gonna have a rough time in there." I told the cops I could get along with anyone and that I wasn't a racist. They both laughed and the cop driving said, "Yeah, well they are and if you don't go in kickin' the shit out of those pricks you'll be comin' out with a very big asshole." I didn't know if he was serious about the gang rape stuff, but it didn't sound good. I took another long drag of that cigarette and tried to imagine what was about to go down.

play the wall

chapter 6

It was evening when we drove through the ill-as-shit-looking South Bronx en route to Spofford. The cops said that even if a white guy makes it over the fifty-foot walls surrounding Spofford, that he'd never make it out of the neighborhood alive and I believed them. There were burned-out buildings, hookers, junkies and a whole lot of motherfuckers up there who looked like they had nothing but bad intentions on their minds. As we rolled up to the correctional facility it was lit up and it looked eerily calm from the outside. That all changed once I entered into the halls and was marched toward the indoctrination center, aka "Indoc," where I was strip-searched. There was yelling, screaming, the sounds of keys jingling and heavy metal doors slamming shut. These were new sounds to me and I took all of them in. I guess fear heightens your senses. As for my sense of smell, it immediately picked up on that institutional cleaning fluid and it made me a little queasy. We entered Indoc and the two Irish cops took the cuffs off, shook my hand and said good luck before they split.

They left me with the other inmates, who looked a lot older than I was. I tried to avoid making eye contact with anyone or showing the slightest bit of fear but I have to admit, I was scared shitless. Right off the bat, one black kid in particular was giving me dirty looks. He walked over, got in my face and said, "You punk-ass, white bitch," he turned to the others continuing, "I got me a Maytag if this faggot ends up in my wing." I didn't know what a Maytag was at that point but it didn't sound cool, so I quickly replied, "Nah motherfucker, you're gonna be my Maytag." This produced laughs not only from him, but from the other inmates, as well. In jail, a Maytag is somebody who, because he's been punked-out, has to wash whoever chumped him off's socks, underwear and sneakers. The reference meant you were like his personal washing machine. He definitely didn't like my response and promised he was going to fuck me up as soon as the opportunity presented itself. We talked shit back and forth and that's when the biggest, blackest, meanest-looking, motherfuckin' dude I ever saw entered wearing a New York Juvenile Correctional Center uniform. This correctional officer (C.O.) wasted no time getting in our faces and screamed at us for talking before we both immediately shut up. Then the C.O. looked at my Maytag friend and said, "You back again? Don't your dumb ass ever learn?" Seems he was a regular.

A doctor came in and ordered us to strip down and asked if anyone had medical conditions, you know, the usual bullshit protocol you've seen in every prison movie. After that we were handed uniforms and we put them on. All of our possessions were taken and put into bags with our names on it, except for our sneakers, which we were allowed to keep. The C.O. told us to line up single-file and then explained three things to us. One: The painted black line running down the center of every inch of floor space in Spofford. Two: The beam in the ceiling, which was directly over the black line. And Three: The enormous, heavy-ass metal keys he had in his hand, which opened the thick metal doors. If we walked off the line or out from under the beam, he assured us that his keys would find their target (your motherfuckin' cranium is how I believe he put it). One kid couldn't follow orders on the way up to his wing and sure enough that C.O. smacked him right upside the head with those keys. This was before inmates had rights and the C.O.'s wouldn't think twice about fuckin' somebody up. I only caught the keys once to the back of my head, during my entire stay there and they hurt like hell, so I never fucked up again.

We were on the way to our wings and the weird thing was, in St. John's I was in 3B, my wing in Spofford, B3. A-wing was for older guys; B-wing was for intermediates and C-wingers were the youngest offenders. At that time, Spofford was for twelve to twenty-year-olds, but the reason everyone looked older was because most of the motherfuckers in there lied about their ages, because they feared going to Rikers Island. In some ways, I believe Spofford was actually worse than Rikers. I mean I'm not saying Rikers wasn't ill-as-shit, but for the most part (in the pre-gang days) inmates just wanted to head upstate where the facilities had gyms, vocational training, TV's, better food, and a sense of getting your time started. So most inmates just minded their business. Besides, if you caught another case while you were in Rikers you could be there for another year, which really sucked. In Spofford, you had a bunch of young, dumb, full-of-cum, wannabe tough guys, who had something to prove. It seemed everyone had something to say about everything and nobody minded their own business. All the cats I knew who did time in Rikers told me that was rule numero uno - mind your own fuckin' business. But that rule didn't apply to the knuckleheads up in the South Bronx.

My friend from Indoc, whose name I never knew, but for the sake of argument we'll call "Dickhead," ended up in B3 with me. He knew all the staff on the wing and a few of the inmates there happened to be from his Harlem neighborhood. While I was in B3 was the first time I ever heard the expression "Yo, homeboy!" Originally the term meant someone who was from your neighborhood. These days, like most other street-slang phrases white people get a hold of to try and act like they're down, the true meaning is watered down and eventually lost.

I remember going to this party in NYC and there were mostly white, professional types there, you know the kind. They looked at me condescendingly because I have a lot of tattoos, which I guess to them, indicated that I was an idiot. I couldn't believe the amount of "Peace out, my niggas!," "Words!" and "Chill-outs," I had heard that night. One white guy even went as far as to explain to this other white guy how the ghetto hand gestures went depending on which street-slang phrase you used. So, I'm in there finding all this shit pretty amusing and talking to a few of the girls because I guess they found me a little more interesting than most of the other lame-asses there. That's when these three herbs in suits came over trying to act all B-boy and I guess to try to humiliate me in front of their boys. "Yo!" one of them piped in, "So, what you do to make paper son?" "Well Winston, Nathaniel, and Bartholomew," I replied, "it's kinda hard to find a motherfuckin' j-o-b wit a felony conviction for aggravated assault and what not, but mainly since I been out of jail I just sling some yayo (cocaine), unless I can find me a bitch to suck my dick and support my broke-ass, while I wait for my guh-a-ment assistance check to show up." Then I gave them my best one-eyed crazy stare and finished with, "Why?: Y'all motherfuckers gots some openings down at your spot?" Well, that sent those assholes on their way and I turned back to the girls and said, "Now where were we before we were so rudely interrupted? Oh yes, the difference between Mayavadi philosophers and the Vaisnava monastic-based lifestyle of India's 19th century monks."

Anyway, in two or three days time, Dickhead managed to turn everyone in B3 against me, including his main homeboy, a brother who also came from Harlem. They were both bigger than me and since I was the only white boy in the entire facility, I knew I had to watch my back. Not everyone at Spofford was an asshole to me though. There were a couple of brothers who thought I was chill and showed me the ropes, which only deepened Dickhead's hatred of me. They showed me how to smuggle a match head and a tiny piece of striker into my cell so I could smoke Kool's (they were the only cigs they gave out in Spofford). They knew who to steer clear of and what everyone was in for (Dickhead: attempted murder for stabbing someone) and they explained the most important term I would learn at Spofford: "Play The Wall."

Playing The Wall meant that when some shit went down like, a riot or you got into a fight, you always, no matter what, kept your back against the wall so no one could sneak up behind you. That shit was crucial information and I would have been clueless without it. Thank God, not everyone up in Spofford had the skin disease and they looked out for me. Actually, I have to admit after almost two years of hanging out with nothing but crazy-ass white people, it was refreshing to be around some brothers again. Most of these guys were handed the shittiest deals from birth - no family structure, the ghetto, poverty, drugs and crime, but they still remained somewhat positive about life. Talk about resiliency.

During the evening hours, we occasionally saw hookers walking the streets near Spofford. We would hang out the windows and guys would scream out at them to flash some titty or a little ass. One night we all yelled shit out the window to this hooker and we got an unexpected surprise. A very convincing black transvestite whipped out a small, baseball bat-sized penis and waved it at us like a wand. This was greeted by shouts of "Oh shit!" and "Faggot!"

Yeah, it was all fun and games and tough guy attitudes at Spofford, but when you got locked in your room and the lights went out, something else happened; everyone became who they really were - scared kids. That's when the loneliness set in and we were forced to face our thoughts and fears, and with that came the tears.

We weren't monsters and each and every one of us had a conscience. We walked around during the day with chips on our shoulders the size of Manhattan saying, "Fuck them," about those we wronged. But at night our true feelings came out. We weren't only crying for our situations and ourselves, but we were crying for the people who we also hurt. Those inmates who were there for rape or murder, they had to think about their victims. Those who were in lockdown for armed robbery, they had to think about the fact that they fucked up royally and it wasn't worth any amount of money to be going through what they were. Whatever the crime you committed, it was during the evening hours when the bullshit, tough-guy walls you put up came crashing down. You had to be real and you had to reflect on your life. When I put all that bullshit aside, I cried, too.

We were the kids who had failed in the foster care system and at places like St. John's. As Brother Mark once said, we were "starting our downward spiral into lives of incarceration." It's a funny thing being alone, because you're forced to confront yourself when you're sitting there with nothing but your thoughts. It's no wonder most of us cried. We had nothing but time to look at our fucked-up lives and who we were becoming. I know I was scared as shit about what the future held, although I would never admit it or obviously let it show. Each morning, another phenomenon took place - our doors were unlocked and we walked out of our cells with our tough guy masks back on. The walls went back up, the shit talking started and no one ever made fun of or even brought up the fact that we heard each other crying at night.

Most of the kids locked up in Spofford laughed at the severity of my charges and wished they were in my shoes. They were all experts on the law, and I don't mean that figuratively. The majority of them were well versed in penal codes and judicial system protocol by the age of sixteen. They knew exactly what the sentences were going to be for most criminal offenses and 90 percent of the time they were right on. I had a court date fast approaching and the word I got from my inmate/lawyers was that the threats of a five-year sentence by the cops were total bullshit. I would probably do anywhere from a year to two in a minimum-security facility. E was already at a place called "Lincoln Hall" about an hour-and-a-half north of the city and that's where I was hoping to serve my time. After a few months of good behavior at Lincoln Hall you could get home visits and they had trade workshops where you could learn to become an auto mechanic or a carpenter. I mean, shit, they even had a barn with horses where you could become a NYC cowboy, just like '70's TV crime-fighter McCloud, who rode the streets of Manhattan on a horse. The problem with going to Lincoln was I had more severe charges pending than E did, so it was a long shot to get sent there.

I spent my sixteenth-birthday in Spofford and a day later I had my first real test. As people lined up for dinner, I was sitting in the last row of chairs in the TV lounge, watching television and minding my own business. Dinner was the one meal that wasn't mandatory and most of the time the shit they served was so nasty I hardly showed up to eat. We were watching a movie and everyone was laughing. Normally that wouldn't be a problem, but we weren't watching a comedy. At that moment, I felt something touching the back of my neck and as I turned around I realized what everyone was laughing at. Dickhead had his johnson out and was standing there humping the back of my head. I jumped up, picked up the chair I was sitting on and cracked him over the head. The blast caused him to scream in pain as a dead silence fell over the entire room. I didn't even have a second to think about what to do next, instinct took over. I was in a blind rage and I immediately stormed over to the chow line, spotted Dickhead's homeboy and hit that motherfucker so hard in the mouth with a left cross that his tooth came out and stuck in my knuckle. I began screaming like a madman, "Come on, motherfuckers! All you motherfuckers!" The staff ran out, tackled me and restrained me on the ground.

The black and Spanish kids at Spofford assumed that just because I was white I had some baseball, apple pie-eatin' easy life, where I shopped at Bloomie's with Mommy and Daddy and spent my summer vacation in the Hamptons. Although I wasn't getting sent upstate for murder or armed robbery, like some of the other residents, that didn't mean I didn't go through my fair share of shit in life. Even to this day, especially in my neighborhood, you'll find loudmouth, little fuckin' wannabe homeboys who start shit with everyone and swear they've had it so rough in the 'hood. I'm like, "Motherfucker, please. This shit ain't the 'hood, kid, it's called the East Village, son, and back in the day when it was the LES, your punk-ass wouldn't have lasted a day going through the shit I endured. So put that in your blunt and smoke it, with your Sony Xbox and $150 kicks Mommy bought you. And by the way, if I saw a herb-ass mark like you down here twenty-five years ago, you'd be walkin' home barefoot, homey, believe that."

Spofford authorities knew scraps went down, but didn't take kindly to the homo stuff. The technicality that got me off, and Dickhead in deep shit was reported as follows: "The inmate actually touched McGowan's neck with his penis." If Dickhead had just whipped it out, waved it around and never touched me, it'd be a different story. But hey, he fucked up. So, fuck him. Dickhead and his homeboy both got their asses busted and transferred to another wing. I had to spend a day in "The Breaking Room, " where they sent you when you went buck-wild and flipped out. If you "broke," as they called it, they'd put you in a padded room until you chilled out. While I was there, I developed a high fever and my hand had swollen to four times its normal size. Turned out Dickhead's homeboy wasn't up on his oral hygiene and the germs he passed along to me, when I blasted him in the face, put me in the hospital for a week with a serious infection.

When I finally did return to B3, I discovered that I had a new nickname, "Mighty-Whitey." Everything was cool and the brothers took a liking to me that is until I learned to play a dice game called cee-lo and started winning their cigarettes. They realized I had an in-depth knowledge of ghetto fashion and music, and I had serious skills on the b-ball court. When it came time for indoor rec., I was always picked for their full-court games. Outside were handball courts and the Puerto Ricans were like, "Mira white boy, c'mon it's me and you, mang!" I never had that much interaction with Puerto Ricans before Spofford, but I definitely appreciated their sense of humor. As a kid my mother always tried to instill fear in me anytime a Puerto Rican walked by, especially since my Uncle Skipper had been stabbed to death by one.

Two things I've learned from fighting on the streets over the years: black brothers will stand there and talk shit back and forth for hours and most of the time never fight. Puerto Ricans will just fuck you up without saying a word.

I had a Puerto Rican homeboy named Chino who got locked in Spofford for armed robbery, possession of a handgun and for shooting someone. He was my doubles handball partner and was one funny motherfucker. He told me he knew some crazy new martial art called, "Puerto-Rican Judo." Well, I had heard of Bruce Lee and I was up on some kung fu and karate shit, but I never heard of fuckin' Puerto Rican Judo. I was like, "Puerto Rican Judo? What the fuck is that, Chino?" He looked at me with his beady eyes and said in his heavy Spanish accent, "Judon't know if I got a knife. Judon't know if I got a gun. Judon't know what the fuck I got."

The Latinos were good at handball, but they were especially funny when they played basketball. They were hacks and had no skills, but they had to play. Spofford rules. They might be able to hit a killer (and non-returnable ball) from any angle on a handball court, but when it came to hoops, these clowns didn't know a jump shot from a lay-up. Most of the Latinos at Spofford were shorter than I was and when Chino and his crew picked me it was, "Yo! Big man, bene ca (come over here) you wit us mang." When the brothers picked me it was, "Yo! Little man, you runnin' wit us, nigga." I guess in some situations, being white had its advantages. I was neutral just like the word, "Yo!" Everybody used it.

After two weeks in lock-down it was time for my court case at Queens Juvenile Court. They took me and Chino and a bunch of other dudes from various wings in Spofford, down to a room where they gave us our street clothes and loaded us into the cage on wheels. All anyone talked about on the bus was their case and what cracked me up more than anything else was the fact that nobody was fucking guilty! According to every last dude, not a single one committed the crimes they were allegedly charged with, but Chino was the exception. He just laughed and said, "Hell yeah, I shot that maricón. He wouldn't give the shit up and tried to play hero."

The other assholes on the bus were getting ready for their Oscar-winning performances in front of the judge. When they tried to rehearse their lines on Chino he would just say, "Shut the fuck up. You're ass is guiltier than shit." Chino didn't need to bullshit anyone. He knew he was fucked, plain and simple, but that didn't matter, because he had other plans.

When we arrived at Queens Juvenile Court, Chino and I had our cases tried in separate courtrooms. I was assigned some rinky-dink, legal-aide lawyer in a dirty suit. Some of the other guys sitting on defendant's row had family members who showed up for moral support. Not me. No Mom. No family members. No St. John's staffers to say some kind words on my behalf. Nobody except the cops from each of my three cases. The judge entered and started reading off cases. One after the other, he slammed down his gavel and threw out sentences like it was nothing…. two years, four years, five years… it didn't matter one bit to him. Most of the charges I heard weren't even that severe, they were small-time robberies and minor drug offenses. The judge's whole attitude was, "Fuck these little trouble makers! Lock 'em up and let the prison system deal with them. Just so long as I don't have to see them in my neighborhood." He hardly ever looked up from his papers to see whose life he was about to make more hellish. That entire day, he only made eye contact with a guy to let him know he was extra pissed and it was personal. "Mr. Johnson," he began. "Or should I say, Justin Brown? Do you think police officers and court-appointed employees have nothing better to do with their time than sit around rewriting all your paperwork because you lied to them about your identity?" The defendant looked up at him stunned as he went on, "Since you're actually twenty-two Mr. Brown and not eighteen, you'll be shipped to Rikers Island immediately, where you'll be awaiting sentencing."

The judge was a prick. Did he even think about where he was sending kids and what they would endure? Hell no. He had no compassion or no words of wisdom. Instead, his catch phrase was, "Get him out of my sight." I recently saw a piece on Dateline NBC about this judge who had the same lock 'em all up and throw away the key attitude. As fate would have it, he got caught taking bribes. When he went to prison he got a firsthand look at where he had been sending people for so many years without the slightest concern for their well being. When he was sent to prison, the judge changed his whole attitude toward the court system and as a result, became an outspoken advocate for changing sentencing laws. Imagine that.

My case came up and the first charge on the court agenda was for selling weed to the narcs at the burger stand. The judge read the details of the case and I was guilty, plain and simple. The judge said, "Mr. McGowan, you'll return for me to impose sentencing at a later date. After that, I better never see you in my court again." Then he slapped his gavel and the word no Spofford kid wants to hear came out of his mouth, "Remand!" That meant I was getting sent back to Spofford to await sentencing. The court officers then took me back down to the holding cells. An hour had passed before I was back in that same courtroom twice more on the alleged angel dust and breaking and entering charges. The judge was pissed, especially since I was so defiant and wouldn't give the cops the info they wanted on the dust case. "Remand on all three charges! And we'll see you back here in forty-five days Mr. McGowan." He smiled. "Spofford's a good place for someone like you. Get him out of my sight!" Yeah, shalom to you too judge!

We were served bologna sandwiches down in the holding room. Then it was time to get back on the cage. We boarded the bus and I went to sit in the back. Chino stopped me and told me to sit in the emergency exit row with him. I laughed and said, "Why, you planning to make an emergency exit, bro?" He looked at me dead seriously and said, "They fuckin' me, yo. My lawyer says I'm gonna do at least six to eight in Elmira. I can't do that, yo." He was implying I help him escape and doing that was serious. Helping another inmate escape would add another charge to the three I already had pending, but this wasn't just some inmate. Chino was my friend and he looked out for me. He gave me cigarettes, kept the other inmates off my back and was just one chill motherfucker. He endured a hell of a rough life and under other circumstances he might have been a really productive member of society, but he was right. This time around, he was fucked.

Chino took a seat closest to a window, as I stood in the aisle temporarily frozen by his proposition. I looked at him perplexed thinking about what I should do. Finally, I took an aisle seat next to him. He nodded at me and shook my hand in approval. Apparently Chino possessed a little-known Spofford secret that if you kicked the emergency exit window hard enough it would pop right open. Although he was armed with this secret there was a guard in the front of the bus and one in the center. If you made any sudden moves, they would be on you immediately. He told me that when he jumped up all I had to do was block the guard from grabbing him and he would be home free. That may sound easy enough, but the motherfucker closest to us just happened to be one big-ass brother. I wasn't sure I could pull it off, but I told Chino I'd give it my best shot.

Chino pounded my fist and said, "I owe you hermano." With that, he jumped up and right away the guard immediately reacted and quickly ran down the aisle. I got up as he arrived at our seat. The guard was screaming for me to get the hell out of the way as he tried to grab Chino. As I exited the aisle, I tripped on purpose, knocking him slightly off balance. That gave Chino the crucial seconds he needed to make his move towards freedom. He kicked the window and just like he said it would, it popped open. He dove out, hit the street, did this acrobatic roll, got up and took off running. The guard was furious, screaming that I helped Chino escape. I shouted back that I didn't even like the dude so why the fuck would I help his ass break loose? Fortunately, I did such a great acting job, the guard believed me. Unfortunately, Chino only had a few days to enjoy his freedom, because he was caught soon after. He was sent to Elmira to serve out the rest of his sentence plus the additional charges for escaping. I never got to say goodbye, but when I got back to Spofford I got free Kool's from his homies for the remainder of my stay.

Have you ever heard of a panic button? Well neither had I, until I dined in the luxurious Spofford banquet facility. There, strategically placed around the room about five feet off the ground, were actual red panic buttons. If some shit went down like a fight and the C.O.'s couldn't contain it right away, they could hit the panic buttons and things would get real ugly quick. As soon as a few people started throwing down it was like a domino effect and everyone started slugging it out. The next thing you knew trays, chairs, food, and fists were flying in an all-out melee. The C.O.'s weren't stupid. They had families to go home to. So, when things were getting out of control, they pushed the panic buttons and broke the fuck out. They'd lock the doors and announce that we had one chance to calm down or shit was going to hit the fan. That was phase one. In phase two, the riot squad stormed the room and enthusiastically busted everyone's ass.

Did I mention there were girls locked-up in Spofford? And these weren't just any girls. They were formed from the same mold as them scary-type bitches that attended the Fourth of July dance at St. John's, but these girls had them beat. They were more brohlick (diesel), more foul-mouthed and had a reputation for starting shit with anyone and everyone. It didn't matter, because they liked to fight. They ate at the same time as we did, but of course, we were separated. Most of these girls had lives as tragic, if not more tragic than any of ours. The fact that they were female meant they were even more vulnerable then we were. I did talk to a few of them on our visits to the Spofford swimming pool (don't think New York Sports Club, think heavy amounts of chlorine, urine, shit-talkin' and fights) and some of the shit they told me was ill. They were daughters of prostitutes and drug dealers and they openly shared their stories about being pimped-out, molested by relatives, being forced to sell drugs and teen pregnancies. These girls suffered more by age 18 than most women suffer in five lifetimes. I can't say I blame them for being that way or doing whatever it was that landed them in Spofford.

According to statistics, most were headed for a life of incarceration. I say, fuck statistics! If someone wants to change, and they're given a chance to change, they can do it. Like the title of a film I wrote says, Don't Count Me Out, all anyone needs is people who care, people who can expose them to an alternate way of doing things. Unfortunately, most kids in the projects and ghettoes of America are never exposed to arts and culture, or other things they need to grow into well-rounded human beings. I'm convinced that they become victims of their limited environments and limited opportunities. I've seen it firsthand after spending time talking to kids in lock-ups and inner city group homes. I know for a fact that if you give any kid love and attention and show them there are things out there other than hustling and getting into trouble, 99.9 percent of them will gladly take a different path.

As simple as that is, it seems like the world's greatest mystery when you talk to most so-called "professionals." What people like me have over most of the people with PhDs, whose lives are spent trying to get inside these kids' heads, is that we've been there. To those who've lived it, the emotional scars and social dysfunction are not abstract principles. We can honestly relate to their pain and suffering. We know what it's like to go through what these kids are experiencing and they recognize it. I've seen some of the most amazing kids in those places, and the people they loved, listened to, and opened up to, weren't the shrinks and professionals. They were the people from the inner city because they had been there. The kids gave love to the adults and advisors whose own love and understanding was truly deep and authentic.

Two perfect examples were Ms. H. and Mrs. W., two of the ladies who worked at The Salvation Army Boys' Home in Manhattan. Ms. H. was a recovering crack addict and had been incarcerated. She unconditionally loved every kid in there and proved it day after day. She would get so angry and even cry when the kids failed. As for Mrs. W., I don't know how many late night phone calls I got from her about those kids, one of which was my nephew. She even suffered a miscarriage from the stress of worrying about children who weren't even hers. These two women and so many others who help troubled kids deserve sainthood. As cliché as the statement has become, it's still true that children are the future. If we just keep locking them up to keep them away from us, or medicating them into silence, where are we heading as a society? With more than 14 million American teenagers on antidepressants, where are we going as a civilization? What mark will we have left on the history of this planet when the future is handed over to a bunch of emotional zombies and their professional handlers?

At Spofford, I felt like I was beginning to fit in. I fought anyone who tried to chump me off, I excelled at sports, had mad cee-lo skills, was an expert in shit-talking, and I had helped Chino earn a few days of freedom. All of that gave me leverage and credibility inside. A couple of days after Chino's great escape, the crew from B3 were ushered into the packed chow hall. As usual, the chow hall was noisy as hell, with the girls being the loudest. The C.O.'s stood around watching everyone as B3 went through the line and got our grits, powdered eggs, Fink bread and swine.

I was at the back of the line waiting to pick up a plastic tray when I noticed Dickhead and his homeboy giving me dirty looks. I stared back and gave them the finger. Dickhead tried to intimidate me by picking up his butter knife and making a slicing motion across his throat with it. This time I flipped them off with both hands, which really got them steamed. I sat down to eat my institutional breakfast and as soon as I took my first bite, I heard two girls screaming at each other. They jumped up and started fighting and I shit you not, within fifteen seconds the entire room erupted in total chaos.

I was an extra on a few episodes of the HBO prison series, OZ, and let me tell you something, TV cannot reproduce the prison experience no matter how hard they try. The Spofford panic buttons were activated and the doors were locked. Food was flying and butter knife-wielding dudes ran at people as chairs and fists flew through the air. I used my plastic tray to shield myself from a few flying chairs and trays that were headed in my direction. I even threw a couple of chairs myself, because I have to admit, participating in total chaos is kinda hard to resist. The problem was, like Ian MacKaye of the band Minor Threat said, "I was guilty of being white."

Being the only white boy at Spofford, I stood out and it made me an instant target. I may have been Mighty-Whitey up in B3, but these other motherfuckers didn't give two shits about who I was, who I fought, who I helped escape, or how dope my jump shot was. I was a cracker-ass-cracker, and they went for me right off the bat. I saw Dickhead's homeboy coming at me with a butter knife and I lifted a chair over my head to crack his ass before he got to me. As I did, I felt a sharp, excruciating pain in the back of my left forearm. I dropped the chair and looked at my arm. It was bleeding and there was a fork sticking out of my flesh. I heard someone laughing behind me and when I turned around, Dickhead punched me in the face and dropped me to the floor. Eventually, the C.O.'s rushed in and fucked up anyone who was still standing, but not before Dickhead and friends stomped the living shit out of me. I'd forgotten the magic rule…Play The Wall, and I paid for it with stitches, a chipped bone, a very sore jaw and bruised ribs.

I spent almost three months in Spofford – was remanded twice – and it wasn't until my third court appearance that I was finally sent up to Lincoln Hall, (where my brother E was) to serve an eighteen-month sentence. The judge (a different judge from my other cases) told me I was very, very lucky to be going to Lincoln. He informed me that if I messed up one more time I would be sent to a place that would make Spofford look like summer camp. I assured him that from this point forward I'd be turning my life around, and I thanked him at least twenty times for giving me another chance. As crazy as it was though, still to this day, I have never forgotten the three months I spent in the South Bronx with my B3 homeboys.

linky-dinky-dog

chapter 7

Lincoln Hall, or "Linky," as it was referred to, was about an hour-and-a-half north of the city. When I got there it was the dead of winter and cold as shit. Even so, I could see that it was a nice facility with lots of trees, baseball and football fields, a large indoor gym and a barn with horses. Not a bad place to land, especially for a troublemaking city boy like myself. Linky had no fences, but if you pulled a MOP - "Man of Property" - the cops and Linky's security staff hunted your ass down before you were sent further upstate to a more fucked up place. There were non-stop headcounts so they always knew exactly where everyone was at all times. The only chance you had to get out was if the guard working the night shift fell asleep. The few kids who actually tried to escape, failed miserably. Linky was designed to prepare you to go back out into the world and be a productive member of society. After a few months, depending on what group you were in (A through D), you could even earn weekend home visits. If you did make it off the property for a weekend visit, you had better make sure you didn't miss that bus or train back to Linky. If you missed the Sunday night headcount they immediately put a warrant out for you. The place was also structured so that it paid to do the right thing. If you fucked up they'd warn you by saying, "You're dangerously close to getting transferred, McGowan." I knew what that meant, so I chilled-out.

When you first arrive at Linky you are assigned to one of the communal cottages. There were senior and intermediate cottages and each one was named after a different type of tree. E was in a senior cottage called The Oak, which was nicknamed "The Smokin' Oak," because someone always managed to smuggle weed in and they always threw wild parties after the lights went out. I was assigned to "The Elm Cottage," an intermediate cottage that had no late night parties and no weed. Well, not yet anyway.

On your second day in Linky they took you to see the head shrink who gave you a psychological evaluation to see if you required meds or therapy. Once, I was in the shrink's office and he wanted me to draw a picture, any picture of whatever immediately came to mind. I didn't like people trying to mill around inside my head, so, remembering a shock value lesson I learned from my punk rock girlfriend, Nancy, I drew a picture of a nun getting gang-raped and beaten by three Linky inmates. Well, let's just say that didn't go over well with the some of the Catholic staffers. As a result of my antics, I was ordered to undergo counseling the entire time I was there. I didn't mind it one bit. As luck would have it, they later assigned me to a female shrink who was hot as hell and would be on my mind many nights after the Linky lights went out for the evening.

The other thing I learned very quickly at Linky was its catch phrase, "Stay Active," and it meant exactly that. You had to Stay Active all the time – no matter what season. In the dead of winter they made you chop firewood, play tackle football or play soccer in the snow and bitter cold. The only time you were allowed to sit around, hang out and shoot the shit, was one hour before bed, or during a "Light Up." Light Ups were the only time you were allowed to smoke cigarettes and shoot the shit. Otherwise you were marching down the road to the mess hall, playing sports or cleaning. There was a small gym/rec. room in each cottage that included sets of free weights. Since our head counselor, Mr. O'Keefe, liked boxing, we also had boxing equipment to work out with. Every Friday night we held boxing matches where guys who had beef with one another were allowed to put the gloves on and beat the shit out of each other. There were some great matches in that room, including one between me and this brother, John Wilson. That night, he gave me a serious boxing lesson and out of frustration I threw him down and quoted Junior Nuts' as I stomped him. "The boots, Jim! Don't forget the boots!" Well, since I bent the rules a little, the staff broke up the fight and I lost my smoking privileges for the rest of the evening.

John Wilson was a funny motherfucker and we eventually became good friends. He had this crazy laugh and looked like a fucked up black version of Howdy Doody, so I called him "Puppet," a nickname that stuck to him the entire time he was at Linky. About ten years ago he walked by me one day on the LES and I knew the face right away, because nobody else looked like Puppet. We both turned around at the same time, he pointed at me and laughed with that same crazy-ass laugh. The first words out of his mouth were "The boots, Jim! The boots!" We sat and talked for hours and he told me about the time he did after Linky. He also kept me up to date on the latest gossip about the other kids that lived in The Elm. He told me many of my former cottage mates eventually ended up serving lengthy prison sentences.

When we did have Light-Ups the groups you were broken into weren't based on skin color, but were determined by musical tastes. Back then, it seemed like everyone had radios and many of the brothers had big boom boxes, which were really popular at the time. The Rockers who lived at Linky made sure that the disco people never had the biggest boom boxes, because that would mean their shitty music would be blaring over the stuff we wanted to listen to. The guy in charge of the rock division was Marty from Astoria, Queens, who was nicknamed "Carrie," because he looked just like a male version of Sissy Spacek's character from the classic '70's horror movie of the same name. Marty always made sure we were at sonic boom levels with our Zeppelin and Black Sabbath as we sat around telling stories and counting the days until we were released. That's how it was at The Elm: rock in the living room, disco in the rec. room and Orlando and his few salsa brothers (from dee Bronx, mang) went to the showers 'cause nobody, including the staff, wanted to hear that shit.

Orlando was a bug-out, plain and simple. He had a 'fro and a crazed look on his face all the time with the coldest, blackest eyes. You just knew it was only a matter of time before this dude snapped. He would occasionally hang out with the white boys because he knew we had weed and would puff with him. If he knew you were holding, he wouldn't let you out of his sight until you smoked with him. Orlando pretended to like rock, just so he could get stoned with us. He went as far as trying to learn the words to some of the songs and hearing him sing them was hilarious, because the fucker barely spoke English. He spoke in a hybrid Spanglish dialect and his famous last words were: "When I get home I'm gonna drink some brews, smoke some joints, get all fucked up and rape some motherfuckin' pussy, mang." Then he would laugh his ass off with this maniacal laugh. It made us all a little uneasy as we knew he'd actually do it, because no woman in her right mind would fuck him voluntarily. Orlando only had one home visit the entire time he was at Linky and the cops had to go to The Bronx and bring his ass back. Unfortunately, I heard from Puppet that Orlando had made good on his promise and ended up in Sing-Sing for it.

Almost thirty years later, I have a confession to make to my Linky rock-n-roll brethren: I, "The Rambler," (a nickname they gave me because of the Led Zeppelin song "Ramble On" and my crazy homeless stories) did knowingly sneak into the rec. room on occasion to listen to some soul and early rap. I still had an ear for all types of music and besides, while the Rockers had weed from time to time, the brothers always had a few ping-pong balls they were willing to share. And what does that have to do with anything you might be wondering? Clearly you people have never sniffed ping-pong balls. Well then, let me clue you in on this piece of underrated institutionalized get-high. We would break open a ping-pong ball, cut it up and hold a little piece of it in a pair of tweezers. Then we would set it on fire, blow it out and inhale the toxic smoke. It gave us a thirty-second head rush like we were sniffing amyl nitrate.

It took months for The Elm staff to catch on, break up our little cartel and fire the brother who was in charge of the recreation department. When they finally did an inventory and realized that more than twenty or so boxes of ping-pong balls had turned up missing, our boy was fired, because he was the only one with the key.

Although a lot of the boys at Linky rolled together, there was also major competition between the cottages. Intermediates battled each other in football, baseball and basketball and that's exactly what they were... battles. When I arrived at Linky it was basketball season and since The Elm's A-team didn't have a point guard, I naturally got the spot. I led the team through an amazing season and to the championship game, but unfortunately we lost the title to The Cedar Cottage. All the same, Linky allowed me get into top physical condition with the Stay Active shit and three squares-a-day. The chopping wood, running (one of my counselors made you run up this steep-ass hill named "Suicide Hill" if you fucked up, which I did on a number occasions) and constant sporting activities, combined with the good food started to put muscle on my frame. I entered Linky a skinny, under-nourished, 130-pounder and within one year I was a solid 165 and had the stamina to exercise for hours. Back then there were no video games, no soda machines, no candy stores, and TV was restricted to an hour a day, so there weren't many fat kids at Linky. I seem to only remember two and if someone did come in fat, they shed the excess pounds in a matter of months.

These days America's children have the highest obesity rate in the world and I say it's all the parents' fault. Parents let their kids eat shitty food and be lazy. Obesity has doubled in kids since '90 and it only seems to be getting worse. Most parents eat crap and don't exercise and kids tend to emulate what they see their parents do. Here's a little statistic for ya - 40 percent of all Americans are now obese, not overweight, obese. Parents take note: Both you and your kids need to get off your asses and get moving, because knowledge is power. If you want a good read in regards to health and nutrition that will really open your eyes, pick up these three books: Fast Food Nation, Diet For a New America, and Mad Cowboy, a book the cattle industry sued Oprah and an ex-rancher named Howard Lyman over. I saw a recent segment on 20/20 that said that the major fast-food companies target inner city, low-income people of primarily African-American decent because most don't have cars and can't drive to the supermarket to purchase quality fruits and vegetables. I saw a KFC commercial a while back and they had the motherfuckin' Colonel pimp-walkin' and talkin' all Ebonic like, "Y'all better get up on these wings, the price is nice for a limited time, dog." I laughed at first, but then when I realized what they were doing, I was stunned.

The African-American guy that was featured in the 20/20 segment was obese and in order to get home, had to walk by at least twenty-five fast food joints. He raised a very good question to the news correspondent, "If I'm poor and I walk into let's say McDonald's, and for $4.99 I can get either a salad or four burgers, which am I going to choose?" As he walked down the entire strip, several miles long, he tried to buy just one apple and couldn't, with the closest place several miles out of town. I've heard several prominent African-American activists say that fast food is a bigger killer than illegal drugs in the ghetto and the facts are well documented. Poor inner-city blacks have the highest rates of heart disease, type 2 diabetes, high blood pressure, obesity, colon cancer, stroke, joint disease, hyper-tension and asthma in the country. These are diseases that can be prevented simply by a change in diet.

During that 20/20 exposé guess what every other commercial was? (I kept score) Ads for drugs to treat a variety of the diseases I just mentioned. And white people don't think you're off the hook either because as a country the latest medical reports say 44 percent of Americans use prescription drugs and 1 in 6 are regularly taking at least one or more medications to control cholesterol, high blood pressure and depression, all of which can be cured through proper diet and exercise. Here's a thought... maybe the pharmaceutical drug companies are in cahoots with the fast-food people. "Yeah Colonel, Ronald, it's Bob from Pfizer. Listen I got a great idea - you get the fuckers sick with all that crap you sell and we'll sell 'em the pills. Together, we'll make a fortune!" Insert villainous laughter here.

My friend, Morgan Spurlock was the genius behind the documentary Super Size Me, which showed you first hand the effects of eating that crap on a daily basis. I strongly believe that the food we ingest not only affects our bodies, but more importantly, our consciousness, our souls. There are three modes of foods: foods in the mode of ignorance, passion and goodness. Foods in the mode of ignorance are over-cooked and decaying, usually rotting flesh with no life force. Meat, fish and eggs are a few examples. They make you sickly by ingesting them either immediately or down the road with diseases that include colon cancer, arterial sclerosis, hardening of the arteries and gout, among others.

Foods in the mode of passion consist of animal products and hot spicy foods. They also have adverse affects on us like ulcers, gout, and hemorrhoids, etc. Foods found in the mode of goodness however, (I suggest organic and if you watch the documentary "The Future of Food", about genetically modified foods, you'll know why) fruits, nuts, beans, grains, seeds, vegetables and dairy products promote longevity and vitality and make us feel good both physically and emotionally. It's also very important that no angry people cook your food because food is directly affected by who's cooking it.

In late '81 I was living at 171 Avenue A, (a recording and rehearsal studio) with the band, Bad Brains. I'll tell you all about that adventure later, but the point is a few nights a week we would have dinners at Gary "Dr. Know" Miller's (the guitarist) wife Lisa's house at 171 Avenue B. We would listen to Bob Marley, Junior Marvin or Black Uhuru and prepare our meals. It was such good vibes and we had our family there - the Bad Brains, Jay Dublee (their producer and owner of 171A studio) and two hippie girls named Mikaela and Pakita. The food was prepared and cooked with so much love. We even "Reasoned" as the Rastas put it, which meant we talked about God, philosophy, life, whatever and I come ta reason and "Overstand" certain runnins about the bloodclot Babylon system mon. Higher consciousness stuff. See, Rastas don't want to understand something they want to Overstand it. When you Overstand, you capture its full meaning. First we Reasoned and Overstood and then when we ate the food we got high from it. Not because it was Rasta pasta like what you get in Jamaica, where they put weed in the spaghetti sauce. We got high from the positive vibrations and love that went into the food while we were shopping for it, cutting it up, cooking it and giving thanks to the "Most High" be it Jah, Krsna, Buddha, Christ or whatever name of God you prefer. As a kid, I never sat down to eat with a family and had moments like that, but later in life that experience was so special for me. Those were some of the best times in my life and even though materially I had nothing more than the clothes on my back, I was 100 percent content because I had my amazing 171 family meals, which truly filled my soul with joy.

The opposite is also true. If you eat a meal cooked by an overly angry person, even if it is vegetarian, you'll get sick. I've experienced that too, because the karma and the vibes of the person cooking, enters directly into the food. If we don't change our eating and lifestyle habits now, we're going to make the doctors and pharmaceutical companies in this country even richer in the years to come. They know exactly what the cause of our sickness is, but there's no money in the cure. The money is in selling you the medicine to treat your symptoms and performing expensive medical procedures. It's like treating V.D. and then going back and having unprotected sex with the same person over and over again. A perfect example of this is when my mom had quadruple bypass surgery and three days later I walk into her hospital room and they were feeding her hamburgers and fries. I was like, "Yo, Einsteins this crap is what clogged her arteries to begin with." After her near-death experience and years of harping on her to make dietary changes she finally listened. E and I put her on lecithin granules (from soy) which strips plaque off artery walls, raw garlic that won't do much for your social life, but lowers cholesterol naturally, and a lot of organic raw foods that we delivered to her. To this day, her arteries have remained fine and it just goes to show whatever housewife came up with that old saying "An ounce of prevention is worth a pound of cure" knew what the hell she was talking about.

I teach nutritional counseling to people and I truly believe in what I'm doing. I know the greatest gift besides spiritualism you can offer someone, is the knowledge of how to make someone healthy. I find if most people had that knowledge, they would make the necessary dietary changes. The government structure of following the food pyramid bullshit led me to begin my search into an alternative diet. I know a little about health and nutrition because I've been a vegetarian athlete for more than 25 years. In the back of this book is a Web address, so write me and I'll send you some free info on the benefits of basic dietary changes that will improve your health right away and keep you informed about my next book "The Go Green Road to Fitness, Health and Longevity."

The future of health is in getting to the root of what makes us sick and diseased, not spending billions of dollars on medicine that only treat the symptoms. Ninety-five percent of disease is attributed to diet, lifestyle and stress. Once people figure that out, we'll put the pharmaceutical companies and ignorant doctors who give recovering heart surgery patients burgers, out of business. There's a great medical reference book out called "Prescription for Nutritional Healing" by James Balch, M.D. and his wife Phyllis, a certified nutritional counselor who wrote about treating diseases naturally. The authors aren't some wacko, snake oil salespeople either. They know their stuff and a lot of what I'm saying are things I've learned from them and others like Anne Wigmore from the Hippocrates Health Institute. The Journal of American Medicine backs up these findings because according to its authors, obesity has almost caught up to cigarette smoking as the number one preventable cause of death in the U.S. It is preventable through better diets and exercise and according to experts, in the next few years, 1-in-5 health-care dollars will be spent on obese people between the ages of 50 and 60.

The problem is that Americans seem to always be after the quick fix with its fad diets, including the Atkins, South Beach and Hollywood diets.

For the past 27 years, I've been a strict vegetarian and at 45, can still bike 100 miles, run 15, swim a few in the ocean, box, dance and do flips in the mosh pit. My energy comes from live food juices, complex carbs like whole grains (no white flour, processed foods or white sugar), green leafy veggies, fruits, nuts, seeds and beans. The options are unlimited. One of the first things people always ask when I tell them I'm a vegetarian is, "What the hell do you eat?" When I tell them, or even better yet, cook for them, they can't believe the variety of healthy foods that are full of flavor. Let's face it, if it tastes nasty I don't care how good it is for you, people, especially kids, aren't going to go near it.

I currently operate Mama Vani's, a NYC catering company, and one thing I know, adding spices to the food we cook is key. One of my secret ingredients is Vedic spices imported from India, which makes the food taste amazing and also offers medicinal properties to those who use it.

Veda means knowledge and the Vedic teachings are written in Sanskrit, which is the oldest language in the world. The Vedas cover everything from yoga, to martial arts, to philosophy. Name it, it's in there. In the Ayura-Veda, the Vedic system of medicine, it says the spice, turmeric helps to purify the blood. It just goes to show that you can eat foods that have wonderful flavors, scents and colors and that also offer positive health benefits at the same time.

I also feed the needy in NYC and it's one of the things I love to do. I think we've become such an "I," "Me" and "Mine," materialistic society that we often forget about the needs of others. This especially holds true in the rat race of NYC, where in the shadows of multi-million dollar luxury buildings and nightclubs are elderly, homeless and low-income families. Since I was homeless and hungry many a night I feel blessed to be able to do this kind of work. When we hit the streets to feed the needy, it's never bologna sandwiches and Kool-Aid, like some of the other groups offer. We serve healthy, vegetarian meals because my philosophy is to give them something with nutrition, flavor and substance, because it might be their only quality meal for the week. On a number of occasions I've heard our appreciative recipients say, "Out of everyone who comes out here to feed us your food is the best."

In addition to giving back to the community through charity work, I've also helped raise funds by organizing a number of benefit concerts. One concert in particular, called "Hardcore Against Hunger" helped raise $15,000 that paid for a new kitchen where we cook our food for the homeless and hungry. Another benefit show, "Rock Against Maya (illusion)" was held in Tompkins Square Park in '82 and helped feed more than 5,000 hungry New Yorkers. Over the years, I've also participated in Thanksgiving and Christmas dinners and one of our volunteers always used to say, "We're only one paycheck away from standing on this line ourselves, dude." How true my man, how true!

I've had some of the most heart-warming and comical experiences while feeding the needy on the streets of NYC. If you want to meet the real troopers and the survivors, come down and talk to the folks who've had it rough from day one and they'll give you a true lesson in intestinal fortitude. You'll also get to experience some of the funniest stand-up comedians you've ever seen.

I remember one hilarious encounter on a hot, summer day while I was giving out food near the St. Mark's Place entrance to Tompkins Square Park. There was a very long line and this really skinny, homeless guy was pushing a shopping cart full of his life's belongings and was waiting to get fed. When he finally reached the serving table, I noticed he was decked out in a Rocawear jump suit and Von Dutch trucker hat. Just as he was about to get his plate of food, another person bumped into him and accidentally spilled a little bit of his lemonade on his sneakers. The guy snapped, "Yo motherfucker! These is two-hundred-dollar Diesel's nigga! Watch what the fuck you doin!" Sometimes you have to act like a referee and squash beef that starts over stupid things like someone stepping on someone's shoes without saying excuse me. Anyway, the dude with the $200 sneaks wiped off his kicks and stepped up to the table. He looked at the food, then up at me and said, "Yo money, I'm on that Atkins shit kid. You know what the motherfuckin' carb index of this is?" Hearing that, I loaded extra heavy portions of whole-wheat lasagna, organic brown rice salad, and five-grain bread on his plate. I then looked up at my skinny friend and said, "Don't worry yo, you good to go, son."

That's what I dig about writing, being able to write about the place I grew up and all the crazy things that go on in NYC. The characters I've met and the stories they have shared over the years could fill tons of books in a library. All it really takes is getting down in the trenches with these unique characters to really experience it. In my own life, I had no choice, because I was living it. If you're not a native New Yorker or were raised in a privileged background give it a try. Come out to Tompkins Square and rub elbows with some real New Yorkers as we serve the less fortunate. Who knows what you might find. On any given day, you'll hear a good joke or two, make some new friends, or find a guy who's sleeping in a cardboard box under the highway, but is still up on the latest fashion and fad diets.

1978 and 1979 were also two magical years in New York. It was right around the time the brothers were making a fashion statement that's stood the true test of time, unlike a lot of the other fashion crazes from that era. I'm talking about wearing "Wave Caps," that are now called "Doo-Rags" which are used to keep your hair tight with waves. In the old days, brothers improvised and used pantyhose that were tied off at the end to keep their shit tight. If the Wave Caps tore, or the brothers in Linky worn 'em out, they'd beg the ladies who worked in the mess hall to bring them their old stockings. The brothers put grease in their hair, donned their pantyhose stocking caps and brushed their hair as they watched the groundbreaking mini-series, Roots. That show definitely caused racial tensions between the whites and the brothers who were living at Linky. No whites went in the TV lounge (except me) while the brothers watched their show.

It was during this time that the Five Percenters, who were an offshoot of the Nation of Islam, started to gain popularity. The Five Percenters referred to their black brothers as "God," and believed that white people were the devil because they contributed to slavery and the oppression of the black man. When they spoke it was always, "True God this, and true God that." You know it's funny, because I didn't realize "God" could get locked up for armed robbery and put on meds.

There was one Five Percenter in The Elm who we'll call "Knucklehead," who happened to be a real racist prick. He always got pissed when anyone, especially a white guy, like myself, called him by his "slave name" (birth name) instead of his Muslim name. Not all the brothers bought into Knucklehead's shit, but a lot did. It sucked too, because everyone got along fairly well at The Elm before this asshole showed up. He was responsible for stirring up a lot of shit between the blacks and the whites who lived at The Elm.

One night I walked in the TV room and sat down to watch Roots as Knucklehead started to stare me down. Everyone was just watching TV and relaxing with a snack of cookies and a pint of milk. Now everyone was kinda mellow and minding their business when things started to heat up on the TV. There is one legendary scene where Kunta Kinte kept defiantly telling his slave owner his name was Kunta Kinte and not Toby. Each time he said his name was Kunta Kinte, he would get whipped across the back. Now, as this was going down, Knucklehead decided to add in his own commentary over the already intense dialogue, "See Gods, when we came here we had African names," and "white devil this and white devil that." So as a way to break up his racist sermon, I made a joke about Kunta's blood looking fake. The next thing I know I heard shouts of "Devil!" as a hail of opened milk cartons rained down on me from every direction. I ran out in a hurry and didn't step foot back in the TV lounge until Roots was over.

The first time I saw E in the Linky dining hall he looked a lot healthier than the previous time I had seen him. He had gained some weight and had a smile on his face, even though he was wearing a bandage on his nose. He was still healing from the surgery he had to repair the broken nose he suffered when the cops arrested him. E made it known throughout Linky-Land that he was my brother. As a result, the seniors from the other cottages looked out for me because E was the man in The Smokin'

Oak. He was a "head" and that meant he could smuggle you in a joint or some other contraband if you needed it, because he had access to the illegal benefits from the outside world.

E held a job at the Linky horse barn and often found himself off the property to work special events like barrel races and horse shows. Since E put the "H" in hustle, you know it didn't take that slick motherfucker long to find out who had the weed at the rodeos. E and "The Horse Crew," as they were known, always ate by themselves in the chow hall because they constantly smelled like rotten horse shit. To this day, I still fuck with E about the fact that he was on the verge of becoming a redneck. On one home visit he actually wore a cowboy hat, cowboy boots, cowboy shirt and one of those big, corny belt buckles. E swears that he was just playing the role so he could get high and meet girls at the cowboy events, but he could never explain the country music record collection. Yeeee-haw, motherfucker!

I was at Linky for about a month when I was told that the Linky staff was taking us off of the property for a special trip. We found out later that the trip was organized for one purpose - to scare the living shit out of us! Now, I don't know if any of you ever saw the Scared Straight documentary about prison life on Channel 9, but The Elm Cottage was one of the first groups to go into New Jersey's Rahway State Prison to participate. It was there that the Lifers' Group, inmates serving life sentences (on charges of murder, rape and bank robbery), scared the shit out of you for close to two hours.

From the minute we arrived in Rahway and stepped out of the safety of our Linky vans to enter the maximum-security complex, we were treated just like prisoners. We were still joking around when the guards lined us up and began shouting, "Shut the fuck up!" and "You better not be talkin' while I'm talkin' inmate!" They instilled fear into our group and warned us about the environment we were about to enter, "If this happens, do that. And if that happens, under no circumstances do this." By letting us know what was up, they now had our complete and undivided attention and all of our clowning around came to a screeching halt. As the alarm sounded and the thick steel bars automatically slid open, we entered the prison. We were now in lockdown and at that point, there was absolutely no turning back.

When I walked inside, the first thing I noticed was the odor. Once again, it was that familiar institutional cleaning fluid scent, but this time it was thicker and much more pungent. The guards then marched us past the whistles and catcalls from some of the illest-looking dudes, but they would pale in comparison to what was waiting for us in that auditorium. We walked in and the guards sat us down in rows of chairs directly in front of the stage.

We were talking and joking around as the inmates walked onto the stage. As soon as we made eye contact with them, this one big jailhouse-built brother took control by running around, getting in our faces and shouting, "You mother fuckin' faggot motherfuckers better shut the fuck up and look forward!" He instructed us that we weren't allowed to turn our heads or even glance anywhere but up at the stage. Then he made us take off our sneakers and toss them into a pile in the front of the stage. He then barked that if were good little bitches they "might" give them back.

The rest of the gnarly-looking fuckers ran off the stage and got in our faces, screaming and challenging us to fight them while they erased our tough-guy attitudes. The leader of the Lifers' Group pulled this short, muscle-bound, black inmate over who was wearing an eye patch. He stood directly in front of me and screamed, "You see this motherfucker! He could kill any one of you little punk bitches with his bare hands." He then took off his eye patch and revealed that he had no eyeball. "Motherfuckers in here stabbed his eye out with a pencil, a pencil! Why? Because they couldn't take the nigga's hood (booty)! Could you faggots deal with shit like this every day of your motherfuckin' miserable ass lives?"

That shit hit home for me, because I knew Rahway was no joke. He told us that we belonged to them for the next two hours and if some shit did go down, the guards wouldn't come in to help, unless they first got in full riot gear. He said by then, the inmates could have easily killed all of us with their bare hands and he was absolutely right. The brother with the eye patch leaned over me, smiled and said, "You's a fine-lookin' little bitch with that long blonde hair." Honestly, the thought of having to fight off motherfuckers like this guy during a ten-year bid scared the living shit out of me. To make things worse, that inmate stood there for the rest of the afternoon smiling and staring me down with his one good eye.

The leader went on to tell us about what he saw happen to pretty, little kids like us who were sentenced to do time at Rahway. Most were raped and murdered and some committed suicide to end their pain and suffering behind bars. He then paraded across the stage in total command of his audience, "You'd be lucky to just have one of us fuckin' you, but when I do get sick of your asshole, I'm gonna sell you to some big, black nigga wit a twelve-inch dick for a carton of cigarettes, he said. "After he fucks the living shit out of you for a while, he'll do the same until the nigger we call 'Tripod' is tappin' that ass and when he's done with you it's so torn out-the-frame you can't even hold your shits in and you got to wear a mother fuckin' diaper!" This place definitely took the whole Maytag thing to the next level.

A couple of kids were singled out to hold some of the inmates' shirts while they walked around the room. They were warned that if they let go they were in for some serious abuse. The inmates took turns speaking and telling their stories and man, I thought I had it rough. Shit, my life was a fuckin' fairy tale compared to these dudes. As the other inmates shared their stories the leader scanned the room for the "Tough-Guy Faggots" as he called them. He found three: this brother, J; a white kid, Darryl; and of course, who else...Knucklehead.

The leader walked up and began shouting every four-letter word in J's face, while covering him in spit. As J went to wipe the spit off, he yelled, "You don't like spit, faggot?" And with that, he spat some more. He then assigned a crazy-looking Italian dude, covered in tattoos to J. The leader turned to the Italian and said, "What the fuck you in here for, Cantone?" Cantone smiled, looked J up and down and said, "Rape and murder." The leader warned J that if he made one more fuckin' face Cantone was gonna fuck him in his pretty little black ass.

Next was Darryl, who for some stupid reason still tried to be a hard rock. The leader walked over, grabbed him by his long hair and told him exactly how he'd, ummm... make love to him. He then made Darryl dig his sneakers out of the pile, but before he could get them three inmates were all over him, one of which snatched his sneakers. Darryl smirked in disgust and the inmate who had his sneakers snapped, "What you think this shit is a game, bitch? I will cut your fuckin' heart out and eat that shit, motherfucker! Wipe that smile off your pussy-ass face!" Darryl lost his grin all right. According to Darryl, the three inmates dragged him to the bathroom where he was roughed-up pretty badly.

Last, but not least, was my favorite, because Knucklehead got what was comin' to him. The leader walked over to Knucklehead and said, "What's your name, nigga?" Knucklehead told him his Muslim name and tried to drop some Muslim philosophy on him. The brother just laughed. "Rashid!" he yelled, "Get your black ass over here!" This big, evil-lookin' brother wearing a kufi, (a knit Muslim cap) walked over and stared Knucklehead down. The leader was on one side of Knucklehead and Rashid, the Muslim brother, was on the other. The leader got in Knucklehead's face,

"He makes his bitches go pork-free so his big, black dick don't gotsta touch no swine when he's rippin' their intestines apart. Now you bein' a Muslim means you're already ripe, faggot." Knucklehead looked at the Muslim and said, "As-Salaam Alaikum (peace be upon you) brother. Rashid jumped in his face and began screaming, covering his grill with spit, "I will fuck you in your mother fuckin' ass punk until that shit bleeds! Don't you ever call me brother, faggot. You hear me? Now apologize bitch and say you sorry!" Knucklehead didn't answer and with that Rashid snatched him up by his shirt, lifting him off the ground. "Answer me bitch!" he screamed. Knucklehead muttered he was sorry as tears rolled down his cheek. "Louder, faggot! Say I'm a mother fuckin' faggot-ass nigga and I'm sorry!" He complied and was dropped and spent the rest of the afternoon holding onto Rashid's shirt very tightly.

Toward the last half hour they were a little more compassionate, pleading with us to turn our lives around, so we didn't have to go through what they experienced. They asked what we were locked up for and the funny thing was a lot of them started out the same way, committing petty crimes and bullshit like that. The Lifer's told us we had an opportunity to change and not go down the same road they had walked, because being locked in Rahway was the end of the road. In fact, it was a death sentence with no turning back.

The inmates told us that every time we thought about breaking the law, we better not forget about them. If we ended up in places like Rahway, they would be the sick motherfuckers who would be waiting for us behind bars. And God help us if we became their cellmates.

At the end of the day, everyone but Darryl got their sneakers back and we were silent as we road back to Linky in the van, except for Knucklehead. He was still popping shit about how in a one-on-one he'd fuck any one of them up and blah, blah, blah. Hearing this, everyone turned around simultaneously and yelled at him to shut the fuck up. We went into Rahway thinking we were tough guys, but we immediately got chumped-off during this humbling experience. I then turned to Knucklehead and said, "By the way, God, you still got a glob of Rashid's spit on you forehead." He wiped it off and everyone burst out laughing as we made our way back to Linky.

I don't think I could ever forget my experience at Rahway. Since that visit, I've done so much in my life and to think that those guys, unless they died, have been sitting in the same place for the last thirty years is bugged out. Unfortunately, as I said before, a lot of the kids from The Elm who visited Rahway with me weren't Scared

Straight and continued to commit crimes later in life. For their sake, I just hope they didn't break the law in Jersey and end up as Tripod's cellmate.

The Linky staff also took us to Fishkill State Prison, a minimum-security prison, located in upstate New York. Unlike Rahway, a lot of the guys locked in Fishkill were there for white-collar crimes and other offenses. One of the inmates I spoke to was an older, white guy, who was serving a seven-year bid for robbing a bank. During our conversation, he tried to get me to get the stolen loot he had stashed away before he got arrested. He wanted me to dig it up out of its original hiding place during one of my home visits and move it to another place. For my troubles, he would give me a handsome cut, of course.

One of the guards at Fishkill later informed me that the inmate was a pedophile and he just wanted me to write to him so he could jerk off on my letters. What a sick fuck!

I was doing well at Lincoln Hall and after a few months, I earned weekend home visits to my mom's house. On these visits I was supposed to be reacquainting myself with my mom and laying the groundwork to live there when I was released, but I did anything but that. Every Friday and Saturday night I would get fucked up to the point where I would stumble home and eat everything in her refrigerator. I hardly spoke to my mother all weekend, and when Sunday rolled around and I was preparing to catch public transport back to Linky the one thing she kept saying was there was no way I was living with her when I got out. Hearing that put me in a sour mood. Not only did I have to go back to Linky in a few hours and deal with all the bullshit, I also had to think about where I was going to live once I got out.

Every Sunday night before I went back to Linky, I had a ritual of getting as fucked up as possible. The Linky bus was free and was always crawling with staff. So a lot of dudes opted to buy a ticket for the Metro-North, so they could get wasted without a hassle. The last car of the Metro-North train was always a sick party, which made the parties we had on the New York City subway line look like retirement home shindigs. Radios blared all genres of music and it didn't matter if you were black or white, as long as you had some weed, drugs or alcohol to share, you were good. When we finally did get back to Linky, we were locked in the rec. room before we were thoroughly searched for contraband and yelled at for coming back wasted.

When it came to smuggling weed back to Linky it took me a while to perfect a little technique I called, the "Linky Trick." What I would do is get a carton of cigarettes and very carefully open it with a razor blade along the glued seam without ripping the box. Then I would take an individual pack of cigarettes and use a very thin knife to open the folded corners of the cellophane. I would slide the cellophane wrapper down without breaking the pull-tab and then tuck the joints in. Then you'd fold the corners back down, place the tiniest dab of Crazy Glue to hold it closed it before putting it back in the carton and sealing that as well. When staff looked at the carton of smokes there was no way for them to know it was tampered with. Other guys went as far as swallowing balloons or putting them up their asses, but I wasn't down with that method. Besides, even if me or E couldn't get any weed, there was no way I was smoking some shit that was up some dude's ass.

Most of my home visits were a blur, due to the amount of intoxicants I consumed. I was like a teenage zombie the entire weekend. It was like I went home, got wasted all weekend, and erased everything I had previously learned at Linky from my memory bank. When Sunday night rolled around, I went back up there and the Linky staff re-programmed me until my next visit.

All of my home visits were fun and I did have some wild adventures when I stepped off the Linky grounds. There was one incident in particular which I refer to as my "Penthouse Adventure" which still has me laughing to this day. It involved this "New Jack" kid, who we will call, "Chris." Now when you're a New Jack coming into a facility that's nothing but little hoodies, you want to impress everyone and have them think you're the man. Well, Chris was no exception. He often bragged about his dad who was a Penthouse photographer, claiming they'd have wild sex orgies and coke parties at his Manhattan apartment. When Chris came back from his weekend visits, he had lurid tales about hooking up with all kinds of strippers and Penthouse Pets.

In most cases kids will bullshit about stuff like that, but Chris backed it up by going right to the Penthouse masthead to prove his point. Right there in black and white, his dad's name appeared under the title of photographer. As a result, Chris quickly gained a lot of what we referred to back then as "Penitentiary Pull," juice, clout, or whatever the fuck you wanna call it. He also got props from us because he snuck in stacks of his dad's porno mags for us to check out. Having the mags on hand was cool, because sex is always on the mind of horny teenagers, especially the ones that are locked up.

Masturbating at Linky was a no-holds-barred event where there was absolutely no privacy. You had to be creative in order to get your stroke on and the first thing you learned was the ritual of getting the job done. Most dudes jerked off at night in the dorm-like facility, and it was every man for himself. When it was time to get busy, you would grab a torn-out page from a Penthouse (they were easier to hide than a full magazine), some lubricant (and you better not run out, because there was no, "Pssst! Yo Devon, let me hold some lotion, cuz."), and a tube sock (extra thick for maximum leak prevention), before the blankets started poppin' away. Twenty-four of us (twelve beds on each side) would be stroking up and down in unison. If the night watchman walked in, everyone stopped momentarily as some dudes would even snore to cover up their pervy activity. When the night watchman left the dorm to complete his rounds, the blankets started poppin' again. When it was finally time for you to hit your mark you put that tube sock on your johnson and let it fly. You know, I kind of felt sorry for the ladies who worked in housekeeping and were responsible for washing the hundreds of tube socks the kids at Linky wore. I wonder if they ever figured out what all that gooey stuff was caked on the inside of every sock.

As time went on, I made friends with Chris, mainly because, being the horny little devil I was, I had to see first hand what really went down at his dad's place. On one weekend, I decided to avoid going to see my mom and opted to check out Chris' dad's crib instead. Chris and I took the Linky bus to Manhattan and before we knew it, we were on Park Avenue. His building was slick as hell: a doorman in a crisp uniform, a luxurious lobby, fancy elevators with gold doors and very beautiful, well-dressed business types coming and going. Up until that point, I only saw stuff like that on TV, or in magazines. But the thing I couldn't really figure out was how a kid like this, from such an affluent background, could be such a fuckin' criminal? Well, I guess the answer was simple – he was a casualty of the '70s, an era where cocaine and unlimited sex seemed to have a stranglehold on society. His dad was so caught up in work, partying at Studio 54, taking drugs, and chasing pussy, he was never there for his kid. Well, Chris did what any other kid would do when they crave attention – they act out.

Over the years, Chris got into a lot of trouble and landed in Linky, instead of family counseling. One of the reasons he ended up there was because his dad didn't want to be bothered with family counseling, so he told the courts it was time to show his son some tough love.

We took the elevator upstairs and entered the apartment where I was introduced to Chris' father. He was a tall guy, who looked in his thirties and was decked out in the classic playboy fashion of the disco era, polyester bell-bottoms, slick shoes and button down, loud-as-hell silk shirt complete with an oversized collar. He gave me a tour of the apartment and it was incredible. It had huge rooms, high ceilings, tons of pricy antiques and dozens of framed pictures personally signed by the hot Penthouse Pets he photographed. We walked down this long hallway, turned a corner and entered a huge living room. Right before my eyes were three of the finest, scantily dressed women I ever saw in person sprawled out on a huge couch. It looked just like a Penthouse layout and it didn't take a math genius to figure out this equation. There were three of them and three of us and when Chris' dad did the introductions, I was undressing each one of them with my eyes. A huge smile then came over my face and I gave Chris a very enthusiastic high-five because I knew what was going to happen next.

We sat on the couch, drank expensive wine, sniffed coke, listened to music and smoked some really exotic Hawaiian pot called Maui Wowie. I was totally wasted and noticed that one of the girls, a blonde with gigantic tits, was smiling at me. Well, that sealed the deal in my mind. All I needed was a sign to make a move and she just gave it to me. I mean, this was the sex-crazed '70's where a wink, a wave, a fuckin' hello with a slight 15 degree tilt of the head to the right while blinking meant a woman wanted to hop in the sack, right? Well, at least that's what I read in Sidney Sheldon novels and Penthouse Forum letters, so this had to qualify. This was a full-on smile and I decided she would be mine that night, so I had to lock it down. Chris and his dad could have the other two, but the bodacious blonde and me - we had instant chemistry. She laced me with several shotguns of weed and when her lips touched mine, she blew the softest stream of warm pot smoke down my throat.

During our smoking session, she rubbed my shoulders while she asked about the circumstances that led me to Linky. As I shared the intimate details of my life she kept saying, "That's horrible," and "That's terrible. You poor thing, how could anyone hit you? Look at you, you're so cute I just want to squeeze you." I had no problem with that, just as long as those two melons she had attached to her chest were squeezing me between the ears. I was playing the old sympathy card angle and so far, it was working like a charm. I poured it on thick and she kept rubbing my shoulders and looking at me with those big, sad eyes of hers. At this point, I could have shattered concrete like a jackhammer with the erection I had throbbing in my pants. That's when Chris's dad stood up and said six words that remain embedded in my mind to this day. It was a cue, if you will, for the wild sex romp that was about to take place. "Well girls, for what it's worth." I got up, smiled and said, "Yep girls, for what it's worth." Wink-wink. I loved his secret code that gave me the green light that allowed the sex games to begin. It was a typical '70's scenario and he was the man to be able to say some shit that enabled three hot chicks to fulfill every sexual desire we wanted to explore. I looked at him and gave him an enthusiastic thumbs up and that's when all three girls grabbed Chris' dad's arm and escorted him to the closest bedroom. I was dumbfounded and confused. I looked at Chris frantically and said, "Let's go, bro, let's get in there. It's an orgy, man! You heard him, he said for what it's worth." Chris proceeded to tell me that the three girls in the bedroom were his dad's personal harem, but I didn't want to hear that shit. "You're fuckin' jokin' right? Tell me you're fuckin' jokin' bro, please," I pleaded. What he said was true and as I listened to the moaning and sexual screams of ecstasy coming from behind the bedroom door everything went south. Now I was pissed and horny. To make matters worse, I lost my high and had a raging set of blue balls that killed me every time I tried to move. I decided to suffer in pain, stand up and slowly make my way to the bathroom.

Having been left out of the sexual escapades, I decided to rub one out in the bathroom. Thank God there was a healthy stack of Penthouse mags in there because it gave me an endless variety of eye candy while I was going at it like a champ. While I got my stroke on, I began talking dirty to the girls on the pages and saying shit like, "See what your friends in the bedroom are missing out on." I relieved myself at least three times in the twenty-five minutes I was in there. Just as I was about to let the ladies have number four a knock came at the door, which startled me and sent me off balance. As I fell off balance, my love potion shot out all over my pants that were down around my ankles. Who dared to violate rule number one of "The Masturbator's Code of Ethics Handbook?" It was Chris and he was banging on the door to let me know that we had to leave before his dad came out with his girls, because they always liked to walk around naked after they had sex. I'm like, "Shit motherfucker, that's all them bitches do is stay naked, now they wanna act shy?" Anyway, I cleaned up the mess and walked out with a big wet spot center stage and when Chris asked what happened I told him I got sick. He looked at me like, "Yeah right" and told everyone at Linky I whacked off in his dad's bathroom for thirty minutes. The kids at Linky got a big kick out of it too, because it was okay to jerk off at Linky, but it was totally un-fuckin' cool to do it on a home visit at a friend's house. The funny thing was everyone (and this was according to the kids from Linky) always got laid on visits and came back with amazing sex stories, but oddly enough, had very smooth and overly-moisturized hands. That was my big Penthouse adventure and "For What It's Worth" later on in life I did date a couple of girls who made it onto the pages of Penthouse and Playboy. Although they were all really hot, they had to be the most mixed-up, dysfunctional group of bitches I've ever met.

Before I knew it, my eighteen months at Linky were coming to a close. I had two weeks left, which was known as being "Short." It was such a wonderful feeling knowing I was going home. I was on cloud nine because I had big plans for when I was released. E was going to be transferred to work on some horse program, while he attended SUNY Cobleskill in upstate New York to study to become a veterinarian. Around that same time, I also got word that this dude from The Oak deliberately broke E's nose by hitting him in the face with a basketball during a pick-up game inside the gym.

While E was at Linky he suffered through two painful surgeries to fix the damage the cops caused him during the liquor store robbery. When I found out what happened at the gym, I escaped The Elm and ran down the road to see what was up. As I snuck into the gym, one of the dudes from The Oak who was E's boy told me the dude I was looking for was in the locker room. I walked in as he was changing in front of an open locker. I snuck up behind him, punched him in the face and knocked him into the lockers. Then I smashed his head several times with the locker door, before he fell to the floor unconscious. I was out of control and consumed by anger as I stomped him. I looked down and the guy had blood coming out of one of his ears. Not wanting to stick around, I ran out of the gym and bolted up Suicide Hill toward The Elm. While en route back to The Elm, I was tackled to the ground and apprehended by a number of Linky staffers. I was then taken to the Linden Cottage, also knows as, "The Cells," which were padded cells that resembled the breaking rooms in Spofford. The rooms were very spartan and the only thing in there was a block of cement and a paper-thin blanket and mattress. There was very little light coming through the steel slats on the windows and it was always freezing cold, because they always kept the air-conditioning on full blast. I was in lockdown for twenty hours a day and was only allowed out for a shower and a few hours of field-daying (cleaning-up).

My original release date was two weeks from the gym incident. It came and went and they kept me in The Cells without telling me my fate. I did hear that the dude I beat up went to the hospital for a few days and according to a staffer at The Cells they were talking about pressing aggravated assault charges. If they did press charges, it meant I was headed upstate to serve some serious time. Since I was stressed about the possibility of doing harder time, I hardly slept or ate. After being locked in The Cells for about three weeks, a Linky staffer took me out of The Cells, put me in a car and drove me off the property. The staffer wouldn't talk to me or even look at me. As I tried to tell him my side of the story he responded by telling me to "Shut up!" I had a sick feeling in my stomach that things were going to get worse. I thought back to those brothers in lockdown at Rahway State Prison. I thought, "So this is how it is. This is exactly what that brother in Rahway warned me of. Here it is...my downward spiral." I guess I was headed to a prison in Elmira, or some place just as bad.

I did everything not to puke in the car and as we drove down the road I looked out the window and noticed something strange. We weren't heading toward the courthouse, but toward the train station. The Linky staffer broke the silence as we waited for the red light. He turned to me and said, "You're never to step foot on Lincoln Hall property again, not for any reason and you're lucky we're not pressing charges. You're being given train and subway fare to your mother's house and that's it. All your possessions up at The Elm were thrown out. Good luck, you're going to need it with your attitude. By the way McGowan, most of us are giving you less than six months before you're locked up again."

I can't even tell you what that feeling of relief and joy was like. Just try to imagine for yourself. One minute you think you're going upstate to a lock-up, and then the next minute you realize you're a free man. He pulled up to the Katonah train station and I opened the car door and got out. The Linky staffer sat there with his big 'fro and glasses staring ahead, waiting for me to close the door. I leaned in, "You're wrong about me. I am gonna make it and I don't give a fuck what you and your dickhead friends think." He laughed, pulled the car door shut and drove off. I left Linky that August morning with nothing except the clothes on my back and just enough money to make it to my mom's house in Jackson Heights, Queens. I didn't give two shits about anything because I was finally a free man living in the world. I bummed a cigarette off someone at the train station and screamed, "Light up!"

snaps

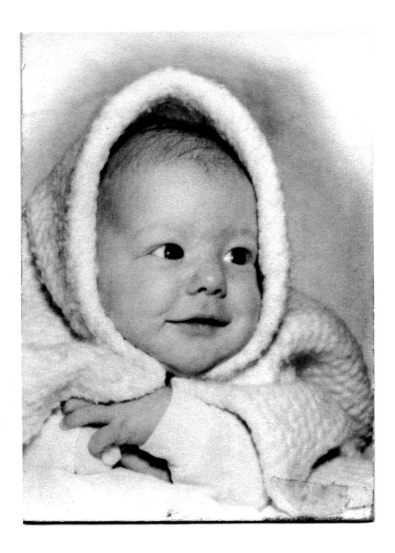

The evolution begins. Born 10.3.62.

Yes, that's me in my father's arms, just a few weeks old.
and E is hiding behind my mom.

Xmas with my mom. Me on the left, Frank in the middle, and E on the right. Frank just broke my plane, but soon after this photo he was paid back in spades.

Top left: The medallion we bought my mom with the money
we stole from the Valenti's. She still has it, over 30 years later.
Top right: The 3 Amigos at the Sheridans' in Brooklyn. E, Frank,
and me right before that Catholic School kicked me out!
Bottom: Frank, Me, and E, school pictures from around 1970-71.

Date	Comments

1/26/73

John could do much better in Math if he would pay closer attention instead of seeking attention for himself from others.

4/6/73 Generally, there has been an improvement in all areas of work. However, John shows an increased absence of self-control in his constant calling out, leaving his seat, and frequent "wise" remarks.

6/22/73 Most of the time, John has been a delight to have in the class. At this time, he would benefit greatly from a closer relationship with a male authority figure. This might help him develop a greater sense of self-discipline.

Quarter	Parent's Signature
2	Mrs. R. Valenti
3	Mrs. R. Valenti
4	Report to be kept by parent.

SCHOOL YEAR 19 73 – 19 74

School JFK   Grade 6   Room_____

Bus _____   Walker _____

No self control! What are you talking about lady?!
Notice the comment after 6.22.73. Only relationship with
Mr. V. was based on ass-whippings.

Top: Ingleside Farms 1975, left to right, me and Frank.
Bottom: Linky Days. Me, Mom, and E the hick.

Where the fuck am I and how many years did I sign up for?

Left: Srila Prabhupada. The real Hare krsna guru.
Right: One of his many books which I'll send you
for free...no kidding.

Bike messenger duties. Shit, Somebody had to pay for rehearsals and recordings! Also, 'Don't be a dick' sticker, what you got if you weren't giving a donation to Wheelchair Santa.

John Joseph (singing) with Harley Flanagan on drums
in the short-lived M.O.I., CBGB, NYC, 1983
Photo by Karen O'Sullivan

Cro-Mags' junk.
I went from puking at Sabbath concerts to almost opening up
for them (Ozzy was shook and pulled out of this show).

Cro-Mags at the old Ritz on 11th Street.
Big Charlie (RIP) doing security.

Top: Me and Mackie Jason (Da Original Rudeboy Ganstas) in the studio recording the Cro-Mags Age of Quarrel.
Bottom: Photo from Spin Magazine article, where I dropped the bomb on the bogus Hare krsna leaders.

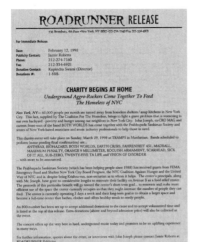

Top left: Concert I organized, we raised $15,000 for
the food relief charity.
Top right: Jinx-Proof Marathon Crew (minus Armando) at the
2007 Marine Corps Marathon in D.C. We all finished!
Bottom: That's me with the white t-shirt (see arrow)
serving the homeless.

Top: Carl, one year before he died of cancer.
Bad-ass was still smoking.
Bottom: Me and E in da hood, 2003.

anchors away

chapter 8

To say I didn't gel with my mom when I got out of Lincoln Hall was an understatement. She kept pushing me to get a job, but I was like, "I just worked my ass off upstate, I need a little down time here." Trust me on this, if a seventeen-year-old, trouble-making teenager has down time, there's only going to be one result. Within weeks I was back at The Dome doing the only job I was ever trained for and hanging out in Rockaway. I had a lot of anger inside me and fought a lot when I first got out of Linky. I was a solid buck-sixty and could scrap with the best of them. I was also drinking and doing a lot of drugs. I had absolutely no clue to what life was about, or where it would take me. I felt alone and confused and that, combined with a temper that my mom said was worse than my father's, made me, as a Linky psychiatrist wrote in one of her reports, "A time-bomb waiting to go off."

E was also fucking up. He was enrolled in one of the top ten party colleges on the East Coast. He was kicked out for excessive partying, which was no easy task. I heard that the fraternity he pledged made the Deltas from National Lampoon's Animal House look like a fuckin' Boy Scout outing. I knew deep down that if something didn't happen for the both of us it was going to be a matter of time before we were both back in jail. It was eating me up inside to know that those bastards with their statistics about re-offending might be right, but where was I supposed to turn?

We were living off momma-dukes and she wasn't diggin' it, at all. Every day she would go to work at Con Ed at 5 a.m., and as soon as she'd get home at 5 p.m., she'd go on patrol. We nicknamed her the "Snoopy Sniffer," because on more than one occasion, she could find a microscopic pot seed or stem in a foot-high shag carpet. She absolutely forbid us to smoke weed in the house, but hey, when you can smoke, eat, watch TV and listen to music, why go anywhere else?

A few years back, there was a hilarious anti-marijuana commercial that hit the nail on the head as far as what we were going to end up like if we continued to smoke weed. There were two thirty-something-year-old dudes smoking a joint while watching cartoons and laughing it up. One guy gets the joint from the other and says, "And they say weed leads to other hard drugs. That's bullcrap. Look at us Tommy. I'm thirty-three. You're like what, thirty-five? None of that happened to us. We ain't messed up on drugs." They slapped each other five and just as he takes a big hit off the joint the front door opens. The guy with the joint, who's room it is, starts waving the pot smoke around nervously before hiding the joint. From outside his door we hear, "Brian, did you look for a job today?" As Brian exhales the weed smoke he says, "Nah, Ma... I uhhh...." The caption at the bottom of the screen read: "Keep Smoking Pot and Nothing Will Happen." Bingo!

Nothing was happening with us alright. My mom also got tired of going to work and coming home to an empty refrigerator and us laying on her couch stoned as hell, watching cartoons, laughing and farting. At that time she knew a U.S. Navy recruiter named Ed McNulty and she convinced us to go talk to him. We went to visit him at the recruiting office, right under the Main Street No. 7 train stop in Flushing, to talk about "The Navy Adventure."

When we walked in it seemed like it was already decided we were going in. He talked about the vocational training, the travel, the pay and an enlistment date. I was like, "Enlistment date? Brother, are you buggin'? We're just rappin' here to humor my mom and keep shit cool, but I ain't plannin' on..."

We started boot camp on January 3, 1980 and it was a case of the hustler getting hustled. Turned out Ed McNulty was as slick as they came. Recruiters get bonuses for every person they sign into the military and he conned me little by little and before I knew it, I had signed on the dotted line. For me, all those perks he talked up – the schooling, the pay and the travel, did not exist. He showed me the list of jobs

I had to choose from - store clerk, paint chipper, glorified pencil pusher, or gunner's mate. E on the other hand was accepted into the nuclear engineering program and right after boot camp was heading off to nuclear propulsion school. I basically got fucked and didn't realize it until I went to boot camp and asked my company commander about heading off to school. He laughed and said, "Oh, I'd say right after you list for another four years because you got fucked on this enlistment, McGowan." He went on to further enlighten me that NAVY was an acronym for Never Again Volunteer Yourself. Now he tells me!

I showed up at Great Lakes (nicknamed Great Mistakes) Naval Station just outside Chicago. I was high-as-shit on dust because prior to getting on the plane we ran around Fort Hamilton, Brooklyn and copped a couple of bags of dust. Getting off that bus on base at 2 a.m., in the freezing cold and getting yelled at while I was coming down from a dust high was an experience I'll never forget. They woke us up at 3:30 the next morning by exploding firecrackers and beating empty, metal garbage cans with broom handles up all throughout the barracks. To make matters worse, they screamed at the top of their lungs and turned over a number of bunks, including mine.

The temperature dipped to minus thirty degrees with the wind chill and my company commander's vibe made it even colder. He was a chief in "The Seabees," a division of the Navy born in the dark days following Pearl Harbor. He was a tough-ass, old Navy son of a bitch who had witty deliveries for every command he barked at you and "God help you if you fuck up in my Navy!"

The Naval boot camp was nothing but yelling, screaming, marching, studying and precisely folding your uniforms and bed sheets. All of that all was designed to get you to pay attention to detail which is a staple of the military. Our company was made up of two-thirds slick talkin', slick walkin' New Yorkers who were all real characters. We had some hilarious times fucking with the rednecks and country-ass brothers from the Deep South. One night right before graduation me and another guy escaped off base and took a train to Chicago where we stayed out all night and got tattooed. We rolled in just in time for the morning roll call and the chief yelled, "McGowan, get in my office!" When I walked in he nonchalantly said, "Okay, let's see it." I guess I wasn't the first boot camper to try to outwit the old chief. When I rolled up my left sleeve and proudly displayed my first tattoo - a skull with a dagger through it and the words, "Death Before Dishonor," below. The chief laughed and said, "That's a Jarhead (Marine) tattoo, numb nuts." He was right. It was a Marine tattoo, but I didn't care.

I believed what I carved in my arm for life. I mean, shit, I had just done time in a lock-up for not ratting someone out and dishonoring my street cred, right? I finished up boot and after an unsuccessful attempt at getting into the Navy's SEAL program (sidelined because of a ligament injury to my knee during training) I was shipped out to Norfolk, Virginia where the real fun started.

The Navy sent me to a pre-commission unit for the USS Arkansas CGN-41. A pre-comm. unit is where you go when your ship is being built and is basically shore duty. The Arkansas was in dry dock in the Newport News, Virginia shipyards and was behind schedule. Because of the injury I sustained while attempting to get into the SEAL's, the Navy doctor wanted to operate on my knee. After talking to a sailor who had to get two more knee surgeries just to repair the first one their hack doctors did, I opted to skip the surgery and take my chances having it heal on its own.

Norfolk itself is nothing but military bases and there was so much military personnel down there you couldn't spit without hitting one of them. This was pre-9/11, when the civilians didn't appreciate just how brave a lot of the service men and women of this country actually were. They had signs like "No Dogs or Sailors on the Lawn." There were 500 dudes to every girl on base and for that reason Norfolk, Va., was nicknamed "No Fuck, Vagina." After drinking a few nights at the bar on base called "The Tradewinds" and experiencing that pathetic scene, I decided to head into town on the solo trip for any future partying.

The difference between the old Navy and today's Navy is back when I enlisted there was no such thing as a piss test. Drugs and partying were rampant and it was like every lost, fucked-up guy who wanted to try and make something out of themselves and become a man (and wanted to have a great time in the process) went into the Navy. Most of them led boring lives compared to the shit I'd been through. Most of their stories in Norfolk were the same: "Yeah, you know I graduated high school, had no job and no money for college. I was smoking a lot of pot and partying and after my dad chewed me out about doing nothing with my life and warned me I was going to wind up in a dead end job like his, I enlisted." Well, with me it was like, "Yeah, I knew if I didn't enlist I would end up just plain old dead." End of fuckin' story. I didn't really like any of the dudes from the Arkansas, so, I kept my past to myself and let that time-bomb tick away.

I often worked out at the base gym and did therapy for my knee. It was pretty much healed, but if I got up too fast it would lock up. I would have to lift it up and try to pop it back into place. Ouch! One day while I was beating a heavy bag at the gym, I met this older guy named Frank, who must have been in his mid-60s. He told me he was a former Navy boxer and he was impressed by my skills with the heavy bag. After a few months of boxing training, Frank convinced me to enter the Smoker Fights down at Little Creek amphibious base.

Against my Marine opponents, I didn't do too badly. I earned a record of 4 and 2, with the four victories coming against slow white guys. The two losses were against cock diesel brothers who boxed my ears in. I would have gone undefeated, but I wasn't allowed to use that underhanded technique I used on a number of occasions and was attached to the famous Junior Nuts quote, "The boots, Jim."

One afternoon during working hours I was driving around near Little Creek in one of the Navy Squid mobiles with a crew of lifers. They were talking shit about re-enlistment bonuses, taking the second-class petty officer exam and a bunch of other bullshit I had no interest in, when we drove past a club called, Taj Mahal. The marquee read: "Tonight Punk/New Wave Featuring the X-Raves. Ladies Free." I made a mental note of where the club was and before we headed back to the base I had the driver stop at a mall on Military Highway where I bought black pants, hair gel and red, black and white paint. When I got off work, I got down to biz for my big night out. I took a white T-shirt and painted a big, black swastika on it with a black circle around it. I painted a red and white circle around that and threw it in the dryer. When it was dry, I cut it out and sewed it on the black shirt. I wasn't a Nazi punk, but I was going for shock value especially since I was wearing a Nazi symbol on a U.S. Military base. I put on my shirt, spiked up my hair, threw on pointy punk shoes, a pair of black pants, and a black, leather jacket, before heading out.

People were totally shocked by what I was wearing. I got the worst looks on base and as I walked out the main gate a group of Marines piled out of the checkpoint building just to sneak a peek. Even at the Taj Mahal they stared. Everyone was dressed in make-up and new wave shit while others tried to look like members of the Romantics or went for the Johnny Thunders junkie look.

That night the X-Raves played covers of the B-52's, the Talking Heads and Blondie, which was cool. I like new wave, but didn't the marquee say it was punk and new wave night? I was hearing lots of new wave and no punk. Finally, they played a Sex Pistols cover and I ran out onto the packed dance floor and pogo'd the shit out of the guys and girls sending them and their drinks flying. They got pissed and got the owner Doug to come over and say something to me about my dancing. He walked up and said, "Hey man, cool out." I looked at him with bad intent and for some reason said in a thick, British accent, "Fuck off, wanka!" A big smile came across his face and he replied, "Sorry dude, I didn't know you were British." Turns out he worshipped British punks who were notorious for violence. It was part of the whole punk trip and so that made it okay. I was "John Boy" from London and I joined the Navy after coming to America and winding up homeless following the recession in New York.

I hung out at the Taj Mahal day and night. Even if I was on duty I would sneak off base for happy hour, have a few beers and take in some good punk music with Doug and the crew. I got in a fight with a few rednecks that came in one night and after kicking some ass I could do no wrong. I was pissed-off, angry and loved to fight and that helped me achieve celebrity status within the small Norfolk scene. I was the first Navy guy they had ever hung out with because that was part of the local code, you just didn't hang out with "Squids," especially if you were punk. God forbid. They had no choice though because I was there to stay. If they didn't like it I would kick their ass, because unfortunately for them they missed out on that Punk 101 lecture that stated mindless violence is a must. So they were all pretty much afraid to fight.

They loved to hear my stories about hanging out at Max's Kansas City, CBGB's and The Mudd Club during the '77 punk explosion. I went to New York at least once a month and brought back clothes and records for a few of them. Little-by-little I phased out the British accent and call me a poser but hey, I was a Squid getting a lot of play with the girls because of it. After a while the people on the scene were like, "You sure are losing your accent quickly," and I'd reply, "Must be from hangin' out with you bloody wanka's all the time."

There were a few really cool punks in Norfolk, but Stan and Barry were probably the coolest. Stan looked like Sid Vicious and knew about all the old English punk music. He told me about the scene in D.C., which was booming and we made a plan to drive up there one weekend and check out a show. Barry was this redneck-type, who was always drunk and ready to fight, which was cool with me. I met two other Navy punks in Norfolk. One was Ray "Raybeez" Barbieri (RIP), who would later sing for the New York City hardcore band, Warzone, and the other was a punk who went by the name Vic Demise. Vic had this insane laugh, loved the Sex Pistols and thought of himself as somewhat of a philosopher. Vic was assigned to the USS Mount Whitney, which was a flagship, meaning it had an admiral on board. As a result, they were really strict about shit like dress code, language and basically everything else punks didn't give two fucks about.

Vic would never let us pick him up because we refused to dress down. He would always make us meet him down the pier, or at the base bus stop. He never wore his punk gear when he left to go out for the night. Instead he'd hide his bondage shirts and his spikes, or whatever else he was wearing, until he got off base. That didn't sit well with Ray and me because he was like one of those weekend-warrior posers who dress up, go to the city and then put their shit away 'til the following weekend. With us you either lived the shit or you didn't and after drinking some whiskey and smoking some weed one night, Ray bet me free drinks for the rest of the night that I wouldn't go to the USS Mount Whitney and get Vic's ass chewed out. Bad bet Ray.

I went back to the barracks, made a few very offensive wardrobe changes and we went to the USS Mount Whitney. I walked up the gangway from the pier to the ship, decked out in punk gear complete with my swastika shirt and every eye on deck was on me. Now, in the Navy, if you were in uniform when you get to the top of the gangway you were supposed to face the flag, salute and ask the deck officer permission to come aboard. If you were in civilian clothes you had to face the flag, stand at attention and then ask to come aboard. Well, I put my own spin on it. I walked up the gangway, got to the top, shot snot out of my nose at the feet of the officer in charge, faced him, flipped him off with both hands and said, "Request fuckin' permission to fuckin' come aboard!" I could hear Ray laughing his ass off on the pier as the deck officer tried to gather himself to find the words to yell at me. "Who the hell are you here to see?" he shouted. "Demise," I said coolly. "Vic Demise." One of the guys on watch knew it had to be Vic since he was the only punk on the ship and he was ordered to go get him. The officer took my I.D., wrote my name and command down, vowed to put me on report and then told me to get my ass down on the pier. Vic finally came up and as the officer pointed down at me I saw Vic mouth the words "Holy shit," as he got ripped a new asshole. He glared down at the two of us, totally pissed off. We flipped him the bird and walked down the pier laughing our asses off. Vic was restricted that night and I was put on report. With our ship being delivered three months late, my command at the Arkansas had bigger problems to deal with then some rowdy, punk rock sailor who didn't give two shits about dress codes. Nothing really came out of the incident, because the report they wrote up got lost in their endless pile of paperwork.

After our escapade at the Mount Whitney we headed over to The Tradewinds on base to fuck off a bit and start collecting on my bet, before going to the King's Head Inn to see some band. As we pushed through the packed Friday night Squid posse that consisted of three to four hundred sailors trying to get laid from the same five fat "Waves" (Navy gals), we definitely stood out. They had on either cowboy hats and boots or rock T-shirts and sneakers. I told Ray we'd drink a few shots each and then we were outta there. We got our drinks, picked a table near the dance floor and sat down to watch the comedy show already in progress.

There were two steppers, line dancers and my favorite, the guys with "WMD," which doesn't stand for Weapons of Mass Destruction. It means - White Man's Disease. In other words, dudes with no rhythm. It was so bad, they looked like they were dancing to a different song than the one that was playing in the club. We were just about to leave when I saw three Navy girls walk by. Two of them had faces that could stop a clock, but the third was absolutely gorgeous. They sat close to us and every idiot in the club was flocking over to their table. It was hilarious because they acted like the other two girls didn't even exist and only asked the good-looking one to dance. She seemed humble about her beauty and didn't want to make her friends feel bad so she turned everyone down. She was about 5'4", cute as a button and had a perfect body. We finished our shots and Ray wanted to split, but I told him we'd leave in a few minutes.

I couldn't take my eyes off of her. It wasn't like I was desperate for sex, because I was getting my fair share in town. This girl for some reason mesmerized me. I knew I couldn't just walk over and throw some line on her because every other asshole had already done that. Besides, corny shit like that just wasn't my style. Then, as if God himself was playing D.J., the music shifted from some country rock song to the Clash's, "Brand New Cadillac," and the dance floor completely emptied. The pretty girl leapt out of her chair, ran out onto the dance floor and started dancing alone. Without even a second thought I jumped up, ran out, grabbed her and started doing that punk dance where the guy shakes the shit out of his girl like a rag doll. The entire club full of Squids just stared in amazement as we danced all night long. I never made it to the King's Head Inn for my night of free drinks courtesy of Ray, but I didn't care. I just captured the heart of the finest girl in the entire Navy and she captured mine. We talked, danced and kissed the night away. After the night was over and I walked her back to her barracks, I officially declared Becky-Lynn Thompson my girl.

Becky was from New Jersey and was cool as shit. Within a few months we moved in together at an apartment down in Oceanview, which was right off the water. She was the sweetest girl, had a heart of gold and as time went on, we became inseparable. We made each other laugh, we went out and danced at the Taj Mahal night, after night, before coming home and making love. She was the first person to turn me on to Bob Marley, who would later become one of my biggest spiritual influences, and I turned her onto all kinds of punk music.

Our apartment off base was a no-frills, no furniture, no amenities kind of place, but it was a place for us to have sex and most importantly, fall asleep in each other's arms each night. I really loved Becky, but unfortunately I was pretty messed-up in the head emotionally and really didn't know how to express it. So we just let the relationship be what it was… a good time. I sold acid and other drugs to help supplement my income because I was the lowest pay grade in the Navy (E-1). I was earning a whopping $199 every two weeks.

We always blasted music at the house and brought the ruckus. We were loud-ass people, with loud-ass, rowdy friends and that really pissed off our downstairs neighbor who was a fat, redneck bitch. She constantly left nasty notes on our door and was always screaming out the window for us to turn the music down. I think she was just jealous that she heard the bed slamming off the floor every night, while downstairs she was suffering from a chronic case of "Lack-a-dickpsychosis."

When we would see her and her fat-ass husband in the hall, or at the supermarket, they looked like they hated each other, so I'm sure the sex was either non-existent, or over very quickly. She even tried to get us evicted by calling the cops one night, then complaining to the management company who operated the apartment building. The next day I decided it was time for some punk rock revenge. I saved up about a dozen or so of Becky's bloodiest tampons and tied them together and attached a note that said, "Suck on these bitch." I lowered the present down by a string and swung it into her living room through the broken screen that was hanging off her window. We woke up the next morning to screams of, "Oh my God. You sick fuckin' bastard!" We laughed about that for days and after that she never bothered us or complained again.

It was the summer of '80 and the Arkansas was almost finished so they started bringing the crew over to familiarize us with the ship. For everyone else that meant seeing the combat systems, nuclear propulsion power plants and missile silo's. For me, it was like, okay you see these decks and bulkheads (floors and ceilings) you're going to become an expert in shining them. You're going to keep them so clean we'll be able eat off them. My big Navy adventure meant I was a "Deck Ape," a "Boatswain's Mate," which was a glorified "Swabbie." I was going to be super-qualified in learning what kind of floor wax the captain preferred in his dining quarters, how to chip away old deck paint and apply red-lead primer and my worst fuckin' nightmare - how to tie fuckin knots, all kinds of fuckin' knots. I would learn about knots 'til I fuckin ate, shat and dreamt about fuckin' tying knots. I'm talking about bowlines, monkey fists, bite on a bowline and square knots. You name it I had to learn it. You had to walk around with a little piece of rope in your pocket at all times and if the second class lifer-dog walked up and shouted, "Bowline McGowan" and I couldn't tie it, or I tied a granny-knot (any knot tied the wrong way), I'd get no liberty that night. I learned to play the game and got pretty good at my knots because I wanted to go home to be with Becky and chill out at the Taj Mahal.

We were scheduled to start our shakedown cruises in the fall to test out the Arkansas in the open waters. Then we were heading to the Naval base at "Gitmo" (Guantánamo Bay, Cuba) for intensified winter training, which meant I had to be around the Squids 24/7, which sucked. There was only one cool guy on my ship, a dude who was nicknamed Moose. He was this big, white, rebellious biker motherfucker from Detroit, who was covered in tattoos and loved to fight when he drank. Moose was my joint partner and being an "H.T." (hull technician) on board the Arkansas meant he knew every square inch of hiding space. During working hours we'd sneak off and find an engine room with an exhaust fan way down in the bowels of the ship, or climb up to the top level of the Arkansas' super-structure where we puffed, while we looked at the Squids hard at work and talked about how much we hated the Navy. There were two drawbacks about hanging with the Moose. One was he liked Southern rock and the other was he hated black people. I told him several times to chill out with the racial remarks and he agreed to at least not express his opinions in front of me. We had some fun times in those early days at sea, but that would change once the Arkansas got her new Divisional Petty Officer BMI Baldwin, who was now in charge of us Deck Apes and out of his fuckin' mind.

Baldwin was in his late-30s to early-40s and stood six-feet tall. He had a shaved head and was a practicing Buddhist. Baldwin was a martial arts expert and even trained the SEALs in hand-to-hand combat. He trained in tae kwon do every day and even though he may have had a belly, he could still send a spinning wheel kick toward your head with accurate precision. As rumor had it Baldwin was moved to the Arkansas after several guys on his last ship, who he was onto for drug smuggling, jumped him out at sea and tried to hit him over the head with dogging wrenches (heavy metal pipes used to lock the handles on the ship's thick metal doors). He ended up throwing one overboard and broke the other two up pretty badly. They never found the guy who was sent overboard and he was later declared lost at sea. As for the other two, they were sent to military prison. The bottom line was you didn't fuck with "Boats," as he was called, no matter who you were. Even the captain of the Arkansas was afraid of him and it was said by many that Boats worked for the NIS (Naval Investigative Service).

Boats was a strange individual who never talked much and would just appear out of nowhere like a ninja. You'd be talking at night on the main deck and then he'd appear out of the darkness with his standard evil look and uttering his catchphrase, "Gentlemen." That's all he would say, and then he'd stare into your eyes. Judging by your reaction he'd know if you were up to no good and God help you if you were. One night we were out at sea and I was way up on the O-7 level (the top of the super-structure) smoking a joint and staring out at the dark ocean. I thought I was out of sight and out of mind and that's when Boats appeared and scared the shit out of me. I don't know how he managed to climb up there without me hearing him because those metal ladders made a lot of noise. Boats made me promise to never smoke weed on board again and he never reported the incident. I kept my word and so did he. One thing you better have in your dealings with him was honor because it meant everything to him. If you said you were going to do something and you didn't do it... look the fuck out. If he caught your ass lying... look the fuck out and duck, because he would launch something (usually a wrench) at your head. This was the old Navy, not this "Don't ask, don't tell" bullshit they're on today.

Every night I studied a little with Boats on the fantail (rear) of the ship along with another sailor, before we would sit and meditate. I never really got any good at tae kwon do, but he did show me some nasty tricks I managed to use to my advantage in a couple of Norfolk bar fights. Boats bent the rules for me on a number of occasions. I was one of the few people he liked aboard the Arkansas and I think it had something to do with the fact that I was a punker and a free-thinker, which meant we didn't give a fuck about the petty rules and regulations as long as we got the job done.

Winter was coming and I heard they were brutal in Norfolk because we were surrounded by water. Becky and I took the bus back and forth to the base every day with the fat-ass Navy wives and their screaming kids. That shit was getting old really quickly, especially if you had a hangover, which I did on more than one occasion. I decided it was time for us to get a car and there were just two problems with that scenario. I didn't have a license and none of the car dealerships on Military Highway would let me finance a ride because of my low pay status. Go figure. So the way I managed to get around the situation was to buy a car from a cook who worked on my ship and collected antique cars. He put up a sign on the ship that he was selling an old, sixty-something Plymouth, the kind that had push buttons for the transmission instead of a stick shift. Since he was a serious car collector he only wanted to sell it to someone who appreciated classic cars and would take great care of it. He was so attached to that car that part of the deal was he was allowed to check it out periodically to make sure it was being cared for properly. Now who better to get his car than a punk rocker with no license, no driving experience and no car care know how?

I did a little research before I met him and acted like I really knew my shit. The bottom line was that he sold me the car and told me I had to transfer the title and get insurance. Well, slight change of plans honcho. I drove it with no insurance, no license and the title still in his name. I owed him $750 of the $1,500 asking price and I kept the title in his name so if anything happened he was 100 percent responsible. I would see him every day and he'd say, "How's my baby doing McGowan. Can I see it? Did you do all the paperwork yet?" My reply, "Oh, the car is just wonderful. I'm having it detailed so it's not on base and as far as the paperwork... I'm workin' on it." He informed me he didn't want to be responsible in case anything happened, so I needed to get on it ASAP. I'd say, "Don't worry, I would never get you in trouble. I'll handle it." And handle it I did.

I parked the car in a secret spot away from the ship so he couldn't see the big anarchy symbol and dents all over it from my lack of drunk driving skills. Since I knew nothing about car care, something very fucked up was happening with the engine (I found out later I needed to put oil in it, who knew?). It got so bad that toward the end of her life that old Plymouth literally sounded like a machine gun coming down the street. It was so loud that people actually ducked thinking they were under fire. I hid it from him that entire winter. One fine spring morning when I put the pedal to the metal since I was late for duty, she had all she could bare. She was smoking, hissing, backfiring and making the usual rat-a-tat-tat-tat machine gun sounds. I raced onto the base and when I got close to my parking spot, with one last gasp of life, she backfired in the middle of the road and died. Smoke poured from the engine, which had now completely seized up. As I got out of the car you'd never believe who came driving by on their way to work? That's right, my little Filipino cook friend. After almost crashing the Navy pick-up he was in, he got out, said nothing and just stared in shock. His eyes filled with tears and his lips quivered as I ran off laughing not wanting to be late for the morning muster. As I took off I said, "You might wanna call a tow truck before you get a ticket on your car."

The great thing about that car was it allowed me to get off base even on days I was supposed to be on duty, which I never could have done taking the bus. I would drive off in uniform and when I got to the Taj Mahal change into the leather jacket and pair of jeans I kept in the trunk. I would then make my way up the stairs for happy hour, listen to punk records with Doug (the owner who usually was the only one there), get a buzz on and then head back to the base just in time for the 7 p.m. muster. That was my Navy life in a nutshell - work by day and punk by night. I was doing quite well for a young Squid in No Fuck, Vagina. I had a fine woman, an apartment, a car for the winter, all the drugs I wanted and was involved in a happening music scene. Despite all of that, it was a very dark and confusing time in my life that left me feeling empty inside. I felt incomplete like something was missing and it irritated the shit out of me because I couldn't figure out what it was for the life of me.

Everything in my life brought me to a point of anger and rage that literally would make me wait anxiously for some fucker to start shit with me, or my friends. This way, I could unleash on their asses and as far as anger management was concerned, I got mine when I got to lose it in a fight and had to be pulled off someone I'd beat unconscious. I wasn't a bully, but an advocate for the weak. Ever since I was a kid and watched my mom being beaten up by my dad and couldn't do anything about it, I knew I needed something to fight for. Protecting people from bullies seemed to justify the cans of whoop ass I was dishing out. Being a punk also helped me channel some of it in certain ways, but I knew that fighting and slam dancing weren't the only answers. I just really wanted the pain to go away. I was a drinker and a drugger who used violence to numb the pain I had inside. I knew I had to get off this train headed for disaster, but I didn't know how. Every day it slowly ate away at me and every day I numbed it with more alcohol, drugs and fights. Then one day in the fall of '80, just as it seemed hopeless and I was destined to become a statistic, I had an encounter that changed my life forever.

As usual I drove over to the Taj Mahal for my 5 p.m. beer, joints and tunes. When I pulled into the parking lot Doug was standing there with the look of a smiling teenage boy who just got laid for the first time and was looking for somebody, anybody to tell, "Smell my fingers, dude!" I got out of my car and he ran up to me, rambling on like a complete madman, "You have to see this band, they're fuckin' incredible, they're amazing. I've never seen anything like it in my life, you're not gonna fuckin' believe it and John.... they're black!"

I followed Doug, who ran up the stairs and there on stage, were four black musicians dressed in funky clothes. The singer was showing the early stages of sprouting dreadlocks and had a certain air about him. They were in the middle of their sound check when the drummer clicked off a four count and the shit really hit the fan. I never heard anything like it in my life; lightning fast chords that they were able to stop on a dime, flip, turn around and race back the other way. The singer moved like no one I had ever seen before. He was fit as hell and had the finesse of James Brown, the anger of Johnny Rotten and a shaking ability that made Elvis look like a fuckin' paraplegic. I was blown away and now I knew why after watching them do a song that Doug ran out and reacted the way he did. As Doug so eloquently put it, they were 'Fuckin' Incredible'- they were the Bad Brains. I waited for them to finish because I had to meet these guys. I knew I just saw the greatest band in the world and I wasn't about to let them get away without telling them that. I introduced myself and oddly enough they didn't have attitudes. On the contrary, they were very polite and well mannered, unlike most dickheads who are in bands and think they deserve to be worshiped.

I have a saying, "Musicians are just assholes waiting to happen." Oh sure, they're always nice guys when they start out, but as soon as they get a little fame look out. Here's the thing, if you analyze what entertainers do, it's not that amazing. In previous ages people looked up to the sages, or holy people with great awe and reverence and emulated them, and the sages never got egotistical, but remained humble. But now in the age we're in, the Kali-Yuga, which in Sanskrit means the Iron Age of Quarrel and Hypocrisy, we are looking up to nothing more than court jesters to guide us through this dark quagmire called life. We're fixated on TV shows and magazines that tell us where they shop, where they eat and what they wear. We suffer through celebrity break-ups, failed marriages, career changes and drug problems, and we live vicariously through these wackos. That's because we're made to feel our lives are useless and insignificant unless we're rich, famous or beautiful. Come on folks, wise up. Most of these people are so fucked in the head they can't even take a shit without calling their therapists to ask which way they should wipe. Believe me, I know a lot of them and what I'm getting at is this; look to the right sources for wisdom and guidance. And all you entertainers…stay as humble as you were in the neophyte stages of your careers and remember… the people you crap all over on your way up, will be crappin' on you on your way down. I mean it's one of the laws of physics after all, isn't it? What goes up, must come down.

I saw a perfect example of this type of humility when I complemented the singer, who went by the name of H.R. (Paul Hudson). He simply said, "It's just Jah you know. Jah give any and all ability. I mon cannot take credit for that." Here was somebody who had more talent and ability in his left big toe than most of us will ever have and he's giving the credit to this other guy? I had to find out who this dude Jah was. I asked H.R. and he told me that Jah was a name for God and that he recently took up the religion of Rastafarianism. Now I was really blown away because these guys were so great and so spiritual. I asked if he wanted to smoke some weed so I could pick his brain and he said, "I and I not smoke weed. I and I sip chalice and give praises to the most high." With that he broke out a huge bag of buds and we went to the back of the club to Reason.

I told him about myself and he just listened. H.R. was good at that: listening. My old Irish aunt, Betty Burke, used to say, "You've got two ears and one mouth, so you should listen twice as much as you talk." H.R. listened as I told him about the crazy shit I'd been through and how I ended up in the Navy. He commented by saying, "Jah brought you here for a reason, Rasta. Check say it was destiny to meet the brethren. The I is a well spiritual youth and looking for Jah. Seek and ye shall find. Jah is what's missing from your life and you can never be happy in this world without 'that' connection. This you must come to Overstand."

I spent an hour with H.R. and his words struck me like lightning bolts. As I drove back to the base I couldn't get our conversation out of my head. Was that the void in my life? Was he right? What does God have to do with punk rock anyway? I was even more confused now and needed further clarification on this stuff. Shit, the Navy was going to have to get someone else to stand the 12 to 4 a.m. watch, because this was my life here and I needed answers to my 4 million questions. I went U.A. (unauthorized absence) from the mid-watch and me and Becky went back to the Taj Mahal to see the Bad Brains perform.

The show was a million times better than the sound check and what fascinated me was, here were these four humble souls, so meek and reserved, but once they hit the stage all holy hell broke loose! What a dichotomy. H.R. was all over the stage ranting like a madman and even did this back flip at the end of the song, "At The Movies," which he landed perfectly on the last note. The Bad Brains were a phenomenon and I was sure I was witnessing history in the making. I went out to the parking lot after the show, hung out in their van and sold Mo Sussman, their big, fat manager, some really good acid and talked to the other guys in the band. I continued my talks with H.R. and he told me they were playing at the 9:30 Club in Washington, D.C. with a band called the Stimulators from NYC.

I left Becky in Norfolk and went to D.C. by myself because we weren't getting along too well at the time. I was just feeling unhappy about my own life and situation. Having to constantly be around a girlfriend made it worse because you were always supposed to be expressing your feelings. My feelings were that I didn't know what the fuck I was feeling.

Seeing the Brains in D.C. was another unforgettable experience. Prior to that I was still pogo-ing and doing a robot-like new wave dance, but the D.C. crowd was sick. I never saw anything like it, stage diving, creepy-crawling, and skanking. It was amazing, and unlike moshing as it's called today, which is nothing more than a bunch of idiot jocks and retards getting their frustrations out by beating the shit out of each other. This was a tribal dance with an art form type quality about it. Back then people caught the stage divers and you didn't throw karate kicks and punches at people's heads because you would be beaten the fuck down very quickly. I remember watching Henry Rollins the singer from S.O.A. (State of Alert) and Black Flag, creepy-crawling around and never even bumping into another person, but looking like one fierce motherfucker doing it. He and a few others went out to the Mecca for punk/hardcore in '80 called California and brought back some nasty moves to the D.C. area. The combination of the band and the crowd all being a part of the show was sick.

The days of cock rock, ego-driven bands that thought they were deities worthy of worship on their stage/altar, were now over. These bands actually liked it when you climbed up on the stage and dove off, as long as you didn't smash into their equipment. I did my first stage dive that night and hit the floor like a 165-pound bag of quarters. Danny Ingram, the drummer from Youth Brigade, jumped off the stage feet first onto my shoulder and almost dislocated it. What a blast!

The opening band that night was the Stimulators and they had this little, punk rock drummer named Harley Flanagan, who was about twelve at the time. He was fun to watch, but the Bad Brains were on a whole other level. I hung out backstage after the show to continue my spiritual talks with H.R. and the stuff he talked to me about was fascinating. At the end of the night he said that Jah would definitely arrange for us to meet again, and after that I found myself going up to D.C. every weekend to catch shows. I saw S.O.A., Red C, Youth Brigade, Black Market Baby, the Teen Idles and a slew of others.

Later on the Stimulators opened for Black Market Baby at the 9:30 Club. They had recently got back from touring Ireland and now Harley was a skinhead. The Stim's finished their set with Kiss's classic anthem, "Rock and Roll All Night," and we all got up on stage and sang along with them. Afterwards the mob, including Harley, went out to Georgetown like a bunch of hooligans to play video games and raise hell. I told him I was from New York and I go there every couple of months. He said he lived on the LES and next time I came home to look him up, so we could hang out. I guess this was fate.

About thirty of us D.C. people piled into cars and vans and drove out to a show at some hick cowboy club called The Branding Iron in Virginia. I guess the owners didn't know what kind of bands they booked for the night because there were tables all the way to the stage with candles on top of them and cowgirls with their cowboys wearing ten-gallon hats. Not a good idea. I can't remember the other bands on the bill that night (drugs), but Red C was definitely on it and they had an Asian kid named Eric L. singing who was really cool. I was hanging out with these two maniacs, Crazy Jay and Billy, at the time and they were always on drugs, drinking and always, always ready to fight. Jay looked like a Jewish version of John Belushi and Billy had this red hair like Howdy Doody, freckles and fucked up stare that screamed, "Look out motherfucker, 'cause you are about to get fucked up!" They wore the sickest spikes and homemade, razor sharp spurs on their boots. I believe it was Jay who took off a piece of someone's ear at the 9:30 Club and got spurs officially banned there.

As soon as the first band hit its first note, we dove off the stage and landed in the cow folk's laps. We slam danced their tables and when they got up to run for their lives, it was like Pearl Harbor because they never knew what hit them. Even after the club owner pulled the plug, the band kept playing until finally, someone ran in and said the cops were there. We piled out of the club and were met in the parking lot by cops with billy clubs who proceeded to whip our asses. Me, Billy and Jay each got cracked, but we managed to get into our cars and race out of the parking lot laughing and feeling no pain. Must have been the 'ludes, dudes.

I even went to New York with the boys from D.C. and caught a few shows. I remember at that time, no one knew how to creepy-crawl, slam, or even stage dive yet. The New York crowd just stood back and watched as we put on a demonstration for them, sometimes even demonstrating on them. Becky and I had broken up by then and it was cool with me because I was in a whole different headspace, a headspace that said, "Fuck romance... be a nuisance." Even my look changed. I wore steel cap boots with bandanas and barbwire wrapped around one of them. On the other boot I had a Chinese throwing star that I made razor sharp by using the grinding wheel on board my ship. I wore spikes and a thick chain like the ones bike messengers use to lock their bikes. It had a quick release, so I could get it off quickly just in case I had to use it on somebody.

In D.C., the Marines always beat up the punks for no reason and it pissed us all off. Then on one night two young punks were beaten up badly and we went looking for the Marines with no luck. A convertible full of Jarheads stopped at a red light on Wisconsin Avenue in Georgetown and the young punks yelled, "That's them!" Danny Ingram and I pulled off our chains and lashed the shit out of these dudes as they sat in their car screaming. Danny got up on the hood and swung his chain down at them. We all kicked the shit out of that car as they raced off. I guess the story made its rounds around the base because after that night no Marine ever fucked with another punk rocker again.

I also remember seeing a bunch of Hare Krsnas who hung around and chanted on Wisconsin Avenue every Saturday night. A bunch of us would dance around creepy-crawling and singing along, but the Krsnas just kept smiling and chanting away. We would follow them for blocks but were always respectful of their religion. We even stopped some idiot rednecks from harassing the Krsnas by surrounding them and threatening to kick their asses if they didn't back off. The Hare Krsnas liked us and little did I know that while I was doing my little song and dance number, Krsna (God) was sinking His hooks into me.

Later that month the Arkansas headed out to sea. Plain and simple, ship-life sucked. After hanging out on the D.C. scene and hearing the stuff H.R. was talking to me about, it really made my head spin about where my life was headed. I asked myself, "Who am I? Where was I from? Where was I going? What was my purpose?" I actually asked Jah, the God of Rasta Far I, to give me some direction and some clue, because I felt totally alienated from the Navy people whom I had nothing in common with. Everyone on the ship was pretty cool and they knew to just let me be except for this one shitbird from Alabama, or some other inbred fuckin' place. This guy found it in his Southern patriotic duty to constantly fuck with me because I was from New York. He was in the Deck Ape division with me so I had to be around him all the time and he was constantly talkin' shit about my clothes, music and whatever else he didn't like about me. Every time I passed him on the ship it was, "Fuck you, New York," and "I'll kick your Yankee, faggot ass." I assured him that sooner or later he was going to get his chance to back up the tough talk and if it wasn't for Boats chillin' me out by reminding me that it would result in brig time and no D.C. weekends for a while, I would have already stomped a mud-hole in his ass thirty times over. I bit my lip and put country-boy on the top of my "Definite Asshole to Get List."

It's a Navy tradition on a new ship's maiden voyage that the captain and all the officers have the first meal cooked on board in the enlisted dining facility, with the enlisted personnel. We were having steak and lobster and somebody must have fucked up because they picked me to serve our born-again Christian captain his meal. The head mess cook put me in a white uniform and gave me instructions on proper serving etiquette that included which side to serve from, what to serve when, how to stand at parade rest behind the captain's right shoulder and other bullshit that went right in one ear and out the other. The captain toasted the ship with grape juice and ordered everyone to eat as much as they could. As for me I was fucking up royally; I knocked over an officer's Pepsi, dropped food, served from the wrong side and I bumped into their arms while they ate. I even burped loudly once, but give me some credit, I did excuse myself.

I could see the old skipper was getting annoyed, along with all the other officer-puke college boys. To lighten the mood the captain broke into a joke-telling session and simply put - his jokes sucked. They were on the level of bible college humor and every brownnoser on board was laughing. Then the other officers piped in with their weak attempts at stand-up and the enlisted continued to laugh knowing if they didn't these pricks could make life on board miserable. A couple of petty officers cracked a few lame jokes and by that point I'd had all I could take. The mess hall fell silent momentarily as everyone waited for the next joke while chowing down on lobster. I looked around and no one stood up. "I got a joke for you Captain," I piped in loudly as the mess cook gave me a signal to be quiet. The Captain looked up at me, his mouth covered in lobster meat and butter. I could tell that he was annoyed that I spoke (I had strict instructions that talking while serving was forbidden) but he played it off, not wanting to seem like the nerd he was by chewing me out. "Well, c'mon sailor let's hear it," he said.

Boats knew what was coming and he was looking at me like, "McGowan don't you fuckin' do it." The mess hall was completely silent as the entire ships crew waited for Mr. Punk Rock's take on humor. I looked down at the Captain and said, "What's worse than having lobsters on your piano?" The Captain thought for a moment and said, "I'd say... to, 'see' food on your face. Get it, 'sea' food?" The officers and enlisted laughed. He continued, "I don't know. What's worse than having lobsters on your piano?" He shoved a fork-full of buttery lobster into his mouth and chewed. "Crabs on your organ!" I shouted. He immediately spit his lobster into his napkin with a look of total disgust on his face. Some of the brothers laughed and when their authorities gave them the evil eye they stopped. The Captain stood up and stared at me. I had a shit-eating grin on my face as he shouted, "What's your name sailor?" "McGowan," I said, "But my friends call me 'Johnny Crabcakes' after a bad case of the crotch crickets if you know what I mean." I reached down my pants and threw in a scratch to the groin just to make sure he got the punch line. Oh, he got it all right.

He gave me a lecture about being a wise guy, chewed me out and then ordered Boats to "Get this vile human being out of my face." Boats sent me to his office and I got chewed out as he fought back laughter the whole time. To make a show of some type of authority he made me strip and wax the floors in the officer's quarters. That was my first experience at sea and I'd have to say it was worth every minute of ass-chewin' because now the brass in the Navy was convinced I had mental problems and that my friends, was part of the strategy.

A week or so later I saw the Teen Idles and the Untouchables play at the Taj Mahal. For those of you who are not familiar with old, D.C. hardcore punk, Ian MacKaye's little brother, Alec, was the singer of the Untouchables and he was out of his mind. The show was sick and they brought a whole crew down from D.C. that slam danced the shit out of anyone who made the mistake of getting out onto the dance floor. I hung out with them after the show and I was shocked at the fact that they didn't smoke, drink or even try to pick up girls. For me, punk meant getting wasted, shacking-up with some girl, then stumbling in just in time for the morning role call. A whole new world of awareness was opening up for me and it wasn't like I couldn't hack the Navy, I mean I'd been through worse shit than anything they could throw at me. I just felt I had another calling in life and the Navy just wasn't a part of it. I spent less time around Navy personnel and more time around the punks on the D.C. and Norfolk scenes. I wanted out, but there was one problem. I signed a contract with the Navy that guaranteed my services for four years. I had a little over three to go and I knew right then and there that there was no way that was going to happen. So, as the saying goes, necessity became the mother of invention.

I had three angles for an honorable, medical discharge - chronic bedwetting, sex addition or sleepwalking. When we sailed down to Cuba's Gitmo, for intense training, what I did was create a hybrid condition out of all three. I got up in the middle of the night like I was a sleepwalker. I then walked to the TV lounge in the berthing living quarters and whipped out my johnson. It was hilarious to see the look on some of the Squid's faces when I urinated right on the floor at their feet. They knew the old myth that said never wake a sleepwalker and they didn't. Instead they followed me as I made my way back to the sleeping quarters. I stood next to my bed and urinated again, but this time on my bed. I lay down in the wet spot and then began masturbating while turning on the perverted shit talk during the entire stroke session. That definitely got the ball rolling, but I knew I had to take it even one step further.

If they couldn't find me during working hours they knew exactly where to look. I'd be in my bed eight to ten times a day doing what any other sex addicted person would be doing, or at least pretending to. I even ordered one of those electric blowjob machines from a porno magazine. You should have seen the look on the division officer's face when he searched my locker one day during a routine locker inspection and found it. He reached in, pulled out this slimy, Vaseline and dry sperm-covered tube, with its rubbery "Life-like mouth that actually moves" (as the ad said in Hustler). He looked at it and said, "What the hell is this?" As I informed him that it was a gadget so I could have my "Blowjobs at sea," he dropped it to the floor and jumped back screaming like a housewife who just had a mouse ran across her path.

After a few days not only my rack, but the entire deck division sleeping area smelled like urine. As word of my pissing and sexual escapades spread through out the ship everyone on board was looking at me like I was possessed. Boats wasn't born yesterday though and knew exactly what I was up to. He told me that when the ship got back to Norfolk they were sending me in for all kinds of tests; very painful tests. I guess I wasn't the first sailor to try and get out of the Navy this way and they had their methods of dealing with Squids who wanted out under fraudulent medical conditions.

The tests they did on me were plucked from the pages of Dr. Joseph Goebbel's old Nazi SS manual. One involved putting a half-inch wide scope into the tip of my penis and shoving it into my bladder to look around. I've seen ironworkers hammer rivets into girders with less force than these Navy wanka's used on me. Then it was hours and hours of psychological profiling, followed by more Nazi tests and talk of a major experimental surgery on my bladder to stop the bed-wetting. The real kick in the nuts came when they sent a 6'5", gay as hell doctor, with hands the size of a small car into the room to "examine my rectal cavity," as he put it in his very feminine voice. As he snapped on those XXXXL sized rubber gloves and lubed up, I jumped off that examining table, ran out of the examination room and declared myself the recipient of a miracle. Praise Jesus! Hallelujah! I was cured. The Navy obviously had my number and I was going to have to figure out another way to make my exit.

Things soon went from bad to worse in terms of my attitude toward Navy life. It wasn't that I wasn't patriotic or anything like that, it was just I felt more and more like I was being pulled toward something else, but I didn't know what. I listened to a lot of Bob Marley at the time along with my usual Germs, Sex Pistols, Damned and Dead Boys records. I found that Bob was hitting on a whole different revolutionary aspect with his music. He had the same attitude as the punks, that everything was fucked up, but instead of just bitching about it Bob offered solutions. He pointed out that the world needed more spirituality, more Jah and that Babylon, which meant the materialistic planet that Earth was becoming, was a spiritual slaughterhouse for the youth. We didn't belong in this material world he said, we belonged in Zion (the spiritual world) with Jah. It just made sense. We're prisoners in this material world and until we start thinking about how to get out of the prison, we're in ignorance just like the prisoner who's thinking, "Ah what the hell, let me make this jail cell the all-in-all. Forget the outside world." I was locked up and the only thing I thought of day after day was getting out and that's why everything Bob was saying made sense. I took his spiritual message, the thoughts that had been brewing in my head from my talks with H.R., the pissed off, get-in-your-face, fuck you attitude of punk rock and kept searching, looking for a sign. On a voyage with the Arkansas, that sign would come to me in big, bold flashing neon letters.

We deployed to the little Caribbean nation known as Jamaica, which was Bob Marley's birthplace. I was psyched to check it out because the Squids that had been there said it was wild. This was way before Jamaica was the popular tourist attraction it is today. Back then, some of the most basic necessities were hard to come by because of poverty. According to the sailors on board you could trade bars of soap, radios, sneakers and all kinds of other crap, the crap that I could get in abundance, for the ganja – the best weed you'd ever smoke in your life. Right before we pulled into Montego Bay, or "Mo-Bay," as it was known to the locals, the docs showed us an on board video about V.D., syphilis and gonorrhea. They said those venereal diseases were rampant in Jamaica and they warned us to make sure we used condoms if we got busy. I loaded up on bars of Ivory Soap, toothpaste and rolling papers before we left Norfolk. As we anchored out in the bay I started to get some sense of what the old sailors must have felt when they brought shit to trade with people in far off places.

One thing about me on the Arkansas was that I was a loner. Whenever we pulled in anywhere I left the ship on my own, which was not recommended for safety reasons, but I never felt like I was ever in any danger. I survived the Valentis, St. John's, the NYC streets, Spofford and Linky, so I was ready for anyone and anything, anywhere. We pulled into Mo-Bay for three days, I went ashore, and never looked back.

Back then you weren't required to wear your Naval uniform on liberty like you are now. It's not that the Jamaicans didn't know my whiter-than-white ass was a sailor, but I thought those Navy Cracker Jack uniforms with the little, white, round hats were corny-looking. I hit the beach in full punk garb and that drew a lot of stares from the locals. My plan was to venture out this first day, make my connections, much like Magellan or Columbus would have done and barter the soap and other stuff for ganja. Then I would figure out a way to smuggle it back to the states.

Montego Bay was an extremely poor area and the minute I stepped on shore the locals were trying to sell me everything from girls to Jamaican rum. I figured most of the sketchy Rudeboy (gangster) looking dudes couldn't be trusted. I knew Rastas stood for peace, spirituality and most importantly lots of ganja. I had my eyes open for them and to my surprise I didn't even see one. I walked through the shops for about an hour and that's when I saw a young Dread who couldn't have been more than twenty-three haggling over the price of some sugar cane with a vendor. I walked up, slipped him a five dollar bill which he accepted and bought his 'cane. He offered me the change and I told him to keep it. We walked around and talked about Jah, the Rasta lifestyle, and Babylon. He said I was nothing like the other sailors he had ever seen or met and that I should leave the Navy. We talked for hours, smoked weed and sat in the warm sun drinking fresh coconut juice. The sun felt so good on my skin, which had suffered through the cold Norfolk winter. As we Reasoned I began to Overstand that splitting the Navy was becoming an inevitable fact.

Together we set out to the country on a bus worse than anything I had ever experienced on the New York City transit line. After about an hour we arrived at this quiet, beachfront village. My Dread friend introduced me to this "Elder" who was a Rastaman with the longest, grey dreadlocks I had ever seen. The Elder talked in a thick patois (pronounced pat-twah) and the young Dread translated most of it for me and told me about some massacre the elder had survived. Many years later I realized that he was talking about the infamous Green Bay killings where Dreads had bounties on their heads and were hunted down and killed. That's what inspired Peter Tosh's Wanted Dread or Alive album cover. We bought some stuff called "Ital" from him and it was served in a wooden coconut shell called a calabash. Ital was pure vegetarian organic food and the Rastaman claimed it was very good for you. This particular dish consisted of seaweed, some kind of greens, beans, and brown rice. Since I was a meat and potatoes guy back then, to me, it tasted like shit. I was definitely going to have to put the whole Ital thing on hold for a while.

After we left the Rastaman's place we went to a wood carving shop near a small beach. It was there he found me the best weed around called "lambsbred," and introduced me to this wood carver with hardly a tooth in his mouth. He claimed he could pack a pound of the lambsbred into three hollowed out statues that he would seal back up, making it undetectable. The way the ship would conduct searches back then was to pick a number like every fourth man coming back aboard before they would get searched. I knew no matter what my number was, I was getting my ass tossed. My plan was to get the weed on board, then before we got back to Norfolk and the dogs came aboard, get it out of the statue. I would then throw the carvings overboard and hide the weed in the bowels of the ship where the dogs couldn't go. I put in my order and told the carver I would be back tomorrow to pick up my statues.

I said goodbye to my young Dread friend and when the next day rolled around, I came back aboard the Arkansas with close to a pound and a half in my wooden carvings. As I predicted the deck officer stopped me and asked me if I had any contraband. I said, "Contraband, sir? I don't ever touch that stuff. That's for communists." He gave me a smirk and he examined the statues and other trinkets I bought to make it look like I was shopping for my mom and relatives. He found no indications of nefarious activities and after I saluted the flag properly and requested permission to come aboard, he gave me a big old salute and a "Permission granted, sailor."

As we steamed our way back to the states I dug out the statues, removed the weed and went to the hiding spot that I already had planned out. In the deck division's bathroom above the middle toilet stall there was a panel that opened up. Once you opened it there was a crawl space inside with hundreds of wires, pipes and different kinds of cables. I crawled in and eight to ten feet later, I pulled apart a huge cluster of cables. I put my weed in the middle of it and wrapped the cables around it concealing it perfectly. Now came the hard part... I had to forget my little package was stashed away until we arrived back in Norfolk ten days later.

As much as I wanted to smoke it, if Boats got one whiff of that stuff I'd be finished. I was still honoring my word that I'd never smoke any weed on board, but I never said anything about smuggling it.

We stopped in Fort Lauderdale on the way back to Norfolk and I went to some punk club down on the strip where I met the hottest little punk chick named Lisa. Since she was Jewish, she hassled me about the fact I was wearing a shirt with a swastika on it. After she was convinced I was no Nazi, we hung out and kissed a little. Lisa told me she was moving to New York and gave me her number in Florida. We went back to my ship at 3 a.m. and since I was cool with the guy standing watch, I brought her on board. We went up to the Captain's dining quarters where the Captain left his Navy hat with all the gold embroidery on it. Lisa grabbed it, put in on and we ran all over the ship screaming and yelling. When she finally threw the hat into the water, we laughed our asses off and kissed some more. She told me that I better call her when I went to New York, gave me a bon voyage kiss and left.

We sailed into Norfolk and when the dogs came aboard they found one of those huge black garbage bags full of Quaaludes, two pounds of cocaine and at least ten stashes of marijuana totaling close to fifteen pounds. My little stash was never found and I gave praises to The Most High, Jah Rasta Far I, for that. After that incident every asshole with a couple of stripes or an officer's insignia watched over the Arkansas crew members like hawks, because no one stepped forward to claim the drugs and receive their 25 years of hard labor inside a military prison. Go figure. Even Boats' attitude changed toward me and everyone else since he took it personally that someone would smuggle drugs aboard "his" ship.

Back in Norfolk I resorted to my old street hustling ways because as the saying goes, "You can take the brotha out the ghetto, but you can't take the ghetto out the brotha." Unfortunately though, I sold a bag of pot to an undercover cop in the parking lot of the King's Head Inn and was arrested and booked. They gave me a court date in May and afterward my locker and person were constantly searched while I was on board. I left the ship and didn't return for 29 days. Twenty-nine was a significant number because a leave of 29 days or less was an unauthorized absence. After 30 days you were classified as AWOL and in a whole world of shit. Up until 30 days, you could still get paid while you waited to go to "Captain's Mast," which was a trial-type situation on board. I came back after 29 days, got my check, and split again for two weeks.

I flew up to New York on People's Airline and if anyone remembers People's, it was the airline where you paid on the plane. Well, I wasn't about to give these fuckers $49.99 of my partying dough. I made sure I was in uniform (for patriotic reasons, of course) and when they came up the aisle with the cash register on wheels, I put on an Oscar-worthy performance. I flipped out, pretended like I lost my wallet on the plane and had everyone on the fuckin' thing looking for it. Everyone chipped in and not only paid my ticket, but bought me drinks and gave me another hundred bucks to party with. As I exited the plane drunk I whispered to the head stewardess standing near the front of the plane, "Hey good looking... there never was a wallet, but thanks for the hospitality." She politely gave me the finger and called me a low-life asshole. Hey I'd take it, I was in New York and I got there for free.

I had a great time that weekend and then went back to D.C. and Norfolk where I couch surfed for another two weeks. I finally stumbled back to the Arkansas on the 23rd hour of the 29th day. At that point they'd had enough of my bullshit. They took my I.D. so I couldn't get off the ship and restricted me to quarters while I waited for Captain's Mast. To prevent me from sliding down a mooring-line like I had done before they made me muster every hour on the hour back on the fantail with the duty officer of the day. At Captain's Mast my old pal, the Christian skipper, who didn't appreciate my lobster joke gave me the max. I got 90 days restrictions, forfeit of two months salary and I couldn't be promoted to E-2 for another year. Now the promotion thing, I couldn't give two shits about. As for the pay, I had sold my little Jamaican stash and had money saved, but being restricted to the ship sucked! I vowed that after we got back from our three month Shellback cruise to Brazil and South America I was going to split for good.

While I was in Norfolk I developed a severe toothache and they sent me to the Naval Station's dentist, with a "Master at Arms" (M.P.) escort in tow. It was determined that two of my four wisdom teeth had to be removed. We were scheduled for deployment to Bermuda and then Brazil in a few days, so the next morning they rushed me over and yanked my teeth out. A few days later we pulled into Bermuda and there's nothing worse than being in a tropical port of call and watching everyone else going off the ship while you're restricted and have to work for no money. My redneck friend was having a blast with the fact that I was in a bad way and kept rubbing it in my face. He would return from liberty drunk with beer muscles and challenge me to a fight. I warned him to back off, but of course he didn't heed the warnings.

My mouth was killing me. I went to sickbay and they said I developed an infection following the surgery. They gave me some antibiotics and told me to gargle with salt water. There's plenty of that all around, right? I was in such severe pain I couldn't even sleep. The pain reminded me of that incident at the Valentis' where I had that abscessed tooth and they refused to take me to see the dentist. My jaw started to swell just like it did back at the Valentis' and each day it was getting worse. One warm afternoon while at sea, somewhere between Puerto Rico and Jamaica, the shit hit the fan.

My mouth was throbbing and the doc on board wouldn't give me any more codeine because he thought I was playing up my condition in order to catch a buzz. At this time, Boats had me operating a deck grinder, which is a big, hand-held sander, with sharp metal teeth that vibrated like hell, that's used to remove the layers of non-skid surface, paint and primer. The vibrating of the deck grinder, the inhalation of dust, the scorching tropical sun and the throbbing toothache, combined to give me one hell of a splitting headache. When I walked by the paint locker on my way to the missile launcher to finish my work, it's safe to say I was in a really shitty mood. I looked in and there was my little redneck friend mixing paint. Now, I try to be humble when assholes start shit with me because as we all know, empty barrels make the most noise. Eventually they push hard enough that something inside me snaps and I say to myself, "If this motherfucker says one more word I'm going to lay his ass out." Well, I was in one of those moods and I told myself I'd had all I was going to take from this inbred fucker. If he said one word he was done. When I walked by, he looked at me and said, "Fuck you, you faggot-ass Yankee."

I calmly walked in the paint locker and closed the door behind me with a sinister look on my face. It was at that point, country boy realized what was about to go down and he tried to get by me. I threw him to the deck and he was shitting his pants, begging for me not to hurt him. I looked down at him, chuckled and picked up a full gallon of paint. I beat him in the legs, arms and back until he was screaming like a banshee and pleading for mercy. Then I beat him some more in soft-tissue areas of his body, being very careful not to break any bones. The beating lasted five minutes or so until he almost passed out from the pain. I simply went to my rack and waited for the repercussions, which came quickly. They came and I was brought to an immediate Captain's Mast. I was told that when I got back to Norfolk I was looking at a court martial and time in the brig for my little stunt. My inbred buddy was covered in some pretty nasty welts and couldn't move his arms, legs and best of all his mouth for days. From that point on, every time he saw me he looked the other way.

I had my own medical issues to deal with though. The antibiotics they gave me weren't working and the infection in my mouth spread. As a result, I was taken off the ship by helicopter and transferred back to Roosevelt Roads Naval Station, also known as Rosie Roads, in Puerto Rico. When I got there I was put on an I.V. drip for a few days and given stronger doses of antibiotics. In a week I was good as new, but my ship was too far south to fly me back out, so they kept me in P.R. Seems the Arkansas forgot to tell the command there that I was a bad boy. After I got out of the hospital I got paid, got liberty and was up to my old tricks on the beautiful island of Puerto Rico.

I hung out with a Navy diver and a couple of "Grunts" (infantrymen) that were stationed at Rosie Roads. They were pretty wild fuckers who loved to drink and fight out in the local bars. These guys were built like brick shithouses and had reps for being real bad-asses even with the locals who lived on the island. While I was there they took me to get tattooed at some shop run by a former sailor who lived way out in the jungle. I got a PiL (Public Image Limited – Johnny Rotten's post-Sex Pistols band) logo tattooed on my right hand between my thumb and index finger. The base, Rosie Roads, was cool because to the authorities there, I was basically invisible. This meant I could just hang out 'til 3 p.m., usually sleeping to recover from the previous night's partying. After that I would find my boys, slip off to smoke some weed and then go out into town in search of what else…hot Spanish women. There was only one problem with the local woman thing, none of us spoke Spanish and we struck out most of the time. One night, the language barrier and a shit-load of alcohol got us into some serious trouble with the locals.

Five of us piled into one of the little cabs with the shiny hubcaps and decorations that always waited right outside the base gate. The cab driver barely spoke English and I asked him in what little Spanglish I knew where we could find some very bonita senoritas. He smiled and said, "Oh, mi amigos want some chocha (derogatory Spanish word for a woman's vagina)? "Si! Si!" we shouted, "Chocha!" He laughed and took us to some bar about two miles out in the country. We opened the door. The entire place was filled with loud Spanish chatter, music and smoke. The second we entered, the place went silent and they all stared at us. We looked around. There wasn't another gringo in the place. We soon realized that our cabbie friend took us to a local's only joint. We walked up to the bar, whipped out our wads of greenbacks and every eye in the place was fixated on the bankrolls. I knew the word for 'give me' in Spanish was 'dame' and beer was 'cerveza' so I said, "Dame cinco cervesas, por favor." We got our beers and made our way through the crowd, which did include a few really beautiful girls. After a while the atmosphere relaxed back to normal and we blended in with the local crowd.

The scene was pretty funny since they didn't understand a word we were saying and we understood them even less. One thing did translate, we knew they wanted to try and win some of our cash on the pool table. Unfortunately for them, one of the guys we were with was a pretty amazing pool player. We won all their money, chatted up their women and basically acted like assholes.

Our guy ran the rack and beat everyone in the place. He didn't give our opponents the opportunity to take one shot. He would break and consecutively sink every ball while talking shit the entire time. Our guy was a corn-fed Jarhead from the Deep South who stood about 6'2" and was able to easily pump out a hundred push-ups without even breaking a sweat. One thing about popping shit is this...you don't need any translation, it's universal. No matter where you go on God's green Earth if you're talking trash to someone they know it and visa-versa. So we weren't exactly a big hit with the local Boriquas at this bar. It was made even worse by the fact that we were saying all kinds of rude shit to their girls involving our new favorite word chocha and buying them drinks with the money we just won off their fellas. Growing up in New York and knowing about the whole Latino machismo thing I knew you just didn't do that kind of shit, and it was only a matter of time before the excrement hit the fan.

I had my eye on one girl in particular and she knew exactly what she was doing by winking and flirting with us. She was looking for entertainment. Her man was getting heated over it and she wanted to see if five strapping young American lads could take on a bar full of angry Puerto Ricans. We were pretty sauced and my Marine friend was about to win another game of pool. At that moment, a girl walked by us and I made some rude comment. She spit at me and walked off pissed to talk a bunch of guys sitting at the bar who were eyeballing us. My buddy, who was oblivious to what was about to go down, sunk the eight ball and shouted, "Hoorah Marine!" As he went to grab his money off the pool table the Spanish guy grabbed it first. Now it was really on!

There's always this surreal moment right before a brawl goes down where everyone just stares at each other and things go silent. Well, we were having one of those moments when the silence was broken by the Grunt who had his money taken. He picked up the cue ball that was left on the table and smashed it into the guy's head, knocking him out. We grabbed pool sticks, chairs, anything we could get our hands on and just started laying fuckers out. By the time the brawl was over we had minor scrapes and bruises, but there was about a dozen or so messed up Puerto Ricans. We figured it was now a good idea if we got the hell outta Dodge.

We were laughing pretty hard as we walked back to the base at Rosie Roads. When you got close to the base you turned a big curve about a half-mile from the gate, the road straightened out and you'd see the Marines at their guard booth. As we made the turn we heard what appeared to be a mob behind us. We looked back and our suspicions were confirmed. A pissed off mob was fast approaching led by a few of the guys we beat up. They were yelling a million miles an hour in Spanish and pointing at us. It seemed like the entire town was with them wielding machetes, bats, clubs, and other nasty noggin crackers. Out of nowhere they charged at a full gallop, which caused us to run the fastest half-mile in military P.T. (physical training) history, straight towards the gate. The mob didn't let up and when we ran inside the gate holding up our I.D.s, the Marines quickly went into their booth and got their M-16s. They aimed at the mob and one of the Grunts shouted, "Pare" which means stop, but they still kept coming. They both then fired shots over the crowd, freezing them dead in their tracks. The Marines then lowered their weapons and aimed them chest level directly into the mob. One of the Grunts was Spanish and said some shit which caused the mob to turn around and backtrack. As they retreated, they were screaming things in Spanish that must have been every explective in the book.

After that incident I pretty much stayed on the base. The Spanish Marine told us the underlying mumbo-jumbo bullshit theme the mob was yelling at us. His translation was something like if they ever saw us in their town again they'd chop us into so many pieces they'd need a vacuum cleaner to pick us up off the road. No worries there amigos, because a week later my orders came in and I was going to Norfolk's Nimitz Hall to wait for the Arkansas to return from Brazil.

It was good to be home and my restricted, no pay status didn't reach the Nimitz Hall command either, which meant I hung out at the Taj Mahal during the week with Vic Demise, Raybeez and the rest of the Norfolk punks. On the weekends I headed up to D.C., and looked for H.R., but unfortunately at that point, the Bad Brains had moved to New York City. That really sucked because I had a lot of questions for him, questions which were going to have to wait to be answered. I passed the time hanging out with guys like Ian MacKaye, Henry Rollins, Crazy Jay, Billy and the rest of the crew. They accepted me as one of their own and we had some great times because back then, being a punk/hardcore motherfucker was dangerous and unpredictable, unlike what it is now – safe and completely predictable.

This shit they're passing off as punk rock these days is so homogenized, so watered down and so full of shit. The once revolutionary spirit punk possessed is dead and buried because the ones we set out to destroy have embraced it and sewn it into the great American fabric. Do any of these chumps calling themselves punks (and you know who you are) write songs like the Bad Brains' "Fearless Vampire Killers," the Clash's "White Riot," the Dead Kennedys' "Holiday in Cambodia" and so on? Hell no. What you have now is a bunch of MTV poser bands with tattoos, piercings and makeup who sing about their relationship problems and how hard it was growing up in their suburban homes and being pissed because Mommy and Daddy didn't understand why they took their platinum card to buy expensive designer punk gear. NEWS FLASH BITCHES!!!! You ain't punk. Back in the early days you caught shit for looking the way we did and we got into a lot of fights because of it. I grew up in New York City where you could pretty much run down a packed subway car during rush hour with your arm chopped off, spraying blood and no one would look up from their morning papers. But, the D.C. area, that was the South my friends. It was a whole lot different, a whole lot more conservative and as you can imagine fights were part of the protocol. If you asked me what was the best thing about being a punk back then I'd have to say the music, the people and the fights. You had to expect that if you walked into some redneck bar in Virginia, or the suburbs of Maryland or into a bar full of military people, you were more than likely going to get fucked with and as the old S.O.A. song said, "Gonna Have to Fight."

Those days are long gone and so are the real deal punks. Unfortunately the younger generations are now being spoon-fed MTV. The only examples of punk rockers they see are the nut-less posers who are nothing but a shadow of what once was. A perverted reflection if you will and I apologize for the rambling folks, but as you can see it's a subject I feel very strongly about. It's for good reason, because posers of all types, be it friends, spiritualists, musicians, lovers (as H.R. states in "Supertouch/Shitfit") can ruin even the purest of intended efforts.

As for N.N.S. (Norfolk Naval Station) everything was pretty much back to normal. As I headed to chow one fine morning I had thoughts racing around in my head about what it was going to be like the day I split this tin-can operation. What I didn't realize was that that day was going to come sooner than I thought. I passed the front desk on the way out the front door of Nimitz Hall and the Irish-American petty officer who was really cool and had covered for me on many of my U.A.'s called me over. "I ain't suppose to tell you this McGowan," he said. "But your ship is pulling in." He gave me that serious look and head nod, and I realized that breakfast was going to have to wait.

I ran up to my bunk, unlocked my locker and threw my clothes into my duffel bag. I grabbed my I.D. and the money I hid and bolted down the stairs. As I reached the front desk, talking to my petty officer buddy was the duty officer of the day. I heard him mention my name along with something about taking my I.D. and restricting me. I stood there frozen like a deer in the headlights, not knowing whether to run or what the hell to do. My petty officer friend looked at me and said, "Hey Johnson. I didn't give you my damn jacket. I lent it to ya. Make sure you bring it to morning muster tomorrow." "Uhh, no worries," I said. "Sorry about that." He shook his head in disappointment, went back to talking to the officer and off I went.

I caught the bus on the base at the last stop and took a window seat on the right side. It pulled away from the curb and traveled down Hampton Boulevard as Smitty the M.A.A. (Master at Arms) from the Arkansas and another sailor started walking toward the bus at a very quick pace. We stopped directly in front of them to let someone else on. While the two waited on the curb for the bus to pass them my heart sunk. Fear and adrenaline shot through my entire body and I slid down in my seat as the bus just sat there idling. That was the longest ten seconds of my life. Just outside my window, bent on my incarceration was a military cop and his lackey. Now, only a thin piece of glass separated me from serious time in the brig. I knew one thing, if they saw me and got on the bus I was going to kick out the window like my boy Chino did back in Spofford and make a run towards freedom down Hampton Boulevard. Then, just as Smitty gazed up at the window the bus pulled away and drove out the main gate. I looked back and watched the two literally jog over to Nimitz Hall, which was just on the other side of the road. That was a close call and if they looked up one second earlier, things would have turned out a lot differently.

I was off the grounds and I couch surfed in Norfolk for a little while. Since I missed my weed case I had a warrant for my arrest. I made my way up to D.C. still not knowing where I was going, how I was getting there or what the hell I was doing with my life. I hardly had any money, I had warrants and no place to live, but for some weird reason I was happy. I felt secure despite the adverse circumstances. I honestly felt a sense of protection like someone or something was guiding me through this. I just knew one thing, wherever I was going and whatever was going to happen, it was going to be one hell of a ride. When I arrived in D.C. via the Greyhound Bus the Navy's catch phrase popped into my head. You know the one, right? "Navy. It's not just a job, it's an adventure." I started to laugh, "Yeah, right. I got you beat in that department, Uncle Sam."

I went down to Georgetown and looked around Wisconsin Avenue for any signs of intelligent life...in other words, punks. There were none. A lot of the D.C. crew (except Crazy Jay and Billy who were basically burn-outs) went to prestigious schools or had jobs and that usually meant no punk rock Monday through Thursday. I walked around for hours with my duffel bag and saw a flyer for a show at the 9:30 Club that coming weekend. I knew I'd run into somebody there, so for the next two nights I slept at the bus terminal. The weekend finally rolled around and it was time to tell the crew the good news... I was now officially AWOL from the United States Navy.

The show at the 9:30 was a pseudo-punk rocker dressed in black named Alan Vega. The fucker was pathetic, but the good thing was that at any weekend show at the 9:30 people came out. Here's this wack looking dude on stage and five or six of us sitting across the front of the stage with our backs to him. That didn't sit well with Alan and he was getting pissed. He made some comments about the people with the spikes, boots, bandanas and homemade razor sharp spurs being assholes. Not very bright was he? We flipped him off and tossed our drinks over our shoulders at the band. Finally out of all the people on the stage, for some reason, Mr. Vega thought it was a good idea to come over and kick me in the ass, but it turned out to be not a good idea. I grabbed his leg, pulled him off the stage and he landed hard on the dance floor. We were 86'd from the 9:30 and headed out into the D.C. night looking for what else - trouble and girls. We found neither, so we went back to someone's house and crashed out.

A few days later I ran into Ian MacKaye and Henry Rollins and told them I split the Navy and was making my way back to New York. They knew I had a warrant, but were cool about it and let me stay at their place until I could find a ride north. Henry worked at the American Cafe on Wisconsin Avenue in Georgetown making sandwiches and I was there just about every day getting free meals. He was always cool with me and was one of the best front men in the business. At shows he'd go berserk and was kind of the tribal leader to some degree on the dance floor. When he'd creepy-crawl, slam or stage dive, all eyes were on his crazy ass. I have to admit I might have stolen a dance move or two from the brother over the years.

Ian on the other hand, was the one with the keen business sense. He and former Minor Threat bandmate, Jeff Nelson co-founded Dischord Records in '80, which Ian ran out of his house. The label was originally meant only as a means for distributing the Teen Idles 7-inch EP. But over the years it has become a legendary independent record label that put out a number of records by Rites of Spring, Jawbox, Dag Nasty, Marginal Man, Minor Threat and Government Issue, among others.

Ian also makes my 'Greatest Front men of All Time List' because he was a motherfucker in Minor Threat. I have to say in all the years I've been going to shows, one of the best to this day was Minor Threat at Great Gildersleeves on the Bowery in NYC. He also gets props for keeping the DIY (Do-It-Yourself) punk ethic alive for so many years by charging $5 to see his post-Minor Threat band, Fugazi, which he helped form in the mid-'80s. Back in the day I would bust on him with all the "Straight Edge" stuff that he preached. I'd say shit like, "Hey Ian, all that Pepsi and meat has tons of drugs in it, so if you really wannabe straight edge..." The last time I ran into him was at Fugazi's NYC's Palladium show in '97. He was on his way to Angelica Kitchen, an organic veggie spot to get some pre-show carrot juice and tofu. Much props Ian.

live from new york

chapter 9

After about a week in D.C., I went to see this band called the Undead and it turned out they were from NYC. Their singer Bobby Steele was one of the original members of the Misfits and I talked them into giving me a ride back to the Big Apple. I got out of their van on Avenue A on the LES with $20 to my name and no place to live. The very first person I saw walking down the street was Harley from the Stimulators. We were both happy as hell to run into each other. As we walked together down the avenue and passed 11th Street and Avenue A, standing in the doorway of building Number 171, like some mystical figure, was the one and only H.R. He just stood there acting like he knew I would show up. "Yes, Rasta. Greetings. Glad you made it," was all he said with one of those big H.R. grins on his face.

H.R. and the Bad Brains were living at 171A (which was written with an anarchy symbol logo), a rehearsal/recording studio/club that Jerry Williams (the infamous Jay Dublee) ran. Jay Dubs was the Bad Brains sound engineer at the time and was one bugged-out looking, cool-ass motherfucker. H.R., Harley (he didn't smoke, he said it was for hippies) and I went inside, shut the door and proceeded to smoke a shit-load of weed, listen to very loud reggae and reason. Jay Dubs knew a lot about philosophy and was a strict Ital-ist like H.R. I crashed on the couch and was woken up the next day by a band coming in to rehearse. I headed out to the LES in search of a pay phone to call the little Floridian cutie, Lisa, I had met some months before. I called her dad collect and he gave me her New York number.

Lisa was living on Waverly Place near Washington Square Park and was more than happy to see me. I couldn't have survived those first few weeks without her because I had no one else. Going to my mom's house was out of the question because, number one, we didn't get along and number two, that's the first place the Navy was going to look for me. Lisa was so cool, so damn pretty and I really fell for her. We were inseparable and had great times together. The best thing about being in New York in '81 was that many of the shows and events we experienced together became legendary events in the punk and hardcore movement.

One such event was the Clash appearing on Broadway. At that time, the band, who were yet to achieve mass popularity, were scheduled to play a bunch of gigs at a club in Times Square called Bonds Casino. The FDNY shut down the May 30th show because the scumbag promoter sold the room out to double its 3,500 capacity for each of the scheduled dates. Thousands of pissed off fans hit the streets practically rioting (I remember throwing a few bottles) and we shut Times Square down completely. The cops came in on horseback and started locking people up. That's when I thought it would be a good idea to leave the area, since I had those warrants out for my arrest. The band decided to add more shows to the already over-sold dates, so that all their fans could see them. I remember at that first show they rolled out this huge banner down the front wall of the club that said, "The Clash." Band members including Mick Jones and the late Joe Strummer were up on the roof as well and when they started yelling down to people in the street the crowd went nuts. Since the band had a total of seventeen New York dates they needed more opening acts and they hooked up a lot bands like Bad Brains, Dead Kennedy's, Lee 'Scratch' Perry, Grandmaster Flash, and the Sugar Hill Gang, and many others. I went to every single date during the New York run and every show was amazing.

There were other great shows at places like the Peppermint Lounge, The Palladium, Irving Plaza, The Mudd Club, Max's Kansas City, CBGB's, Trudy Heller's Playroom (I saw one of the Beastie Boys' first shows there opening for the Bad Brains), Danceteria, The Ritz, Great Gildersleeves, and the list went on and on. I remember at a Black Flag show I was sent flying across the dance floor by none other than the late John Belushi, who was a huge punk/hardcore fan and was at a lot of the early shows. John was a big dude and when he slammed his way across the dance floor you'd just see bodies going airborne. It was pretty funny to see these little punk dudes try to slam into him because they'd just bounce off his large frame.

Do you remember the band, Adam and the Ants? They were corny, weird fuckers, who played cheesy new wave and their fans tried to look like the douche-bag lead singer, Adam Ant, with war paint on his face and weird clothes. They even danced weird. Black Flag's fans were some of the craziest fuckers around and a war developed between the two clans. Well, I wouldn't exactly call it a war it was pretty one-sided. If you saw some "Ants," as we called them, you'd stomp them out. I had this shirt with the logo from Black Flag bug-spray that said, "Black Flag Kills Ants on Contact." John Belushi came up to me that night at the Black Flag show and said he liked the shirt, so I told him where I bought it. A short time later I remember seeing a photo of him in some magazine wearing that same shirt.

New York was the place to be back then and every touring band from Canada's DOA to the West Coast's Angry Samoans, Dead Kennedys (amazing show at Bonds with Bad Brains) and Fear, as well as the onslaught of great bands from D.C., made their way to the Big Apple. New York was the musical testing ground as Frank Sinatra himself sang, "If I can make it here…" You weren't shit unless you could come here and win over a tough New York crowd. The other cool thing was unlike these days, you actually had to be talented to be in a band. Not everyone with a guitar and a rock-n-roll dream was in one. There were people called audience members and they actually came to shows because they enjoyed them and not just to hand out flyers for their band. I believe three things pretty much killed the music scene in NYC (which is on life-support as we speak). Number one - the total and complete over-saturation of horrible bands with members who heard somewhere that being in a band makes you cool. Yo, I got news for you: if you were a douche bag before you got in a band, chances are either you'll remain that way, or become an even bigger one. Number two - MTV. Why? Because instead of being original, bands just copy what's on hot rotation. Also, if people can sit on their ass and watch music videos all day, who the hell needs to go out to see a concert? And last but not least, Number three: Mayor Giuliani's Nazi task force which targeted the quality of life issues and shut down all the clubs to make way for the yuppies who moved into Manhattan. Rudy ran up our rents and started complaining away about the noise. The noise of the street and its culture is what made New York, New York. Gool-liani's Holocaust has left only few survivors in its wake. Not even CBGB's survived. There you have it folks, my opinion for what it's worth. Now if you don't mind, I'd like to bask in the sunshine of NYC's glory days.

At that same Black Flag show where Belushi knocked me on my ass, I reconnected with a bunch of my boys from D.C. It was cool to see those maniacs again and we really slammed the crap out of most of the people there. I was with Lisa as the fellas hit the dance floor. I noticed a few people from New York had finally caught on to the whole slamming thing. I skanked across the floor with my twenty pounds of chains, spikes and spurs. I was wreaking havoc on the others on the dance floor, when I was introduced to a sick son of a bitch from Kiev, Russia named "Kontra." His introduction was a punch that caught me right in the mouth.

Kontra earned a black belt in order to become a better fighter on the mean streets of Russia. His fighting stories followed him all the way to America and he was given the nickname, "Karate Man," by his Russian comrades out in Brighton Beach, Brooklyn. As I wiped the blood from my mouth in the pit, I felt retribution was in order. On the very next song I took him out with a very precise, feet first stage dive. After the show I pointed at Kontra and asked Lisa who that guy was to which she replied, "That's Crazy James." I actually liked the fucker and we became best friends from that moment on.

Although I was living in NYC, I really didn't have an official place to live. Sometimes I stayed with Lisa, sometimes I stayed with Kontra at his parents' house and sometimes wherever. I think Lisa wanted me as a boyfriend, but I was just too damn wild to tame and the wishy-washy girlfriend stuff just wasn't in the cards for me. She got sick of me showing up just to crash at her apartment, now located in Midtown Manhattan. We pretty much broke up any relationship there was, but remained good friends. I remember she tried to bleach her hair blonde and it came out this fluorescent yellow tennis ball color, so I nicknamed her "TBH" which stood for "Tennis Ball Head," which pissed her off. Years later when Lisa would see me with her friends she'd introduce me as the only boy she ever loved. Lisa, wherever you are, I love you, too, for everything you did for me. Thanks.

Kontra and I hung out just about every day and I would go sit in on rehearsals with his band, "The Crypt-Crashers." He also owned this deli in the heart of Bensonhurst, the land of the Guidos, and he caught shit every day for the way he looked. There was one asshole in particular who was a real idiot we referred to as "Tommy Two-Fares." He got this nickname because, plain and simple, "Eye-talians" who lived so far out of Manhattan that they had to pay two fares (bus and a train) to get into Manhattan, were usually a little short on scruples. It was 1981 and this fucker still had on Jordache jeans and the rest of the played-out '70's Guido disco gear. Whenever I stayed at Kontra's house I would go to the deli and help him in exchange for food. But his constant complaint was that I was always eating way more than I was working.

Kontra and I met two hot Canadian girls and they had a nice hotel room, so we hung out with them for a couple of days. The girl I was with was named Margo. She was into S&M and if I wasn't hitting her hard enough when we had sex she'd bite me and scream, "Come on, hit me harder you fuckin' pussy! Kick my ass!" Well, what guy wouldn't like that said to him by his chick? Relax feminists. It's a joke. The other girl, Kim (RIP), who Kontra was with, was shy and quiet. I didn't get the friendship between the two girls because they were like oil and water. One night we hung out on the LES with them and my brother E, who had surprisingly become rather straight-laced while on leave from the Navy. He told me that he brought some of his Navy buddies from his ship up to New York and promised them one thing - girls, girls and more girls. To a bunch of horny sailors who were just underwater on a submarine for six months, that's all you had to say and they were there. E took them out to a resort on Long Island's Fire Island for some serious woman hunting. Although E had never been there, he heard there were a lot of very drunk, bikini-clad girls running around ripping each other's tops off and humping anything with a pulse.

Now to get to Fire Island you have to take a ferry from Long Island and once you pick the side of the island you want to be on you're pretty much stuck there if you miss the last ferry back. The four of them checked into the hotel and E said the guy at the desk was looking at them funny. The other three said E was just fucked up off the weed they had just smoked and they brushed it off. They got to the room and started the party off by doing some more drinking and smoking. How lucky they were they thought; four Squids stranded on an island full of beautiful woman for the weekend. Sounds just like a romance novel, don't it? As they laid out their clothes for the evening one of the Squids looked around the room at the decor and noticed an uncomfortable amount of paintings on the wall of half-naked, muscular men. No biggie, guess it's the Greek god theme. E went into the bathroom to take a shower and as he pulled the shower curtain open, stepped in and closed the curtain, something scared the shit out of him. No, it wasn't Norman Bates from the movie, Psycho standing outside the shower, dressed in drag, holding a large kitchen knife. It was an enormous, penis-shaped soap dispenser and when you pumped the balls, the soap ejaculated out of the tip of the penis. He leapt out of the shower, threw a towel on and ran back into the room. "Yo, this is a fag..." before his buddies cut him off. "We know," they said, in unison as his boys flipped through the TV channels that played nothing but gay pornos.

No problem they thought, let's get the fuck out of here and get another hotel room. They made a run for it and as they walked down the road with their bags E said it was like a scene from Sodom and Gomorrah; naked dudes were having sex in the bushes, naked dudes were having sex on the beach, naked dudes were having sex on top of cars, naked dudes... well, you get the point. E asked someone where the uhhh...'Straight Area' was and while the guy sized-up my brothers package he said, "Honey, I hope you can swim, 'cause it ain't on this side of the island, sugar, and the last ferry out of The Pines just left." They got down to the pier and it was true. They had missed the last boat. They were stuck. They slept on the beach and in the morning went to a cafe to get something to eat where they talked very loud and macho-like about their girlfriends, football and car racing. When they did finally touch down back on the mainland, they got on their hands and knees, kissed the ground and vowed never to tell anyone on their ship about what happened. If motherfuckers even thought your ass was gay in the old Navy you would get keelhauled. The others decided to take their chances without E as their tour guide for the rest of their stay in New York. So, E figured he'd come down and hang out with me for a bit.

He took us out for drinks that night and paid for everything just like a big brother should. While we were bar hopping Margo found this piece of garden hose and she kept whacking E really hard with it. He kept telling her to chill out and looked at me like, "John what the fuck is up with this bitch?" He got a little weirded-out when I told him to beat the shit out of her because she was into S&M and liked it. After an hour of this shit E finally snapped, grabbed the hose from her and beat the living shit out of her with it. She loved every minute of it and when it was over she whispered in my ear that she had an orgasm. Around sunrise E called it a night, gave me a $100 and split. We used the money to buy Tuinals and more booze, before we went back to their hotel room.

Kontra passed out right away and we started drawing on his face with a magic marker. Then being the fucked-up, stoned assholes we were, Margo suggested that we shave Kontra's eyebrows off and we agreed. Kontra was already one of the weirdest looking fuckers, but when Margo shaved them shits off he looked like an alien. We were dying of laughter for about an hour before we passed out. We woke up the next morning and were sitting and talking to Kontra with his shaved eyebrows and magic marker covering his face. We did our best not to burst out laughing. Kontra said we had to get goin' out to Brooklyn to open the deli. He went into the bathroom to take a piss and as he flushed the toilet, he turned on the water to wash his hands. We waited and then we heard a blood-boiling scream better than any scream queen in a horror flick. He rushed out, "What the fuck! Who the fuck did this?" He was pissed. "How the fuck can I go to the deli like this?" I knew what he meant and I stopped laughing, but Margo kept laughing hysterically.

Kontra dragged her by the hair to the bathroom and screamed, "Its funny, bitch? You think it's funny? You like pain?" He pulled her face down to the sink and punched her. I grabbed Kontra and chilled him out, but he was right to go nuts. He was in a load of shit. His parents were going to flip when they saw him and we argued all the way to the deli. We bought an eyebrow pencil and painted eyebrows on him for the first couple of days. When he finally calmed down, he even laughed about it. He said, "Fuck it," and started drawing big K's, for Kontra, and other designs all over his face. As a result, no one came near the store and Kontra had to take some time off work. His mom had to be there full-time and she was so pissed that she threw him out of the house.

I frequently ran into Harley and we would hang out at his mom's tiny, little hippie apartment on 12th Street off Avenue A. The first time I went over there we had to make our way through the gauntlet of Spanish thugs who held the block down. When we entered his building we passed this bugged-out looking dude in the hallway who said "Hello," to Harley. After the guy walked out Harley told me the guy was Allen Ginsburg, some famous American Beat Generation poet who lived above him. Now, usually when you go to a friend's house their mom hops into the kitchen and whips up some snacks. Since I was homeless and hungry at the time, I was naturally looking forward to a sandwich or something. But all Harleys' mom did was sit in her bed, read her book, smoke weed, and drink wine. Mrs. Cunningham from Happy Days she wasn't, but she was cool and I liked her.

Harley actually ate less than me on a daily basis and he lived at home. So since my mom's refrigerator was always full, I took him out to Queens one day when she was at work and conned the old landlady into letting me in. I told the landlady I was on leave from the Navy for the weekend and wanted to surprise my mom. Oh, she'd be surprised. I cooked everything in the refrigerator and left the dishes for her to clean. The other place Harley and I went to was a recording studio where he played me some of the tracks for his solo project. Those tracks would later become some of the music for the Cro-Mags' album, The Age of Quarrel.

When I wasn't hanging out with Harley or Kontra, I'd be over at 171A with H.R., Jay Dublee and the rest of the Bad Brains who lived there. Late at night I would get to watch the Bad Brains jam and write some of the songs that appeared on their legendary, self-titled cassette-only debut. H.R. told me to stop eating meat and 'Ital Up' as he put it. I still remember the first time he took me to Angelica Kitchen when it was on St. Mark's Place. He ordered this dish for me called a "Dragon Bowl" and I had a 'what the fuck is this shit' look on my face as they brought a bowl of brown rice seaweed, greens, tofu and sprouts. I ate very little of it, said a quick goodbye to H.R., before running around the corner and woofing down a burger or two at Mickey D's. But when he took me to places like Vegetarian Paradise on Bowery and Canal, a Chinese veggie spot that made all kinds of fake meat, or the Caldron on 6th Street and Second Avenue and ordered me a veggie turnover, I started thinking this veggie crap ain't so bad. Besides, H.R. was paying and that was a definite plus, too.

At that point I remember feeling like I was being pulled between two worlds. One world involved me still doing drugs, drinking, fighting, sleeping with as many girls as I could and eating an occasional rotten, green meatball. In the other world I associated with conscious individuals, talked philosophy, drank vegetable juices, avoided casual sex and tried to walk the Earth as Rasta says, "A Prince of Peace." But conflict is what makes life exciting, isn't it? My two worlds were in direct conflict with each other and on a hot summer night outside of 171A, they were sent on a collision course.

I can't remember who was playing at 171A that night, but I do remember that it was packed with about seventy-five, or so, punk rockers. I was talking to Jay Dublee and in very high spirits. Then someone gave me a Quaalude and I started drinking a little bit. When I got loaded I was never the sloppy-type drunk. Instead, drinking did to me what it did to my father… it made me extremely violent. If I was hanging out with Kontra and we knew some shit was about to go down one of us would say, "S.O.A." In other words, be in a "state of alert." It was a code word so we would know to watch each other's backs. Kontra wasn't with me that night and if he was there I think things would have turned out a lot differently. Inside 171 were four Puerto Ricans and they were fucking with everyone while the band was playing. The leader of the group was this stocky, crazy-looking son of a bitch. He walked up to people who were watching the band and poked them with this big knife, while his amigos bitch-slapped people. I asked Jay Dubs who these dudes were and why no one was kicking their asses. He said everyone was afraid of them because they were from a gang called "The Hitmen."

The Hitmen hung out on 11th Street where they had their dope spot (one of the highest grossing heroin spots in the U.S. back in the late-'70s and early-'80s) and since 171A was right there, they would come in from time to time and fuck with everyone. I was looking around and surprised to see that no one was fighting these guys. I wondered where their balls were? If these guys did that kind of shit to the punks at Max's, or to some of the D.C. crew I hung out with, somebody would have been guaranteed a trip to the hospital. I told Jay Dubs we should jump these guys and fuck them up. He asked me to be cool and out of respect for him I was, but that was before the stocky dude walked over and poked me in the stomach with his knife.

I looked him dead in the eyes and told him that if he did it again I was going to cut his fuckin' balls off with that knife. Big boy was a little drunk and since the band was so loud, I guess he didn't hear me. After the band was done and everyone emptied onto the sidewalk, he came up to me and went to poke me, again. I moved out of the way, stepped in and cracked him with a solid right hand to the jaw, which sent him to the ground. He looked shocked as I got on top of him, grabbed him by the hair and bashed his head off the concrete, knocking him out. I got up and the punks were stunned. There was that moment of dead silence, which was broken by his three friends yelling at me in Spanish and charging with their knives raised. I immediately took off my heavy chain belt and lashed all three of them. This caused them to pause briefly like, "Oh shit! White boy got game." They charged again and I ran around the street, swinging my chain each time they lunged forward.

A few days earlier I got in a bar fight and broke two fingers on the hand that I was holding the chain with. As I swung the chain, I lost it. Now, you'd think at that point as I dodged around the middle of Avenue A narrowly avoiding getting stabbed a dozen or so times, that one of these so-called punk rockers would come to my aid, right? Shit. Not only did they not help me, but when the stocky dude woke up from his beating it was now four guys against me. As I ran out of O.J. Simpson moves, the punk rock chumps standing in the doorway of 171A tried to close the door on me as I rushed to get inside. I put my foot in the door and was yelling at them to let me in but they were trying to leave me for dead. Nice guys, huh? Finally with a rush of adrenaline, I pushed through a small opening in the door and just as I did, one of my Spanish homeboys reached in and plunged a knife into my left shoulder. The punks inside locked the door and, you better believe, as I sat on the couch with my shoulder bleeding I told off the cowards who tried to lock me out. They had nothing to say. I shook my head in disgust and waited a couple of hours to make my way out of the neighborhood and up to Lisa's apartment in Midtown.

Lisa cleaned out the stab wound. Luckily only the tip of the knife went into my shoulder. The wound wasn't that wide, but it was deep and I did develop a terrible infection because of it. I couldn't move my arm for a week and word got back to me that the Hitmen were "Going to kill that fuckin' white boy." I heard that they waited for me every night outside the studio and flashed guns, knives and bats. For me it was mission accomplished, because they never came inside the studio again. It sucked though, because no one wanted to hang out with me for obvious reasons. Even Harley's mom forbid him to be around me, because she said I'd be dead in a few weeks and she didn't want her little boy suffering a similar fate. I couldn't go past First Avenue and I guess the saying I heard back in my drug mule days with Mikey Debris and Canito was ringing true except with a new twist... if I went to 'A' I wasn't just adventurous, I was dead. I missed all the shows at 171 and the other punk club called A-7 (located on Avenue A & 7th Street). But worst of all, I couldn't hang out with the Brains, Jay Dubs, or anyone. The only person who would hang out with me was Kontra because that fucker had my back to the death. He couldn't go home because of the eyebrow shaving and deli thing, and I was left without a place to crash. Since we were both fucked, we decided to fix up this apartment and squat in an abandoned building at Rivington and Eldridge streets. That's when we ran into the other local drug gang, the notorious, Allen Street Boys.

All we knew about the ASBs was that they recently had a war with the Ghost Shadows, who were an Asian-based, Chinatown gang. There was a memorial mural on the wall of one of the project houses on Allen and Stanton streets, RIPing some of their homies who died in the shoot out. We didn't know that for the entire four days we busted our asses working away in that apartment, which literally had three feet of dirt in it, we were being watched. We carried down broken furniture, mattresses, and three or four broken stoves. Then garbage bag after garbage bag full of dirt and debris filling close to thirty bags. By the time we swept up, filled the last bag and mopped it was dark out. We looked around at our dope, spacious apartment and gave each other a celebratory high-five for a job well done. As I literally took down that last tiny bag of garbage, put it curbside and headed back into the building two figures stepped up behind me. One put a shotgun to my head and the other jammed a pistol into my back. All they said was, "Thanks for cleaning up for the Allen Street Boys, punyetta. Now you and your boy get the fuck out." I had no problem with that and assured them that I couldn't think of a finer couple of lads I would like to have our apartment than them.

They marched me up the stairs and stood on each side of the doorway, hiding in the dark, unlit hallway. I banged on the door that Kontra had dead-bolted from inside and he opened it. "Kontra," I said. "We gotta get outta of the apartment now." He stood in the doorway, looked at me like I was crazy and rambled in that thick Russian accent, "What? What are you talkin' about? Why? Why do we have to have get out?" My two friends stepped out from the shadows and the dude with the shotgun, pumped it, jammed it under Kontra's chin and said, "You wanna know why motherfucker? This is why bitch! This is why!" They could have shot us dead right there and we knew it. We didn't even get our clothes. We just bolted and went over to Second Avenue to get a drink and calm down. We found out later that they turned our apartment into a drug spot where you put the money through a hole in the door and the drugs pop out.

Once again, I found myself with no money and no place to live. As for Kontra he was back at his mom's in Brighton Beach and I didn't get the invite. I had to sleep on park benches, trains, rooftops or wherever I could. It sucked not being able to go to Avenue A and hang out. After a month had passed, I'd had enough. It was time to go down there and face these dudes who were keeping me out of my neighborhood.

When I walked past First Avenue I had a sick feeling in my stomach and I was practically ready to puke. I didn't know what to expect and as I headed north on Avenue A toward 11th Street the feeling intensified. I tried to psyche myself up and as I did one half of my conflicted conscious chimed in, "Hey, it's like fighting the bullies back in school, dude. You might get your ass kicked, but at least they knew you fought back." Then my other half kicked in and the battle was on. "Turn around, man. What do you have to prove? You already fought the fuckers and kicked their asses for the most part, and maybe they're not going to just beat you up. Maybe they really are going to kill you. Is it worth it?" A block-and-a-half away, I froze in my tracks on 9th Street and Avenue A, wrestling with the decision I had to make. I came this far, do I turn around and head out of the neighborhood and give it more time to chill out? Or do I walk into the unknown and deal with everything right here, right now? I ran over all the possible scenarios in my head and made my decision.

I continued north and sure enough right there on the corner of Avenue A and 11th Street stood the stocky dude I punched at 171 with a bunch of his friends. I walked right up, stood in the middle of them and said, "Here I am. What's up?" I think I really surprised him and then he informed his crew that I was the blanco maricón he was looking for before they surrounded me. Dr. Know (Gary Miller) and Darryl (Jenifer) from the Bad Brains came outside of 171 and jumped right into the middle of everything, "Yo, everybody chill out!" Doc yelled. He and Darryl pulled the dude off to the side and explained to him that I was just sticking up for my friends and that they would have done the same shit if the shoe was on the other foot. After Doc talked to him he walked over to me, stuck out his hand, smiled and said, "I like you. You got balls. I'm Crazy Eddie." I was back on the scene and just as a footnote; Crazy Eddie and I are still friends. Whenever I see him during one of his short stints out of prison, he tells all the younger Spanish kids he's with, "This was the only motherfuckin' white boy I ever met down here with heart."

Jay Dub's let me move into 171A and I became Earl Hudson's drum tech. Since I wasn't afraid to fight dudes with knives I was also doubling as security during the Bad Brains' East Coast shows. During the '70s I'd seen the greatest rock bands of the time: Led Zeppelin, Black Sabbath, the Who, Aerosmith and a host of others, but I have NEVER seen a band that could come close to the Bad Brains on stage, especially during those early days. Their sheer physical and spiritual power was so amazing that it made your hair stand on end and gave you goose bumps. Night after night, every show was better than the previous one. On tour, the Bad Brains, Jay Dubs and I were all developing a close bond and became a team. For all my work with the Brains, I never accepted a dime for my drum tech, roadie or security services. All I needed was a place to sleep and some food and I was happy. The Brains had fans that would have followed them to the ends of the Earth because we believed in what they were doing. I was such a big fan that by the third or fourth song, you would catch me doing the sickest stage dives into the crowd. For the rest of the show I'd be on the dance floor and not worrying about Earl's drums, which is why they later had to hire another roadie named Alvin.

I went out on those first few gigs eating burgers and came back a strict vegetarian, and it wasn't because anyone was preaching to me. It was because I saw that H.R. had more strength, vitality and endurance than any burger eater I'd ever seen on stage. I remember thinking, "This dude's tapped into something with this veggie shit." I gave up meat, alcohol, drugs (weed wasn't a drug to the Rasta's and I was cool with that) and even sex for a little while. We made a stop in D.C., for a show and I hung out for about a week. I got a job stocking shelves at a health food store called "Fields of Plenty" through a dude named Major. He was a friend of the Bad Brains and I remember complaining to him that somebody needed to invent some health food with taste. Major, who just came back from picking up his lunch, had a Styrofoam food container in his hand. He opened it up and said, "Try this. I got it from the Hare Krsna restaurant."

I never saw food that looked like that. It was colorful and it smelled good, too. He let me try a vegetable dish (subji) and some halvah (a sweet), which blew me away. These people got it down and I asked him if he was sure it's the same guys I used to make fun of dancing around in orange bed sheets every Saturday night on Wisconsin Avenue. He assured me they were one and the same, and that according to their philosophy anyone who eats this food gets spiritually uplifted. He didn't have to sell me on that because the taste alone did it for me. Every day Major would come back, set his container down in the office and since I wanted as much 'spiritual advancement' as I could possibly get, I would sneak some puri, some veggies and a chunk of halvah. I'd devour it while hiding under a grain bin somewhere. After a week he walked up with my check and said, "Alright fucker, now you can stop stealing my food and go buy your own." I did and it was so good I ate the entire meal in about thirty seconds.

At the Brains' gigs the spiritual conversations backstage grew deeper and the shows were more meaningful because H.R. wasn't just content letting you get caught up in the moment of the music. He always reminded you while he was doing his thing on stage that it was all about the "Spiritual Revolution" and that alone was what gave their music it's power. He always gave praises to The Most High and, as I said, when you glorified him about being the best front man that ever lived, which he was hands down, he would say, "It's just Jah brethren." That's the problem with 99.9 percent of the music out there today. It's devoid of any kind of spiritual message or philosophy and full of false ego. That's why the shelf life of bands is so short. If you tap into the spiritual powerhouse that has unlimited reserves and stay humble about your ability, your music will stand the test of time and live forever. Bob Marley is a prime example.

When we returned to New York after the tour was over, H.R. and I started an organization called the "United Freedom Fighters," or U.F.F. We had a few meetings, which included the late singer of Reagan Youth, Dave Insurgent, and a bunch of others dudes who played in bands. We sat around and talked about God, philosophy and revolution against the Babylon system. To H.R., the youth were everything. As Bob Marley said in one of his songs, "The Babylon System is the vampire, sucking the blood of the children day by day." We talked about doing benefit concerts, taking trips to Africa, organizing martial arts classes and shutting down slaughterhouses and abortion clinics in the U.S. That is until the first joint was rolled. Then the meetings turned into a free for all and lost focus. That's what intoxication does... it destroys motivation and austerity. Austerity means deliberately undertaking some hardship to achieve a higher result. You come up with great ideas, sure, but you have no follow through. The U.F.F. lasted about as long as a dog crossing the FDR Drive during rush hour traffic.

I loved living at 171A Studio. It was this culturally happening spot where there was always music, weed and good vibes with good people. We were the misfits of society, each of us in our own way. We didn't fit in anywhere else and we were making our own family - a family of whites, blacks or whatevers. The only thing you had to do to be in the inner circle was hate everything Babylon stood for. There was unity between us and I felt like we had each other's backs until the end. The late Dave Rat (RIP) opened the Rat Cage Record store and later started his label in the basement of 171A, where he released the first records by the Beastie Boys and Agnostic Front. Dave was one strange cat, like so many others who passed through those studio doors on a daily basis. I met a lot of cool musicians and bands as well; Richard Hell and the Voidoids, Henry Rollins auditioned for Black Flag there, dozens of early punk bands from all over like Black Flag, the Angry Samoans, Circle Jerks and the Subhumans played there. More importantly I witnessed history in the making - the Bad Brains' late night recording sessions for an album that would become "The greatest punk/hardcore album of all time," as Adam Yauch from the Beastie Boys put it - The ROIR Album.

Those sessions were so magical you just felt something amazing was taking place. It was like God was present in that studio playing those songs and the Brains were just the mediums channeling it. I remember watching Jay Dubs work tirelessly night after night to pull those performances out of them. The sessions would go on for seven, eight, sometimes ten hours at a pop and many times the sun would be coming up before they ended. I still think no producer has ever come close to making the Bad Brains sound more like the Bad Brains than Dubs did on that first album. Not Ric Ocasek (former Cars lead singer who produced Rock For Light), Ron St. Germain (I Against I and Quickness) or Jimmy Quid, who produced the "Pay to Cum/Stay Close to Me" first single. They knew the Bad Brains were something very special and wanted to be involved, but they were no match for Dubs. That's why when you put the first Bad Brains record on it takes you back to the early days when you just knew you were witnessing the greatest band to ever walk the face of the Earth.

After their sessions, H.R. and I would make our way to this little bakery on First Avenue between St. Mark's and 7th Street that made fresh whole wheat Italian bread. I remember the smell of the warm bread filling the air for blocks and blocks. The old guy who worked there would always leave the door open to cool the place down, but kept the sliding gate locked. He was a mean fucker, because when we banged on the gate to try and get him to sell us some bread, he screamed at us to get lost. After seeing us night after night and witnessing H.R.'s sadhu-like humility he finally caved in, sold us some bread and actually became friendly with us. We would buy a couple of loaves, some bananas, avocados and peanut butter, then go back to the studio, make sandwiches, smoke some more, and Reason about life and God. By the time we crashed the sun was usually coming up. We would stand outside looking toward the East River and H.R. would hold his arms up toward the sky and yell, "Jah! Rasta Far I!"

A few of us hanging out started our own jam sessions. We played reggae, ska, punk and everyone took turns on different instruments. Since I was Earl's drum tech I would always hop behind the kit, but I sucked so bad I would get yanked off pretty quickly. H.R., who is Earl's brother, told me I had too much energy to be sitting down (I think he was just being nice) and that I should sing. I told him I didn't know how to sing and he convinced me I was a natural and to prove it he hooked me up with this 6'6" insane guitar player (insane meaning crazy, nuts, fuckin' loo-loo, not necessarily talented) named Bob.

Bob lived out on the Bad Brains farm in Herden, Maryland he stored his sound gear. One day Bob just disappeared and never returned (he was AWOL and the military got him). He got nabbed by the cops a pair of sunglasses. During that time the Brains got evicted and since they want to just leave Bob's gear in the house, they took it with them when they moved to New York. Bob got out of the brig and found out the Brains were in New York with his shit, so what does he do? He stole a moped, jumped on I-95 and rode all the way from D.C. in a torrential rainstorm, before showing up at the Bad Brains front door in New York City ten hours later. Shit, I would have loved to see his big ass on that tiny, little fuckin' moped getting soaked, while cars were flying by him on 95 North.

Bob's playing ability (or lack there of) really wasn't all that great. He would stand there towering over me, playing the same note, over and over and over, as fast as he could for one minute. Then he would turn to me and say, "You got some words for that? You got some words? C'mon! Write some words and just scream in the mic?" We had a couple of sessions where I didn't even sing a single word and then finally, the first time I let loose it felt great. I was letting out years of pent-up aggression and it seemed to come pretty naturally. Unfortunately, the band with Bob never materialized because some time later he was found murdered in his Staten Island apartment. I still wanted to thank him for dragging those first words out of my mouth at 171A. Rest in Peace, Bob.

At this point, I must thank one person for instilling the confidence in me that I could sing. If not for H.R. believing in me, life would have been a lot different. Up until that point I was a spectator just standing on the sidelines listening to music. I always felt drawn to it like I should be more involved in it for some reason. Over the years, music was the only relief I had for all the pain in my life. It was a portal to other worlds, a lifeline to connect with other people's emotions and feelings at a time when I held so much inside. It was a release and no matter what I was going through as long as I could hear some music, it made all the shit bearable. As far back as I can remember I would dance around with my aunt and my mom with their beehive hairdos, listening to Motown 45's on their little record player amidst the chaos and crap with my dad. It made me feel like everything was okay and I was safe. I would sit outside Tommy

Sheridans' door for hours while he played Cream's "Sunshine of your Love" over and over and over again. I was hypnotized by the sound of his guitar and the words of Eric Clapton as he played along to the record. If it wasn't for my little AM radio under the blanket at the Valentis' I wouldn't have made it through that hell either. From my Garden City David Bowie and Parliament days, to the Madison Square Garden concerts of Rockaway's beat acid trade, music was my savior. It helped me get through some of the toughest times in my life and there's no way on Earth I can ever repay H.R. for putting me in the game, except to say thank you from the deepest regions of my heart, brother. I was no longer just a spectator, I was a singer and I was on a mission to find a band, but not just any band. This band had to be a vehicle for what I had to say and believe me, I had a lot to say.

Late in the summer of '81 I started hanging out with Harley again. He spent a lot of time at 171A because he was good friends with the Bad Brains, since he shared the stage with them playing in the Stimulators. I remember Harley and Darryl would wrestle around in the studio for hours like big brothers. Darryl was an amazing bass player and Harley learned to attack his instrument the same way - with a vengeance. Right around that time is when Harley put together the first Cro-Mags line-up at 171 with him on bass, the late Dave Hahn (Bad Brains manager and former production coordinator) on drums, Dave Stein (who played in a band Even Worse) on guitar, and me on vocals. We started writing songs and we used some of Harley's solo stuff, but the project was doomed to fail since a few months later Dave H. announced he was going into drug rehab and Dave S. said he was off to college. Harley wanted to play this show at the Peppermint Lounge as a goof under the name "The Disco Smoothies," but I was way too serious about my shit and turned down his offer. Harley doesn't like to mention the actual facts because he loves to claim that I wasn't the first singer. Instead, he got this dude John Berry (who was in the Beastie Boys when they were a NYC hardcore band and prior to the addition of Adam Horovitz to the line up) to sing and they did their Disco Smoothies show. It seemed the REAL Cro-Mag line-up would be put on the back burner for a while.

One little funny tidbit I remember about 171 Studio was we would smoke in the control room, which was right by the front door. There was an exhaust fan that sucked the smoke from the room and blew it out onto the street. The pipe was about eight feet off the ground and when you passed by 171 on the sidewalk there was always a thick cloud of weed smoke emanating from that pipe like something straight out of a Cheech and Chong movie. People's noses would twitch (cops especially) and they would stop dead in their tracks, look around and try to figure out where the hell it was coming from. Occasionally we would even get some of the Spanish guys from the neighborhood knocking on our door going, "Yo mira, that shit smells good. Can I get some, mang?"

Right next door to 171 was a joint called, The Crow's Rest, an after hours gambling/get high spot, especially designed for pimps and playas, run by this big, fat pimp from Harlem named, Brownie. When the club changed owners in the late-'80s and '90s and became a live music venue, it was named Brownie's. Brownie was a bug out. He loved his coke and liquor and when he pulled up in a purple convertible Cadillac at 3 a.m. with a pimp hat and bitches in tow, you knew you weren't getting any sleep in 171. At that point, the party was just getting started for him and the only thing that separated The Crow's Rest from us in the studio was a thin plaster wall. They blasted music, had a lot of fights over gambling issues and on occasion fired off a few shots at each other.

At that point I was a living, breathing, eating vacuum for anything related to spirituality. I was moved by H.R.'s revolutionary spirit and devotion to God, but something was missing. That something was a philosophical understanding as to why he did the things he did on his path. Religion without philosophy is fanaticism and when I would ask questions about certain matters like reincarnation, or how the soul fell into the material world in the first place I would get an answer like, "Don't worry about all that. It's just Jah ya know." Well, being a punk rocker meant questioning authority even if it is the "Higher Authority," and that's where Jay Dubs came in. Jay gave me books on philosophy like George Gurdjieff's The Fourth Way or Ram Dass's Be Here Now. I read Krishnamurti's literature on Zen Buddhism, The Autobiography of a Yogi by Paramahamsa Yoganada, and on and on. If it pertained to philosophy I read it. As soon as I would finish a book, Jay would give me another one. He was my transcendental librarian and he also answered any questions I had and God knows, I had a lot.

Jay Dubs also schooled me on health and nutrition. He turned me on to raw foods and I attended seminars and meetings, which were fascinating. A whole new world was opening up and I had such a great feeling inside, because I knew karmically that I was in the right place. I took it as further evidence that I was closing in on something, but I didn't know what. One thing I did realize though, there was a reason

I went through all the trials and tribulations in my life. Everything thus far brought me to the point I was at and I knew it. Sometimes only when we suffer do we look for truth. And although it's no fun when we're going through it, in retrospect, a lot of the stuff in my life turned out to be a blessing in disguise.

I owe a lot to Jay Dubs. He is one of the most humble people I've ever met in my life. He had the patience of a saint and would give you his last organic orange if you asked him. Dubs lived the life; he wasn't a talker and he sure as hell wasn't a hypocrite. He wouldn't preach to people, he would only give you answers to your questions if you asked for them. He let me and the Bad Brains live in his studio and never asked us for a dime. He roadied, drove, did sound, fed you, shared his weed with you and was just the best friend you could ever have. If I did something that was off, he wouldn't criticize it, he would just point out that there was another way, a way in fact, that was the right way. Dubs never dealt with right and wrongs. He wasn't caught up in dualities, but just dealt with alternatives. He was a real punk rocker because he really made you question everything.

I got so much knowledge from Dubs but, when I asked him where God fit in all of this philosophy stuff, he would say we're all God and that once we get out of the illusion we realize it. "Wait a minute," I said. "If we're all God as you say we are and we fell into illusion, that would make illusion stronger than God because it's covered us." Hmmm. The other problem I found with the books I read was there was no mention of the spiritual world, or of God having any personality. If I had personality how could someone who I'm supposed to be so attracted to have no personality? I mean c'mon. Have you ever had to hang out with a person with no personality? Ain't fun, is it? Philosophy without religion or devotion is mental speculation. What I found as my search went on was that each of the above mentioned authors had a different take on things. They all speculated and as human beings we have four defects: we are illusioned; we have the tendency to cheat; we have imperfect senses; and we make mistakes. So how can any philosophy we concoct be perfect?

I hadn't found any path yet which contained the perfect combination of philosophy and devotion. What I did was take what I learned about Rasta Far I for it's devotional qualities and combined that with the knowledge I was getting from the philosophy books I read. That would have to do for now and what I noticed about being on the scene back then was that as soon as you became a "Seeker of the Truth" engrossed in talks of a higher nature, you became an outsider. As Bob Marley himself said, "Many people will fight you down, when you see Jah Light." Everyone on the scene turned their backs on me. Even Kontra didn't want to hang out anymore. He was happily dating my ex, Lisa and didn't want to hear about all this "spiritual mumbo-jumbo bullshit," as he called it. All the punks seemed content to just complain about life and not do a damn thing to change it.

What became clear to me early on was that punk failed in its mission of revolution for one reason; it offered no solutions. Punk said in essence, "Okay everything's fucked up." But my question was, "Okay what now? What's the solution? How do we fix it?" And I don't mean like the prisoner making his prison cell nicer. In other words, don't try to talk politics, replacing one - ism with another. I mean how do we get out of the prison? That's the real revolution. A revolution on the highest level. The government doesn't want you sitting around pondering this kind of stuff because if you stopped to think, "Hey man, I'm gonna die one day. What's the use of all this materialistic bullshit if it's done at the time of death? I need to get some info on what's coming around the next corner, after this body is finished." See, if that happened, the machine would break down. That's why in America especially, there's so much crap to distract us from the real goal of life, which is the revolution against the cruel prison keepers and ultimately our eventual escapes. Their tools of the trade - sex, drugs, lame rock-n-roll, alcohol, sporting events, cars, TV, newspapers, bling and the other bullshit they stuff down our throats on a daily basis. I love the line on "Freedom" from Rage Against the Machine's first album, "What does the billboard say come and play come and play, forget about the movement." That's the government's job - keep you numb and dumb to what's really going on and cloud up your mind with useless crap, intoxicants and poisonous food. You think them fuckers couldn't get the drugs off the streets of America if they really wanted to? You don't think they know how poisonous fast food is? C'mon people wake up.

And God help you if you're anyone with a revolutionary message. Come to think of it, a lot of people have died sudden deaths haven't they? Bob Marley, John Lennon, Malcolm X, Martin Luther King. Even Srila Prabhupada himself was quoted as saying, "If THEY knew what I came here to do they would have killed me." That's why this battle can't be fought materially. The only answer to solve the world's problems is to replace material solutions with spiritual ones and when I refer to spirituality I'm not talking about these dogmatic religious processes that have the masses brainwashed into thinking that their God's better than the next guy's and if they don't agree, we'll just kill off the competition. Real spirituality has nothing to do with that. Religion is faith and faith can change. One day you can be Hindu and the next Catholic, Muslim, or whatever. One thing that never changes is our Sanatana Dharma, or eternal occupation, and that occupation is service. Just as the hand is part and parcel of the body and is meant to serve the body, we are part and parcel of the Supreme Being and as such you are meant to serve that Supreme Being.

If you read any of Srila Prabhupada's books you'll find out that what's contained in their pages is revolutionary, because the real revolution is all about throwing up the middle finger to this fucked up way of life and getting back to our original, blissful spiritual nature. The real issue at hand is that we're caught in samsara, which in Sanskrit means the cycle of repeated birth and death, and if we are on a screwed up journey what we need is the map to get on the right road. That's what the Vedas from India are. They are the road map to get us out of the cycle. I'm not preaching here. What I am doing is saying that if you're looking for a way out, or if you know there's more to life than meets the eye, check it out and see for yourselves. If now on the other hand you're asleep at the wheel and you think you're enjoying, don't let me stop you. But what you need to remember is that train called death is speeding down the track closing in on you at every passing second. Sooner or later, you're going to have a nasty head-on collision with it as Krsna Himself says in the Bhagavad-Gita, "Time I am, the destroyer of worlds."

As my search for knowledge and truth deepened I would get the answers to my questions. Even as a little kid I knew life was about something bigger and something deeper. I wanted something more than just a normal life which basically involved going to high school, then college, finding a job, having a wife and kids and then death. My life was anything but normal and I constantly had this feeling as early as I can remember. I had to figure out the puzzle and answer questions like, who am I? Where am I from? And most importantly, where the hell was I going? Even from age nine when I saw a dead body, my first reaction as I looked at him in that coffin was, "What's the difference between the guy lying here and the guy I saw two days ago running around?" I constantly looked up to the heavens and asked God why I was being put through this hell. As I found more answers at 171A, I realized that things were happening exactly the way they were supposed to on this bumpy ride called life and it couldn't have been any other way.

Not all the punks on the scene were so dull spiritually. I met this really cool dude named Tomas from Spain. He was a real political-type and a thinker. We would get into some serious discussions about everything and one of our rituals was going down to St. Mark's to panhandle so we could get money, buy weed, smoke it, talk philosophy and meditate. Tomas had a Mohawk that was 100 percent natural. He didn't need to cut it that way, because he was suffering from Alopecia Areata, a disease where the hair on your entire body falls out. Bottom line, if God gives you a Mohawk, you know you're punk!

In November of '81, I was invited to my mom's house for Thanksgiving, but I didn't really want to go because I still held a lot of resentment toward her. Tomas said we should go and I realized I had to learn to be more forgiving about the past in order to grow in the future. As we sat at the dinner table chatting away and about to say grace, my grandfather told Tomas to take his hat off. When he did, there was dead silence. Then my grandpa being the class clown he was yells out, "Holy shit, Pilgrims. It's the last of the friggin' Mohicans!" They couldn't stop laughing and neither could Tomas and I.

Tomas was very intelligent and had a really cool vibe. He was soft-spoken and very humble. He was squatting in this empty apartment on 10th Street between B and C, and offered to let me move in. Since 171 had no shower or kitchen facilities, I jumped at the opportunity. He said he didn't know how long we had until we would get evicted, but I figured what the hell, I'll stay here until the landlord comes knocking and then I'd figure out something else. What was really cool about staying with Tomas was we were both on the same path in life. We were searching. We talked philosophy for hours on end, went to yoga classes almost every day and spent our nights hanging out at 171 or going to gigs. I still remember our first yoga class at the Integral Yoga Institute on the West Side because I was sitting next to this old lady and every time she bent into a stretch she ripped the loudest fart, which broke my meditation and made me laugh my ass off. After class the instructor made an announcement that for the benefit of the others, it wasn't a good idea to eat before class and I said, "Yeah, especially when you got no BMC (bowel movement control)."

We even went out to Queens once to hear Krishnamurti speak, or at least that's what I thought was going to happen. All he did was walk into the room, sit down close his eyes and then every one else followed suit. I looked at Tomas like, "What the fuck is this?" After about forty minutes had passed the dude next to me, who was asleep with his head on my shoulder, started snoring. I so wanted to push him off, but I didn't. After an hour Krishnamurti opened his eyes and the dude up front rang this little bell signaling everyone else to break their meditation, or in other words, wake the fuck up. The guy whose drool now covered my shoulder looked at me and said, "Did you feel it?" I pointed down at my soaked shirt and said, "What? Your hot-ass, bad breath on my neck?"

This dude Krishnamurti had some racket going. He charged twenty bucks, never said one damn word and then sold a shit load of his books in the lobby. I truly felt like I just got hustled. It was like the more we kept looking, the more we found that these people posing themselves as spiritualists were full of shit. The sannyasis in the yoga centers, who are supposed to be in the renounced order of life, were having sex with their female disciples. The so-called philosopher gurus charged twenty plus dollars to hear them speak, or in Krishnamurti's case, sleep. It just seemed like everywhere we turned on our search we ran into snake-oil salesmen. We saw the most bizarre example of this from Michael Cesa on 10th Street who called himself "The Pope" (who was later known as the "Pope of Pot"). He ran a storefront called, "The Church of the Realized Fantasies," and get this ravers and club kids…he gave out hits of free ecstasy (which was still legal at the time) as the Blessed Sacrament during Mass. The Pope was a blatant homosexual and he would invite boys back to his church, get them high on X and have his way with them. Sounds a little like the Catholic Church, doesn't it?

It's said that this is the age of the cheaters and the cheated. If you want to cheat spiritually then you'll join a bunch of cheaters and the leader, who's the best cheater of all, will cheat you too. But, if you truly are searching for the truth you'll find it. Well, I was and so was Tomas. After all the meetings and seminars we went to, we knew our search had to go on. But in the meantime there was a punk rock revolution happening, and this time, this revolution was going to be televised.

It was Halloween '81 and Tomas and I were wondering what the hell we were going to do that night. That's when I ran into Ian MacKaye and some of my boys from D.C. They told me that, Fear was going to be on Saturday Night Live that evening and they could get me in if I showed up to NBC studio inside Rockefeller Center. I invited some of the New York punks and later that evening as we waited on line to get into the studio hallway, the scene was complete and total chaos. A few of the normal audience members were absolutely terrified as we screamed punk lyrics, slam danced and basically raised hell. Some NBC producer-types came out, saw what was going on and separated the two groups. They were led into the studio and allowed to take their seats as a small contingent that included me, Tomas, Ian MacKaye and a bunch of the D.C. posse, were taken backstage to the dressing room. When I walked in, John Belushi was hanging out and drinking with Lee Ving, the singer of Fear.

As it turns out, they sent those producer clowns to get us because Belushi wanted to meet everyone and make sure we really showed America what punk rock was all about. The way this whole thing went down (as I mentioned on MTV's news documentary, Social History of the Mosh Pit) was Lee was friends with Belushi and he convinced the SNL executive producer and creator Lorne Michaels to let Fear be a musical guest. Lee invited the D.C. punks, they invited me and I invited the NYC punks. Belushi was a really cool dude. He was like a ball of energy that could explode at any moment, kind of like that scene in Animal House where he stands up in the cafeteria and yells, "Food Fight!" I shook his hand and introduced myself, hoping to jog his memory by telling him I was the guy with the Black Flag Kills Ants On Contact shirt at their last New York show and how he sent me flying across the dance floor. He just laughed and said something like, "Yeah, man. I was really fuckin' wasted that night." We hung out with him for a little bit and assured them that this country was about to witness history in the making - their first slam dancing.

After about twenty minutes, the producer dude came and got us and led us and the forty or fifty other punks into another room, which was empty except for a piano and a few chairs. There was this window that faced the studio and you could see all the sets and the stage where Fear was about to play. The NBC dude told us that for the first song and the duration of the show we were to stay in this room. When Fear played their final song at the end of the show we would be led onto the set where we had to behave ourselves. Well, that did not sit well with us and as soon as he left the room we trashed it. We practically ripped every string out of that piano, broke chairs, walls, sinks in the bathroom and slam danced down the halls only taking a break to cram against the window and watch Fear play their first song. Then it was back to raising hell and after a while a guy came and locked the door to the room so we couldn't leave at all.

Finally, it was time. Our moment of glory was upon us. We were led down some stairs, then a hall and finally stood in front of a huge door that read: studio entrance. The door opened and the bright stage lights blinded me like one of those

UFO landing scenes from a movie. We were given some more instructions on how to behave by several very nervous NBC studio personnel. As we were led inside I thought to myself, " How fuckin' funny is this? I'm AWOL from the Navy and a wanted man, and here I am about to be on national TV."

As we walked onto the set, our chains, spurs and steel cap boots clanked away. We must have sounded eerie as hell to the straight-laced audience. Once they got a glimpse of us the audience collectively gasped and then some big, scary-looking punk rocker pointed at them and yelled, "You motherfuckers are gonna die!" This had them cowering in their seats and a few were so worried they even got up and left. We went to the front of the stage and waited anxiously for Fear to emerge as Belushi joined us. He looked pretty high and was slamming people around before the music even started playing. The stage was covered in dozens of pumpkins and at first I was like, "What's up with the pumpkins?" Than it hit me, "Oh, shit that's right. It's Halloween."

What's bugged-out though is I'm sure some of the audience members probably thought we were some kind of Halloween gag and were part of the show. Get it? Fear = scary punkers. Fear walked out on stage and grabbed their instruments and when they did we went nuts, screaming and yelling. People started slamming into each other, and everyone, including myself, looked for the cameras. Punks always talk shit about posers and this and that, but let me tell you, when a punk's got a camera rolling on him believe me, they know how to ham it up with the best of them. At that point actor Donald Pleasence, the host for the evening, came on and announced Fear and more importantly, warned the audience that this was no Halloween gag. I got a copy of the tape from Spit Stix, Fear's drummer and Pleasence's exact words were "They're really nice people ya know." Pleasence laughed and continued. "They uhhh…look very frightening, but they're really very nice…our Halloween guests. By the way tonight…look out for surprises. Ladies and gentlemen, Fear." With that Fear broke into "Beef Bologna" and I hit the stage, launching out over the crowd in perfect stage dive form.

The place went absolutely nuts as the dance floor exploded into complete and utter chaos. Some punks were running in the aisles and diving onto audience members sitting on the folding chairs. Those poor bastards ran for cover along with the NBC staffers as Belushi went wild, skanking across the dance floor and laying people out. The NBC cameras only shot what was happening on stage, but out on the dance floor a fight was brewing between the D.C. and New York punks. It left a couple of the D.C.'ers hurt (I believe one even suffered a broken nose) and by the time Fear played their last song, "New York's Alright...If You Like Saxophones," fistfights broke out all over the studio. I was neutral because I was cool with people from both camps. Besides, I was way too busy trying to get on camera to get caught up in dumb shit like that. NBC security people were trying to get us out of the studio and a few of them made the crucial mistake of coming out onto the dance floor. Not a good idea and towards the end of that song the fighting got worse. That's when Ian MacKaye grabbed the mic and yelled live on national TV, "Fuck New York! New York Sucks!"

Even Lee tried to cover that one up by saying, "Awe, he don't mean that," and Fear quickly went into, "Let's Have a War." Sure that'll help the situation Lee. NBC cut the show off the air as soon as Ian cursed (I believe that was the first time that ever happened) and they ran a tape of an Eddie Murphy skit, but back in the studio we were still going nuts. We now had ten security guys in NBC jackets trying to get us out of the studio and screaming that they were going to call the cops if we didn't leave. Since Fear was still playing, we weren't going anywhere.

As a way to defuse the situation, the head honcho of security came on stage, grabbed the mic and told us that the police were on their way and blah, blah, blah. It didn't matter, because Tomas picked up a pumpkin and threw it, hitting him in the head and knocking him down. That's when the pumpkin fight started. Pumpkins were flying everywhere. A camera was knocked over, monitors were smashed and mics were thrown. The fisticuffs died down and we were still laughing our asses off when the cops rushed in with riot gear. The D.C. and N.Y. punks took off running side-by-side with the cops in hot pursuit who were trying to take our head's off with their billy clubs. They chased us down the halls of Rockefeller Center and out into the NYC Halloween festivities where we easily blended into the crowds of ghouls and goblins walking the streets.

On the following Monday, the New York Post front page headline read: "SATURDAY NIGHT LIVE RIOT DESTROYS $250,000." SNL claimed in their book that it was a lot less, but I just think they didn't want to look like a bunch of schmucks for not seeing that disaster in the making. I mean c'mon guys, you let a band named Fear play on national TV on Halloween night and invited seventy-five or so of their craziest slam dancers to the set, Belushi included. Smooth move. One thing's for sure though, we definitely gave the good old U.S. something they never saw before. To this day that is the one episode of SNL, NBC has vowed to NEVER re-air. (Elvis

Voice Here) "Why thank you very much."

Everyone was blown away seeing the whole thing on the tube, and after a week or so, my 15 minutes of fame was up. Back at 171A the Bad Brains road crew including Jay Dubs, Alvin and myself formed a band. Dubs played guitar, Alvin was on drums and I sang. We had Teddy Horowitz, who later called himself Poppa Chubby, on bass and we called the band what else - Bloodclot! Why? Because every time something broke down on stage usually Doc or Darryl would yell, "What the Bloodclot! Fix the Bloodclot amp! Fix the Bloodclot mic! Fix the Bloodclot this and fix the Bloodclot that!" Since we were the dudes who were in charge of fixing the Bloodclot situations as they developed, we could see no other fitting name for our band. Actually, "Bloodclot!" is a curse in Jamaican patois, which has something to do with a woman's monthly cycle if you get my drift. We wrote songs like "Kill the Beast," which made reference to Babylon-types bearing the 666 mark of the beast. "Presidential Policy," "Excess" and several more which were all pretty self-explanatory. Bottom line, opening up for the Bad Brains night after night was an honor. One I'd never forget.

super touch shit fit

chapter 10

Everything was pretty good in my life at that point. I had a band, friends and place to live. I even had a little money in my pocket because Tomas and I cleaned out a few basements around town in buildings that were being renovated. We got the job because none of the construction crews were punk rock enough to pick up all the dead rats. It was around 9 a.m., on Thanksgiving Day and later on in the afternoon Tomas and I were going out to my aunt's house to have some veggie food with my mom and family. We were just waking up when we heard a slight knock on the front door. I started to get up to see who was there when the door was kicked open and in came a swarm of city officials who were carrying dozens of boxes. The city was caught up in the holiday spirit and decided to evict us on Thanksgiving. We tried to grab some clothes to put on, but they were like robots, systematically snatching everything in sight. They never said a word as a few of them threw our shit into the boxes and took them outside to the curb. As I finished getting dressed on the street, we looked at the boxes that contained our life's possessions and we were like, now what? At that moment the first snowflake of what would become the Thanksgiving '81 snowstorm hit.

I rang the bell at 171. Jay Dubs answered it. He looked at our wet boxes of personal possessions and it didn't take him long to figure out why we were there. He shook his head, smirked and said, "C'mon in." That was it. No speeches, no lectures. Just c'mon in. That's how Dubs was. He knew I couldn't just leave Tomas out in the cold so he let him crash in this little storage, crawl space under the engineer booth. I slept on the couch along with the Brains or anyone else who was in need of a place to live. We spent Christmas and New Year's there and in early '82, I prepared to go on the Bad Brains legendary tour of the South with the Throbs from Florida. Before that happened I needed money for food, so I landed a job that turned out to be the best career move I ever made.

Prana Foods was a little health food store on 9th Street and 1st Avenue. It was previously called Bhakti Natural, and was run by the Hare Krsnas. Back then LES only had two health food stores, Greenberg's and Prana. The good thing about Prana was they had a juice bar that made sandwiches, falafels and juices. One day I went over there with H.R. and met this guy he knew named Vinny who worked the juice bar. Vinny Signorelli was the drummer for the Dots, an old punk band from the '70s. Jimmy Quid who was also in the Dots was the guy who produced the Brains' first single "Pay to Cum/ Stay Close to Me" and through that connection Vinny got to know the Bad Brains. Vinny was really cool and never charged his friends for any of the food. Big mistake Vin, 'cause after I found that out I was there every day, sometimes twice a day. I noticed the help wanted sign in the front window and asked Vinny for the job. He got the okay from the owner, Bruce, and I was hired.

This store was hooked-up with Integral Yoga on the West Side. It was there I was able to get free yoga classes for Tomas and me. I later worked there and my co-worker, this older hippie-type named Tom, knew I was into music. He kept telling me about this guy who delivered our sprouts who had a son who was one of the best drummers in New York. His name was Mackie Jayson and he went on to play in the Cro-Mags, Bad Brains, Fun Lovin' Criminals and Urban Blight, among others. Now here was the catch with working at Prana - for the first month, according to Bruce, I was doing what he called "Karma Yoga," in other words I wasn't getting paid. Nothing, nada, nunca, and I was cool with that because not only did I stuff myself all day long and take bags of groceries home every night, but I had the Bad Brains and every fucker from the neighborhood showing up at the juice bar window to get free food. Bruce stood and watched one day as I gave out bag after bag of juices, sandwiches and groceries and never got a dime for any of it. Finally, he walked up to me and said, "Uhh, excuse me John. Did any of those people pay for that food?" I replied, "Why, no Bruce. It was some of that 'Karma Yoga' you told me about, dude." Well, I guess according to his philosophy it was cool to be on the receiving end of the benefits of that yoga system but not the giving end. He informed me that he was putting me on salary from that moment on and my philanthropic days were over.

The best thing about working there though was that I spent countless hours talking philosophy with Vinny who it turns out, lived in a Krsna temple for a little while. I had my hodge-podge philosophy and what ticked me off was everything I said philosophically, Vinny defeated easily. Then he asked me a simple question. Who is God? Well, I went on and on talking about God being energy and this and that. Then I asked him who he thought God was and to this day I'll never forget his answer, "God is a person." He went on to elaborate, "His name is Krsna which means the All Attractive," and he told me that Krsna possesses all six opulences in full: all beauty, strength, fame, renunciation, knowledge and wealth and that how, even in this material world when we meet someone with even a little bit of beauty, or wealth, or any of the other opulences, we're immediately attracted to them. Just imagine how attracted we'd be to a person who possessed those opulences in full. This was stuff I'd never heard before and as our talks continued everything he was saying made so much sense, but I knew there had to be a loophole somewhere and I was going to find it. There was no way the guys dancing around in bed sheets and playing drums and cymbals on street corners had all the answers, I mean c'mon... that ain't possible is it?

I asked Vinny to give me a book about it and he said the next time he went to the temple he'd get one for me. He assured me that before that happened Krsna, who was situated in my heart and directed me on my path, would make an arrangement for me to see that this was for real. Two days later while I'm taking a bag of organic groceries to my mom in Jackson Heights, I came across a Hare Krsna in robes handing out books in the 74th and Roosevelt Avenue F train station. I rushed over to him and he said, "Hare Krsna," to which I replied, "Hare Krsna." He handed me a book called "The Science of Self-Realization." On the cover was a photo of this really intense looking master and he informed me that it was his guru Srila Prabhupada. I had no money and he wouldn't give me the book for free so I argued that he should just give it away and that charging people for spiritual knowledge was wack. His point was that this was about me surrendering and doing service to Krsna and that he was a monk and didn't profit by doing what he was doing. He accepted two bottles of organic juice for the book and in one day I read it from cover to cover. The next day I rushed into Prana Foods with the book in hand ready to tell Vinny about how he was never going to believe what happened. When he saw me he laughed and said, "I told you." I informed him that I still wasn't sure about this stuff that I would continue studying it. What I was really doing was looking for inconsistencies and believe it or not, I found none. Vinny gave me a couple of other books and I passed them on to Tomas when I was done and soon after, he started coming over to Prana to talk with Vinny. After a couple of weeks Vinny invited both of us to the Hare Krsna temple in Midtown for the morning program.

The first thing I noticed as I walked into the temple building on 7th Avenue was how good it smelled. The incense, the flowers and that food being cooked in their spices, created this amazing combination of scents that captivated your sense of smell. The second thing I noticed was how beautiful and colorful everything looked in the temple room. The paintings on the walls, the decorations...these people had it down and all of this, combined with the sounds of devotees chanting so early in the morning, gave me the strangest sense of peace. Although the sights and scents were intoxicating, I was sure I could find a flaw with what I was experiencing. To understand why I was feeling this way, you have to put yourself in my shoes for just a minute. Everything I went through in my life was associated with trust issues because most of the people I met up until that point had an angle, a gimmick or a con. I considered myself a streetwise hustler/philosopher and I was sure these Krsna guys had an angle. I was determined to find out what it was and yell out, "Ah ha, I knew it! The bullshit detector has done it again!"

It was almost 7 a.m. and Vinny told me there was a spiritual program from 7 to 8:30 and then afterward we ate. Well, at exactly 7 a.m. this monk stepped out from behind this curtain on the altar and blew this conch shell as loud as he could. All the Krsnas gathered in front of the altar as the curtains opened and I remember just standing there and staring. On the altar were these deities of Radha-Govinda, which were so amazing and beautiful. I bowed down quickly with everyone else and then stood up while this song played which everyone sang along to. Vinny told me that George Harrison from the Beatles played bass on it and that he was into Hare Krsna. After that they did their chanting on drums in front of a statue of their guru Srila Prabhupada and then there was a class followed by the most incredible food I ever ate.

I came back a lot in the days that followed and asked a lot of questions. For every question I asked, I got an intelligent, satisfying answer. I took some more books home still determined to find something, anything they couldn't explain, but it never happened. I stayed up all hours of the night reading and taking notes from their books. I would show up the next day with my list sure that I'd come up with a question that would stump them. NOT. If I asked a question about reincarnation, they had the answer. If I asked a question about karma, they had the answer. Even when I asked the question which always got the "It's a mystery my son" answer from the priests, which was, "If we were pure and in the spiritual world with Krsna (God) as you say, then how, and more importantly why, would we ever come to this material world?" The answer I got - envy. We wanted to enjoy like Krsna and we actually wanted to come here because we were envious of God. Krsna even begged us not to go and told us we wouldn't like it, but that's how powerful and blinding envy is. Take a look at any person who is riddled with envy, they'll even risk their lives to bring down whoever it is they're envious of won't they? Money isn't the root of all evil my friends, envy is. And as I looked back at some of the most fucked up people I knew in my life, the one quality they had in abundance was envy. That answer just made so much sense and so did all the things A.C. Bhaktivedanta Swami Prabhupada put in his books. He translated more of the Vedas (means knowledge in Sanskrit) than any person even to this day and his books are praised by scholars and are studied in universities all over the world.

If you love heroic stories, Srila Prabhupada's story alone is enough to inspire you to read his books. His guru back in India told him to go to the West and spread the knowledge of love of God and at almost seventy-years-old he crossed the oceans on a small steamship with nothing more than seven U.S. dollars and a case of books. He suffered two heart attacks on the rough journey over and came to NYC's Bowery where he began translating the Vedas and going out into public to chant the holy name's of Krsna. He was robbed of his typewriter and dealt with cold never witnessed in his life back home in India. He survived things that would make any normal man cave in, but he knew he truly was on a mission from God. When he went to chant in Tompkins Square Park in 1965 in front of a tree (it's now a city landmark and even has a plaque) hippies like Allen Ginsberg and his crew became attracted. Something special then started happening: people joined him, people helped him and the

Hare Krsna Movement took root in America with its first temple on the LES called "Matchless Gifts," because of the Swami's love and devotion to Krsna and his Spiritual Master. He knew people in the West were suffering from lack of spirituality, and out of compassion he risked his own life to come here and help us. That is the definition of a true hero.

The knowledge contained in the Vedas truly is a matchless gift. They are the roadmaps out of this material world and the process of Bhakti-Yoga contained in them is a science. According to Webster's Dictionary the definition of science states, "Systematized knowledge derived from observation, study, etc." In other words you have a formula, you apply it and you get a result. To the degree you apply the formula, to that degree you'll see results. There's no cheating. If you change or speculate on the formula and think, "I don't want to add two parts per million, I'll do it my way and add one part per million." The result will be altered. So, in the Bhagavad-Gita Krsna gives the formula. He says, "To those who are constantly devoted and worship Me with love I give the understanding by which they can come to Me." Simple formula. It's about love and devotion, and the result - we get out of the entanglements of this material world and go back home, back to Godhead with Krsna where we enjoy our eternal spiritual nature, which is full of bliss.

That's why the association of spiritually minded persons is so important because without them we wouldn't have a clue as to why we're suffering. Srila Prabhupada's arrival in America opened up a lot of eyes and never before did someone show me a picture of what God looked like. I always saw the Christian pamphlet of the guy with the white beard and no face sitting in heaven on a throne. Well, if I'm supposed to love God how can I love Him if I don't know anything about Him? You guys have been in love at some point I'm sure, right? If I told you there's someone on the other side of a door, but I can't tell you what they look like, or enjoy, or anything for that matter, could you develop any love for that person? Not unless you're crazy, or extremely hard up. Well, these people knew what God looked like, what God enjoyed, what His names were, even His pastimes on Earth. After a few weeks of having my ego smashed to smithereens and hanging out with the devotees who were very humble while they were doing the smashing I might add, I realized that the Hare Krsnas had something really deep. They had more devotion to God (their day started at 4 a.m.) than anyone I ever saw including H.R., and they had the philosophy to back it up. If you don't believe me, challenge it like I did.

By the time we were ready to hit the road for the tour of the South I was pretty convinced that what I discovered with Vinny's help was the real deal. At that point, I was reading a lot and began chanting the Hare Krsna mantra on beads (Hare Krsna, Hare Krsna, Krsna Krsna, Hare Hare, Hare Rama, Hare Rama, Rama Rama, Hare Hare).

Tomas stayed in New York and minded the studio with Jerry's boy from back home. As for our mode of transportation, Alvin had borrowed a van from this band called Joey Miserable and the Worms. It had a big colorful worm painted on it that wrapped around the entire van. We loaded it up with as much brown rice, veggies and tahini as we could and headed out.

Being on the road was so cool because we drove a lot, Reasoned for hours and smoked a shit load of weed. Jay Dubs even gave me my first vegetarian cooking class where he taught me how to prepare the "Yot," which was the evening Ital meal made by putting the brown rice into our pot, then the root veggies and lastly the leafy green veggies. The steam from the rice cooking would cook the veggies and when it was done it looked like a colorful pot of goulash. We'd throw some tahini on it and chow down. We ate that almost everyday and I have to tell you after a few days of that shit I was definitely missing that bugged-out looking Krsna food.

Our first stop on tour was North Carolina and I remember staying at the house of this dude who harvested pecans and grew his own weed. The thing that really blew me away about him was he had a 500-pound, male lion on his property. You had to see H.R.'s face light up when he brought that beast into the house. "Rasta Far I!" was all you heard over and over again. To the Rastas, lions are mystical animals, you know, with that whole conquering Lion of Judah stuff. So, to be this close to something so amazing was pretty cool for him. All I kept thinking about was this big-ass cat could kill all of us in about one minute flat. The other thing I was thinking about non-stop was the fact that I was about to play my first live show. After spending a couple of days eating so many pecans I got sick, we then drove to Charlotte where we had a show in some space in a run-down shopping center.

I have to say the first time I stepped on stage with Bloodclot to perform in front of a live audience didn't make me the slightest bit nervous. All the singing along to those songs on my radio under the blanket at the Valentis' had prepared me for the stage. It felt so natural and I got this weird feeling of déjà vu. It was exhilarating; my adrenaline was flowing and I was on a total spiritual high. I would always watch

H.R. pray before he went on stage and I knew I had to meditate and think about what it was I was about to do. Ego in check? Check. Remembering that this was all about the revolution? Check. Amped-up and ready to kick some ass? Check. During that first performance I ran all over the stage bouncing off everything and shouting my lyrics into audience members' faces. The rush of performing had me hooked; I was now officially an addict. After that first gig Poppa Diddley (Earl) changed the Throbs' name. They were now called Crucial Truth and Bloodclot borrowed their bass player so we could open up on every show of the tour. The next gig we played was in Raleigh at a club called The Big Bad Wolf, and that show would set the tone for the rest of the tour.

I realized something very quickly as soon as we stepped into that redneck biker bar and that is, no one knew the Bad Brains were black. It seemed Dave Hahn the Brains' manager failed to mention it to the club owners when he sent out their record and press kit, which contained no photos. I remember hearing one of the biker bouncers whisper to another in his best Dukes of Hazzard twang, "Hey, Jeffro. The band is niggers." Jeffro replied, "I know Bubba and what the hell is wrong with them boys' hair?" Dreadlocks. We weren't inside that club for more than five minutes when a beef started at the front entrance because Jay Dubs (who was a vegan and didn't wear leather) was wearing this pleather jacket while there was a sign on the wall that clearly stated: No Leather Jackets. They tried to make Jay remove it, but he insisted it wasn't leather and an argument ensued. Finally they said something to the effect of, "Take the fucking jacket off or you and your nigger friends can get the fuck out of the club." I remembered expressing to him what an asshole he was and things really heated up at that point, but H.R. cooled us out and we went backstage. I looked at the expression on his face and I knew this was going to be one hell of a show.

I was right. After three or four songs H.R. made some comments about the Nazi club owners and racist bouncers telling us how to dress. That incited the kids to tear up the club and surprisingly enough when the tough guy bikers with the big mouths saw the punks in action they did nothing to stop it. After the show we had just finished packing up our gear and were hanging out with some of the punks while we waited to get paid. They were happy that someone finally stood up to the assholes who ran the club. They told us that at every show the bouncers would mess with the kids on line by smashing down their Mohawks and all kinds of dumb shit like that. Anyway, as we're yuckin' it up this big fat dude and about eight bikers carrying baseball bats walked in. The big guy grabs a bat from a biker, walks onto the dance floor and yells, "Where's that nigger lead singer who wrecked my club?" I immediately told all the punks, which numbered about fifteen, that they were going to get their chance to make a statement to these dickheads. I told them all to grab chairs and a few did. I stepped out onto the dance floor with a piece of metal from one of Earl's cymbal stands in my hand. I told the owner that we were ready to fight if that's what he wanted. Isn't it funny how even the biggest bullies will punk out if you stand up to them? They backed down quickly and we were informed that he was keeping the money we were supposed to be paid for the damage done to his club. Then two big, white redneck cops came in and asked the good old boy club owner if everything was all right. I guess knowing he had other shows happening and needed these kids, he told the cops it was cool and we left without our money. I ran into some of those kids almost ten years later and they told me they never forgot what went down that night. They also said that after that incident, the bouncers at The Big Bad Wolf had a new, humbler attitude toward the kids.

After Raleigh we made our way to Tampa, Florida to play three nights at a club called Miss Lucky's. At that point, we had no money and the club owner refused to pay us until the last show, so we slept on the floor of the club and basically starved for three days. The turnouts in Tampa were poor and after the last show the owner never did show up with our pay. Instead he sent some bouncers to kick us out of the club. At that point Alvin started buggin' and was trying to take the van and go back to New York, with or without us. I was ready to knock his ass out, tie him up and throw him in the back of the van if I had to. Doc opted for the more civil approach and was able to talk him out of it and we continued on the tour.

As we traveled through Florida, we got more of the same treatment - dirty looks and certain obscene middle finger hand gestures from the locals. As we made our way to Jupiter, we expected more of the same, poor turnouts and shitty treatment, but to our surprise that night's show was packed out. Bloodclot opened the show and we basically did all the same ranting, stage diving and slamming. When the Bad Brains came on and the club owner saw four black guys doing it, practically inciting a riot as the fans were going berserk, he pulled the plug on them. In the middle of one of their songs the power went off and we were basically ordered to get the hell out, but we did get paid, thankfully.

The next day H.R. and I went to the woods to Reason while the sun was setting and turning beautiful shades of red and blue. We smoked from his water pipe called a chalice, read verses from the Bible and talked about Jah. That was such a spiritually powerful moment for me and it's an image that remains burnt in my consciousness. So many things were realized on that first tour, but the main thing was how special the gift of music really is. Over the years it's taken a poor kid like me all around the world where I had the best times with people I really cared about. I met a lot of really cool people and the other thing touring will let you see right off the bat is who's who in your camp. In other words, who's going to crack under the pressure of the road. On that first tour Alvin cracked. He was starting a lot of shit with everyone (must have been all the hamburgers) and came close to getting bitch slapped by me a couple of times for being too aggressive toward some of the fans who came up on stage. I had to stay cool with him because he was the drummer for Bloodclot. Alvin meant well, but he was just a crazy motherfucker and couldn't help it. I had some good times with him, but I didn't appreciate some New Jack coming on board, barking orders at me and smacking the young kids around. Alvin always popped shit about how one day he was going to kick my ass and I just kept telling him that when that day came I was going to make him eat those words. Well, that day came a few years later when he tried to attack me with a hammer and a knife. Just for the record, I'll let him tell you guys who won the fight.

We got back to New York and even though it was the dead of winter and freezing, it was good to be back. There were no rednecks and the scene was buzzing about the Irving Plaza show on February 27th featuring Bloodclot, Heart Attack, the Necros and the Bad Brains. The Brains were amazing that night and once again H.R. did his patented back flip, landing exactly on the last note of "At the Movies," before the crowd went fuckin' nuts. That night was extra special because I watched my favorite band play and I got to rock the house in my hometown.

The other thing I liked about being home was that I could go to the temple with Tomas and Vinny. That spring we traveled upstate to a big festival where I hung out with a number of devotees. The more I hung out with them the more I liked them, because they lived the life and were very austere. I was soaking up as much knowledge as I could and I learned a lot about all the yoga processes and what they were meant for. Now I'm not going to bullshit y'all, it was definitely the food that kept me coming back and the Krsnas knew it. They encouraged me to eat as much as I could and then eat some more because prasadam (which means the Lord's mercy) purifies your entire being. All I knew was after a day of chanting, philosophy and eating that food, not only was I happy as hell, but I was high as a kite without ever taking a single hit off a joint. I read somewhere that in the '60s Srila Prabhupada's devotees distributed these leaflets out in San Francisco's Haight-Ashbury that said in big, bold letters, "LEARN HOW TO STAY HIGH FOREVER." What an ingenious marketing strategy. Hippies joined by the bus full.

There was talk of a Bad Brains West Coast tour and I was psyched because it was their first time there and I knew people were going to go crazy. Unfortunately the good vibes and brotherhood between the Bad Brains and me would soon come to an end as a dark cloud by the name of Judah hung above us. Judah, or Judas, as I'll refer to him from this point on was this so-called Rasta from D.C., who preached hatred of white people. H.R. hooked up with him and I distinctly remember one van ride up to a gig in Boston where for five hours I listened to a tape of Louis Farrakhan spewing racist comments about white people. In one part of his Nazi-type lecture Farrakhan said that God created white man so that the black man could see just how despicable man could become. I confronted H.R. about it and he said, "You ain't white, man. We're talking about the other white people." I remember holding up my whiter than white hand, putting it in front of H.R.'s face and looked at him like he was crazy. I knew what he meant though. I didn't share the same values, or act like most white people, but if he judged me initially on the color of my skin he would have never spent the time he did teaching me so much and there were tons of other, 'white' kids out there who were just like me. It seemed H.R. had fallen victim to the skin disease.

One thing I've learned from the multitudes of interactions I've had on this planet with all kinds of individuals is that you can't judge people by their skin. As for Judas, I was a white devil no matter how down I was with the Bad Brains. He wouldn't even look me in the eye or answer my questions because he knew I had his number and saw right through the bullshit he was peddling. In the Vedas it says, Aham brahmasmi (we are spirit) so any religion that propagates crap like, "Whites are the Master Race" or "Blacks are God's Chosen People and White Man is the Devil," is inferior. The soul is neither white nor black and to identify with this material body is ignorance. Throughout history there have been plenty of devils no matter the race. It is my personal belief that the karma of these racist idiots is that they have to take their next birth as the race they so despise.

What really bothered me about what was going on was the fact that the Bad Brains were my family; I never saw skin color and I would have risked my life to protect them. I was a roadie who never took a dime for my services and I would have given them my last penny if they needed it. Why? I believed in the unity and revolution they spoke about and their method of delivering it: blazing punk rock. I believed the world needed to hear it. But now that message had changed. What was once so positive was now dogma and racist viewpoints. The "Whether you are black… or whether you are white… we all have to unite," lyrics faded behind the racist rants of Farrakhan quotes. Judas kept H.R. at arm's length at all times and preached to him constantly, literally brainwashing the dude. I remember hearing one conversation about, of all things, not playing punk music anymore. I was like, "Yo, numb nuts. Punk rock is what made the Bad Brains who they are so why don't you take your Farrakhan bullshit and your fake-ass patois accent and shove them up your Rasta-Imposter ass."

H.R. definitely acted differently toward me and that's when I got one of the biggest shocks of my life. We were leaving for the West Coast tour the next morning and I was at 171 finishing the pre-tour packing. I was so happy to be hitting the road again since I had never experienced the California punk scene before, but heard so much about it. I walked by Earl in 171 and I said something to the effect of how great it was going to be out there. He looked down at the ground and said, "Squidly, you're not going." I said, "What are you talking about?" His response, "Because you cited-up other runnins." In other words, my philosophy. I found it ironic that they would kick me off the tour for that reason. At first I was floored and devastated. Then I was pissed. I was pissed that my spiritual god brother, H.R., didn't even have the balls to tell me himself. Instead, he waited until the night before I was supposed to go, to have someone else tell me. I pleaded to Doc, Earl and Darryl, but it was no use. They said it was H.R.'s decision and H.R. was conveniently nowhere to be found. I never even saw him before he left. My spiritual brother ex-communicated me and I'll give you one guess as to who took my place? That's right, Judas.

I felt totally betrayed by H.R. and was close to tears that night. The next morning Tomas returned to 171A and was surprised to see me. I was in a very depressed state and even he couldn't believe what H.R. did. He was supposed to be my brother and for him to treat me like that really hurt. I took it personally. I heard the tour went well but it was a flop financially. Between them not paying Jay Dubs back and running up a huge phone bill booking gigs, the New York scene lost one of its prized possessions…171A. As for me, I don't hold any grudges against the Bad Brains and to this day, we're still friends. In February of 2006, I filled in as their vocalist during two of their shows at CBGB's.

Besides, the decision of not allowing me to go on the West Coast tour wasn't the other guys' decision. It was H.R.'s and he was just being misled by pseudo-spiritualist parasites who never had the type of commitment and dedication that we, their white devil brethrens had in terms of helping the band. There are a lot of wolves in sheep's clothing out there waiting to take advantage of people who are looking for God in this life. I feel the Bad Brains truly were on that path and were true spiritual warriors. They just hit a bump in the road.

As for me, I decided to take my Krsna Consciousness to the next level and move into a temple and as I did, I found out that wolves don't only come with dreadlocks and call themselves Judah.

let the scams begin

chapter 11

At this point, I really felt I had to dive into my spiritual journey, so I decided to get out of New York and go somewhere tropical. Beacuse I had warrants out for my arrest, my choices were obviously limited. Tomas was also down with getting out of the city and taking a spiritual vacation away from the pangs of material life. After talking to Vinny we chose to venture down to the Puerto Rico temple, which was situated in the hills of Gurabo across from the El Yunque Rainforest. Vinny had lived there when he joined the Hare Krsna Movement and told us stories about how beautiful it was down there. Since Puerto Rico was still part of the United States, I didn't need an I.D. to get there. Besides, some of the other devotees who visited the temple told us about chanting in the rainforest, swimming in waterfalls and getting up before dawn to watch the sunrise over the hills while they meditated. The day was filled with work on the organic farm and at night the devotees would gather in the temple to chant and dance, take hot milk and read about Krsna's pastimes, before taking a rest. Vinny said he never felt more peaceful, content and connected with Krsna then when he was a brahmacari (monk). He was right, because as you take to the spiritual path in life all fear dissipates.

Every human being knows in their heart of hearts that they should be living for the search of truth. When you don't, it's like this looming uneasiness in the back of your head that never goes away. For those of us who choose a life of pleasing ourselves and don't surrender to Krsna's internal energy (love), or have chosen to call themselves atheists, Krsna comes to remind us of who's in charge in the form of death. Death is the representation of Krsna's external energy. We living beings are from His marginal energy and can choose either path. The choice is ours. Death for a devotee is simply a stepping-stone, because the devotee steps on the head of death to get to Krsna.

Death for the non-devotee though, is a whole different ball game. They have to be ripped away from their family, big house, bank account, cars, etc. I'm not being sectarian either, a devotee is one who is devoted and follows the laws of God and that could be a Muslim, Hindu, Christian or Buddhist. It doesn't matter. What does matter is that you develop love for God and when you love someone as we see in relationships in this material world, we want to serve that person. That's true love. If we only cultivate material desires and that's what we've put our faith in our entire lives, imagine how painful it's going to be at the time of death when we have to give it all up? Really, stop and give that point some thought.

Vinny told us that what was so cool about the devotees was you didn't need to call or write. You could just show up and say, "I want to surrender to Krsna," and they'd embrace you like family. I was sold. I worked a couple of weeks at Prana and paid for our airline tickets before we set off to Puerto Rico with the clothes on our backs, a wheatgrass juicer and about 300 pounds of sprouting seeds. We were really into the raw foods and wheatgrass juice thing so we figured, "Let's grow some kick-ass wheatgrass and juice for everyone there." You had to see the look on the faces of the devotees when we got out of the cab at the temple with nothing more than the twelve 25-pound bags of sprouting seeds. They took us to what was no more than a hut with a couple of wooden beds and told us to put our seeds down. Then we were instructed to follow them, because the temple president wanted to see us right away. It was kind of weird, because these devotees weren't like the ones I met in New York. When we walked toward the main building we got some odd stares.

Being on an island up in the hills with the weird vibes going on had me feeling a little bit of a cult-like Jim Jones-ish atmosphere going on. They walked us to a door, knocked and then walked off as we were ordered to enter. Sitting inside on a raised seat was this short, muscular, black devotee wearing a flower garland, named Vakresvara Pandit, aka V.P. He told us to have a seat on the floor and we did so with the biggest smiles on our faces. We waited to be welcomed to the temple and given an enlivening pep talk about how surrendering to Krsna is the highest thing you can do with this human form of life. It never came. Instead, he stared out at us with a scowl on his face and said, "Who the hell told you to come to this temple?" I was caught off guard. "Excuse me," I said. He reiterated, "Who the hell told you to come here? Why did you two pick this temple?" I looked over at Tomas and he was in total shock. I told Vakresvara we wanted to surrender to Krsna and that my friend Vinny once lived here and referred us. He shook his head in a way that said he didn't believe us and said, "That's not what you're doing here and I'm going to find out the real reason you're here and when I do you'll be sorry. And what's with all these friggin' seeds." I told him how we'd share it with all the devotees and he snapped, "We don't want your crap. And as far as raw food here, you'll eat what we give you or else you can starve." Well it was obvious Vakresvara didn't write How to Win Friends & Influence People. After barking some more instructions at us, which made me feel like I was back in boot camp, he told us that if we screwed up once we were gone. Tomas and I walked out of that office completely bewildered, but still determined to give it our all.

We went back to our hut and I noticed mosquitoes were filling the evening air. Since we were near the rainforest it got so bad, so quickly, that you couldn't take a breath without swallowing a bunch of them. Everyone else in our hut had mosquito nets on their beds and when I asked where to get one they told us we had to ask Vakresvara. I ran back down to his office and when I told him we needed a net he looked at me with this wise-ass smirk and said, "Guess you shoulda brought one instead of all those seeds, smart guy. Sorry... (chuckle, chuckle) we're fresh out." That night was hellish and I didn't sleep a wink because I was constantly being bitten all over my body. The mosquitoes, combined with the sounds of a pig slaughterhouse located across from the temple, made our so-called spiritual adventure seem more like a Freddy Kruger nightmare.

When morning came Tomas and I literally had hundreds of mosquito bites all over our bodies. Vakresvara got a big kick out of asking us how we slept. Bottom line...I did not like this dude at all. He was a prick and I wondered how this guy could be representing such a beautiful movement that talked of love of God and compassion towards all living entities. That morning he taught a class and the entire time he kept saying really nasty stuff and staring out at us. The class ended by him staring us down and saying, "If you don't like it here, just leave. We're not even going to give you a ride back to the airport, just get your asses out on that road and hitchhike." We wondered what the hell he had against us and why he was treating us that way. All we wanted to do was become devotees.

At breakfast we were served the hottest, spiciest cooked-down-food I had ever eaten. When I told Vakresvara that the New York temple always gave us fruit in the mornings, he said even though we were on a tropical island there was no fruit. The food was so spicy I got sick. Immediately after breakfast we were taken to this very steep hillside where we performed hard labor for eight to ten hours chopping trees with an axe. Each day, we baked in the sun with very little water and no sunscreen or hats to keep the sun off our heads. He kept us out there from breakfast to sundown, only breaking for super spicy meals. I could just picture that sick son of a bitch standing there over the cook going, "More chilies, more chilies ha, ha, ha..." After the fourth day we were severely sunburned dehydrated, covered in mosquito bites and blisters on our faces. At this point, our hands were raw from swinging an axe ten hours a day without gloves. Tomas reached his breaking point and said that this was too cult-like and not what he expected to find. He was leaving and convinced me to go with him. When we bounced, Vakresvara stayed true to his word and made us hitchhike back to the airport. Despite our treatment, I left Puerto Rico with my faith in the process still intact. I brushed this devotee's weird behavior off as an isolated incident, but some years later I would realize that what I witnessed was only the tip of the iceberg. It would be a fraction of the widespread corruption that was being carried out not only by Vakresvara, but by all the so-called leaders of the Hare Krsna Movement.

I was back in the city and I practically kissed the dirty-ass floor at 171A when I arrived. We told Vinny about how we were treated in Puerto Rico and he was shocked. We basically picked up where we left off, going to the temple in the morning and hanging out at night. Little-by-little things at 171A started to go wrong beginning with the phone getting shut off for non-payment. As a result, none of the bands could call to book rehearsals as the studio was slipping deeper and deeper into debt. Tomas split New York and I took up with Harley who just got back from California. Dave "Rat" Parsons moved the Rat Cage to 9th Street and we hung out there every day. Dave was one hell of an artist and he was the one who drew the artwork of the lightning bolt hitting Washington, D.C.'s U.S. Capitol Building on the Bad Brains legendary 1982 debut record.

Dave Rat always had the best weed and Harley and I knew this, so we went over there every day to smoke. Since we were a couple of broke punk rock potheads there's no better weed than O.P.'s (Other People's). What made our smoking sessions with Dave bugged-out was that right around that time he was making his transformation to become a woman. First a little eye shadow, then some make-up, then woman's stockings, under his pants and a lacy kind of feminine shirt. Then he'd add some highlights in his hair and then a little more make-up. It got to the point where Harley and I didn't know what to expect when we hung out. We would walk down the stairs and take a deep breath before we walked into the Rat Cage so we wouldn't crack up in the dude's face. One day we were wasted and I couldn't contain myself any longer. I blurted out, "Dude, what the fuck is up with all the make-up and shit?" Dave seemed stunned that I asked as Harley was just trying not to laugh. Dave's response, "What? You know I'm into Siouxsie and the Banshees." We wanted to believe him, so we looked at each other for a moment, still a little unsure of his answer. We nodded and sighed in relief. "Shit," I said. "You had us worried there for a minute, we were starting to think you were turning into some kind of fruit-cake or something." A lot of Siouxsie's male goth/new wave fans did dress that way and Dave was no exception. I mean, he did have a girlfriend, so we walked out of the Rat Cage laughing at the fact that we even thought for a moment Dave was becoming a weirdo. Or was he?

Shortly after that we found a woman's lingerie catalog in the Rat Cage addressed to Miss 'MIR' Parsons. No big deal, right? Except MIR was Dave's graffiti tag and Parsons was his last name. Now the make-up and other shit we were willing to overlook with his Siouxsie excuse, but knowing that Dave Rat was sitting next to us like one of the boys, with a lace thong up his ass really hit home. We left there trying to make sense of it all and made plans to meet back over at the Rat Cage later that evening for a spliff and to hear what records Dave got that day. As dusk settled in I was walking down St. Mark's to meet up with Harley, when I saw the most horrendous-looking drag queen. She whizzed by on a skateboard wearing a dress, fishnet stockings, orange hair, 10-pounds of make-up and combat boots. I laughed my ass off all the way to the Rat Cage and as I burst in to tell Harley and Dave that I just saw a dude who had him beat in the make-up department I noticed Harley had this totally bewildered look on his face. Dave emerged from the back room and I soon discovered that the skateboard-riding drag queen I had just witnessed was Dave's big, 'coming out' victory ride down St. Mark's. We were speechless, but Dave, or should I say Miss 'MIR' Parsons, acted like nothing was up. He opened his boxes, put on the latest releases by Black Flag, rolled up a joint and said in his deep voice, "Their new album kicks fuckin' ass." We just kept looking at each like, "Is this fuckin' dude gonna tell us about his wardrobe change or what?" The answer was no and when the joint came back around to us soaked in this cherry-red lip-gloss, Harley held it and stared at it. We looked at each other, then at Dave and said simultaneously, "Uhh... dude. We gotta split." We broke out of there and never hung out at the Rat Cage with Dave ever again.

In reality Dave was cool as shit. He just chose a different lifestyle at a point when we were judgmental about anything that had to do with those issues. My philosophy now is more or less live and let live. A few years back, Dave called me from Switzerland where he was living, about fifteen times to invite me to his show at Manitoba's on Avenue B. He was leaving messages calling himself Daisy, so I guess that meant she was still into the whole drag thing. I showed up at Manitoba's to see Daisy sing and play her ukulele in front of a crowd that included the usual skinheads, punks and Rockers, as well as a few of the old timers from the 171 era. The minute Daisy (who had on this white, lacy dress with puffy sleeves and ballerina slippers) saw me, she ran over jumped up and threw her arms around my neck like a woman greeting her man who had just came home from the sea. My girlfriend was laughing her ass off and I didn't mind because even though Dave was now Daisy, she was still my friend. A lot of the Manitoba regulars just stared, but knew better than to say anything. After a couple of minutes I peeled Daisy off me and told her how good it was to see her. We reminisced about old times at 171A, the Bad Brains, Max's and the Rat Cage, before she performed a set of all Bad Brains songs. The set was entertaining as hell and I later found out, it was her dying wish.

Daisy had cancer and it was slowly killing her, but she didn't come to New York looking for sympathy. Her wish was to come to the place where her Daisy persona was born and to let us see her perform. Although Daisy recently lost her battle with cancer, she did live long enough to make her final transformation. Even though she was suffering through a painful death, she wanted to leave this world as a woman. She defied her doctor's advice by taking hormones and traveled overseas to complete her sex change operation. Dave Rat left this world as Daisy, as much a woman as the surgeon's knives and injections allowed her to be. No matter what anyone says, or what I may think about how freaky that is, no one can take away the fact that Dave 'MIR' Parsons truly believed he was meant to be Daisy in this life and believed it up until the moment she left this planet.

Since 171A was in danger of being shut down due to the huge amount of back rent being owed, the Bad Brains held a benefit at the New York Theatre Ensemble on Fourth Street to try to save it. The show barely raised any cash and as a result, a historical piece of NYC punk rock culture was lost. As for me, I still wanted to live in a temple and give the monk life another shot. After I saw an article in the Hare Krsna magazine, Back to Godhead, about these devotees in Hawaii who had a sailboat and sailed around the Hawaiian Islands chanting out on the open seas, I called the Hawaiian temple. I was invited out to put my Navy know-how to work on the Jaladuta 2, named after the Indian steamship that carried Srila Prabhupada from India to America in 1965.

The temple property on Coelho Way in Oahu was incredible. It had the second largest banyan tree on the island of Oahu where the guests would eat under it during the Sunday Love Feast (named "Love Feast" by Srila Prabhupada because the food is offered to Krsna and the guests with love). Being in Hawaii was so different from my dealings in Puerto Rico with Vakresvara. The devotees here were friendly, especially the resident sannyasi (renounced monk) Narahari Swami. He was the devotee who was featured in the Back to Godhead article and he personally invited me to come out to Hawaii. He got the sailboat from a gentleman in Washington State who donated it to the Hare Krsna Movement and Narahari sailed it across the Pacific Ocean to Hawaii.

Temple life in Hawaii was great. Each morning, I got up two hours before sunrise (called the Brahma-mahurta). It's the most peaceful time on the planet and the most advantageous for meditation. Previously that would be the time I would be going to bed, but getting up early gave me so much power spiritually. On Saturday nights I went out onto the streets of Waikiki and chanted like the Krsnas did back in D.C. I remembered thinking; "If only those fuckers back in D.C. could see me now, they'd shit themselves." I also started working on the Jaladuta 2 and honing-up my skills. I started learning how to read maneuvering and navigational charts for the islands, but all that sailboat stuff was short lived because the Hare Krsnas had a major brawl going on in downtown Honolulu. Little did I know I was about to get thrown in the center of the ring.

One morning I was eating breakfast and I overheard a devotee who was an amateur heavyweight boxer talk about a street fight he had down on Kalakaua Avenue with these people he called "Mokes." A Moke was a derogatory term for the local Hawaiian dudes. I found it odd that they were referred to like that, especially by a devotee who was not supposed to be identifying with the body, but seeing everyone as a spirit soul. As it turns out these Mokes were robbing the devotees who collected money along one of Waikiki's main tourist areas. Now, the devotee with the boxing background tried to prevent this from happening, but was roughed up in the process. Not knowing what else to do, he asked for help. Since it was a noble cause and I liked to fight, I volunteered. I finished up my meal, got into the van with the devotees and headed down to Waikiki Beach.

I watched these Krsna dudes, who were all in street clothes and wearing hats to cover their shaved heads, hustle hard. I have to admit, I was impressed with their skills. They would stop the tourists with a flower on a bobby pin like they were the official Hawaiian welcoming committee. They would always use the standard bullshit lines like, "Aloha, welcome to Waikiki!" They would try to be funny and ask the woman who was there with her husband if she's tookin' or lookin' before putting the flower in her hair, depending on their marital status. If they put it on the right side that meant you're single and the left signified that you were married. They'd say, "Here's your welcoming gift." Sounds like it's free right? Then they handed them this Hawaiian postcard mounted on a piece of wood covered with polyurethane. They made these things at the temple and were pieces of crap worth about fifty-cents. See the psychology was to make these poor fuckers feel guilty as shit about the fact that at that moment while they were enjoying hula dancers, sun-bathing, moonlit strolls on the beach and the $10.99 – all-you-can-eat luau's over at Big Mike's Pig and Poi Shack, there are sick and dying children around the world eating grubs and drinking water infested with feces. These devotees even showed the tourists pictures of this to hammer home their point. After that happened, I think it's safe to say the money was rolling in by the wheelbarrow.

The profit margin was considerable when it came to the postcard scam since that so-called "gift" cost about a half-a-buck to make. And the flowers the devotees handed out to tourists were actually stolen each morning from cemetery graves all around the island. Most of the devotees who pulled these scams were working for free. Well most were, but a few were financing their luxury condos with what they made on the streets. But the evil vacationer who would only commit sin had he or she been left with their money, made spiritual advancement for helping those devotees live their lavish lifestyle. I'm not shittin' you, that's exactly what I was told. The last part of the whole Waikiki transaction (which took place only after the devotee got the money) consisted of giving a tourist a book. When people tried to read the small print on the cover which clearly said the literature was from the Hare Krsna Movement, they would turn the book over, open it up and keep flipping through the pages so they wouldn't notice it. Legally the only way they were allowed to be out there was if they gave them a book, since they were covered under the First Amendment of the U.S. Constitution, which grants freedom of religion. A lot of people would come back though and be like, "This is Hare Krsna and I want my money back," and they'd say, "Sorry the cult leader just came by in his golden Rolls Royce and picked up the money. No can do."

Sometimes the tourists asked what ISKCON (which was on the charity I.D.s and is an acronym for the International Society For Krsna Consciousness) stood for and they'd reply, "International Society Keeping Children Off Narcotics" or "International Society for Kindness and Consideration," or some other bullshit. Hands down, these guys put my beat acid gig to shame and as I observed their hustle I was like, "Uhhh…excuse me fellas, but I uhhh…happen to have some street skills myself (I never told them in what exact capacity), so if you hook a brother up with some of dem joints I'll get down and show y'all what I can do." Since they had no idea of my past earning potential I was told to just watch their backs and that's exactly what I did those first few days in Waikiki.

I was fascinated by the thought that I could get my hustle on and make spiritual advancement at the same time. Hustling is my passion and it always has been ever since the days at the Valentis'. Put me in some fucked up circumstances with nothing and watch me get out of it, because I looked at it as a challenge. I was like the MacGyver of street scams and even though I was in Hawaii and living this renounced life, for me that old saying still applied, "You can take the hustler out of the hustle, but you can't take the hustle out the hustler."

In any hustle, whether it's selling beat drugs with Mikey Debris, breaking and entering with J.K., or late night garage shopping with Junior Nuts and Dougie, there's always one or two individuals who reach the upper echelons of the hustle. In the Waikiki Krsna scam, that individual was this dude named Shari. You will now see firsthand, just how good this guy was at raking in the dough and since I always appreciated the fine art he mastered, you'll understand why I was absolutely mesmerized by this individual.

Shari stood about 6'1", was a fast talker-type and weighed a whopping 130-pounds soaking wet. Now since he presented no physical threat and was the one making all the money, naturally he was the one getting robbed. The other devotees were okay, but Shari was in a league of his own. As I break it down for you, you'll understand why the governor, the mayor, the cops, the businessmen and just about everyone else in Hawaii except for the Mokes, hated the Hare Krsnas. Shari learned to speak Japanese while he ran a hustle in Japan with another Krsna devotee named Guru-Kreeper. Together they terrorized the Japanese people and scammed them out of millions of yen. Since both devotees were wanted they decided to flee the country. Shari made his way to Hawaii where his Japanese came in handy because once a year it was open season on Japanese tourists where Shari could easily make up to $2,000 a day.

In '82 the Japanese economy was booming and the Japanese people loved to throw around a lot of that hard-earned cash, especially on travel. It just so happened that Oahu was one of their favorite vacation destinations. They were the largest source of tourist income on the island and, as you'd expect, the authorities wanted to protect their investment by keeping them away from us. Thanks to the First Amendment, there was nothing they could do to enforce this. We were only allowed to be out there if the Japanese received literature about the Hare Krsna philosophy, which they couldn't read anyway because it was printed in English. So with the book distribution and some fine acting on Shari's part, who smiled the entire time as he basically threatened to nuke their country again, rape their wives and rip their heads off because their ancestors killed his grandparents on this exact spot during the attack on Pearl Harbor, he got away with it. You may not be able to see the subtleties of what he was doing out there, but according to the leaders of the Hare Krsna Movement he was saving those poor Japanese bastards' souls from having to go to hell.

I noticed right off the bat that Shari was different compared to the other devotees because he didn't waste his time with that postcard crap. He only gave out flowers to the Japanese, and if someone warned you that a particular individual was going to hustle you and told you exactly how they were going to do it, would you still get hustled? Most of you wouldn't (except for the idiots who come to New York and get warned about the three-card monte scam and still play). For the most part you guys would avoid the hustle. Well, the Japanese travel companies would bring the Japanese tourists right by us in big tour buses and the tour guide would point at us while talking over the loudspeaker. They'd tell them not to stop and take flowers, that we were very bad and evil people who would rob them. The Japanese tourists would pile over to the side of the bus to stare at Shari, or whoever else was working out there. They would wave their flowers that were on bobby pins at the Japanese and smile while making these faces like they were deranged, brainwashed cult members saying, "We're gonna get you...we're gonna get you." It would freak the hell out of the Japanese and it was so funny to see their reactions. Their eyes would get really big like a deer in the headlights. They would just stare frozen with fear with their faces pressed up against the bus window.

I remember the first time I saw Shari work the hustle, I was laughing so hard I almost pissed my pants. A Japanese couple walked up the street with their hand trucks piled to the top with boxes of macadamia nuts. They just loved them nuts. They would buy hundreds of dollars worth of the things and load them up several feet high and wheel them down Kalakaua Avenue while they shopped. When they passed by Shari he held up a flower and said, watasumonoga arundakedosa, or in other words, "Here's a present for you." Yeah right, it's only going to cost you a few hundred bucks. Immediately the dude would shout, irane-yo, irane-yo, which means, "I don't want it" and literally bolt off dragging his wife and nuts (macadamias that is) down the street.

Now pay attention, 'cause here's where the bobby pin came in. Shari who loved a captive audience, would yawn, stretch, check his watch, look at his fingernails, pick his teeth and then let the couple get about fifteen feet. The Japanese thought they got away and were safe and some even giggled about it. Then Shari gave us the thumbs up and effortlessly launched that hula flower through the air and the bobby pin balanced it so it hit its target with pinpoint accuracy. I shit you not, it would land right in his wife's hair and most of the time they wouldn't even notice, before Shari would have to yell, orega yattanjane-ka which means, "I gave it to you!"

The husband would look around as Shari pointed to his wife's hair while calmly walking up to them. Once the husband saw the flower in her hair he would freak out and start smacking the shit out of her trying to get it out. Shari would settle him down by calmly saying, kanewa irane-zo or "It's free." By this point, the husband and wife were both trembling in fear. The husband, who was holding the flower would say, hontouka or, "Really?" Why yes my friend, of course. Shari would put it back in her hair as both husband and wife smiled away, forgetting about their previous instructions where they were warned that guys like Shari were the anti-Christ.

Shari's slick-ass would then break off a petal and conceal it in his hand. With the slight of hand of a magician he would tuck it in behind the flower as he put it in her hair. His next move was to show the pictures of starving babies in India, Africa and the Middle East. The pictures depicted babies with bloated stomachs and infested with flies. He would inform them that we needed a donation and the Japanese tourist would say, ikurada or "How much?" Shari's reply, gojuu doru dayo (it costs fifty-dollars). The husband and wife would say, gojuu doru nanka aruwakenaidaro (we don't have fifty-dollars). Then Shari would stick out his chicken chest, get in the guys face and say, sonna kuchino kikikatanaidaro, which means, "What the hell is this? Don't be so impolite!" The husband either gave up the dough or took the flower out of his wife's hair to give it back. When he did give it back the broken flower petal would always fall to the ground. Shari would look at them like they just shot his dog, point to the flower peddle on the ground and say, "kowareteruzo henpin dekinai jane-ka. You broke it, now I definitely can't take it back." They would fork over the fifty bucks and Shari would call each one of us over and say, koitu bangurades shu de hataraiterundakedo, koitunimo 50 doru na which means, "My friend here works in Bangladesh give him fifty, too." Then the next guy worked in Africa, him too and let's not forget those poor people in India... one more fifty, please. He got about two to three hundred bucks off the dude and he would do that all day long with nothing more than a flower.

He even played a little cat and mouse game with some of the Japanese and it gave us a good laugh. A couple would be looking at us as they approached, but do their best to pretend not to be. They'd get up the courage to walk by looking terrified the whole time as they stared straight ahead. Shari would act like he didn't see them. He would almost let them off the hook then at the last minute throw his arm up in the air with that flower and shout, mate (wait) yaruyo (I have a present) and they would take off running down the street while their gifts and nuts were flying all over the place. We would just crack the fuck up. We had a Krsna gauntlet going and what we were doing out there amounted to little more than strong-arm robbery. The local

Hawaiians would watch us and get pissed, even the tourists watched it go down in total disbelief. That's why the Moke thugs figured it was okay to rob the devotees. I mean, shit, they were just robbing someone who was robbing someone else. I believe that's called karma, ain't it?

The Hawaiian locals have an endearing term for white folks. They call us, "Howlies," and the Mokes lovingly referred to the devotees as fuckin' Howlie Krsnas. They would wait until the middle of the day when Shari had about $600 or $700, walk up and say, "Hey you fuckin' Howlie Krsna… gimme your shit, bra (bro) or we gonna have beef, bra." If Shari resisted he was punched or whatever else was on the beat-down menu for that day. As for the cops doing anything to stop it, forget about it. They actually encouraged the locals to do it because they hated us harassing the tourists.

What really cracked me up was the lack of street smarts the devotees had. They had no clue how to deal with these guys and they actually resorted to baking cookies every day to try and make a peace offering. I couldn't believe it. The devotees were like, "Excuse me, 'Mr. Six-Foot-Four, Two-Hundred-and-Forty-Pound-Monster who's Stoned out on Hawaiian Bud and got the Munchies' would you like a delicious oatmeal-raisin cookie?" Well let's see now…that's a no-brainer. In this hand I have $400 and in the other hand I have a freshly baked cookie. Even the Mokes, who weren't exactly known for their smarts, had an easy time with that one. They would walk up and say, "Hey you got one cookie, bra?" The devotees would reach down into the bag, hand over the cookie with a smile and before they could say "Hare Krsna" they got laid-out and robbed. I finally told the devotees that they were going about it the wrong way. My philosophy was they had to meet aggression head on with not only more aggression, but with tact.

See I had a common bond with the Mokes. We shared a certain kind of mentality because they were in fact, up to my old tricks out on Kalakaua Avenue selling weed to the tourists… seaweed. They were beat artists and I knew I had to get down in the trenches and fight dirty with these motherfuckers and communicate on their level. I began telling the tourists that the Mokes were ripping them off and that's when things got really heated. I got into a few pushing and shoving matches, even went toe-to-toe with a few of them. After I proved that I was more than game, I called a sit down. I pulled their head honcho aside and broke it down mano e mano, scammer to scammer. "Look," I said. "You guys got your gig out here and we got ours. I'm willing to fight to protect our gig, just like you would be if someone tried to fuck up your hustle. I ain't letting that bullshit go down no more, so either we get along, or none of us are gonna make money out here, because I will tell every fuckin' tourist on this island that you guys sell beat weed."

It worked and the Mokes agreed to back off and never mess with us again. I even clued them in on how to make beat acid, which they did very well with, I might add. The guy was stunned that some dude who wears orange bed sheets on a daily basis would have the balls to stand up to him. He was even more stunned when I showed him the acid gig and told him about my concert days in the '70s. The big guy shook hands with me and said, "Hey brudder (brother), you the coolest fuckin' Howlie Krsna I ever met, bra. Anybody ever give you beef, bra, you tell me, bra. I gonna take care of it."

The temple was very happy with the turn of events and because of my street credibility they finally decided to load me up with flowers, wooden postcards, some basic lines in Japanese and books. I was unleashed onto the public at Waikiki Beach and I was huge. My first day out I gave out a lot of books and I collected more money than anyone except Shari. I was really into talking about the philosophy with people, but I was a little off kilter with my approach because no one on vacation really wants to hear about the suffering taking place in this miserable material world. They see it all year long and come to Hawaii to try and forget about it for a week or two. That's why when you showed them pictures of the starving kids they just forked over the cash. Only a few took back their donations after they asked what organization we represented and I informed them we were Hare Krsnas. It was then that another devotee informed me ISKCON was an acronym for International Society Keeping Children Off Narcotics, wink, wink. It was all good in the 'hood because the key was to come back to the temple at night with your pockets full "By Any Means Necessary," as Malcolm X put it.

I got smooth with the Japanese intimidation thing as well, that is until I unknowingly got in the face of a couple of yakuza (Japanese Mafia) members from Tokyo. They threatened to chop me up into little pieces and feed me to the sharks. After that I was just a little more humble, at least until I checked to see if the guy had a full-body suit tattoo and a severed pinky finger. Anyway everything was going well on Kalakaua Avenue. I was really bringing in the loot earning upwards of three, four, five hundred dollars a day. If I hit up a few Japanese tourists I could clock $700 to $800 a day.

One great thing about living in the Hawaii temple was the fact that I was very regulated with my life and my spiritual practice. I was in bed every night by 8 p.m. and up by 2 a.m. I meditated from 2:30 to 4 a.m., went to the morning program, then before breakfast went for a five-mile run and practiced martial arts. By 9 a.m. I was the first one in the van to go down to Waikiki and when we arrived, God help you if you fucked with us because I would fight you to the death. I was making a lot of spiritual advancement because I believed back then as I still do today that what Srila Prabhupada brought to the shores of America is the "Absolute Truth." If you follow the Absolute Truth strictly you develop a taste for spiritual life and lose your hankerings for materialistic life. Were we being deceived by the leaders? Hell yes! Did we know it? Hell no! Because had I known what was going on, believe me, heads would have been rolling.

In the late-'70s and early-'80s the Hare Krsna Movement was transforming into a weird cult. When Srila Prabhupada left the planet in '77 the problems started and still continue to this day. The trouble within the movement boils down to one thing and one thing only - the scum who, without any authority, seized control and took over. The bogus leaders, who appointed themselves as Srila Prabhupada's successors, changed everything Srila Prabhupada had previously established and used their henchmen to enforce all their bullshit. Srila Prabhupada never would have allowed the donation scams that were going on in places like Japan and Hawaii. In '76 Srila Prabhupada found out that a tape was circulating around the movement by one of the big collectors which broke down how to be a better scammer and how to use the tricks of deception when soliciting donations. When Srila Prabhupada found out what was going on he was furious. He ordered all fraudulent collection methods to be stopped at once because it would ruin the movement. The fact was Srila Prabhupada only wanted books to be sold as a way to collect funds and nothing else.

These guys were nothing more than a bunch of thieving con artists. They allowed the Krsna children (who later won a multi-million dollar lawsuit against the movement) to be molested in the Krsna schools. They sold and took drugs, and even gave their disciples mood-altering drugs like Prozac and other substances to keep them in line so that their multi-million dollar enterprise kept functioning. They stole millions under tax-free status, had rampant sex (abstinence is part of the religion), and even ran a grave robbing business in Miami where they stole jewels from corpses. Shit, one so-called guru actually built a fuckin' UFO to fly to the spiritual world, stole millions and lived a life of luxury, sponging off of his disciples. Another bought a multi-million dollar chateau in the South of France and had sex with his massage therapist while we literally fed the food thrown in the garbage by the guests at the Sunday Love Feast. One low-life, fake guru said recently that although he had fallen from grace, he was so addicted to the lifestyle of being worshiped he couldn't give it up. These guys even murdered people who spoke out against their bullshit including a devotee named Sulochana in 1986. Even though the so-called guru Kirtananda recently admitted to molesting little boys while he was a guru, he's still worshiped like a god by his blind followers. Another guru has ordered his disciples to kill anyone in other countries who speaks out against him.

If you've read the book Monkey on a Stick: Murder, Madness, and the Hare Krishnas by John Hubner and Lindsey Gruson, it chronicles and exposes all the insane stuff that was going down in the West Virginia Hare Krsna temple. The so-called guru Kirtananda who the book's about, and who later served ten years in a federal prison, also told his disciples to kill anyone who spoke ill of him and they did. Another one of the bogus gurus ran one of the biggest ecstasy operations in England until he was decapitated in the middle of a crowded mall by his one of his Irish disciples, because the fake guru was having sex with the guy's wife.

They took advantage of the innocent devotees who joined and let me clear that up right now, it is the minority who were and still are corrupt. They've done so many horrible things and unfortunately that's all you ever hear about in the media because as we all know, negativity sells papers and earns TV raiting points. A majority of the Hare Krsna followers are sincere, amazing people who have given their lives to the service of both God and humanity. That's exactly what attracted me to the movement in the first place, and make no mistake about it, what Srila Prabhupada set up and the way they are running the movement today, are two different things. We believed back then that Srila Prabhupada gave them the authority to become guru (which he didn't) and that they were his successors, which meant that they were carrying out his orders. They had the oldest, most scientific spiritual literatures on the planet, the Vedas, which gave them the authority to act like they were the all-in-all and according to them we were to worship them "As good as God." If you didn't, or if you asked questions concerning any improprieties you saw, you were thrown out or suffered a worse fate.

These were just some of the methods they used to deceive and control people, the cult leader's "Tools of the Trade". We were also told to not talk to our family members because they were meat-eating dogs who just wanted to take you away from Krsna. On the other hand, Srila Prabhupada never said that and wanted the devotees' families to be involved as much as possible. I remember hearing about this big lawsuit against the movement while I was in Hawaii and when I inquired about it I was given a bullshit story. The real deal was that one of the scammers with some clout had the hots for a young girl named Robin George who joined one of the temples. When her parents got wind of some sex crap that was going down, they wanted to take her out of the movement. So what this guy basically did was kidnap her and shuffle her around the country hiding her in different temples so her parents couldn't find her. Nice, huh? Eventually the girl and her parents ended up suing and winning millions, which was a big financial set back for the movement.

Even Dhanadhara Swami, the so-called guru of the hardcore Hare Krsna band Shelter (and so many other hardcore kids), allowed dozens of kids in the Hare Krsna school to be molested by a low-life scumbag. He even terrorized the kids to keep them quiet. Dhanadhara beat them, even broke little kids' noses when they told him that his friend was raping them. Dhanadhara was informed last year that some of the kids would take their names off a huge lawsuit they had pending if he would renounce his guru position. He declined, instead he chose to go on as a bogus guru, and so the kids proceeded with their lawsuit.

Another whack-job named Murli-Vadhaka raped dozens of little boys at the Hare Krsna school in Lake Huntington, New York. Now get this, he was about to get voted in as a guru, until the kids that he raped protested. That piece of shit quickly dropped out of sight and no charges were ever brought up against him for the dozens of kids he molested. Someone I know recently saw him in a temple in Hartford, Connecticut that's mostly families with kids, and he was serving the food at the Sunday Love Feast like everything was cool.

One of these fake gurus in India recently raped more than twenty young boys in the Krsna school. Several devotees gathered and taped the children giving testimony to what the guru did to them. Hearing of this, the guru sent a mob of machete-wielding thugs to confiscate the tapes.

These scumbag pricks should be in jail or end up dead just like the pedophile Catholic priests or anybody else who touches a kid. Since I had that shit done to me as a child, I would personally love to get my hands around their fuckin' necks. Even in prisons like Sing-Sing and San Quentin, the places that house some of the worst criminals on Earth, sexual offenders who touch children are considered the lowest of the low. They're referred to as "Short Eyes", and if the inmates find out about their crimes, their days are numbered.

Now I find it hard to believe that criminals in prison know how to deal with molester scumbags and a movement that is supposed to stand for righteousness and truth, did nothing. As a matter of fact, to this day, not one single molester within the movement has been brought up on charges. Not one. Just recently a teacher in India was merely asked to leave after it was discovered he was molesting several children that were under his care. Do you know what Srila Prabhupada said should happen to anyone who harms a child? That person should be hung. Well, it seems that the current leaders missed these instructions and that's why I encourage the kids who've had shit done to them to take matters into their own hands. As a matter of fact, one of them did find Dhanadhara a while back and he gave him a taste of his own medicine, by beating the living shit out of him.

These parasites have done so many things like that, which not only cost Srila Prabhupada's movement huge amounts of money, but also gave it a bad name. We were out their conning the public while the leaders were conning us. And I never kept a single penny. These guys on the other hand have very hefty, hidden bank accounts. One of the self-appointed guru scammers, Tamal-Krsna (who was accused of poisoning Srila Prabhupada), recently died in a hellish car accident in India. It was later discovered that he had $6.2 million stashed away for a rainy day, while temples were closed because of the lack of funds. Now the funny shit is when the current leaders talk about the dude's death, they make it sound like he left this world under these auspicious conditions. Gimme a fuckin' break. He died having his head practically severed, and his brains splattered all over the place as he begged for water on the side of the road. Yeah, real fuckin' auspicious. I just have one message to the rest of you scammer fake gurus...YOU'RE NEXT! God sees all, and each and every one of you parasites will get your karma for the shit you've done and are doing, trust me.

In retrospect, I guess I was a perfect candidate for the bogus cult they were running. Now, I'm not making excuses for some of the things I did, but I was duped. Just look at where I came from. My life was hell thus far and now I was being offered nirvana, the spiritual world, but for the price of my soul. My philosophy is fool me once, shame on you, fool me twice, shame on me. I was born having to literally fight in this material world, that's the way I've lived my life and I'm sure as hell not one to back down from a fight for the right cause. This movement and what it has to offer the world is far too valuable to just walk away from and leave in the hands of these bastards. Myself and a lot of revolutionary-minded devotees are hip to their bullshit and have taken up arms against them by creating the IRM (ISKCON Revival Movement). If you want to see the crazy shit these subhuman leaders of ISKCON have done, it's all laid out in detail, just go to the IRM's Web site: www.iskconirm.com. The IRM devotees have faced great adversity, even death, to get the truth out there. A good friend of mine was marked for death in India by a so-called ISKCON guru. The bomb that he had one of his brainwashed disciples build in order to kill this devotee blew up its builder in Mayapur, instead. Even though the newspapers in India said there was bomb-making material found and it was in fact a bomb, the bogus leaders covered it up and told the movement it was a gas explosion.

What I would find out later, in terms of how deep the deception and downright criminal activity went, blew my mind. It's going to blow yours, too, when we get to it, trust me. These guys make Jim Jones and Charlie Manson look like fuckin' Boy Scouts. When their web of deception began unfolding before my eyes the one emotion I was consumed with was anger, and not just at them but at myself as well and for one simple reason - I forgot my roots. I forgot where I came from. I violated the first law of punk, which clearly states, "Always Question Authority."

What is it with Marines and me? Is it because I got Squid written all over my face and there's always been a rivalry between sailors and Grunts? Does it say I hate Marines across my forehead? All I know is whatever it was, from D.C. to the shores of Waikiki, the Grunt boys and I (except for my bros in Puerto Rico) had beef. According to Shari the very large Grunt who was storm trooping toward us sporting an evil grin smacked and even punched some of the other devotees on several occasions because Jesus told him to do it.

As he walked up screaming biblical crap in Shari's face he spit at him. When I went to grab the guy, he made the crucial mistake of swinging at me. I ducked and cracked him with a good shot to the face, which stunned him. I grabbed him and dragged him over to the cement flower boxes, which lined the street outside the International Market Place. The boxes had metal spikes wrapped around each of its four edges, which acted as a barrier for people who tried to mess with the flowers. As a kid I learned to fight with the terrain and use what's at your disposal to win a fight. If you had to smash someone's head off a wall, the concrete, a parked car, rip off a car antenna and use it like a whip to the eyes, you did it. The key was DO NOT LOSE. I bent him over backwards on the steel spikes and punched him. Then I jumped up and landed on his chest with my knees, which sent the spikes plunging into his back. He screamed like a banshee as he fell to the floor, bleeding profusely. These two huge cops heard the commotion, came running up, threw me up against the wall and busted me.

The police report said I caused him serious facial damage and came close to puncturing one of his lungs. They showed me the pictures of the dude and he had a black eye and deep gashes in his back. They asked what kind of a peace-loving Hare Krsna would do such a thing? One of the cops kept insisting because of my Death Before Dishonor tattoo, I was a member of the military who was AWOL. He also said that John Thompson, the name I gave them off my ISKCON charity identification card was a fake alias. I thought for sure the gig was up. As I sat in my cell I prayed to Krsna to protect me and get me out of this situation, but it seemed hopeless. The cops said they weren't letting me go to court until I told them my real name because they knew I was lying about my identity. They even paraded a guy in front of my cell that they beat the living shit out of because he gave them a phony name and that caused them to do hours of extra paperwork.

I was in the holding cell for several hours and just when I was about to tell them my real name and take my punishment, a voice called out, "John Thompson!" I looked up from the floor of the cell where I was sitting. On the other side of the bars was this guy in a suit that said, "Hello John. I'm your attorney. We're going to court." He got me out of the holding cell, told me to shut up and not to make any statements to the cops. Who was I to argue? He was a professional, right? I could see that the cops who arrested me were really pissed they couldn't crack me because they knew I was actually AWOL. The one cop who had it in for me vowed to keep tabs on me. One thing I definitely learned in that cell though, prayer works. Good lookin' out Krsna. When I arrived in court I found out the devotees managed to find two witnesses who saw the Marine spit at Shari and then swing at me. As a result, the case was dropped by the state, but not by this dickhead Marine who threatened to get me as I left the court. Two days later he walked up and stood by as three of his

Marine buddies harassed Shari, broke up our donations, pushed him and then spit at me. I challenged all three to a fight, not in the street like last time, but in the underground parking garage down the block. They laughed and accepted the challenge. As we walked up the street they said I got lucky with their buddy (who stayed behind because he was warned to stay away from us by the judge) and as they put it, "My momma wasn't even gonna be able to recognize my ass when they were done with me." We went to the bottom level of the garage and as I put my bag down I immediately punched the first one and knocked him out cold. "Now, it's two-on-one," I said. The other two had this look on their faces that said, "Maybe we made a mistake." As we squared-off I decided to take on the bigger guy first. I grabbed him by the back of the neck and pulled his head down. I jumped up and landed a flying knee strike to his face, before he went right down. I then proceeded to ground and pound as they say in the street-fighting world, talking crazy shit with each punch and elbow I landed on his face and head. After a few blows he was out. I got off him, turned to the last man standing and said, "I guess it's just you and me now, huh?" I didn't even get a chance to beat the last guy down, because he took off out of that garage like a bat out of hell.

I went up to the street, put on my flower bag and went back to harassing the tourists. Shari walked up and asked me what happened, assuming we didn't fight because I was rather calm and didn't have a scratch on me. I told him I didn't think they'd be coming back, but I was wrong. They did come back - to shake my hand. As they stood there with ice packs on their faces (the original Marine I went to jail for split) they congratulated me and said they've never seen anyone fight like that. They promised to never bother us again and that they were going to tell the rest of the Grunts to do the same. Shari was stunned. I thought it really took balls for them to come back and humble up considering they were all twice my size. They kept their word and we were never hassled by another Marine out on Kalakaua Avenue.

After about a year on the islands I started to feel homesick for New York. I met some punk rockers down at Waikiki who were on vacation and just saw the Bad Brains play in California. I left soon afterward and after all the money I collected for the movement, the temple wouldn't even buy my plane ticket home. I had to borrow cash from my brother E. Later on I heard about the bullshit that was going on in that temple. Narahari (the renounced swami) had sex with a blatantly gay devotee named Diva. Every night when we went to bed Diva would slip out of the room and go to Narahari's hut in the back of the property to, as he put it, "Massage the Swami." Yeah, right. We know what you were massaging, dude. In addition to participating in gay sex acts, Narahari was also growing weed on the big island farm (he had a college degree in horticulture). He even stole the temple's prize possession, the Jaladuta 2 sailboat, and sold it. He now makes a living on the islands marrying people underwater in scuba gear. Can you say Jaws?

I was back in New York and hanging out on the scene, but things were somehow different. I mean sure, I was having fun going to shows, smoking weed and hanging out with girls. But after living as a monk for over a year and really getting in touch with my spirit and God I just felt incomplete. I felt like something was missing. It was at that point I took a trip out to Long Island with the Bad Brains who were opening for Peter Tosh at Stony Brook University. It was good to hang out with the old crew, especially since Judas wasn't hanging around the Bad Brains anymore. We had a big soccer game prior to sound check with the Bad Brains posse facing off against the Peter Tosh posse. We lost the game because the Dreads smoked a lot of ganja, but even when they were lifted they could play a sick game of soccer.

I met Peter briefly and asked him all kinds of questions. To my surprise he wasn't as dogmatic as a lot of the Rastas who are very one track minded. Peter was more universal. We talked about yoga and martial arts (he held a black belt). He also told me about the time when he and Bob Marley first saw pictures of India's Shiva worshipers (Shivites) with their twenty-foot-long dreadlocks, smoking ganja and hashish. He said they were blown away because they realized there were other Dreads in other parts of the world. Peter told me no matter what to stay on the path and that Jah will guide and reveal all in time. He said we must never go with the flow that we must always resist the tides of Babylon. For everything I was going through at that time his words hit home. That day meant a lot to me and it's an experience I will never forget. We must never be afraid to stand on our own as individuals and stand up for what we believe. Rest in Peace, Peter.

I continued going to the temple in Brooklyn and spent a lot of time on my own. I needed money being out on the streets and from time to time, I sold dime bags of pot. That's when I was introduced to a customer named Arthur "Googie" who was the former drummer of the Misfits. Googie was a hothead and had a reputation for knocking out high-profile people. He knocked out his own singer, Glenn Danzig, because Danzig made him look like a conehead in the photo that appeared on the "Walk Among Us" Misfits record. He even smacked around actor Matt Dillon and hit Rockets Red Glare (friend of Sid Vicious and rumored to be the real killer of Nancy Spungen) over the head with a garbage can. He broke my old Navy buddy Raybeez's jaw and during the Misfits' West Coast tour he took on half the crowd with one of his cymbal stands. Googs was one year older than me and when we talked about where we came from it turned out his family had a summer bungalow in Rockaway. As a kid, he remembered seeing me hanging out with Jimbo and the rest of my crazy crew.

The conversation eventually got down to the fact that Googs wanted me to front him $20 worth of pot, which I did, even if he had no intention of paying me back. That's just the way he was. Everyone on the LES knew you didn't trust Googs with two things - your girl or your weed. I mean, you could leave $10,000 in front of the fucker and he wouldn't take a penny, but leave a bag of weed and his ass is definitely tapping the shit. Leave him alone with your girl, he would definitely talk shit about you and try to pass along his number.

I saw him on several occasions after I gave him the weed and I never asked him for the money or brought it up. That would piss him off because he wanted a confrontation. After a while he just walked up all pissed off and red-faced and handed me the money. He said he was trying to test me because he heard from his friend and other people that I had a rep for fighting. He couldn't understand my calm demeanor and I explained how it came from meditation and vegetarianism. And with that, we started talking about spiritual topics. I told him about Krsna and he said that he remembered seeing the Hare Krsnas chanting out on the boardwalk in Rockaway back in the early-'70s. He had his doubts about a lot of what I was telling him in terms of the philosophy, but at the same time he found it interesting. I told him that just as I got signs that I was on the right path in my search for the truth, Krsna would prove to him that this was the real deal. After talking for a few hours, we shook hands and he split to his crib uptown.

Googs was a superintendent for a big high-rise apartment building near the U.N. on Manhattan's East Side called "The Delegate." He worked like a bull busting his ass waxing floors, painting, doing plumbing work and taking out hundreds of 50-pound garbage bags. That was one of his classic one-liners, "Yo, shmedrick. I sling garbage all fuckin' day, I will fuck your ass up" and it was true. I helped him on several occasions and it took a lot of strength to carry those heavy-ass bags up the stairs and out onto the street. That's what gave him his knock out power.

The next morning Googie was taking out the trash when something told him to look in this one particular bag out of the fifty or so he was putting on the curb. He opened it up and right inside was a copy of the Bhagavad-Gita As It Is by A.C. Bhaktivedanta Svami Prabhupada. He was speechless and dropped everything he was doing. He jumped on the Second Avenue bus to try and find me downtown and tell me about what had happened. He didn't have to look too far, because I was standing at the bus stop and finishing up a conversation on the pay phone. He ran up to me with this crazed look on his face and said, "What are you doing here?" and I replied, "Just hanging out." That's when he pulled out the Gita, stuck it in my face and told me how he got it. I just smiled and said, "I told you dude." A couple of months later Googs got the words "Hare Krsna" tattooed on the outside of his bicep.

It says in the Vedas that when you truly are searching for the truth you'll be led and directed to it by the Lord in the heart, or Visnu. Visnu instructs us from within and the guru is the Lord's external representative who is here to further instruct us. Personally speaking, I don't always listen to that inner voice of reason that guides me to the path of enlightenment and says, "Listen, Johnny Bloodclot. If you do that you know what's gonna happen, bro." Instead being a conditioned soul, the polluted thoughts of my mind sometimes win the battle and get me into a world of shit. One thing I can guarantee you is that if you talk to anyone who's come in contact with the knowledge Srila Prabhupada disseminated about the Supreme Personality of Godhead, Krsna you'll find so many stories like Goog's and mine. There are too many of these incidents to just brush off as coincidence. "I was gonna go this way and something inside told me to go that way instead and that's when I met this devotee and got a book."

Later that week I went to the Brooklyn temple's Sunday Love Feast and I took Googs with me. He was definitely a little bugged-out by the chanting, incense and people with shaved heads and robes, but at the same time he dug it. I saw some of my old Hare Krsna friends from the 7th Avenue temple and I told them I was in Hawaii for the last year and shaved-up and everything. They told me the guru (I use the term lightly) from Hawaii, Ramesvara Svami, was at the temple. It was at that very moment, he came by with some other devotees, including the Brooklyn temple president. Ramesvara recognized me immediately and before we go any further let me give you the background on him.

I personally believe he came to the movement with honest, good intentions to serve the mission, but just like the others, became hungry for power, money and a level of worship not even the president of the United States gets. He eventually got caught having sex with a fifteen-year-old girl and when the rumors first surfaced around the movement he totally denied it. He even had me set up a meeting with all his New York disciples and it was held at the actor Rip Torn and the late Geraldine Page's brownstone in Chelsea. I had made their daughter Angelica and their son-in-law Keith devotees and they were one of his aspiring disciples. Ramesvara swore to us that the rumors were not true, that the movement was out to get him for some reason and this was all some kind of conspiracy. Several weeks later he left with millions in tow, married some woman and invested in real estate out on Long Island with the money. Believe it or not, he's considered one of the lesser of the bad guys within the movement.

Anyway, Ramesvara talked with me and I told him I left Hawaii because I missed New York. He told me to move into the Brooklyn temple and I said I'd think about it. As I walked away I overheard him say, "That guy is a huge collector. We have to get him in this temple no matter what." They put the pressure on me to move in and sure enough in the weeks that followed I was back in orange robes with a shaved head.

I was immediately sent to St. Louis by Ramesvara to be personally trained on how to move books in the airports by three of the legendary Hare Krsna book distributors. Each day, these devotees were moving hundreds of books and clocking hundreds of dollars for the movement. I have to tell you in all honesty, I was into the philosophical aspect of what they were doing. They spent time with the people and really made them appreciate the books and spiritual enlightenment they were receiving. I didn't take to the airport thing very well because I had a hard time dealing with the happy American family vibe and the suit and tie business travelers. I was a little too rough around the edges for the airport hustle and as soon as they saw that it wasn't my propensity, I was immediately sent back to New York. Upon my arrival in the Big Apple they didn't waste a minute of time.

Back home, I was trained by the best in the business to do "The Pick." If there were ever a Hare Krsna Olympics these guys would have received the gold medal in three separate events. The first is "The Change Up." This is where you tell a mark you have a lot of ones and fives and ask to give them change for a $20 or a

$50 bill you so keenly observed in their wallets. Then you give them very little change back, pressuring them with each bill you do give back to donate the rest. Since most people were in a hurry they would cave in and give us the cash. The next operation was "Cloak and Dagger." Devotees had a serious collection of costumes, fake I.D.s, wigs and business suits, which could only be outmatched by members of the CIA. The last technique was known as "The 100-Yard Dash." When people saw through the smoke and mirrors and mumbo-jumbo soliciting tactics and realized they gave their hard-earned money to a Hare Krsna member they would demand their money back. We just bolted and never gave back donations unless it was at gunpoint. That's exactly why there were no fat Hare Krsna collectors out on The Pick. You had to be fast on your feet to get away with the cash if things got hot.

Every morning at around 9, after four hours of chanting and spiritual practice, you had forty to fifty "Pickers," as we were known, getting ready to go out and deceive...I mean, save the world. The cast of characters included clowns, people in wheelchairs, Raggedy Anne, mimes, deaf people with those cards they hand out asking for money and depending on the time of year: Santa Claus, the Easter Bunny or perhaps even a Thanksgiving turkey. We hit the subways, airports, parking lots, the Olympics, concerts, tractor pulls, football games, shopping malls, Department of Motor Vehicles and anywhere else large numbers of people congregated. Shit, even when Pope John Paul II came to America there were these guys posing as Christian monks in those brown robes, selling buttons with the Pope's face on it and making $2,000 a day.

The leaders of ISKCON, or the IS...CON ARTISTS as I like to refer to them, had a multi-million dollar tax-free business built off scamming and deceiving people. When I hear that old stereotype, "Oh yeah, I know the Krsnas, they're the ones who try and sell you a flower for a buck at the airport," I just laugh and say to myself, "Dude, if you only knew." They said it didn't matter that we deceived people dressed as Santa Claus or clowns because the money was being used in the Lord's service and they (the victims) got the spiritual benefit. I turned in every single penny I collected in New York because as we were told time and time again, "To take even one red cent meant you were going to hell." Now you tell me, what Fortune 500 Company wouldn't want to have employees like us? They told us we had to, as they called it, "Liberate" the money from the evil doing non-devotees who were just going to hell with it because they were spending their money on illicit sex, eating meat, gambling and getting stoned. The sad thing was, that's exactly what a lot of these leaders did with the money they stole.

I didn't want to do the cartoon character thing (not yet anyway), so I was introduced to the "Pick a Wig Drawer," which held some twenty to thirty very, weathered and worn wigs. I chose this red-haired, straw-looking thing that looked like an elephant ate it, shit it out and then stomped all over it. Since I had my head shaved and sported a sikha (pony-tail in the back), I had to wear a wig to cover it. Otherwise, people would know I was a Hare Krsna. God forbid. The very next day, I was immediately put out into the parking lots to collect money with these bumper stickers. After a day of grinding it out, I did pretty well and beat out everyone in the temple. Since I did so well on my first day, the temple leaders knew at that point, I was a collection goldmine. The wig was obviously so fake that the very first person I hit up asked me why I was wearing it. Hearing that, my quick-thinking, street-hustling improvisational skills immediately kicked in. As I gave her a look of despair I lifted up the front of my wig to show off my baldhead and replied, "I just finished chemotherapy."

Each morning while the entire congregation gathered in the temple room they would read out the "Laxmi (sounds like locks-shmee) points," the scores of how much money you collected. One Laxmi point equaled one dollar. When the devotees heard how many Laxmi points you earned the entire temple would clap. If you were the big man of the day, which I frequently was, you got all the extra perks. Do you know what extra perks are for a cult member? You got to eat one of the so-called guru's (one fake-guru was usually giving head to his gay lover the previous night) chewed-up, half-eaten, spit-laden leftover samosas from breakfast. According to them you were going to make great spiritual advancement just by eating it. If you thought that was good, just hold on because believe me, it gets even better.

Now, if you were the highest earner for the week, you got an even holier perk - you were the one who washed and massaged the dude's feet with a combination of yogurt, honey and ghee (clarified butter). Then you got to drink the concoction down because just by drinking their toe-cheese you were guaranteed spiritual liberation. Needless to say, I passed on that entree.

It was all about the Laxmi points and once they realized I was a goldmine I was given a new identity. They knew I was AWOL from the Navy and with the deception tactics of The Pick arrest was inevitable. I now adopted the identity of a redheaded stepchild named Edward Leonforte and I had several pieces of I.D. to back it up. Edward was another devotee who lived at the temple. To the leaders there he wasn't as valuable as I was because he couldn't bring in the kind of dough I was earning. So what did it matter if he racked up a few criminal cases of fraud under his name for the sake of all mankind? As a matter of fact, I was arrested no fewer than five times. Several years after I left the temple, I saw Ed and he said, "Hey Jayananda (my spiritual name). I hope you're not still using my I.D.s, because I just got a couple of notices to appear in court for not paying traffic tickets for going through red lights on a bike." I acted insulted as I stood there on my bike in full bike messenger attire and said, "Of course not. How could you even think I would do something like that? By the way, just out of curiosity, was it at 57th and Madison, or 42nd and Fifth?" It was neither he stated. He got those two summonses a week later.

When it came to hustling donations, they gave me the minimum weekly quota of $2,500, which I was able to do with my eyes closed. If the devotees didn't make their weekly quotas they weren't allowed to come back to the temple on Sunday night. I was now a full-time Picker and one of the biggest in the temple, along with another devotee named Adi-Purusa, with whom they built up a furious rivalry so that we'd collect even more donations. I was also initiated and given the name "Jayananda," which means "All glories to the transcendental bliss of spiritual life" in Sanskrit. Now some of you may be appalled by what you're about to read, but some of you will see the creative genius of the scam these guys perpetrated and hopefully gain some insight into the minds of the cult leaders. As for me, I was just doing what I thought was the right thing at the time. Just like the Manson Family members who killed and committed other crimes, the Jim Jones cyanide drinkers, or the Rashnish (a bogus Indian guru) followers who let his fat, smelling-like-curry, nasty-ass bone their wives so Siva would bless them. See, I was a foot soldier for the Hare Krsna Mob, a member of the Swami Organized Crime Family, and now if you will, please allow me to tell a few stories about the methods I used to collect close to $150,000 in the fourteen months I lived in that temple.

Concerts were my bread and butter out there on The Pick. Let me send Billboard magazine a heads up right now. Fellas, if you want to know who's selling records and who ain't, you don't have to wait for the SoundScan numbers to come back. All you have to do is ask a Hare Krsna Picker because they know who's hot and who's not just by how many people are turning up in the lots. Now, to understand why this gig was so huge you first had to understand the psychology behind us going to the concerts in the first place. Most of the concertgoers were either teenagers, or people in their early-20s who had bought their tickets way in advance. Since they had been anticipating the show for months, they made sure they had everything ready when the day finally arrived. When it came time for the show, they lined up the perfect date, the perfect group of friends and the perfect amounts of drugs measured out in perfect amounts for their parking lot party. This was their big night - the one they'd tell their grandchildren about. Now, making their story even more memorable is where I came in. I mean, just get a load of one of my typical parking lot encounters.

Darkness fell over Uniondale, Long Island and I was just about finished making the rounds in the lots at the Nassau Coliseum working a Van Halen concert. At this point I had been in the temple a few months and had the whole concert thing down. In the temple the other Pickers referred to me as a "Heavy," or in other words, I was someone who scared the living shit out of people. My tools of the concert trade included my overly official-looking I.D. that I wore on a chain like an undercover cop, a dummy earpiece like the Secret Service dudes, a fanny pack and a flashlight. I kept the "Don't be a Dick" and "Life is Short - Party Naked," and other joke stickers in the fanny pack. I usually kept the band stickers down by my privates, because the feds who took all the bootleggers T-shirts in the lots would take the stickers as well, because they weren't officially licensed merchandise.

During the summer months, you would sweat like hell and the stickers would peel a little and get caught up in your short and curlies. Then you'd give them your line about giving them a citation for being under the influence of Van Halen or Ozzy (or whatever concert or event you worked) and go to pull out a sticker. When you reached down, you'd literally have to rip them out of your underbrush (which hurt like hell) and they'd yell, "Yo! That's fucked up, dude" because there were always a couple of big old pubic hairs stuck to their sweat-soaked sticker.

Each event, whether it was a concert, football game, car race or whatever, always consisted of three phases. The incoming parking, the event itself (where we got in by using fake vendor's licenses) and finally the blow-out, which was basically one big traffic jam which allowed us to work the line of cars with whatever it was we were peddling. It was all according to time and circumstance and our tactics varied for each event. For instance, if I went to a college football game in Alabama and tried to do what I did at the concerts I would have got my ass handed to me by a bunch of rednecks. At concerts like this one, for instance, I would go inside, walk up and down the aisles with four or five different Van Halen stickers stuck on a big cardboard sign that said: "Four Stickers/$5." While at football games, you worked the beer lines; car races, the bathroom lines and the infield by going from motor home to motor home during the race. Every event was different and we had to change our tactics accordingly or else we got nipped-out (busted) by Alice, which was our code word for cops. When it was all said and done, you'd average about $1,000 for a five-hour shift, but I was above average. In fact, I was great! Now just a word of advice kids, before you try this at home, spend some time with your local bogus Hare Krsnas, because if you mess up it's either jail or a good ass-whippin'. So have the best in the biz show you the ropes on this hustle.

I was cleaning up at this Van Halen show and had made somewhere in the neighborhood of three bills just on the incoming parking. I had just hit up my last car in the lot and was about to shift personas from an undercover cop to that of a vendor who was late for work. That's when I noticed this car in the back of the lot. I could see they were sniffing coke inside, so I figured what the hell, I'd do one more car and then head in to walk the aisles with my cardboard sign. There were six people in the car and under these circumstances I knew I could get at least five bucks if not more from each of them. I purposely kept out of sight, sneaking through the lot unnoticed until I got to the back left bumper of their car. Then it was time to swing into action. I crept along the driver's side until I was right below the driver's window. They were so caught up in sniffing that they didn't even notice me. I popped up right outside the driver's window, hit him in the face with the blinding brilliance of my super bright Mag-Lite and yelled, "Freeze!" The driver, who was chopping up a large amount of coke on a mirror, panicked and threw it up in the air, which sent that huge pile of cocaine all over everyone in the car. I had to fight back the laughter as I shined the light in the faces of my new friends, who were all in total shock and looked like a bunch of powdered donuts. See, that's where the acting part came in. You couldn't smile or laugh - you were undercover.

I quickly flashed my fake I.D. for obvious reasons and then talked to my back up in the hidden mic under my shirt. "Yeah, I'm at the suspect's car now, a black Chevrolet, license plate blah, blah, blah (I memorized the plate). Yeah Sarge, there's major contraband in the vehicle. Better bring a paddy wagon there's six of them. Roger, ten-four." Then I looked around the floor of the car a bit with the flashlight and ordered the driver (who was ready to go into cardiac arrest) to roll down the window. After barking the command several more times because he just sat there frozen, he finally did so. As I kept looking around the car moving the flashlight from face to face I asked them all for some identification. I collected their I.D.s and I studied each one briefly. I then said in my best official voice, "Gentleman, we have reason to believe that you are all in violation of penal code three, section one-hundred-eight, that is (I pulled out a stack of Van Halen stickers from my crotch) you're all under the influence... of Van Halen!" I gave them the stickers and the dudes in the back all grabbed their hearts as they started having serious palpitations. Some of them laughed and some were close to tears. The driver was still in a state of shock and I comforted him by saying, "Dude, it's okay. It was a joke." I continued with the pitch. "Now I'm not gonna take you guys in on your first offense, but we are gonna have to fine you guys five bucks each, for excessive partying, to help feed needy kids." Naturally realizing they weren't going to jail, they were all like, "Holy shit! Hell yeah dude, that was fuckin' fucked up, bro. You got it man!" They'd gladly fork over the cash and one even demanded I take $10, which I had no problem with.

The driver however, didn't budge with turning over the funds. I poked him lightly. "It's five or I'm taking you in, brother." He mumbled, "Get away from my car." I asked him for the donation again to which he said clearly, "Get the fuck away from my car!" Now I wasn't one to take no for an answer (that's why the leaders loved me) so I continued, "Uhh, I gave you stickers, man. They're five bucks, bro. C'mon, your buddies all paid up." He was furious and trembling with anger. "That was $200 worth of pure, fuckin' Colombian coke, asshole." I looked at him and tried to lighten the mood with a joke, "So, uhhh, I guess a donation's out of the question?" He screamed like Tarzan on steroids and practically ripped off his door getting out. He was a big son of a bitch and I wisely dropped all their I.D.s and took off through the lot with him in hot pursuit, still covered in coke and yelling every curse word under the sun. He never was able to catch me, thank God. And by the way, Van Halen kicked ass that night. When it was all said and done, I made close to $700, which was better than any concert I ever did with Mikey Debris.

Retarded-Crippled Wheelchair Santa. First off, I have to admit that necessity became the mother of invention on this character that I helped create. Allow me to, as we say on the streets, "Break it down for ya." The bogus leaders of the Hare Krsna movement weren't the kind of people who wasted time, especially when it came to making money. In other words, while The Salvation Army and the other groups waited until after Thanksgiving to send their Santas on the streets, these guys had us out there in early November to get a jump on things. That's because all throughout ISKCON in every temple all over the world, November marked the beginning of "The Christmas Marathon," which by the way doesn't involve running, except occasionally from the cops.

Now, instead of pitting devotee against devotee in your local temple, it became a global competition to see who could collect the most money and give out the most books. Although they tried to make it look like the books were the real emphasis, it doesn't take a rocket scientist to figure out what it was all about. Like the Wu-Tang Clan said, "Cash Rules Everything Around Me... C.R.E.A.M. get the money, dolla' dolla' bill, y'all!"

Most of the leaders could care less about helping anyone get out of their suffering material condition by giving them spiritual knowledge. It was all about the C.R.E.A.M. baby, and the reason I know that is because a lot of that money we collected found its way into the secret bank accounts they set up all over the world. One so-called guru even spent $10,000 to buy his gay lover a Persian rug for them to have sex on in the Trump Towers, while "Bank Account Swami" (Ramapada), who's nothing more than a crook, had and still operates a loan-sharking business. His scheme involved hustling money from the temples and his disciples, then lending it back to them at astronomical interest rates. Nice gig, huh?

What they set up in the Hare Krsna Movement around the world is still going on as we speak. It's a type of pyramid scheme where the guys at the top of the pyramid (gurus and senior devotees) profit from all the hard work done by the guys operating on the bottom. The only reason some of these cats at the bottom stay in the movement is because they hope to one day reach the top and exploit the others now at the bottom. I know for a fact that the temple president in New York opened a recording studio after his fall from grace in the '80s. His cohort Vakresvara Pandit (from Puerto Rico... dude gets around right?) bought sports cars, guns and condos in Virginia with the money he stole and got from Bank Account Swami. Believe me, I haven't even begun to scratch the surface because hundreds of millions of dollars have been stolen in the last twenty-five or so years, all of which was tax free! Their current money making scheme (which is making them a killing) is selling religious visas to people from India. I just hope an al Qaeda terrorist doesn't figure that one out. Now that you know just a little of what was going on behind the scenes with the money we collected, all unbeknownst to us of course, you'll really get a sense of how we were being hustled. That's why, as of late, the temples all over the world (except those in Poland because they're a little slow to catch on) are pretty much empty. The rigorous collection schedules burnt everyone out.

In New York, The Christmas Marathon was an all out effort, where seventy devotees worked for a month and a half straight. If you didn't work the streets, you had better be part of the support team which cooked, cleaned, did laundry or whatever else needed to get done for those who were pounding the pavement. I heard through the grapevine right before the marathon started that you could really rack-up out there as Santa Claus. Since there were no events in the area for the Sticker Pick I decided to give it a try. They had me go out to the strip malls on Sunrise Highway on Long Island and people just didn't want to see no motherfuckin' Santa Claus' in November. Cars honked their horns and people screamed, "Hey asshole, you're early!" Storeowners threw me out and told me not to come back. It was brutal out there. Some kids even egged me.

But, being the persistent monk I was, I never gave up. My rebuttal to the storeowners became "We had a lot of backed up orders at the North Pole, so we had to start early this year." They obviously found it funny because it started to pay off in large dividends. My donations went from a $100 a day to $200 then $300, then $500 and before I knew, it was the middle of November. I was in full swing on the marathon and then the Indian summer hit. For three straight days temperatures soared into the 70s and I baked out there in that red Santa suit and white beard and wig combination. By the fourth day, I had the worst jock itch and rashes running up and down my legs from sweating profusely while I walked the five to six miles collecting donations. To make matters worse, the knee I hurt while I was in the Navy swelled to the size of a small grapefruit. I couldn't walk and just when it seemed like my gig was up and my marathon over, our resourceful Pick Leader told me, "You can't walk, no problem. Here's a motorized electric wheelchair! You can go work the lots in Staten Island as an invalid."

Yes folks, I was to play a cripple who never lost the meaning of what Christmas was all about - giving. I was going to be out there braving the elements collecting money for starving children all around the world. As I climbed aboard the motorized wheelchair, which would be my home for the next week or so, I brainstormed. Wait a minute, I thought. What if I went out as a crippled Santa? That would even be bigger than just some regular old invalid. Even better, what if this particular Santa was not only crippled, but retarded as well? This would be FUCKIN' HUUUUGE!!! When The Pick leader walked out and saw me in full Santa attire, in character, in that wheelchair, his mouth hung, his eyes bulged out of his head and he cracked a smile. "Wow," he said. "No one's ever stooped that low." He was thoroughly impressed.

The van dropped me off at the back of the mall parking lot in Staten Island so that no one would see me not only walk, but lift the two-hundred-pound monster of a wheelchair out of the van. The driver parked up front in between a few cars and if I got nipped I was to whistle and he would come and get me. As I drove my wheelchair up to the front of the lot where most of the cars were parked, I played it off to a 'T'. I used the bent portion of my left wrist to work the joystick and even cocked my head to one side. I had an empty paint can wrapped in Christmas paper, with pictures of starving children all over it. As I passed a few cars that were exiting, I saw the look on the faces of the people inside. They were totally fuckin' shocked. The horrified children then burst into tears as their mothers hid their faces. Hmmm, I thought, that's my angle. I went from car to car as the people left the mall, only hitting up mothers with kids. When I would approach the kids would cry, "Mommy, mommy! What's wrong with Santa?" Then I would reply in my best retard voice, "Santa says please help the starving children," and hold up my can. The mother would hide the kid's eyes and give me ten bucks just to go away. It worked like a charm, car after car and lot after lot. That first week I hit up all the stores around Staten Island, Long Island and even New Jersey. No security guard ever had the heart to throw me out and in one week I did close to 3 Gs in collections.

A week or so later I went back to that first lot on Staten Island and got ready to start the second round. Well, about an hour into it a black security guard who looked like he just got out of Rikers Island came out and told me to get out of the lot. Staying in character I answered okay, but I had no intention of leaving. As soon as he went inside I started working again, but that's when the snowstorm hit. I didn't mind getting wet, but the problem was my wheelchair's tires lost traction and were now just spinning in the snow. Since I couldn't catch my victims and corner them before they got to their cars (most ran as to avoid having their kids see me), I wasn't making any money. That's when I decided to go in and work the aisles of the stores. It was hilarious. Moms with their kids would be looking at stuff on the shelves and hear the motor of the chair from down the other end of the aisle. They would turn around, spot me coming and just stand there in shock. Then came the crying from the kids and of course, the money. I even got bold and worked the checkout line at a supermarket. While I was hustling I had an old lady pat me on my head, talk to me like I was a five-year-old and tell me what a special Santa I was as she put five bucks in my can.

I was doing bigger business than I ever was out in that cold-ass lot. As I made a beeline for a group of shoppers in the frozen food section I heard someone yell, "Hey you!" I slowly spun my wheelchair around and it was that same black security guard running toward me at full gallop. "I told you to get off the property!" he said. "No… no… no you did not… you…. you…. sai… said to get out of the lot." I said stuttering, but the brother wasn't having it. "Your honky-ass ain't no retard, so cut the bullshit. You got your motherfuckin' warning now I'm callin' the cops." I was out of there like Vladimir. I put the chair into high gear, got outside and whistled. The van came screeching up to a halt and its doors flew open. I jumped up out of the chair and sure enough the lady who gave me the five bucks was standing right behind me. She was stunned as I picked up the heavy wheelchair, threw it in the back of the van and jumped into the front seat. "You piece a crap. You should be ashamed of yourself," she screamed. As I closed the front passenger door I pulled off my Santa wig and revealed my shaved head. "Have a Merry Krsna and a Happy New Year," I yelled as we burned rubber and chanted all the way back to the temple.

After a week had passed, my leg was healed and I got out of that wheelchair. The devotee, Adi, who was in direct competition with me for marathon collections, now had passed me. The race was now on. During the last week of the marathon, I donned the Santa suit, traveled around and averaged eighteen-hour days hustling. We were doing huge amounts of money running into malls (kids would go nuts at the sight of us), bars, shops, gas stations, McDonald's and strip clubs. Shit, we even worked traffic lights at busy intersections. Any place there were groups of people, we were there. Finally, it came down to the last night and we knew by counting our money that it was almost dead even all the way up to the end.

The night before Christmas Eve we were somewhere upstate in Dutchess County, New York. It was freezing cold around 11 p.m. and we found one last bar to hit up for all the marbles. It was the bottom of the ninth, bases loaded and whoever hit the grand slam was going to be the hero for padding their guru's bank accounts. His was the homosexual who blatantly stole money and got blowjobs in gay bars. Mine was the child molester who raped a fifteen-year-old girl and split with millions of dollars. As we pulled up in the van we noticed that the parking lot of this particular bar was full and that meant only one thing; it was packed. We stared at each other for a second as if we were two prizefighters meeting in the center of the ring before the first round. We both jumped out of the van. As he ran in the front door, I decided I was going to go through the back door and work the bar toward the front. I saw another parking lot that was empty on the side of the building and ran down the embankment to cross it. As I got about fifty-feet out on the lot I heard a cracking noise. I then realized that this was no parking lot, but it was a small pond, which was frozen over and covered in snow.

I crashed through the ice and sunk to the bottom of the freezing cold water with my can of candy canes. I sunk about fifteen feet and couldn't see anything other than my entire life flashing in front of me. What a way to go, I thought, as a bogus Santa in some scummy pond upstate. But, instead of panicking I crawled along the bottom of the pond and finally reached the shore. I climbed out and crawled up the embankment. My Santa suit was completely soaked and felt like it weighed two-hundred-pounds. My beard was waterlogged and hung off my face by the elastic band. My Santa wig, as well as the rest of me, was covered in algae and pond scum and my can was also full of water. But I still had candy canes and that meant the competition wasn't over yet. I ran to the front door, burst in and yelled, "Ho, Ho, Ho, Merry Christmas!" The noisy patrons who were gathered around my competitor, forking over the dough, turned and looked at me. It was dead silent in there and finally someone shouted, "What the fuck happened to you Santa?" I yelled, "I missed my landing and the sleigh fell through the pond outside." The entire bar erupted in laughter and they all ran away from the other Santa and came at me stuffing bills in my can in exchange for my soggy candy canes. I won the Christmas Marathon and, just as a foot note, after all the devotees worked so hard that year on the marathon, the scum who ran the temple stole the entire collection. Oddly enough after the last night of the marathon, when all the money was in the treasurer's office he somehow forgot to lock the hundred and some odd-thousand dollars in the safe. All the thief had to do was break through a thin sheetrock wall, open the door and all the money was conveniently just sitting right there. It was so obvious what had happened and even the cops said it was an inside job. Real spiritual, huh?

The Hopathon/Walkathon gig was another moneymaking experience and it involved myself and another devotee, who was the one that came up with the idea. We usually did the Walkathon as a way to raise funds, but since it was Easter we invented a Hopathon. The other devotee who worked the Hopathon would wear this baseball hat that had iron-on letters that said, "HOP." The only problem was his ass wasn't doing any of the hopping, I was. I hopped from store to store on Long Island in a big-ass, hot as shit, heavy bunny suit. I had to stay in character the entire time hopping everywhere and not saying a word.

Here's how the Hopathon scam went. We had these bogus forms and I.D.s made up at the printers that looked official. The forms said the Hopathon was a fundraiser to fight heart disease for the American Heart Association. The inside joke became we were fighting heart disease alright; the disease of materialism in their hearts which would be eradicated as a result of them getting caught up in our scam for God. What's really twisted is that at that point I was operating on autopilot. In other words, I was programmed to not only follow and believe all the bullshit they were telling me, but now I was using my own intellect to devise strategies to make more money. I also had convinced myself that what I was doing was the right thing. We would burst into the store like gangbusters and as he ran around, sounding-off like a maniac carney who's trying to get you to pay one dollar to see the three-legged lady at a carnival freak show, he'd scream, "Sponsor the bunny! Sponsor the bunny! C'mon sir, it's just ten bucks to sponsor the bunny to hop a mile to help fight heart disease!" While he talked constantly I hopped all over the store knocking into everyone and everything. The head of the costume was so loose and had two little eyeholes that would end up on the side of my face as soon as I moved. Most of the time the store owners would give us $10 or $20 just to get out and leave their customers alone. We would do anywhere from $400 to $700 a day, sometimes even more, and we turned everything in. Shit, we even felt guilty about buying two bottles of spring water on a hot day, so we drank from someone's dirty garden hose.

Traveling/The Pick on Wheels. I guess you can call it, "Have stickers will travel." Now you'd think that with the amounts of money we were making the leaders would want us to be comfortable when we traveled thousands of miles, risking our lives to make them tens of thousands of dollars-a-week, right? Wrong! This is a cult we're talking about and the only ones who had creature comforts were the creatures that ran it. For everyone else, it was ungots. What they did was get these cargo vans and build wooden decks in them. Underneath went our thousands of stickers for the monthly events that were mapped out, a couple changes of clothes (no personal items, no room) and the cooking pots. They built an area in the middle of the deck to hold a propane tank for cooking. That van was home for the next month, two months, or however long we were out. Four or five of us were packed in the cargo vans like sardines and when we finally did get to sleep you couldn't even move. We showered by filling empty, one gallon spring water jugs and dumping them over our heads in the woods or the back of a supermarket at four or five in the morning. The supermarkets were the best place for our showers, because they usually had water faucets to hose down the dumpsters. It was perfect for refilling our jugs a couple of times and rinsing off really well.

I was down in Tennessee that January or February after The Christmas Marathon and we snuck behind this supermarket in the cover of darkness to shower. It was so cold that when we dumped the water over our heads our feet froze to the ground. So there we were a group of five, butt-naked Hare Krsna's with shaved heads and ponytails jumping around to keep warm. That's when we got hit with a spotlight. Then came a voice over a loudspeaker in one of those deep, Southern drawls, "This is the police. I don't know who the hell you are, or what the hell you are…" His partner piped in, "This is like something straight out of a Twilight Zone episode, Ned." He continued, "But ya's best get your asses in that van and get out a' here real quick like before I haul ya's in." We jumped in that van covered in soap and got the hell out of there in a hurry. To this day, I know those Dukes of Hazzard-ass cops tell that story around the water cooler. "Ned tell 'em 'bout the time we seen them Martians out behind the Winn-Dixie on Route 3 doin' some kinda naked water ritual dance in five degree weather at four in the mornin'."

We developed a couple of techniques for taking showers because one devotee got really sick and was covered in these horrible boils. When we called the temple to ask if we could spend money to get a hotel room so he could soak in a tub of hot water, their response was, "Hell no!" So, once again, necessity became the mother of invention. The first showering technique was simple. You'd park in the lot of a motel and wait for the early check out people to split and leave their door open. We'd quickly run in and shower before the maids got there.

The second was the "Patel Motel Scam," named after Indians from India (all named Patel). Before they owned all the candy stores, 7-11s, gas stations and porno movie stores, they owned these sleazy hotels that rented rooms by the hour that were places to go have sex with hookers, or whoever. What we would do was have one devotee walk in there in complete Hare Krsna garb, sheets (dhotis) and shout, "Hare Krsna! Hare Krsna!" The owners loved to see a Krsna devotee out in Nebraska, or Mississippi, or wherever, because it reminded them of home. No matter where they were from in India one of us was just there on pilgrimage. Bombay, no problem. Delhi, no problem. Mayapur, West Bengal…still got the dirt of the Holy Land in my shoes, pal.

We would talk shop a little and then cut to the chase. We were on pilgrimage in America and we were very tired and in need of shelter for the night. That usually got us a free room and breakfast from his wife. I remember one incident where I was at a Patel Motel trying to get the room and the Indian guy was such a cheap prick he just wasn't having it. He kept saying that he had no rooms and that having four Hare Krsnas in his lobby was ruining his business. I looked behind the desk and saw that he had plenty of keys hanging on the wall. Number one, he was lying and number two, next to the keys on the wall was a photo of his wife and kids. Just then this very heavy African-American hooker entered, walked up to the front desk and planted a kiss on the guy. "Hey sugar, how you doin' Gopal baby?" Then she went behind the desk and grabbed a set of keys from the wall like she owned the joint. "I'm only gonna be a half-hour. Why don't you come up afterward so I can take care of my bill for the week." She exited, gave us a smile and now it was clear; it was definitely time to hit Mr. Patel with some K.G.T. (Krsna Guilt Trip). I heavied him out about how he should be ashamed of himself for running this type of motel. I also vowed to put the Hare Krsna whammie-jammie curse on his house of ill repute, insuring that Laxsmi (the Goddess of fortune) would never bless him or his family, because in India, it's all about the family. "Oh and uhhh…by the way," I said as I pointed to the picture of his wife and kids, "Does, 'Mrs. Patel' know about your little arrangement with Shakweesha?" We got the best room in the house. It's no wonder it took a Hare Krsna to come out with the book "How to Live on a Dollar a Day."

Being on the road provided some good laughs from time to time, but it was tough and we always worked our asses off. We drove all night in shifts and in the daytime we hit parking lots, malls, car races, football games or whatever else was on the schedule. At night we worked concerts, tractor pulls, baseball games, even fast food joints. In the early-'80s every temple across America had several "Sticker Pick Van Crews" out there. You couldn't even go to a junior high school basketball game in bum-fuck Idaho, or any event, anywhere in the United States, without someone coming up and telling you they were giving you a citation for not partying, or smiling enough and fining you five bucks to feed the needy. If there was an in-coming parking, there was a Hare Krsna there. After a month or so of non-stop Picking it wasn't out of the question for a van to have upwards of $20,000 in it. If you multiply that by four or five other van parties for each temple working other areas of the country you're talking about some serious dough. We never spent a penny on anything for ourselves; we basically got fed and that was it. We were told that "Austerity was the wealth of the Brahmans," and so we pushed ourselves beyond the limits of human endurance. Devotees fell asleep at the wheel and crashed, developed all kinds of illnesses because of the lifestyle and some even died. One van party consisted of a friend of mine named Kevala-Bhakti, who began traveling in the dead of winter. So, to keep warm in the minus twenty-degree night, they turned the van on and ran the heat. The carbon monoxide leaked inside and killed three devotees. Kevala-Bhakti laid in the van under the dead bodies that were on top of him for days until he was found.

We suffered and endured while most of the leaders flew first class around the world, ate amazing food, broke the principles of the religion and hoarded money. The first thing that raised my suspicions was the fact that despite the money we were bringing in, we were told that the New York temple was always in financial trouble and had to do these Sticker Pick, mini-marathons to help save it. It just didn't make sense because the numbers didn't add up. Just as I was pissed off at the Valentis when I found out I was being used as a pawn to make them money, I was determined to get to the bottom of what was happening in the New York temple. If I was being hustled, there was going to be hell to pay and heads were gonna fuckin' roll.

I actually remember the exact moment the realization came that what I was doing out there on the Sticker Pick was complete bullshit and I had enough. As

The Pick leader coined the phrase, I was 'Fried.' I was at a car race that summer in ninety-degree heat and had just finished working the in-coming parking. I was about to go inside to work the motor homes on the infield when I stopped to take a dump in a Porta-Potty. There was shit piled up to the toilet seat, flies buzzing away and a stench that no human (except redneck race fans) should have to endure. That's when it hit me - the piece of toilet paper with doo-doo that someone stuck to the roof of the Porta-Potty, that is. I screamed, "Fuck this, I'm outta here!" I told the party leader I was done and demanded that he send me back to New York.

Back in the city I told the temple authorities that I wanted to set up a food program at Tompkins Square Park on Manhattan's Lower East Side. I argued that we were collecting money to feed the needy and we weren't doing a damn thing for them. They agreed to let me run the program on the one condition that I got back out on The Pick soon. Every Sunday I was out there serving hot meals to the seniors and poor people. One day I happened to run into Harley. After he made fun of my orange Krsna bed sheets he told me he put the Cro-Mags back together. He told me I should leave the temple and come join the band. I told him being a monk was my life and as we parted ways, that thought stayed with me that day and for the next few weeks. That Thanksgiving I set up a meal for the needy at P.S. 122 on First Avenue. The feeling I got helping others who had nothing to eat and no one to spend their holiday with made every single second of suffering I endured out there on The Pick worth it. As the months went by I noticed more and more odd things happening in the movement. Much more would come out later, but at that point I was naïve enough to believe all the bullshit explanations they gave me. I went on as a devotee Picker until I served lunch to Annie Lennox from the Eurythmics whose first husband at the time, was a Hare Krsna devotee.

I felt a strong calling back to my musical roots after meeting Harley that day in the park. Also, just hearing Annie talk and being in her presence made me realize that it was possible to get a message to the masses if you really had something to say. I had something to say and I decided it was time to split, but you couldn't just walk out the front door of the temple. Oh, hell no! That was impossible. There was too much peer pressure and too many cult tactics. I had to hatch a plan and once again, my quick-thinking street skills kicked in when I needed them.

Every Sunday night at the end of the Sunday Love Feast we would take out the week's worth of garbage from the temple. There would be close to a hundred of those big, black garbage bags piled up on the sidewalk sometimes five or six feet high. Since I helped with the trash, I grabbed two empty garbage bags, went upstairs and put my belongings into them. I went to the roof of the temple with the two bags and walked over to the edge. I launched my stuff over the side of the seven-story building and at that very moment, two people walked out of the temple directly in their path. I shouted at them to get out of the way and they did just in the nick of time, cursing at me in Hindi because the bags narrowly missed their heads. The bags landed perfectly on target, right on the pile of other trash. I ran downstairs, grabbed one last bag of trash and walked out the front door. As I dropped the bag of trash on the pile, I grabbed my two bags, ran down the street and got on the F train to the LES.

I showed up at the squat at 713 East 9th Street between Avenue C and D and hooked up with Harley who let me stay in his apartment. I told him I left the temple and was ready to be in the band again. Unfortunately, he found another singer, this cat named Eric Casanova who was his boy. Even though it was a minor setback, I was just glad to be out of the temple. We put a band together called Mode of Ignorance (M.O.I.), which featured Harley on drums, me singing, Doug Holland on guitar and Nunzio from Antidote on bass. Once the temple realized I split they sent out the bloodhounds because they weren't about to just let their top collector get away that easily. They heard through a couple of the other hardcore kids who went to the Brooklyn temple that I was down at the squat. They assembled a posse to convince me to come back. To set this up properly I have to tell you about the living conditions at "The Eastern Front," which is what we called the 713 squat.

There were no windows or electricity, barely any walls and most of the stairs in the hallway were missing. If you didn't know the layout of what stairs were missing, you fell through. There was also no plumbing and that meant no flushing toilets and no showers. We solved the toilet problem by shitting in plastic bags and having a competition to see who could throw them out the back window of our apartment and hit the windows of the adjacent building. It was pretty nasty and after a while every other apartment in the building got in on it. After a few months the entire back of our rent-paying neighbor's building was covered in shit, toilet paper and used condoms. When the warm weather hit you could literally see the swarms of flies hovering around. I solved the shower problem by resorting to my old Krsna tricks - bucket showers. Right outside our building was a fire hydrant, so I got a wrench and went to work. Harley and I put on our boxer shorts and went out in the sub-zero temperatures with our empty gallon water jugs and our bottle of Dr. Bronner's liquid soap. You had to see the look on the faces of the Puerto Ricans and brothers who lived down there when they saw these two tattooed, motherfuckin' freaks in ten degree weather, lathering up, jumping around and showering. We stopped traffic, literally.

Now early one morning in comes these three Hare Krsnas, in nice new dhotis. They took one look at this place from the outside and are already freakin' out. I remember hearing a knock at the door and Lucifer, our pit bull, attacking it to bite the shit out of whoever was on the other side. I told Lu-Dog to go lay down and I opened the door. I was shocked to see three devotees (one of them messed up his leg from falling through the stairs) and they were shocked to see where I was living. Of all the people to send to try and get me to return they sent my old buddy Vakresvara Pandit (from Puerto Rico) and two of his cronies. They looked around at my place from the doorway (couldn't let them in because Lu-Dog had good enough sense to want to kill them) and tried to convince me to return. They dissed me saying I was living in a palace in Brooklyn and now I was in hell. They told me I hit rock bottom and it's not too late if I come with them now and blah, blah, blah, blah, fuckin' blah. After they finished their ten-minute sermon I told them I wasn't leaving with them. Bottom line…they had to leave without their number one Picker.

When these guys leave the movement they leave with millions, when I left I only had two garbage bags full of my clothes and not even a penny in my pocket. The Eastern Front was a dump, but I was happy at my dump. I was happy to have to beg for food and I was happy that I could sleep at night. I also had a clear conscience. I was deceived by scammers who made me think that what I was doing out there on The Pick was the right thing to do. I accept that, but I really did believe in my heart of hearts that everything I did was an honest attempt to help people. I did believe that the money was going to print books, feed people, open temples and change the world for the better. According to my bogus, child molesting, thieving guru I was now a servant of the "Mode of Ignorance" (thus the name of the band). But as Srila Prabhupada himself always said, "It is better to be an honest street sweeper (or homeless hardcore punk rocker) than a cheating spiritualist."

In the several months that followed their visit, the shit hit the fan. It was early-'84 and I started going back to the temple for the feasts and they were working on me trying to get me to move back in. I was pretty close to doing it, too, and that's when three things went down that started me on my investigation of the facts. The first thing involved a guy who was coming around the temple and showing some promise in joining. He was a known weed and cocaine dealer who also collected classic guitars (which he had dozens of very expensive ones). Our buddies who came to talk me into coming back, Vakresvara and Laxsmi-Nrshringha, got the guy to move in. They also informed him that there was no need to give the drugs back to his dealer. I mean, what the heck buddy, what are friends for? We can throw it away for you. Yeah, right. They took pounds of weed, coke, money and classic guitars, sold everything and kept all the money.

They weren't done with him yet, though. See, this guy was married and when he joined the temple he joined with his wife. There was another devotee (Ramabhadra) who ran the temple gift shop and it was known by a few of us that he was gay, which was forbidden in Krsna Consciousness. Since this wasn't allowed, he needed a cover-up wife. They stole the poor guy's wife and when she caught the gay shopkeeper having sex with another man in the temple, he beat her silly each day and left welts all over her body. She kept quiet for a while, but would eventually wise-up and get as far away from him and the movement as possible. The ex-dealer never recovered emotionally from everything they did to him. He even served time in prison and after everything became severely depressed and was recently deported. Nice people, huh?

The second thing that sent my head spinning was something that happened at a Sunday Feast. Vakresvara Pandit pulled me aside and said, "Listen, I got a friend who donates large quantities of marijuana to the temple and if you know where we could get rid of it downtown we could make the temple a lot of Laxsmi points." I couldn't believe this guy had the balls to ask me to help him sell drugs in the temple while he was the vice president (I guess vice was the operative word). I turned down his offer and told this heavy-set devotee woman they were trying to marry me off to. You know when big gals ain't getting no lovin' they got nothing else to do but gossip all day. She told everybody! Vakresvara had to resign and that meant a major loss of serious money. The following week he approached me and threatened to kick my ass. I called him a scammer and a low-life con artist. I told him to bring it on, but he had other plans. Some months later he acted like everything was cool between us. He even invited me down to the Virginia woods to work on the condos he bought with the money he stole from the temple. I needed a job and he made it seem like all that stuff between us was water under the bridge, so I accepted. The night before I was to leave for Virginia I had a talk with Googs and I told him about all the crazy shit I saw going on in the movement. He told me point blank, "John, if you go, you ain't coming back. They're gonna kill you for blowin' the whistle." I took his advice and I firmly believe that had I gone, I would not be here right now telling you this story, or any of these others about Vakresvara Pandit.

He raped a thirteen-year-old devotee girl a few years back and still, NO charges were ever brought against him. He is welcome at any temple. As a matter of fact he was just given a hero's welcome (by, of all people, the temple prez, his boy Laxsmi) at the temple in Alachua, which is mostly made up of families with teenage children. If it were me, I would have welcomed that cocksucker with a fuckin' bat across his face. He also robbed a bank in South America, ran businesses under ISKCON's religious tax-exempt status and kept the money. He also raped women and forced them to get abortions (which are strictly forbidden in the Hare Krsna religion), sold guns and was a bully enforcer for the corrupt leaders. I think it's safe to say, for all the shit that fucker's done, a little street justice is in order for his ass.

The third and final thing was an incident that took place with a mutual friend of Googs and mine named Nick Cooper. Nick was from SoHo and his mom owned an art gallery down there. His father owned ROIR records, the company that put out the first Bad Brains record, which is how we met. Nick was interested in philosophy and was cool, so we finally decided to bring him to the temple. This particular Sunday Love Feast one of the gurus, Bhavananda, a supposed pure devotee of God from Australia, was giving the class. The three of us walked into the building and Nick commented on how good the incense and food smelled. We entered the hallway outside the temple room, took our shoes off and as I opened the door to the temple room Nick's face turned white. He pointed to Bhavananda who was sitting on his golden throne with his flower garlands and shouted, "That guy's gay! He's gay!" We immediately closed the door and asked Nick what the hell he was talking about. See, according to the philosophy, we are supposed to kick the living shit out of him for what he just said.

Nick then informed us that just two nights prior that so-called guru was at his mom's art opening in SoHo holding hands and kissing another man. We refused to believe it and threw Nick out of the temple. Months later, a devotee Ambarisha (Albert Ford, the grandson of automaker Henry Ford) walked into his penthouse at the Trump Towers and caught Bhavananda the pure guru, having sex on that $10,000 Persian rug with his boyfriend. He forced old fudge-packin' Bhav to resign at once. He went back to Australia and started a gay porn business with the money he stole from the movement.

In the years that followed I discovered more and more atrocities committed by these scumbags. Although they deny everything, all you have to do is turn on the TV or pick up a newspaper and find out the truth. It was exposed on NBC's Dateline and ABC's 20/20, and in the New York Times. You'll see there was a multi-million dollar lawsuit awarded to the hundreds of kids who were raped and abused at the hands and these scumbags and they're paying it off as we speak. In 2006 I toured in Europe and was told that in Hungary young girls were raped on the farm. The movement hushed it all because they claim the preaching in Eastern Europe is going great. On Memorial Day of 2006, I had to update this book because another one of these poor kids, who had the crap beaten out of him by Dhanadara Swami to keep quiet about what was being done to him, put a bullet in his head to end his suffering.

Like the Genghis Khans and Attila the Huns of the world they raped, pillaged, stole and even murdered. They decimated Srila Prabhupada's movement and now just like any other cult, they try and recruit young, easily cheatable adolescents to be their indentured servants while they milk the rich Indians for their money or sell them green cards. One thing I want to know is what's wrong with the parents of these children devotees who were abused? Why haven't you prosecuted these scumbags for what they've done to your children? I would gladly, with the help of my friends in law enforcement, help you bring all of these scum of the earth to justice. If they were my kids, I would take justice into my own hands even if it meant me going to jail. We in the IRM (ISKCON Revival Movement) are here to help ALL devotees especially those who have been wronged. Call us justice seekers, vigilantes or whatever. We are onto them and have made it our business to expose their bullshit. And just a word of advice for the pieces of shit who did all this stuff… sleep with one eye open you fuckin' parasites. Because when everyone else finally realizes what you guys did, and they will, there won't be a corner anywhere in the three worlds where you'll be safe.

They had it all in the early days of the Hare Krsna movement. The Beatles were hanging around (especially George Harrison) and there were many rich and famous people attracted to the message. At one point it was the fastest growing religion in America. Not by these scoundrels' endeavors, but by Srila Prabhupada's pure devotion to God and his loyal disciples who worked endlessly to push on the teachings. As I put distance between their sick cult and myself, I decided to channel the energy that came from the anger and do something positive. Those feelings, mixed with all the crazy shit I went through in my life, fueled the lyrical content of one of the most influential punk/hardcore bands of all time… the Cro-Mags.

survivor of the streets

chapter 12

When I left the temple Harley and I became really tight. He was like my little brother and I would have seriously hurt anyone who fucked with him. People would come up to me and say, "Yo Bloodclot, if that nigga Harley wasn't your boy I would fuck his ass up." I didn't blame them because as much as I liked Harley, he could be a real dickhead at times. The Cro-Mags at that point had a Nazi skinhead reputation because Harley and Eric dressed like skins. Harley got a swastika tattoo and they engaged in gay bashing with the other knucklehead skinheads they hung out with. After I left the temple he was forced to chill out with beating up homosexuals. Harley and Eric made the front cover of this big gay magazine that had a picture of them about to fuck someone up. The caption read, "GENTLEMEN... BEWARE OF THESE TWO SKINHEADS." I had to step in and cool shit out because the homosexuals who lived in the neighborhood hired some Puerto Ricans to fuck Harley up. I had to go to Crazy Eddie and squash the beef between Harley and the gay dudes.

As a way to counter the attacks the homosexuals started camouflaging themselves by dressing like skinheads! They had on the ox blood Doc Marten boots, the braces (suspenders), flight jackets and shaved their heads, which really pissed

Harley off. The gays made skinhead-ism a fashion statement and you know they have a reputation for having a keen fashion sense. The bottom line was when they dressed like skins, all the gear had to be impeccable. It was like Queer Eye for the Skin Guy! Harley quickly changed his appearance by wearing sneakers and growing out his hair. Another reason the skins chilled out was because the gays started hitting the gym and fighting back; with success I might add. Have you ever seen the size of some of those dudes? I wouldn't fuck with them. Harley told me a story once about some shit that happened to some of his skinhead buddies while he was in San Francisco and it's hilarious.

One night these skins devised a plan to earn some drinking money by robbing a gay dude. They had one of their cronies lure the guy into this alleyway thinking he was going to get some action. The rest waited patiently, hiding behind a dumpster. They stepped out and surrounded the dude. When he realized what was up, he simply smiled and said, "Oh, you boys want to play rough? That's good, because there's only one thing I like better than sucking cock...and that's kicking ass!" The dude was a black belt and laid them out in a matter of seconds unleashing very precise kicks and punches. The truth is, a lot of these so-called tough-guy skinheads who went around beating up gay people in New York, were actually gay themselves and gay-bashed to smoke screen their own sexuality which was way, way in the closet.

One skin named Yoda who beat up gays on a regular basis, stayed at this girl's house I knew. He was outed by her because she woke up in the middle of the night to screams and moans coming from her living room. When she walked out of her bedroom she found her gay roommate servicing Yoda's rump in the middle of the floor. Another skin, the notorious "Tony Dust," became a gay hairdresser (pardon the cliché) up in a gay community in New England, while others were found to be showering and sleeping together at the infamous Norfolk Street skinhead apartment. The real kick in the nuts was when a friend of mine named Karen, whose girlfriend lived across the street from CBGB's, told me how she would look out her friend's window and see a lot of the skins getting blowjobs in an alleyway by the hideous bearded, black transvestites who hung around the Bowery back in the day. So guys, the next time you want to beat someone up because he or she is gay ask yourself, "Do I really need to be doing this?" Because karma has a way of coming back around and when you finally do come out of the closet, you just might be the one getting gay-bashed.

The LES was still a pretty dangerous place back in the early-'80s. We had a couple of incidents where Spanish dudes tried to take over some apartments in our building to use as a drug spot, but we weren't havin' it. We used to hang out on the roof of the squat, smoke weed and look over the entire LES. You would hear the salsa music blasting, see the hustlers hustling, the poor ghetto kids playing and the bags of trash flying out the windows. That was one thing you had to watch out for back in the day because people didn't like carrying their trash down six flights of stairs. They would just heave a big-ass bag out their window. Once I was even hit by a dirty pamper and I wondered – "Is that like the old New York superstition about pigeon crap? Is that good luck, too?"

One morning we were sleeping in the squat apartment and I heard a knock on the front door. Before I could open it, the door was kicked open and five or six heavily armed men ordered all of us to the ground. Now I'm thinking, great here we go again, another drug gang taking our apartment. But it turned out these guys were homicide detectives. Harley took the apartment from a Spanish dude who mysteriously disappeared. As it turns out, the dude murdered someone in the 'hood and that's why he split in a hurry. A few nights later Harley came and found our front door barricaded from the inside. He went upstairs, climbed out the window of the apartment above ours and climbed down the fire escape to get in through our window. Just as he was about to enter he saw the light of the moon reflect off something shiny. Harley looked in and there in the shadows, lurked a figure. He yelled, "Yo! It's Harley, Who the fuck is that?" Out from the shadows came the Spanish dude holding a very large pair of scissors and I believe if Harley went in the window the guy would have definitely killed him. Harley told the dude that the cops were there two days prior and he split right away. I actually knew the dude and I don't know if he was ever arrested for that murder, but last I saw him was a few years back on Broadway going uptown. As we locked eyes I smirked and said, "What up LES?" He nodded then walked away very, very quickly.

All-in-all though Harley was changing for the better. He started to read a few of the books on Krsna consciousness and asked a lot of questions, which I answered. He stopped drinking (in part due to an ulcer) and even became a vegetarian. I knew that when he was convinced about the depth of the philosophy he would want me back in the 'Mags. I was writing a lot of conscious lyrics and I was right about Harley wanting me back. After the two Cro-Mags shows Eric did at CBGB's Harley had enough with him. Eric barely sang any words and the ones that he did remember, "Kill the Ayatollah," were cartoonish. During the first show, Harley kicked Eric on stage because he was fucking up so badly. At the second show, Eric sat on the drum riser looking at Harley like, "What do I do, dude?"

The band on the other hand was great. Harley was a madman on stage, Kevin "Parris" Mayhew was an excellent guitarist (for an uptown momma's boy... story at eleven) and Mackie, who I had heard so much about back at the health food store, was one of the best drummers out there. Soon after that second show Harley fired Eric and informed me that he wanted me to sing. Kevin wanted Roger Miret from Agnostic Front to be the singer, and even though I argued that I was the original singer before Kevin was even in the band, I had to audition. They set up the battle of the front men and after I literally bounced off every wall in the rehearsal studio, threw flying karate kicks off the drum platform, (mostly at Kevin's head) and screamed like a madman, Harley just gave Kevin this 'What did I tell you motherfucker' look. Then he turned to me, gave me a hug and said, "Squid, you're in."

I was once again the official Cro-Mags' singer and the first order of business was to start practicing as much as possible. I wanted the band to become more than just an urban legend with Cro-Mags' graffiti tags all over the LES. We set up dozens of rehearsals to get the band tight. I started filling in the lyrics for the songs Harley and Eric wrote words to and I also wrote lyrics for a bunch more. I took a difficult job as a bike messenger to help pay for the band's practices. My day started with waking up in that freezing squat and going for a five-mile run along the East River. Then it was an ice cold shower at the fire hydrant, followed by an eight-hour bike messenger shift that included fighting the New York City traffic. Work was followed by rehearsals a few nights a week and all of the hard work was paying off because the band started to sound great. I hear a lot of people in the arts talk about suffering for your craft. For me suffering wasn't enough. Suffering was for pussies. I was ready to die for my shit and if you got in my way, you got run over. Plain and simple...the Cro-Mags were quickly becoming a force to be reckoned with.

I got along great with Mackie. He was an uptown West Side hoodie at the time and a well-known graffiti artist. Mack was about the clothes and the flash, which they refer to nowadays as bling. He was the sickest drummer I ever saw, next to Earl from the Bad Brains, that is. I remember seeing Mack at those early Brains shows just watching Earl, studying him and taking mental notes. See, Mack wasn't satisfied just being Earl's protégé. This son of a sprout farmer didn't stop until he became the baddest drummer in the motherfuckin' land and to this day, he still is. I dug Mackie and he turned me on to so many different kinds of music like Return to Forever, Brand X, the Mahavishnu Orchestra, all bands that featured the best drummers including Lenny White, Phil Collins and Billy Cobham. The running joke was Mackie would never invite anyone up to his apartment. After we would come home from tour Mack always made us drop him off a few blocks from his house with his heavy suitcases. When he walked off he'd look over his shoulder to see if we were following him in the van. His reason was he said, he didn't want niggas like 'US' to know where he lived. Shit, ain't that the pot callin' the kettle black 'cause we were all hustlers back then.

As for Harley and me, we were living and breathing the Cro-Mags. We lived the life and grew up on the streets. We fought, we suffered, we begged, we borrowed and we stole. We had a really close friendship and we hung out so much we were able to finish each other's sentences and jokes. After I left the temple there was a real spiritual connection developing between us, one that made us even tighter. He saw where I was coming from and also saw that the philosophy behind my lyrics was what the Cro-Mags needed to complete the puzzle. The Vedas had the answers and they held the key. We knew that if we were able to incorporate them into an already mind-blowing live show we would be unstoppable. The one thing I wanted to make sure of was that I didn't come off as some type of lunatic preacher on stage. I wanted to present the public the life I led and the experiences I went through in the hope that they could gain something from it. Why? A lot of people were going through the same shit as me and maybe not to the same degree, but who isn't suffering in this material world? The first step is realizing that you are suffering and that you don't have to.

Living in the squats and the other shit might have been an adventure, but make no mistake about it, it was for real. We saw life and death shit happen in front of us every day because we were down in the muck and fighting in the trenches. A woman who wrote a feature on the Cro-Mags for Spin Magazine called us "Extra-Terrestrial Sewer Workers." The sewer was our home and its inhabitants were our peeps. We weren't like those rich kid weekend-warriors who I'm sure are all writing books as we speak chronicling their one summer adventure squatting, panhandling (not that they had to, it was just cool) and shooting dope on the LES. But unlike them, we couldn't run to Western Union every Friday to get our money from Mommy and Daddy who were living in Greenwich, Connecticut. The difference between them and us was that they could leave anytime they wanted and go back to their nice homes. For us, the sewer was our reality.

And speaking of rich kid momma's boys, that brings us to the last piece of the Cro-Mags puzzle, Kevin. Kevin or Parris "Mitchell" Mayhew as he refers to himself lately, was from a different world. He hated the fact that I was in the band because I was injecting a spiritual message into it. Harley stopped hanging out with him once I left the temple and I guess there was some kind of weird jealousy going on with him. Kevin was from the Upper East Side and it was scary how he would come downtown and jock Harley. He would stand out on Avenue A practically on a soapbox, preaching the glories of Harley. I was like, dude chill-out, somebody's going to think you want to blow the guy or something. He had the $2,000 B.C. Rich guitar and nice clothes. It's not that I'm jealous of that crap, but it was just his douche bag, "I'm better than you" attitude. He flaunted his shit in less fortunate faces on several occasions and that made me want to slam my fist down his throat. Nowadays he walks around like a tough guy and talks so much trash on the Internet about how he was the Cro-Mags and this and that. Let me straighten all this out, right now. Back in the day, he used to hide behind his amp when the insane Cro-Mag fans stormed the stage to thrash around and stage dive. He'd whimper to Harley and me in the middle of a song to kick them off so they wouldn't damage his expensive guitar that his parents bought him. I remember laughing my ass off at one CBGB's show when he caught a good kick from Harley. In the midst of the chaos Harley turned around and there was Kevin doing his best Willie Nelson impersonation that included sitting down on the drum riser, strumming away and looking oh, so jolly. There was no room in this band for a person who sat down (except the drummer) and there sure as hell was no damn jolliness allowed onstage.

As a band, minus Kevin, we were ill as shit onstage. We had a rep for having the sickest fans and the sickest crew. We fucked anyone up who crossed us, but don't get me wrong folks, we liked to yuck it up even more. The funniest moments I love to think about are the good times. As short and fleeting as they were they were still unforgettable. There was a time when, just for a brief moment, we were in line to be what the record industry calls the "Next Big Thing." Some of the shit that happened to us was gut-busting funny and some was insane. Our story was not only unique it was also magical. What made it so was the backdrop, the canvas that the Cro-Mags painted on…the LES, which came complete with all its crazy characters. Without the people who filled our Lower East Side stomping grounds and our experiences with them, we would have never had so much shit to draw inspiration from in our writing, or had the laughs we had.

I'm sure most punk and metal music fans are somewhat familiar with the Cro-Mags' history. Perhaps some of you were even around and watched it go from the equivalent of a bad-ass, motherfuckin' R-rated, Charles Bronson flick to a lame, soap opera-like war of words, complete with all the bad acting, treachery and nauseating dialogue. Maybe some of you have even logged-on to the Internet lately and read different versions of what happened. According to Kevin's and Harley's Web sites their memories of those times and certain events both vary greatly.

But I'm going to take you guys back in time to the real deal. I'm going to take you back to a time before there was an Internet, when stories were still passed down via word of mouth. I'm going to tell it the way it really went down. I'm going to tell you the funniest tour stories and I'm going to show you how we handed out the Cro-Mags version of some "Street Justice." Then after the laughs and holy shits, I'm going to tell you about how the knife was plunged in my back as the lyrics of "Don't Tread On Me" so eerily foreshadowed my future with my band mates. This is how the Cro-Mags became an urban legend and this account will be free from personal motivation or didacticism because quite honestly, I don't have any lessons to teach here. The story itself does the teaching. It alone provides the meaning, and that meaning is whatever YOU walk away with from it. Now sit back and relax, loosen your bra straps and belt buckles and prepare to laugh your asses off because just when you think you've seen it all, you'll find that with the Cro-Mags and all our "Malfunctions," just being "Seekers of the Truth" was never enough.

I guess the place to pick up the action is '84 to '85; that's when the Cro-Mags started making a real name on the scene. Word was spreading like wildfire in the underground punk, hardcore and metal scenes that we were the band to see live. Our shows were getting more and more popular and more and more insane as the days passed. We played harder and faster than anyone else (minus the Bad Brains, of course) and our shows were some of the most violent around. It was a controlled violence though; it was dance. There was a rhythm to it and perhaps to the outsider, the mosh pit may have looked like a bunch of people beating the shit out of each other, but in reality it was anything but. The Cro-Mags always spoke of unity at the shows and if some jock or redneck type did start some shit, I guarantee you after the Cro-Mags cronies got done with his ass, his mosh pit days were over.

Harley and I put our shit on the line every single night. We put 1,000 percent of our entire beings into every show. If we didn't bleed or break something, we were pissed and felt we let our fans down. In the mid-'80s we played with the Bad Brains, Scream (Dave Grohl's first band), Motorhead, Megadeth, Venom, G.B.H. and so many others. I do remember how cool most of the musicians were back then. Although these days the word "cool" may be an oxymoron when used in conjunction with the word "musician." Back in the day, it was protocol. If you weren't...well, we'll let the bands who tried to fuck over the Cro-Mags fill you in there.

In '84, Kevin and I financed the recording of the first demo tape and we recorded it at Jay Dublee's brother's studio on Park Avenue. Kevin's dad owned a country music label in Tennessee (guess that's where he got his Willie Nelson moves) and he pressed up the Age of Quarrel demo cassette. It was raw as hell because Jay Dubs produced it. I came up with the idea of calling the first release Age of Quarrel because it was taken from the Vedic term "Kali-Yuga," which in Sanskrit means, "The Iron Age of Quarrel and Hypocrisy." These were the times we lived in and the lyrics I wrote directly reflected that. Even Kevin liked the name and those things couldn't be pressed quickly enough because a real strong underground buzz was surrounding the Cro-Mags. All of our hard work and dedication started to pay off.

Harley and I were still living in the squat and the city had the T.I.L.T. program going where you could buy the building you were squatting in very cheaply if you fixed it up. I set up a benefit at Manhattan's Danceteria to help fix the roof and get some plumbing put in because the whole shitting in a bag/fire hydrant shower thing was getting old. I wanted a place to call my own for once in my life and I worked tirelessly to make the concert happen. The show was called "Benefit for the Eastern Front" featuring a bunch of local bands. Around that time, real estate investors started to realize that there were a lot of vacant buildings with squatters in them and if they could get us out, they could make a lot of money.

The benefit was a success and we raised $2,600 to fix the roof, but the scumbag developer who was after our building sent in his goons a few days after the benefit to wreak havoc. In the middle of the night his goons padlocked the doors in the hallway of the top floor apartments and threw firebombs through the fire escape windows. The fire trapped three people inside and they burned to death. Did the cops even bother to do an investigation for arson and murder? Hell, no! To them, a few less squatters around was a good thing. Down there people were losing their lives, their homesteads and their apartments, one after another. These were the kind of life and death struggles that occurred on a daily basis. Now they're replaced with the life and death struggles to make it to the front of the line at the Starbucks, to be the first name on the list for a table at Cafe---- (insert some stupid French name here), or to get a parking spot for their $50,000 car after the Department of Sanitation's street sweeper rolls by.

So many characters were around the Lower East Side back then and they gave this place a certain charm and charisma. Unfortunately they're gone now and when I walk down Avenue A on a Saturday night I see nothing but coffee shops, fancy restaurants and bars complete with drunk yuppies puking on the sidewalk. I almost feel bad for the people who hang out and live down here because they missed out on seeing this neighborhood the way it really was.

In the '80s "Operation Pressure Point" started the ball rolling for the change on the LES. Operation Pressure Point was an all-out war against drugs because the investors were not going to invest big money in the neighborhood if it wasn't cleaned up. I got tossed at least once every other night by the cops and it pissed me off because I was like, "Yo, assholes I live down here." It didn't matter though, if you were white you got tossed for trying to buy drugs. If you were black or Spanish you got tossed for being black or Spanish because to the cops, most of who came from the suburbs, that meant you were selling drugs.

Over the years, the sights and sounds of my Saturday night strolls through the neighborhood sure have changed. I think the moment we realized shit changed for good was when that first tour bus company rolled down Avenue A with tourists aboard that red, double-decker. We stood there with our jaws hanging open and when the blatantly gay tour guide made his announcement over the loudspeaker, "Folks if you take a little gaze over to your right you'll see a few of the colorful people who decorate the East Village and give it diversity…" the tourists piled over to one side and began taking photos of us like we were animals on safari. One asshole from someplace like bum-fuck Oklahoma yelled out, "Jesus, y'all, look at that freak on the skateboard! (Daisy in drag, wearing combat boots) Quick Martha get me a picture. The fellas down at the plant'll love that one!" Now we had the problem. We bombed the shit out of them with any produce we could get our hands on from Kim's fruit stand before that bus got the hell out of Dodge in a hurry.

What that did was spark an ingenious venture I should set into motion. What if I operated a tour company that showed you the real LES complete with all the crazy stories, about crazy motherfuckers I saw down here on a regular basis for years? How fun would that be? This wouldn't be like one of those Hollywood tours where they hand out maps and you get to see where famous people live and all that boring bullshit. This would be a tour that really gave you some vacation memories to last a lifetime and a hell of a lot of photos to take back to your town. Oh sure, we'd hand out maps, but they'd be a lot different. And now for the benefit of those who missed out on the real LES allow me, John 'Bloodclot' Joseph, to act as your tour-guide as you climb aboard the "Cro-Mags Caravan Tour Bus From Hell." I will take you on a trip down memory lane so you can see how the Cro-Mags lived and laughed through a typical Saturday night once upon a time.

Just as those Hollywood tours make everyone grab the bus at a famous landmark like the Hollywood Walk of Fame or some crap, we'd do the same. You'll be meeting the bus at St. Mark's Place. To make sure you can easily find it, if you look on your map there's a star with a hypodermic needle stuck in it because it was the meeting spot for all the punk dope fiends. They would meet there every day around 3 p.m. to figure out which spot had the quality dope. If you do get lost you'll be able to spot it easily because as soon as you get to Astor Place you'll see a gigantic mural on the side of a building of an old punk-dude wearing an eye patch. That dude was John "Spacely," who was the star of a low-budget druggie, punk movie called "Gringo". Spacely as he was known was quite the punk celebrity as far back to the Dictators, Dead Boys and Sid Vicious days. But unfortunately heroin and punk rock are a lethal combination and it got the best of him. RIP Spacely.

The other reason we want to pick you up on St. Mark's Place between 2nd and 3rd Avenues is so you can run into the local hooligans like us and do a little shopping before you get on the bus. You'll be shopping Cro-Mags style at the trendy punk clothing store Trash & Vaudeville, and guess what? Everything's free today! We're going to wait for some S.P.P.s (Suburban Punk Posers) to walk out with their nice, big bags and surround them with menacing stares. When we point to their new stuff, that's it. They just drop their stuff and take off running. You can either take what you like or sell their shit to the next group of idiots who come there to buy a real-life Sex Pistols bondage shirt for $150. We consider it a toll, a right of passage, which all S.P.P.s have to pay. In years past, I remember seeing a few of the fuckers we ripped off doing the same exact shit to the next generation of posers. I'd walk by in a Darth Vader-esk type of way and say, "You've learned well, my son. May the force be with you."

We've finished shopping now so… ALL ABOARD! If you look to your right we're passing Kim's Video, but years ago it was a three-level bathhouse called "The St. Mark's Baths". This wasn't just any bathhouse. This place had a Sodom and Gomorrah quality to it and I'll give you a little morsel from the old Bloodclot memoirs. One night, I went in there with my Russian nut-job boy Kontra and our girlfriends to get some drinks because we wondered what the hell went on in that place. We were pretty drunk as we sat at the bar with half-naked gay dudes making out with each other. It was pretty freaky and the bartender came over, pointed to our girls and said in a very rude tone, "Get these cunts out of here." Well, that kind of attitude didn't go over well with Kontra and me. He reached over the bar, grabbed the dude and I popped him in the face. This sent a posse of the biggest gay bouncers in leather running after us with bats. We picked up barstools and whatever else we could and fought for our lives to get out of that place.

We're just passing Second Avenue and today is your lucky day because you're just in time to catch Poppo working his corner. Poppo's an African-American panhandler who always wears a kung fu suit and Chinese slippers. When I first split from the Navy I squatted in a building with him on St. Mark's Place between 1st and 2nd Avenue. Part of the deal with staying there was I had to wake my ass up at 6 a.m. each day and go to the roof to try and keep up with him in his kung fu martial art animal forms. Poppo was a bad ass and he's still around the neighborhood. I'll see him from time to time and although he's an alcoholic who talks to himself and more or less practices drunken monkey styles most of the time, he can still drop a monkey fist on any of your asses in a split second. How do I know this, you ask? Because I still sneak up on him and yell, "Poppo!" and he'll spin around and throw a precision punch which he'll stop an inch from my face. Once he realizes it's me he says, "Hey Brother (my name since day one)," and hugs me. I'll give him some money and say, "Just testing you Poppo." And when I walk off he'd mumble some shit and do that fake Chinese laugh you hear in the kung fu movies with bad over-dubs, "Ha, ha, ha, ha, ha."

Now we're off to Alphabet City where the girls are loose, the cops are crooked, the dope is strong and the crack heads shit anywhere because the curb your dog signs don't apply to them. Coming up on your left, the individual with the brown paper shopping bag…that's "Mr. Belt Guy." Mr. Belt Guy's an old bugged-out Ukrainian who got his name because he always walks around with a shopping bag full of dozens of belts. See, he's figured out the perfect demographic to market his merchandise to…junkies. Mr. Belt Guy only knows three English words he needs to know down here to pay his rent, "You buy belt?" That would do it. The junkies would line up and buy him out every day. I wouldn't run off the bus to buy any of those even though they are a steal at $5 each. Now you might be wondering, "Just where does Mr. Belt Guy get those belts?" Well we wondered that exact same thing until one day when I was with a friend of mine and that mystery was solved. Mr. Belt Guy walked up and tried to pawn off his goods and the guy I was with looked at a particular belt with this fucked up look. Turns out the belt with the "T.S." initialed buckle and the rebel flag belonged to a friend of his who had just died. Turns out, Mr. Belt Guy's friend was the night janitor at the city morgue and he would go down there at night and steal the belts off the corpses.

Ladies and gentlemen here we are on Avenue A and on the right is an LES landmark: Ray's Candy Store. Ray has the best milkshakes and he was another individual who, just like Mr. Belt Guy, knew early on to take advantage of the local indigenous population because junkies love sweets. Uncle Ray and I had a lot in common because Uncle Ray went AWOL in 1956 from the Turkish Navy and came to America. In his case if he ever does go back to Turkey, according to him, he faces death by firing squad. The stars in the heavens are lining up for you on this tour this evening. That crowded sidewalk in front of Ray's with the two police barricades blocking the sidewalk that allows only a small space in between for people to pass through single-file, and that rolled up carpet everyone has to step on to get through means only one thing…. Kevin Carpet is out tonight. See K.C. gets off sexually by having people step on him while he jacks-off inside his carpet. We recently threatened to beat the shit out of him because he was paying young punk girls on the scene twenty bucks each to step on his balls in an alleyway while he lay under a mattress. So now he's improvised and come up with a new scheme… the amazing "Sidewalk Masturbating Carpet Gig." As soon as he sees me he'll get out of the carpet, stand up without saying a fuckin' word and walk off nonchalantly while dragging his carpet in nothing more than tightey-whiteys and a pair of sneakers. Back in the day I vowed that eventually Harley or me had to write about this shit. We then looked at each other, laughed and said forget it, because no one would ever believe it were true.

Okay…we're off again. That little spot there on the corner (it's now 7-A Cafe); that storefront club is where a lot of famous jazz musicians sat in and jammed. My boy, Charles "Bobo" Shaw who played drums with Joseph Bowie, Frank White and Frank Lowe, among other greats clued me in that the reason they liked this particular club. It was easy for them to come down, cop their dope in the 'hood, get high, play the hell out of some jazz and pick up some ladies. If you listen you can hear them play their instrumentals while the martial art screams from Sifu Rodan's students at the University of the Streets Dojo on the second floor provide the vocals. Then there's "Mushroom Man" working away on the block. We call him Mushroom Man because the little old Polish man with a hunchback made that mushroom looking hat on his head out of paper and plastic bags. He constantly sweeps around 7th Street between 1st and A, and he never takes money from us and he never talks. He just waves you away anytime you try and offer him something and then walks off to go sleep in a nearby doorway. One winter the cops found his dead body frozen on the ground and when they peeked into his hat they also found more than $100,000 stuffed inside.

We're about halfway through our tour and at this point we have some live entertainment because there's a show going on at A-7 which is now Niagara, a bar located on the corner of East 7th Street and Avenue A. Let's get off the bus, pop our heads in and check it out. Back in the day, a crazy motherfucker named Black Dave, who knew everybody in the neighborhood, ran A-7. You didn't fuck around in Black Dave's club. I found that out the hard way one night because Kontra and me sold his boy a 'C' note worth of beat coke. When I returned a few days later Black Dave chased me down the block with an axe.

Black Dave was one of the original apostles of freebase and crack on the LES. He was smoking that shit back in the day when nobody even knew what it was. He originally owned the space that's now the Pyramid Lounge on Avenue A and he sold the lease one night for $250 in order to get some rocks. Dave was mad cool because he always paid the bands and always hired a lot of local musicians to work there. I remember one show where the Bad Brains played and there was at least three hundred fuckers packed in this tiny little area slam dancing the shit out of each other. There was another three hundred out on the sidewalk ready to riot because Dave over-sold the club and they couldn't get back in once they left. Now you ask where was Dave during the chaos? He was in his office (which was in the middle of the dance floor) behind his Fort Knox-type door complete with seventeen paranoid crackhead locks, freebasing with his friends. He would stick his head out of his door during the chaos of the Bad Brains' "Supertouch/Shitfit" or "Pay to Cum," and was always high as hell. The look on his face said it all, "How the fuck was his runner gonna get through all that shit to go get some more coke?"

Back then A-7 was our club. We ran it, we policed it and we booked the bands. I've seen all the clubs down here either close up or get bought out by yuppies and turned into some bullshit cafe or restaurant. It pisses me off that some Euro-trash yuppie had the audacity to open a fine dining eatery at the original 171A space and call it the Alphabet City Kitchen. Now it's time to head across the street to Tompkins Square Park and calm down by smoking a big-ass spliff we can cop from the Rasta-Imposters who hustle there. Now once you're good and high I'll tell you some spooky stories.

Is everybody nice and high? Yeah? Good, because you are in one of the most bugged-out city parks in the entire U.S. of fuckin' A. It was built on top of a sacred American Indian burial ground and I guess that's why it attracted some of the ghoul and goblin-types that it did in the '80s. Back in the '60s it was the place where the political hippie-types like the Yippies, as well as cats like the famous Beat Generation poets, including Allen Ginsberg, hung out. It was the place where Srila Prabhupada first chanted in public in America. There's a plaque from the NYC Landmark Foundation to commemorate the occasion. When Srila Prabhupada chanted with Ginsberg and the others he commented that he saw the ghosts flying out of the park because the transcendental sound vibration of the mantra annoyed them.

After the Summer of Love ended and we headed into the mid to late-'70s the vibe in Tompkins Square Park totally changed from peace and love to drugs and guns. It became a daily occurrence to find people either overdosed or murdered, but everyone took it in stride. Then in the '80s when we entered the park the first thing we'd see were the tents and shanties that were erected in the center lawn. Inside you had some homeless people, but it was mostly crackheads, junkies and crusties (these smelly-ass punks that don't bathe, eat out of garbage cans and act like they're roughing it on the streets). The ones I've seen coming out of Western Unions or bank ATM's to pick up their allowances sent by their families.

It wasn't unusual to see people in Shantytown shooting up, smoking crack, or having sex in public. These fuckers had an attitude like they were paying rent out there. If you did tell them to take it inside their shanty or tent, they'd tell you to fuck off. Directly across from Shantytown was the band shell, which had no bands playing in it. Instead, there were a hundred or so people that were living in it. One night I walked through the park and there were at least seventy-five people on that stage arranged jailhouse style (biggest or illest up front…chumps to the rear). They were looking in the same direction as though hypnotized, while they blatantly smoked their rocks, drank or did whatever they wanted like they were in the comfort and privacy of their own homes. Nobody made a peep and when I got closer I noticed that in the front of the stage was a tiny twelve-inch black and white TV plugged into the power source. They were watching the movie "Fort Apache the Bronx." I guess that's what you call the ghetto version of a drive-in…a crack-in.

Most parks in the city calmed down after the '70s and became places for families to go and spend quality time together, maybe even have a barbeque or a picnic. The family outings and picnics in Tompkins Square Park were either a homeless dude roasting a skewed pigeon over a metal garbage can (no shit, I've seen it), or Daniel "Wacko" Rakowitz serving the homeless a huge caldron of soup, who's main ingredient consisted of his Swiss girlfriend/roommate Monika Beerle's chopped up body parts. The reason most of you probably never heard about that one, is because the last thing the real-estate agent said to the yuppies who were about to pay $2,000 a month for an apartment was, "Hey did you know this place was a cult murder sight and that head Chef Monsieur Daniel ran the Rakowitz Cafe out of this exact apartment?" I've been back over there and met people walking out and they had no idea what transpired there. I happen to know about the case firsthand because I squatted in an apartment directly under the one where Rakowitz killed that girl. When I started smelling a really foul odor in my place, I told my super and friend "Crazy Cubano" Dave and he said that a rat probably died inside my wall and eventually the smell would go away and it did. Right after Chef Daniel made his famous pot of human gumbo, that is.

Wanna hear a bugged-out story? Crazy Dave was the superintendent for 700 East 9th between C and D and the building's owner was in some type of litigation with the bank so no apartments could be rented to anyone under any circumstances. The building was a rat-infested piece of shit and Crazy Dave was a lousy super to say the least. One night I fell asleep and left half a slice of pizza on a table near my bed and woke up in the middle of the night to the sounds of a huge fuckin rat. I yelled at it, threw my shoe and the fuckin' thing still did not budge. Instead it turned around and looked me dead in my eyes like, "What bitch? Go back to sleep faggot," and pimp-walked away with the slice in his mouth."

Even the rats on the LES had attitudes and this building wasn't even fit for them to live in. It smelled, the power didn't work most of the time and the lock on the front door was broken. That just left the door open for all kinds of undesirables who would wander in at night. On one occasion Crazy Cubano and me came home from a punk show and walked in the building to a strong odor of burning crack cocaine. We walked toward the staircase and heard moaning coming from under the stairs. As we turned the corner to investigate, sitting up against the wall was this Spanish crackhead girl with her pants down and her legs cocked open. She was smoking a stem with some crack in it and at the same time her gal pal (who was on her knees with her pants down as well) was servicing her with this two-foot dildo that looked like a baby's arm. I thought, "Now there's an anti-crack commercial for you." Cubano snuck up on them, kicked the one holding the dildo in the ass and scared the shit out of them. He knew them on a first name basis and cursed at them in Spanish. They then ran out of the building half-naked, dildo in hand and crack vials left behind. The translation of what Crazy said was, "Take the dildo and get the fuck out…but the crack is mine, bitches." Cubano laughed as he gathered up their rocks and said, "Only in New York Johnny. Only in New York."

Crazy Dave was definitely out of his fuckin' mind and just the sight of him was enough to make you write home. He had a thick Cuban accent, fucked up dingy grayish teeth, a bad bleach-blonde dye job and the worst fuckin' tattoos you've ever seen. It literally looked like a three-year-old took a black magic marker and scribbled all over his ass for three hours (Note to self: mention Harley did them all later). He would always talk about their meaning which made no sense at all and discussed how he was going to tie them all together one day and form sleeves. I'd be thinking, "Dude, if Da Vinci was a fuckin' tattoo artist he couldn't do shit with that mess." Mix that with a loud mouth that constantly ran at 10,000 rpm's, throw in some wild, homemade punk clothes and that was Dave in a nutshell.

Crazy Dave was a crackhead who constantly needed money to get high. Since he knew he couldn't rent apartments legally what he did was hook people up as roommates who barely knew one another and charge them an average of a hundred bucks a week. One of Cubano's tenants was Rakowitz, who he often smoked crack with. Cubano paired him up with Ms. Beerle and I'm sure she found Rakowitz interesting in the beginning. He was originally from Texas and had this long blonde hair and a beard. He was a neighborhood pot dealer who constantly walked around in hippie clothes with a large rooster on his shoulder and boldly proclaimed that he was the reincarnation of Jesus Christ. Well I guess after Monika got a good look at this fucker's mind she ended their little fling and wanted him out of the apartment. Now, that just didn't sit well with old J.C. (Rakowitz). He proclaimed loudly, "You don't diss Jesus, bitch" (that's exactly what he told Cubano) before he beat her to death with a blunt object.

The first sign that something was up was the fact that Cubano noticed he hadn't seen the girl around for some time and she was late on her rent. Then little by little he started finding her shit in the garbage. When Cubano asked Rakowitz where his roommate was, he said, "I killed her, chopped her up, made soup out of her and I fed her to the homeless in Tompkins Square Park." Cubano laughed it off and said, "Come on, mang. That shit ain't even funny, yo. For real, mang, where's she at, yo? She owes me money." Rakowitz repeated himself, "I killed her. I chopped her up." To confirm it he said he could show him pieces of her brain in his drain. Cubano was convinced this psycho was telling the truth, remembering that there was that ultra-foul smell in the building.

He bolted over to the 9th Precinct and ran in screaming, "Mira, I'm dee super for 700 East Ninth and deece crazy motherfucker mang, he killed his girl bro, chopped her up and fed her to the homeless people in the park, mang!" The cops took one look at Cubano's crazy ass and threw him out of the precinct. Dave ran back to the building got some of her clothes, ran back to the cops and screamed some more showing them her clothes as proof. This time a cop physically escorted him out and told him that if he came back they would lock his ass up. Great work Kojak.

Finally the girl's mother who didn't hear from her daughter in quite some time came over from Europe and filed a missing persons report at the 9th Precinct. When she wrote the girl's last known address it was none other than the one Cubano, the crazy punk rock super, was screaming about. When the cops finally showed up and questioned Rakowitz he denied everything. I saw him later that evening while I was riding my bike down St. Mark's. He stopped me and said, "Hey, did you hear the news? They're trying to say I murdered my girlfriend." I looked dead into that fucker's cold black eyes. I said, "You know what…you probably did you sick son of a bitch," and I rode away.

A few hours later Rakowitz confessed to the murder and took the cops to the Port Authority Bus Terminal in Times Square where he had her skull and bones stashed in one of the lockers. He bragged to Dave about killing others and claimed he and his cult members dined on their internal organs and then fed their remains to the homeless as well. Rakowitz is still locked up at NYC's Kirby Forensic Psychiatric Center on Wards Island, a prison for the criminally insane. If you were one of the homeless that happened to pass through the park back then, see him and his boys serving away and decided to sample the free eats at the Rakowitz Cafe… I hope it was good eatin', homey.

Soon after that the city knocked down the shanties and the band shell by showing up at sunrise with a bulldozer and dump trucks and getting busy. They tested the soil under the Shantytown and it tested positive for hepatitis and other nasty diseases from the junkies and crusties who were passing their bodily waste products. They put the park on lock down and I was glad to see it happen because it was fucked up and smelled like hell. You had kids in the playground picking up needles from some asshole who shot up the night before, or stepping in a big pile of crackhead shit near the monkey bars.

When the city kicked out the homeless and tried to enforce a 1 a.m. park curfew the famous Tompkins Square Riot of 1988 took place. I saw the whole thing from start to finish with my two nephews who were four and five at the time. It was brutal as the cops covered their badge numbers and nametags with black electrical tape and started hitting people, including women, in the face with billy clubs. The cops even herded a pack of protesters onto First Avenue between 7th Street and St. Mark's. The cops trapped them in the middle before a police helicopter came in about forty feet off the ground and kicked up this huge dust cloud that was so bad you couldn't see two feet in front of you. When the dust cleared that whole group of people were lying on the ground beat to shit.

Well, now it's time to leave this beautiful park and all its beautiful memories and get back on the bus. At this time, some of our favorite people are out for their evening strolls. Let's go and remember…stay together.

This famous street is called Avenue C….C as in "crazy" and back in the day if you came down here alone, you were. It's also one-half of the drug dealers famous mantra, "C and D, C and D!" This avenue had an ample supply of C-ocaine and D-ope and look who's checkin' you out to see if you got anything worth stealing. That's "Eddie the Puerto-Rican Cutman" and he didn't get the name because he worked in some boxer's corner either. Please keep your arms, throats, fingers and especially purses, inside the vehicle at all times. Eddie's more than likely jonesing right now and he would slice and dice you up (thus the name Cutman) quicker than a sushi chef on a piece of warm tuna for his next bundle of dope.

Passing on our left we have "Bags," who gave himself the name in reference to the size of his nut sack. Notice the perpetual fifty-yard stare and seductive tattoo on his chest that proudly proclaims to the ladies in bold letters, "I Eat Pussy." Yep, Bags is a real ladies man and his idea of romance is a $3.99 all-you-can-eat buffet at a Mexican joint run by the Chinese (Chexican). The food is so hot the roaches make beelines for your glass of water. On one occasion he took his girlfriend for a meal and then they went home afterward, made wild passionate love all night and into the morning. According to Bags who always kissed and told, none of her orifices were off limits and he bragged about being an ass man. Two days later Bags accused his girl of cheating and giving him V.D. because his wiener started burning like a three alarm blaze. He went to the doctor and when the doc looked at Bags' penis he couldn't believe it. He took a pair of tweezers and went to work, emerging seconds later and holding something between them. He looked at Bags, held up the tweezers and said, "Son, you don't have a venereal disease. What you do have is a chili-pepper seed stuck in the tip of your penis." Hmm, now how do you suppose that got there? I think I'll leave that one to your imaginations. Once again you're strongly advised not to make eye contact and to keep appendages inside the tour bus, because Bags is a man-eater. He's used those razor sharp teeth to bite off the nose of an occasional biker, the finger of CBGB's owner, Hilly Krystal's son and a few other motherfuckers' toes here and there. Seeing him out of prison is as rare as seeing a duck-billed platypus cross Madison Avenue in rush-hour traffic wearing fishnet stockings and sippin' on gin and juice.

Now the crown jewel of the John "Bloodclot" Joseph's Cro-Mag Caravan Tour is just passing in front… shhhh… keep it down people or you'll scare him off. This is Bubba Phet, the African-American scammer on wheels. These days he's considered an endangered species on the LES. To see him riding a skateboard may give him an innocent, almost child-like appearance, but don't let that fool you. He's an absolute ruthless hustler, who has his seven-month pregnant white girlfriend pay the rent by doing lap dances in the sleaziest strip club on The Deuce and commenting that it's payback for slavery. He makes a living by driving around his quadriplegic uncle (who won a large settlement in a medical malpractice lawsuit) in his van, feeding him cocaine and swiping several grams to sell since his uncle can't turn around to see that Phet is tapping his shit. Uncle Doc knows what's up, but he doesn't say shit because Phet's the only relative willing to disconnect his catheter so he can get some hooker booty up in The Bronx. See although everything else on the brother might be flaccid, his swanson is alive and well. Doc's even commented on it saying, "You can take a brotha's arms, take a brotha's legs, take a brotha's sight, take a brotha's speech, but you take a brotha's dick... and you might as well drive my mother fuckin' wheelchair off a cliff."

Phet's crowning achievement was renting electricity to a Haitian dentist who had an office below him. What he did was run extension chords out his window and down to the illegal chop-shop dentistry practice. What makes it illegal you ask? The fact that this particular dentist isn't registered or licensed by the New York State Dental Association to practice because they don't exactly give out licenses to dentists who make replacement teeth out of cats and dogs. That's right, he grabs stray pets, or goes to the pound to adopt and kills them for their bones. He's even been heard bragging in his thick, Haitian accent that they're ten times stronger than any porcelain tooth. Since the illegals are afraid that if they go to a real dentist they'll get turned in to INS (the Haitian dentist propagated that one), he has a very thriving practice.

Phet is the kind of brother who'll walk around talking about million-dollar rap deals into a cellphone that doesn't work. So ladies, if he promises to put you in his video, don't believe the hype, he just wants to bone you and steal your credit card in the morning so he can get the new Air Jordans. Fellas if you're the type to go on porn Web sites and buy stuff look out, because Bubba's caught on to the whole Internet craze. Bubba has his very own Web site at www.laceandsoil.com and it's an on-line site that specializes in selling used woman's panties. Now, the only problem for the perverted fuckers buying the shit is the doo-doo and urine stains in the panties are his. That's right... big, black, fat-ass, nasty Bubba Phet can be seen each day walking around his house in butt floss. To make the panties seem authentic, he personally puts the skid-marks on every pair he sells. He even instant messages his unsuspecting clients over the Internet, "Sure baby, I can put more stains, hold on. Oh, they're way up in my pussy and ass now..." Stay up, Bubba Phet, you're one of a kind!

This concludes our tour. I hope you've enjoyed it as much as I've enjoyed taking you on this journey and showing you a bit of the Cro-Mags' stomping grounds. It was a pleasure to show you some of the colorful individuals who decorate the good old LES and give it its diversity. It's no coincidence the cover of our debut album, "The Age of Quarrel", was a photo of a nuclear explosion, signifying the end of the world.

Sometimes the Cro-Mags cronie chaos spread to other neighborhoods in the city and one experience in particular brings back fond 'holiday' memories. Back in the mid-'80s Harley started tattooing to make some extra dough and well, how should I put this? He sucked!!! But you had to be cool to get your skin completely fucked up and ruined by a Harley Cro-Mags original. At first, everyone wanted Harley to tattoo them and as a result, there was a long waiting list. People wanted to brag to their grandchildren, "You see this black blob of shit right here covering my entire chest and this chicken scratch on my forearm? Do you know who did that? Harley from the fuckin' Cro-Mags, that's who!" He practiced on skinheads and potatoes because according to him their I.Q. was about the same. His résumé included the Crazy Cubano Dave massacre and a big American flag on this guy Brian's neck. After the painful nine-hour tattoo session that would have taken any real artist an hour, Brian looked at the finished product and said, "Yo Harley, it's backwards, man!" Harley's reaction was simple, "Oh, shit, sorry dude. My bad. Just look at it in the mirror and you're good to go." Needless to say the guy's nickname became "Brian Flag." There was a dozen or so victims who sat through countless hours of grueling torture at the hands of Harley just to have the ink disappear six months later because he didn't put it in deep enough. That really cracked Harley up, too, because he saw it as a way to have a constant flow of repeat clients for years on end.

One day the unthinkable happened and I believe it was what was known as a Deus ex machina, a Latin phrase that means, "God from machine," or an act of God. To save epidermises of future generations and stop the heresy being committed by Harley against the religious-like cult known as the "Ink Slingers" (legitimate old-school tattoo artists), Harley's tattoo equipment was stolen. He left his power supply and tattoo guns at somebody's house and this low-life cokehead named Marshall, who lived up by Central Park, stole them. So off we went with our posse to get his shit back. It was myself, E, my brother Frank, Rich Stig, Harley and someone else who I can't remember. Stig knew Marshall and told us he saw Harley's shit in the guy's house. On this particular night there was only a few people hanging out there so we decided it was time to pay him a little visit, Cro-Mags style.

Marshall was a paranoid coked-up fucker who never answered his door unless he knew you were coming. So, Stig made plans to drop by that night. He drove us in his beat-up car somewhere into the eighties between Columbus and Amsterdam. When we got in the building, we just stood outside Marshall's apartment door. The plan was Stig would knock, then we'd push our way in and Harley would grab his shit after we taught this prick a lesson about stealing from the 'Mags. As we stood in the hallway the yelling and music inside was so loud Marshall couldn't hear Stig knocking. So I turned to Stig and said, "Dude, it sounds like there's a fuckin' party going on in there." Stig told me that Marshall always played the music loud and assured me (guaranteed me), that there would be four, maybe five individuals at most inside and just the sight of us rushing in would make these cocaine freaks shit their pants. I told everyone I was going to count to three and then kick open the door before we'd rush in and handle our business.

Everyone got ready and in position while Harley kept saying that nobody was to touch Marshall because he wanted him. I counted off, "One... two..." and just then the music stopped. We all looked at each other like what the fuck do we do now? I looked at Stig and gestured for him to knock. We stood on the side of the door so when Marshall looked out the peephole all he saw was Stig. He knocked and we heard footsteps. Then one by one, the dozen or so bolts, locks, security bars and door chains were undone until finally the door opened. There he was...our buddy Marshall. He said, "Yo, Stig. What's up, bro? That's when we all stepped behind Stig and my suspicions were correct there was a large group of knuckleheads inside partying.

Marshall was in shock and I looked at Stig like, "Nice one, jack-off." Harley stepped up to Marshall and said, "What's up? This is what's up bitch." And he slammed him dead in his face and dropped him to the floor. The timing couldn't have been any better because right as we were ready to bum rush the show someone put on a Black Flag record. We stormed in and started fuckin' people up. I yelled for Harley to grab his gear and he and Stig made a beeline for Marshall's bedroom. I remember walking over to the biggest fucker and planting a front kick right under his chin that knocked him the fuck out. E and Frank were enjoying the same success on their end and within a few minutes it was all over. Some were beat the fuck up and the others, who only got a slap, kick or punch, cowered in fear on the floor. Harley emerged from the bedroom smiling, holding up his tattoo guns as Stig was right behind him with the power unit. Mission accomplished…time to extract.

We ran out, jumped in Stig's car and peeled out, heading East toward Central Park West. As we approached, a cop ran toward our vehicle screaming into a walkie-talkie. He pointed at us and ordered us to stop while he reached for his gun. Sure we were speeding and just ran the light, but I thought his show of force was still a little extreme for a couple of minor traffic violations. He was blocking the entrance to Park Drive South, so I told Stig to hang a right. As he hit Central Park West at about 50 mph he made a screeching right turn, which practically put the car up on two wheels. He slammed on the breaks and that sent us flying forward and almost through the windshield. Now remember, I said that this was a fond 'Holiday' memory. And what makes it one? It was the day before Thanksgiving. Still not 'Holiday' enough for ya? I was also with my two brothers and my best friend in the whole wide world. You're still not warm and fuzzy inside yet? Shit, you guys are tough. Okay, let me ask you a question. Does anyone know what happens on Central Park West the night before Thanksgiving? (Insert Jeopardy! theme song) That's right! They blow up the huge floats for the Macy's Thanksgiving Day Parade. Blocking our path was a seventy-five foot, seven-story Snoopy balloon. We looked south down Central Park West and all we could see was dozens and dozens of the huge 'Holiday' floats and tens of thousands of kids with their parents looking on, lining the sidewalks behind police barricades.

I yelled at Stig to take off and we peeled out again, zig-zagging through the Snoopy, Bullwinkle, Charlie Brown and Grinch floats, with cops running after us. Now, I'm sure the spectators thought it was part of some kind of stunt show. We looked for an exit off Central Park West, but they were all blocked. Finally, as we saw an opening, a squadron of cop cars and vans blocked us in before we screeched to a halt in front of thousands of onlookers. The cops ran up to the car with shotguns and handguns drawn and screamed, "Drop the guns! Drop the fucking guns out the window now!" We looked at each other like, "All this for some tattoo guns?" Harley slowly rolled down the window as the cops locked, loaded and took aim. He reached out of the car and dropped his two tattoo guns on the sidewalk. It was so quiet you could hear the metal guns clank and bounce off the cement. Now even the cops were confused. See, Marshall had called the cops and told them that we broke into his house and robbed him at gunpoint and in the process gave them a description of our getaway car. The cops thought we had guns and eventually pulled us out of the car handcuffed us and took us into the precinct. As that went down, the parade onlookers clapped and cheered in appreciation of the fine stunt work they just witnessed.

As for the scene in the holding cell, it was right out of that Abbott and Costello skit, "Who's on first? What's on second? I don't know's on the third." Since I was AWOL I'm telling E, "Listen I can't be John, you're John because if they think I'm John and they run my prints or some shit, I'm fucked." E's like, "No… let Frank be you, I'll be Frank and you be me." Then Frank chimes in, "I can't be E. I'll be John. John you be E and E you be Frank." This went on for about five minutes until the officer walked in and said, "Which one of you guys was in the Navy?" We froze and looked at each other. Then E said he was. "Are you AWOL?" the cop said. "Hell no," was E's reply and he even told the cop to check him out. Marshall told them I was AWOL, but didn't know that all three of us were in the Navy at one point. Fortunately both my brothers had earned honorable discharges.

Another cop walked up to the cell and said, "Okay what the fuck happened up there?" It was then that my rebuttal ability gained from the beat-acid and Pick days paid off. "Officer," I said, "We just went up to this guys house to a party. We didn't break in. He invited Richie Stig. We get in and these low-lifes are using cocaine, so we decide to get out of there. I go to the bathroom just before we split and what do I see on the bedroom table? Harley's stolen tattoo gear and when we tried to take it back, a fight broke out." Since Marshall had a criminal record for burglary and the cops believed us, all the charges were dropped except a misdemeanor assault charge. The cop was being so cool he even let us pick who would cop to it. Since it was Harley's shit, he gladly took the slap on the wrist. We were released and when we got out of the precinct we smoked the biggest spliff out of the stash of weed I had hidden in my draws. The next day the McGowan brothers had a turkey-free Thanksgiving dinner at my mom's house and if that story of holiday camaraderie, holiday ass-whippins, holiday parade floats and holiday sacrifice on Harley's part doesn't get you choked-up, make your eyes misty and make you want to put on Bing Crosby's Christmas Album and start roastin' chestnuts on an open fire while Jack Frost nips at your nose…you got problems you sick fuckin' fuck.

Let me tell you one more story (although there's dozens) of what happened when the Cro-Mags were allowed off our leashes to wander other neighborhoods, scare pets and their owners. For this one we have to head south to an area called Tribeca, because we were invited to have a little going away tour party at this super-dope duplex apartment. Our host was none other than the lovely and talented actress, Miss Brooke Smith, who played Catherine Martin, a character who was abducted by Buffalo Bill in the film "The Silence of the Lambs." Brooke was really cool and a nice person and I still don't know how she ever got mixed up with a bunch of dicks like us. And I mean dicks in a "We Don't Give a Fuck, Punk Rock Kind of Way," not the dickhead/dick kind of way. Brooke was a fan and friend of the band and once drove us to Montreal for our first gig out of the country in her mom's station wagon. How we pulled that one off I'll never know. The car barely ran and I crossed the border using the photo I.D. of a guy named Charlie Bananas' who looked nothing like me. Thank God this was pre-9/11.

Brooke's mom was Lois Smith, a big talent agent at the William Morris Agency, who knew all the celebs. The reason I'm bringing it up is because when they went out of town and needed someone to watch their place, feed their pets and water their plants, they told Lois and Brooke got the gig. This duplex apartment was in the famous Thread Building on West Broadway and 6th Avenue, which belonged to model/actress and daughter of Ingrid Bergman, Isabella Rossellini. Brooke instructed us that we could only have a few people over, so when the mob walked in the lobby, punk as a motherfucker with our pit bull Lu-Dog on a big chain, the old tough-guy New Yorker of a doorman was less than enthused. I believe the words he used were, "Keep it down ya bunch a pricks ya, or I'll throw your asses outta here." He called up and announced that Brooke had a Mr. Bloodclot and guests waiting to see her.

Brooke opened the door and when she saw our posse she was a little ticked off. She begged me to keep everyone in line and not wreck anything. I gave her my word, but made no guarantees. This apartment was out of control with antiques everywhere, including an original American Indian headdress and a couple of Oscar statuettes that belonged to Isabella's mom. Lu-Dog had someone to play with and his name was Wheedalini, Isabella's dachshund. Lu really liked the dog because the minute I let him off his chain he went right for it chasing the long-ass dog all over the apartment.

There were photos of the ballet dancer Mikhail Baryshnikov inside the apartment because he and Isabella were boning at the time. I couldn't believe the clutter of mementos, photos and little trinkets around this place. She was like a pack rat that kept everything on display. I came from a world where if you came back to your boardwalk camp, staircase, or squat and some homeless fucker didn't steal your stuff you were lucky. I have two pictures of my entire childhood (both pre-Valenti) and I was blown away at how someone could document their entire life like that. I'm sure if I looked hard enough I would have found her first tampon dipped in gold and mounted on a wall somewhere.

As a youth I always lived by the monks' philosophy (not by choice), "Never possess more than you can carry on your back," and for some reason I never envied people who were more materially wealthy. We can't take it with us when we go, so why be attached, right? Now that kind of philosophical outlook on life is exactly what made it so easy to go buck-wild in Isabella's apartment. Before you knew it we had her stereo blasting and we were slam dancing off the furniture. I was looking around and I found a Polaroid camera and I started taking pictures just to document our party. I took photos of our mosh pit, a male punker with the most horrible pimply, rashy-ass wearing Rossellini's lingerie and someone squatting over her garbage can, laying an enormous turd in it. I even held Wheedalini over my head and launched him through the air like a missile while Harley waited about ten feet away to catch him. While the dog was in mid-flight someone took the photo. I wrote on it, "Giving Wheedalini Flying Lessons."

Next it was time for the mandatory group photo. We got together, shirts off and ink out. Harley wore the Indian headdress and crossed his arms over his chest while clutching an Oscar in each hand. I had Lu-Dog on his chain ripping apart some antique doll or something and we all had big spliffs dangling out of our mouths. Now being the assholes we were, Harley and I thought it would be funny if we hid them so that Isabella would eventually find them in the bookcase to get a good look at the hooligans who invaded her space. We thanked Brooke for a lovely evening and we left. Isabella if by some miracle you read this, I just wanted to let you know that rash you broke out on your ass after wearing those yellow panties, that wasn't an allergic reaction. It was because Chris the Crustie had scabies when he put them on.

the age of quarrel

chapter 13

It was around '84/'85, after we did the hard work playing shitty gigs, sleeping on people's floors, traveling in beat-up vehicles and sometimes having only one yogurt a day, when the Cro-Mags started to build a strong following. That's when the parasite managers started flocking, hoping to make some cash off our blood, sweat and tears. The parasitic germ that attacked the Cro-Mags went by the name of the Chris Williamson Virus aka CWV. The symptoms of contracting CWV are: feeling great at first because the disease actually fools you into thinking life is great and couldn't be better. Then slowly it sucks your energy, makes you irritable and the final straw - total and complete shutdown of your creative flow before... musical death. The fact was it didn't matter who got involved as our manager, all you had to do was come to a live Cro-Mags show and you knew we were destined for big things. Every crooked manager will tell you how you were nothing before they got involved and how they made you, but the fact was we were selling out shows and touring long before CWV struck. To his credit though he did get us on some great tours and shows through his production company Rock Hotel, but at a price, which amounted to nothing more than slavery. Please allow me to elaborate on CWV's intricate plot to fuck us over so badly that still to this day, after so many Cro-Mags records have been sold around the world, I have yet to receive a single penny in royalties. That's right…not one fuckin' red cent!

I should have seen the warning signs the first time I had a run-in with the virus. Rock Hotel gave us an opening slot on a show and 99.9 percent of the bands that played his shows had a squabble over the money because he always came up short. One thing you definitely didn't do under any circumstances was dog the 'Mags and after he shorted us I got into a heated argument with CWV. The fucker actually tried to push me against the wall and I pushed him back. I told him that if he ever put his hands on me again I'd kill his ass. Now, you'd think that would have 86'd us and ended any future business dealings, right? Wrong. He liked the fiery attitude and offered us more shows, before he asked to be our manager, which we accepted. Around that time Profile Records wanted to sign the band and CWV saw that as an opportunity to further his position in the music business by using us as bait. At the time Profile had an impressive roster for an indie label that included Run-D.M.C. and Motorhead. The problem was they ripped off every one of their bands and they were such scumbags they needed an armed off-duty NYC detective to sit at the front desk with his gun out, for all the rappers, dance hall and Rudeboy reggae artists they robbed.

So the way CWV slipped into our musical bloodstreams was to say to Profile, "Okay, you want the Cro-Mags, right? Well my production company Rock Hotel wants a label. You let me run Rock Hotel Records as a subsidiary of Profile and the Cro-Mags will be on Rock Hotel/Profile." That was how Rock Hotel Records was born. We were their debut act. Now you might be asking, "What's so bad about that?" But get a pen boys and girls because here's your first lesson in the music business. It's what's known as a 'Conflict of Interest.' If the manager's job is to fight to get us paid from the label, but the manager owns the label, he isn't going to fight himself to pay us, now is he?

When CWV struck, he struck hard, because our publishing was cross-collateralized. We'd never get any money from record sales or writing credits. Our merchandising rights were signed away. And guess who took the advance on that and all of our gig money too? It started to get heated between us and I tried to convince the other band members that CWV was a scumbag and was ripping us off, but no one would listen. I caught him with the merchandising document on his desk before the '87 tour and confronted him about it. He was furious and

I told him I was going to get him fired. He said point blank, "No, I'm getting you fired," to which I laughed. He knew I was AWOL and said on several occasions that if I, or my friends, ever put our hands on him I'd be in jail. The Cro-Mags way of dealing with adversaries would not work with this fucker. I knew karma would have to serve him whatever he had coming.

We assumed the role of the ho and CWV was our pimp. We would go on tour playing sold-out venues, come home, get pimp-slapped, get our money taken and then have to go back to a squat, or sleep on a friend's floor without a penny in our pockets. In order to survive, I was forced to go back to being a bike messenger when I came off the road. When I broke my hand and had to ride with a cast, he couldn't give two shits. He still took all our money. The sad fact was I had nobody to blame but myself. I learned the hard way and for anyone getting involved in the music business never sign a single document without having an entertainment lawyer read it first. Then get another lawyer to make sure that lawyer is on the up-and-up and hasn't sided with the label for an under the table pay off.

I remember when I signed with Rock Hotel/Profile I thought it was so cool of CWV to save us money on a lawyer by having his attorney explain the entire contract to us (duhh). He ensured us that Rock Hotel was giving us a really, really great contract. I had a lunch date with a hot girl that day so I basically said, "I don't need to read this shit. I trust you guys… give me a pen." A few years back I showed the contract to an entertainment lawyer I knew and he almost fell out of his chair and suffered cardiac arrest. That's why it's called the music business, because without the business there ain't no music. So make sure you handle your business properly because there ain't no 401K for punk rockers.

We recorded Age of Quarrel at East Side Sound Studio on Allen Street in NYC. From the outside the place looked like an abandoned building but that was just to throw off the derelicts in the area. Once you got in there it was like you stepped into a spaceship. I found out that CWV overcharged the label for the studio costs and pocketed the difference for recording costs. Now, guess who had to pay that back? There's one word you learn very well in this industry and that word is recoup. They may take you out to fancy dinners to wine and dine you like a bitch they know they're going to fuck, but there's a reason the douche bags are keeping every single receipt right down to the one for the condoms they bought for the call girl they ordered the night before. After you sign the contract on the dotted line, guess who's paying it all back? That's right. You, the artist!

Right before we did the album we asked Doug Holland from Kraut to join the band to beef up the live sound and add some stage presence. After the album was completed Harley and I were seriously considering firing Kevin. We were sick of his whiney, pussy-ass uptown momma's boy I'm-better-than-you attitude. Look at any of the old photo shoots of the 'Mags and it's like that kid's game where the mother has four potatoes and one orange and she sings to the kid, "Which one of these is different from the others? Which one of these just doesn't belong?" Well, you knew who the fruit was with us and I wished we shit-canned his ass right then. But we decided to wait until we could find a replacement.

We finished Age of Quarrel in record time. I was rushed through my vocal tracks and sang all fifteen ear-shattering songs in one day, which is unheard of. The record was released in '86 and we were ready to hit the road for a tour opening up for one of the greatest English punk bands of all time, G.B.H. They were the nicest bunch of fuckers with bad teeth you'd ever wanna meet. The ongoing joke on the tour became what the acronym G.B.H. stood for. Every day Harley and I came up with something new. One day it was the "Gaping Butt Holes." Then it was the "Gay Ball-sucking Homo's." And finally, I think we settled on the "Gigantic Bleeding Hemorrhoids," but it actually stood for "Grievous Bodily Harm." The G.B.H. tour was a great success, but not financially, of course. We played in front of great audiences in the Midwest, L.A. and Canada. They make such a big deal about violence in the mosh pit nowadays and all this bullshit, but I'd put any one of the old-timers against the most feared mosher of today and he'd slam dance the shit out of 'em. Most were unique individuals back then. Some were just down right out of their fuckin' minds, but a lot of them were serious thinkers who thought outside the box. If it weren't for punk and hardcore they'd be fucked because society wanted nothing to do with them. It's kinda like that saying about America, "Send us your weak, your tired, your weary…" except with us it was like, "Send us your fuckin' lunatics, your rejects, your dysfunctional misfit family members…"

It was a lifestyle, a way of life and over the years I can't even count the amount of fuckers who weren't in it, as they say, "For all the right reasons," then just faded away and went to live some quiet life of desperation in the suburbs. They became statistics within the job market, unemployment, the poverty level, or families whose households consist of 3.5 members. They gave up on their feelings, their beliefs, everything. Time will do that to you. As you grow older every single thing you think you believe in this life will be tested and if you aren't true to it to the depths of your soul, time and finally the ultimate test - death - will snatch it away from you like an expert pickpocket. Time is the ultimate bullshit detector. It will test you and if you aren't for real you'll cave in and surrender to this cutthroat, rat-race society. As for me, I can't. There is no turning back. It's like I've passed the halfway point on an ocean swim and now it's further to go back. The thought of just giving up never crossed my mind because there's something in my nature that forces me, even at 45 years on this planet, to go against the grain. For me, to stay under the radar, to rebel and start shit, to keep fuckers on their toes and thinking is the only way, because falling in line is just plain suicide. I didn't choose punk and hardcore, it chose me and, for whatever reason, it ain't about fashion, or even the music for that matter, it's a state of consciousness. Once you realize that, there's no way you can ever sell out.

One thing about being on tour was I had to experience starvation all over again. In New York I could always hustle up a meal somehow, but on tour there was no backstage catering, per diems, or tour bus 'fridge full of little munchable goodies like all these bands have today. It was hard for me because not only did I play my ass off on stage every night, every morning I ran serious miles, then trained like a son of a bitch. I would get low-blood sugar and go the fuck off, if I didn't eat. One day I hit the wall and went ballistic in a supermarket kicking in the yogurt containers and screaming that I better get a meal or was going to fuck somebody up. But if I had to do it all over again, I would. Adversity builds character and character is something most of these so-called punk bands of today lack.

There's no struggle. There's no starvation. There's no rednecks wanting to fuck them up. Shit, even the rednecks are dressed like punks these days. These bands get signed to big deals right out of the box and go on tour in brand new, shiny tour buses, have $100-a-day per diems, managers, bodyguards and personal assistants. Shit, that ain't punk. Back in the day, we were lucky if we made a $100 a show, which usually went towards gas and other expenses. Everything's nice and safe for them, but we experienced shit in our broken down vans, clubs and squats that these guys will never get to experience. Simply put...we lived punk while these people dress punk.

The road reveals all and it will either make you or break you and you really find out what people are made of. The pressure out there is intense and as I said before pressure is the only way to find out a person's true character. Before I start this, I do have to say in their defense, I know I was a jerk-off at times, too, and wasn't the easiest person to get along with. On that note I'll start with the one dude I never had beef with, Mackie. Mack was a neat freak, which was cool because the last thing you wanted is a smelly fucker in the van. Kevin became an even bigger douche bag, if that was possible. Harley was a total egomaniac and a big baby who had to have his way about every little thing. He brought whoever was his girlfriend at the time on every single tour. It's like dude, just because you can't wipe your ass without your girl holding the toilet paper don't mean the bitch got to be on the tour, in the van, in the rooms and everywhere else, getting involved in band business. On one European tour Harley's 'rhoids were tearin' the ass out of him, so he gets on all fours in the middle of a parking lot, drops his pants, pulls his ass cheeks apart and says, "Baby, blow on my ass." Sure enough his girl who was high on dope or whatever, crawls over, puckers up, puts her mouth an inch from his crack hole and blows like a fuckin' champ on homeboy's ass. Harley then looked over at our drummer and just smirked proudly, because he had such a good woman. So here's the rule for that one band member who wants to bring his girlfriend out on the road...unless she's willing to blow on everybody's hemorrhoid-filled ass at a moments notice, the bitch stays home.

Doug was the dude in the band who always fucked the ugly girl in town. But the thing about Doug was he always had an excuse, "Dude what a body, you could never tell just by looking at her, but when those clothes came off, holy shit." Now I can understand if you're a drinker and occasionally put the old beer goggles on and end up in the sack with a creature or two, but when you repeatedly bag the town mongrel that's a red flag. The first time we got wind that Doug was an ugly girl addict was on the G.B.H. tour of the U.S.

We played The Electric Banana in Pittsburgh which was run by an ex-New York mob guy who had a habit of pulling guns on most of the bands before he told them to fuck off when it was time to get paid. Since we were hardcore New Yorkers he liked us so much he not only paid us, but also gave us a bonus and made his wife cook us veggie pasta. After the show we stayed at this girl's house and Doug slept on the living room floor with her friend who was the fugliest little punk rocker with pimples and B.O. We listened to them have sex and in the morning just knew Doug was going to brag about his sex-ploits. You know, how hot she was once he threw that pillowcase over her face and shit like that. Sure enough he's in the van yakking it up about how he gave her her first orgasms (five as a matter of fact) and all this crap. We were like, "Dude that bitch had a face that could stop a clock, so shut the fuck up already." After an hour of driving in the hot-ass van with no air-conditioning, we were sweaty and irritable. That's when we started to smell a very strong odor of urine coming from Doug. As it turns out, those five orgasms weren't orgasms after all – she just pissed all over him during sex.

The next major act of courage on Doug Holland's résumé was in Winnipeg, Canada, which we nicknamed "Win-A-Pig," after an incident where Doug did just that. After our show we went back to these people's house for one of those cliché after parties where one asshole gets drunk, develops beer muscles and wants to fight everybody. I met this pretty Asian girl, so eventually one thing led to another. Here I am sucking on her nipple when I get this piece of hair in my mouth and naturally, I tried to pull it out. Now I'm not exaggerating when I tell you this, the shit was like sixteen-inches long and turned out, to be connected to her nipple. This chick had two, foot-and-a-half-long, jet-black strands of Fu Manchu hairs hanging from each nipple. It was so freaky that I nearly puked. I got out of there in a hurry and we went back to the party to find Doug making out with a 250-pound behemoth of a woman, who was all over him like white on rice. People at the party were actually calling everyone in town to tell them that Susie (name changed to protect the overweight) might actually get some tonight.

Little Susie was on a three-year hiatus in the sex department, but tonight she had no worries cause 'Dougie Do-Right' was on the case. People started showing up from all over Win-A-Pig by the dozens just to see who was making out with this chick. Once the two lovebirds hit the bedroom, a line formed outside the door like people waiting to see a religious epiphany. If we were smart about it, we could have charged admission and financed the entire tour. Well, after a night of earthquake-sounding bed banging and screams, it was time to go, but the problem was Susie didn't want to release Doug. I looked in the bedroom and there she was smothering him. All you could see was Doug's little tuft of red hair. He looked up at me with the most desperate look on his face and mouthed the words, "Help." After prying her off with a crowbar we waited in the van while Doug said his goodbyes to Susie. As a goof, we took bets on how long it would take him to give us an excuse for hooking up with her. When he finally got in the van we drove off and to our astonishment, Doug didn't say a word. We looked at him and waited. Still nothing. Doug had out-done himself on this one and he knew it. So Harley and I helped him out.

Harley piped in first. "Man, that was the best blowjob I ever had. She coulda sucked a basketball through a garden hose."

Next, it was my turn, "Yeah and that chick's ass just looked fat, but once I pulled down those size 64 granny panties, it was all pure glutumus-maximus muscle, dude."

Doug just looked at us and said, "Fuck you's. Fuck both of yous," and we cracked up at his expense all the way to the next show. To this day, every time Doug starts acting like a playa I humble him by reminding him of his Cro-Mags road days and his little Susie in Win-A-Pig.

After the tour was over, we got back to New York and went our separate ways. After you've been in a van for two or three months straight with the same fuckers, smelling their farts, breath, feet and armpits, the last thing you want to do is see them when you get home. Once we got back to the city we discovered that Age of Quarrel was flying off the shelves across the country, but that didn't mean shit for us because ho's don't get paid. I went back to being a bike messenger and tried to find a place to live while we waited for word on the next tour. I decided to team up with the rest of the McGowan Clan because my younger brother, Frank, had a line on a dope, two-story house in Maspeth, Queens. He and his family (two sons and a wife), along with E, were ready to move in. There was a bedroom on the first floor for about $200 a month, so I jumped on it.

So here we were, one big happy family together again just like old times, right? Well, not exactly. Frank's wife, Wanda, didn't like the fact that I was there. When Frank first hooked up with her in '82 and brought her down to the LES to meet me, my eyeballs almost popped out of my fuckin' head. Frank married the crazy bitch I made out with one night back in '77 while on the Irish Riviera. Back then she was a loose chick who went by the name of Poco (after the band). I almost shit my pants when I saw her and I told Frank to immediately get a divorce. Now, you could understand why there was tension between us.

As for E, that motherfucker was notorious for eating the last of your shit every night. You'd be dead broke and down to your last little bit of cereal, or two apples, and you'd be looking forward to your breakfast, except when you opened the 'fridge all your shit would be gone. After the food trials and tribulations we went through as kids you'd think the nigga would even save you a half-a-bowl of cereal, or one apple, or even a half of a fuckin' sandwich, right? Hell no, not this fucker, he left you ungots and must have been thinking he was back at the Valentis' on his midnight bread drawer runs.

The way we got to rent the house was funny. Once again, I relied on my brethren from India to provide me with shelter, but this time the victim was named Umon. He and his wife reminded me of an Indian version of Nick and Rose Valenti. She had a hairy upper lip and a mole and he was skinny and constantly smoked. Frank, Wanda and their two kids got dressed up when they went to meet Umon for the first time and look at the house, complete with tacky colors inside – Valenti style. Umon kept smiling, patting Frank's sons on their heads and repeatedly saying in his super-thick Indian accent, "What a nice American family. So, so nice all of you are." Guess he shoulda read Robert McKee's "Story," Chapter 5, pages 100-102, 'cause the brotha got fooled by the characterization. If he did know the true character of my brother Frank and his twisted wife and life well, let's just say we would have never gotten that house and leave it at that. Since that was not the case, he gave us the lease and took the first and last month's rent. Last meaning that was the last money he ever got from us. Once the neighbors got a look at who was moving in, they were pissed at Umon for renting his house to a bunch of lunatics.

Yes people, we were the neighbors from hell that you read about. Within weeks the scene on the block went from serenity, peace and quiet, to pit bulls barking, Wanda and Frank screaming and constantly fighting. Punks showing up 24/7 and blasting music and weed smoke bellowing out from every window. Frank was an auto mechanic and ran a chop shop and a repair garage out of our backyard, both of which were obviously illegal. He had turned the entire street into a junkyard with beat-up cars, greasy engine parts and spray paint fumes so bad that you choked on them half-a-block away. Well after two months of the neighbors complaining to Umon and us not paying the rent, Umon took us to court. But unfortunately for him, it turned out E knew the two most powerful words in Landlord/Tenant Court, "Tenant Application!"

Tenant application means we were filing charges against Umon for violations in the house, which were plenty. That meant, until he fixed every last one down to the loose screws in the light switch plates, we didn't have to pay rent. Back then you could stall for months on end and just keep going back to court before you got evicted. Our case was made even stronger because we had two small children in the house. It took two months just to get a city inspector to come by and then after six or seven months of going back and forth to court, living rent free, you'd move and never pay the back rent. Nowadays the courts are hip to that scam and make you put the rent money in an escrow account so that when the landlord finishes the work and clears up the violations they still get paid.

Umon couldn't believe that this kind of shit could go down in America because it seemed they forgot to tell him this one in his, 'Get Rich Quick in America Seminar' back in Bombay. The look on his face in court was priceless. "What? What the hell is going on! I want my money or I want them out," he'd shout at the judge, who was one of those good old boy types who liked to keep American dollars in America and kept siding with us every month we went to court. Umon even showed up at our (notice I said our) house one day and tried to walk in the front door to do some inspecting of his own. He had to be physically stopped and thrown out on his ass by Frank and E, before he ran to the cops. When he returned with the cops he started yelling in a mixture of Hindi and English, "Doo bah did dee dah bah dee dee 'want my money' da dondi did dee boo dee dah … now!" E calmly stepped up with the court papers and said, "Officers I believe these will explain everything," he said. "We are currently in litigation with Mr. Umon."

He handed the cops the papers and after they read them they said, "Mr. McGowan, do you want Mr. Umon in your house?" E replied casually, "No officers, now is not a good time," and with that the officers turned to Umon and said, "Mr. Umon, please leave Mr. McGowan's house." Umon was on the verge of tears and yelled, "What? It is my house! I bought it! I own it! What do you mean his house? It is not his house, it is my house!" The cops had to literally drag him away while he repeatedly screamed, "It is not his house it is my house!" Finally, Umon fixed everything and we made plans to meet him one morning at the house to give him his check for the seven or eight months of back rent. We pulled a midnight move the night before and left his ass sitting high and dry on the doorstep.

I was homeless and couch surfing, staying wherever I could. At that point, the 'Mags started doing bigger shows in New York, opening up for Anthrax at the Beacon Theater and Venom at The Ritz on 11th Street. We also played at the Cabaret Metro in Chicago with Venom and nobody in the mostly metal crowd knew who the hell we were. To make matters worse right before that show an article came out in some big metal magazine with Cronos, Venom's lead singer, who was quoted as saying that he hated skinheads and he ate them for breakfast. So as we walked out on stage and went to play our first song Harley's bass rig blew out. We argued with Cronos because he didn't want to lend us any of Venom's gear. Meanwhile for the ten minutes it took for Cronos to finally say okay and then have his roadies hook it up, the entire fuckin' crowd kept shouting, "Skinheads suck! Skinheads suck!"

Now first of all, I wasn't a skinhead. I had a Marine-style high and tight cut. Kevin looked like fuckin' Opie Taylor from The Andy Griffith Show with that dopey-ass haircut. As a matter of fact, the only one with a shaved head was Harley, but it didn't matter as we soon found ourselves under a barrage of bottles and spit. Now most bands in that pressure situation would have crumbled, maybe even ran off stage fearing for their safety, but we were the fuckin' Cro-Mags and for us it was just another day at the office.

As the minutes went by the intensity in that room was getting thicker and something inside me snapped. The adrenaline ran through my body and I became euphoric. I jumped off the stage and pushed through the crowd eyeballing every fucker in that place with bad intentions. I knew we were about to hit them with some shit they'd never seen before. I taunted them, egged them on, even challenged them to be the sick fuckin' metalheads they were supposed to be (Venom's fans had a rep). Finally our roadie gave the green light and I jumped back on stage. As soon as we hit the first note of "We Gotta Know" we won every fucker over in that room. By the end of that song instead of the crowd chanting, "Skinheads suck" they chanted, "Cro-Mags Rule!"

In Ohio, we opened for the German speed metal band Helloween, whom we nicknamed Helloweenies. These rich boy wanka's had like $100,000 worth of gear and stage props and they refused to tear down their two-story, wannabe evil castle drum riser. Petey Hines, who was playing drums with us at the time, had to play up on it, which was funny as hell. After a little encouragement on my part the 'Mags fans broke their little stage toys up a bit and they bitched about it later. I think it was Harley who told them where they could go with their complaints. After this run of shows word soon got out that we were one band you did not want to go on after because we were a tough act to follow.

Just before hitting the road in '86 to do a short stint on the East Coast, I helped out the Bad Brains at a New Music Seminar show at The Ritz. Also on the bill was Megadeth and, I believe, Slayer. I have to say whoever the hell was behind this booking needed to have their fuckin' heads examined because booking the Bad Brains and death metal bands together was just asking for trouble. Well, trouble did come via Megadeth's lead singer, Dave Mustaine. During that particular show, we shared a dressing room with Megadeth. Back then, the way the dressing rooms were set up at the old Ritz was you walked in and the headliner (Bad Brains) had the middle room, while the opening act (Megadeth) had to walk through the Brains' room to get to theirs. The Bad Brains were there with their wives and kids, all Rasta-ed out, eating veggie food and quietly reading their Bibles. In walks Mustaine, who's obvious high on dope or something. He takes one look around the room and starts swearing at the top of his lungs like a sailor. "Motherfuckin', cock suckin', pussy-lickin." I walk over to my man very humbly and say, "Hey bro, could you chill out on the language? There are kids in here." He says, "Fuck you man, who the fuck are you asshole? You're just a fuckin' roadie!"

Now I really wanted to lay this guy out right then and there, look down at him and say, "Did I mention I also double as security?" I resisted the urge and chilled-out after some coaxing by H.R., who was in the Zen-like trance he always achieved before he performed. I didn't feel the need to tell Mustaine I was a Cro-Mag. I figured I'd let him find out the hard way and he walked away mumbling, "Now I got the fuckin' help trying to tell me what to do, what the fuck is rock-n-roll coming to?"

The problem is when you let some fuckers off the hook from a beat down they make the unfortunate mistake of taking kindness and compassion for weakness. So when Megadeth finished their set a sweaty Mustaine passed through our room, picked up one of those large, square black tubs of ice and threw its contents in the air. It landed all over the kids, the women, the band and the crew. I jumped up, grabbed a fist-full of his long, blonde permed-hair, wrapped it around my fist and slammed his cranium so hard off the wall that I'm sure he saw fuckin' Tweety Birds circling his head. At that point I got to see H.R. in one of those rare moments where he snapped. I held Mustaine (who by the way was ready to shit his pants) against the wall by his hair and H.R. got an inch from his face. He stared him down and pointed in his face before saying, "You want violence? We'll show you violence like you've never seen before." Believe me, I've seen H.R. in action and I know the internal power this man has. When he reaches that state of anger I'd put him up against anybody. Mustaine wisely apologized and basically begged us not to kick his ass, but I was still waiting for the signal from H.R. and this fucker woulda been going back to the

West Coast minus a few teeth. H.R. told me to let him go, so I did. Now, just for the record: Mustaine was as quiet as a church mouse the rest of the night as the Brains went on to do an especially super-charged show that evening.

Now, the ironic thing was a couple of months later I got word that the Cro-Mags were going out on a U.S. tour with Motorhead and guess who? That's right, Megadeth! When I found out that news I remember thinking, "Hmmm…this should be interesting." Just before we hit the road I was told that a very famous Hollywood producer and some director saw one of the Cro-Mags shows and they wanted to meet with me and talk about putting us in their upcoming movie. The producer was Julia Phillips whose credits include Taxi Driver, The Sting, and Close Encounters of the Third Kind. I met with the director and he was really cool. He said Julia really wanted us in her movie and I was stoked to hear that because Taxi Driver is one of my favorite movies of all time. When I asked the director what the movie was about he said, "We don't know yet. All we know is that we have to have you guys in it." The meeting went well and it was a lock, we were going to be in her movie and the plan was after the California and Texas leg of the tour she would fly us back to New York for the one day shoot, before we picked up again down South. I only had one stipulation for us doing the movie and it was this: we had to play a live show and we had to let the real Cro-Mags fans in. If she really wanted to capture the essence of the 'Mags on celluloid there could be no actors faking the funk. Sure we'd give her the lip-synching scenes she needed so they could be shot in the crowd safely, but to see the chaos that ensued at every one of our shows, we had to do the shit for real. I mean that's why she gave us the spot in the movie in the first place, right? She agreed and we signed on.

In October of '86 we flew to Los Angeles with our road manager, Roger, and were picked up at LAX in a brand new motor home. I had never been in a motor home up until that point and to see the full kitchen, bathroom and TV (with VCR) on board was un-fuckin' real. It had more amenities than any place I ever lived, except the McGowans' home in Garden City. Unfortunately we were told not to get comfortable because we had to switch vehicles once we got to the Santa Monica Civic Auditorium where one of the Motorhead/Megadeth/Cro-Mags shows was booked. They told us not to worry, because we were going to trade the motor home for one of those slick tour buses. We pulled up at the arena and the motor home dumped us off along with the gear. Roger went to find our manager, CWV, and as we walked around the back of the huge arena to see our tour bus we were already arguing over who got what bunk and all that other shit. That's when we saw the brand new Prevost sitting there idling. We stopped in our tracks and looked at each other. I knew what each one of the band was thinking "This is it fellas. We fuckin' made it." Yes, this is what all those shitty, yogurt-eatin', catchin' scabies at some fuckin' dirty punker's house tours, were for. At that point I actually believed CWV's catch phrase, "I'm doing this for you guys." Shit, it was more than a catch phrase, it was the fucker's mantra and I never believed it until I stood there looking at that tour bus. See, that prick finally came through and was actually spending some money for us to be comfortable on tour. I was misty-eyed.

The lights were on inside so I walked up, banged on the door and it slowly opened like something out of Star Wars. I believe the term we all used simultaneously as we stood there in awe was, "Whoa." The door opened completely and after a few seconds, standing there was Lemmy Kilmister, Motorhead's lead singer and bass player. We did the meet and greet thing and then I said, "I guess the party's on our bus tonight, huh Lemmy?" He looked at me perplexed as I attempted to board our bus. He interrupted and said, "Hold up, this ain't your vehicle, mate. This is our bus. Your vehicle's parked just behind ours on the other side." I apologized and told the guys that our bus was just behind Motorhead's. So we grabbed our bags and walked quickly around to the other side of Motorhead's tour bus.

As we turned the corner we stopped dead in our tracks and dropped our bags in disbelief. There was no bus or motor home parked there. The only vehicle in the entire fuckin' lot behind Motorhead's bus was a beat-up, '71 white Ford cargo van with no windows and the words, "Kendik Plumbling," written on the side. Roger appeared and I looked at him and said, "This is a fuckin' joke, right? There's a bus coming, right dude? Tell me there's a bus coming, Roger?" Roger fell silent and shook his head from side to side. He was instructed not to tell us about our luxury ride until we got to the venue. The motor home thing at the airport well, that was just a ruse because CWV knew if we were picked up in the Kendik, as it came to be known, well let's just say the shit would have hit the fan right then and there. The CWV said a tour bus just wasn't in the budget and according to him, this van was a steal at $400. Yeah, a steal for who, scumbag? The fact was that prick was flying around first class to the shows and we were paying for it. When we confronted him about our show transportation he actually laughed in our faces and said, "Hey, look at it on the bright side... at least

I got Motorhead to carry all your gear instead of having that crammed in the van with ya's, too. Then you's would really be fucked." I think at this point, it's safe to say I practically had to be physically restrained.

After we put our bags in the Kendik we headed into the venue. As pissed off as I was I decided it was best not to say anything to Mustaine about the Bad Brains incident, but let him bring it up and see what's become of our little rift. As I got into the Santa Monica Civic Auditorium Mustaine was sitting on some road cases that were on the venue's floor. We walked over, introduced ourselves as the Cro-Mags and to my surprise, that son of a bitch didn't remember me. He was all smiles and even invited us to smoke some of the best weed in all of Southern California, which we gladly accepted.

So I'm sitting right next to Mustaine and he keeps looking at me. He finally takes a hit, exhales, points at me and says, "Dude, you look familiar. Do I know you?" I was like, "Nah, man. I never met you before, bro." Doug and Harley struggled to hold back their laughter. I wasn't done with him just yet. He broke out his bag of weed, rolled another joint, lit it and took a hit. While he held in the smoke he eeked out, "Nah, I know you. I just don't know from where." I told him he must have confused me with somebody else, because I never met him in person and that I've only seen him in magazines. This went on for like ten minutes. He asked me if we went to the same school? Did I ever live in the Bay Area? Did I used to fuck a girl named Peggie Von Slassenhooters? My answers to all of the above were, "No, no, and no."

At this point a frazzled Mustaine jumps up and says, "Dude, c'mon. Stop fuckin' with me. I know we met before. Where the fuck do I know you from?" I was holding all the cards. I had the upper hand and I knew it. I casually took a hit off the huge spliff, exhaled and pointed at him. "Alright," I said. "I'm going to give you one clue and if you don't figure it out, I'm never going to tell you." Mustaine was all smiles, "I knew it! I knew I knew you fucker! Alright, alright, what is it, what's the clue?" "You ready?" I said. The anticipation was killing him. "Yeah, yeah, yeah... c'mon motherfucker!" He yelled. I stood up and got into character, that being a very intoxicated Mustaine. "Fuck you man, who the fuck are you asshole? You're just a fuckin' roadie!" His mouth hung open, his eyes got as big as two softballs and he muttered the words, "Holy shit," as he stood there staring off into space. I knew that entire evening's events just flashed through his mind because he rubbed his head right where I smashed it off the wall inside The Ritz months earlier.

I stood there waiting to see what his reaction would be. Thirty-seconds later he looked at me and said, "Bro, man. I'm so sorry, dude. I was really fucked up back then and I know I acted like a total asshole." He held out his hand and I shook it and accepted his apology. On a side note, Dave was a really cool fucker when he wasn't high on dope. He was the nicest guy on that entire leg of the tour. He always made sure our catering was on point and the soundman keep our sound tight, which was totally unheard of for opening bands, especially on arena tours. Unfortunately, Lemmy and Mustaine didn't get along and Megadeth was later booted off the tour after a few shows in California.

As for the 'Mags, we got into the Kendik, headed up the Northern Cali coast and that's when the fun started with the vehicle. See, a lot of the vans that were built in the early-'70s had the motor inside and this thing was so fucked up we had to shout just to be heard over the revving engine. To make matters worse, the carburetor wasn't working properly so we had to have the engine cover off while we drove. Whoever was in the front passenger seat had to hold the valve door open the entire time. That meant the dirt and debris from the highway shot up into the van and one evening we even got blasted with some leftover road kill. It was not just inconvenient traveling in this thing, shit I've been inconvenienced my whole life; this van was fuckin' life threatening. We would be driving along at 55 mph and then all of a sudden, without warning the van would backfire and drop down to five miles an hour. Roger would have to put the pedal to the metal shouting at the top of his lungs like Scottie from Star Trek, "I'm giving it all she's got captain!" I can't even count the number of times we almost got taken out by some tractor-trailers that were driving behind us. After the first day of traveling in the Kendik we crossed out 'Plumbing' from the side of the van with one of those big, black graffiti markers and added the words "We" and "You and We Will." Now the side of the van proudly proclaimed in big bold letters: "We 'Kendik' You and We Will," which cops in every city didn't find too amusing.

Inside, the Kendik was one fucked-up row of seats with springs popping out, digging into your ass every time you hit a bump. After the second day on the road every square inch of wall space was covered in anti- CWV graffiti. Last but not least, no tour horror story would be complete without a crazy tour manager. Roger began bugging-out on the tour under the pressure and became a born-again Christian psychopath who constantly quoted his favorite part of the Bible – The Book of Revelations. In other words, all he ever talked about was the end of the world and the destruction of the evil non-believers that included the psycho-Krsna-cult band members he was driving. Roger, or "The Bull," as we called him, was a cock-diesel motherfucker and when he flipped-out and started talking all that crazy shit about the fact that he could drive the Kendik off the side of the mountain we were on and how we couldn't do anything to stop him, uuhhh, let's just say it freaked us out a bit. I volunteered to do a lot of the driving, even with no license and being AWOL from the Navy. Now, take all of that shit, mix it with the explosive personalities of the fuckers in the band (minus Kevin the dweeb, of course) and it's no wonder when we stepped out of that van onto the stage we killed it every fuckin' night. As a matter of fact, Lemmy was quoted as saying, "The Cro-Mags were the only opening band I ever came out to watch every night of the tour because you just never knew what to expect from those crazy bastards." Coming from Lemmy who is the front man for one of the greatest bands of all time that was an honor. Oh, by the way, when Roger got back to Chicago after touring with the 'Mags, his family had him committed to some psychiatric hospital. I guess we had that effect on people.

During the Motorhead arena tour we got really tight with Lemmy. He was, and still is, one of the coolest fuckers in the music biz. These days, with all the douche bag assholes with attitudes that are in bands, it's good to know there are still some real solid people out there. Personally, I think Lemmy didn't know what to expect from us as a band. Several months before the Motorhead, Megadeth, Cro-Mags tour kicked off we were supposed to open for them at The Ritz, but their roadies did one of those three-hour sound checks while Lemmy and the boys were running around the LES looking for something (now what could that be?). We were so psyched to play that show and we had tons of people there to see us, but our set got bumped because they were running late. I don't think Lemmy did it on purpose. I just think the fucker was a little burnt-out and lost track of the time. I flipped the fuck out on him after the show, cursed him out and threatened to kick his ass, something any old-school punk would have done. I mean, could you imagine what Lemmy would have done if someone did that shit to Motorhead back in the day?

We both apologized then the 'Mags and Motorhead were like one big family. One thing about Lemmy was if he liked you, you knew it, because he fucked with you and most bands probably took the ribbing from him, kept quiet, went to their tour buses and wrote in their journals. A typical entry would be something like this: Dear Diary, Oh my God! I can't believe it... Lemmy called me a fuckin' pufta!" Don't laugh people, Kevin kept a journal and I guess it's because if you know in your heart of hearts that this is the biggest thing you'll ever accomplish in your pathetic life, you want to write about every fuckin' event from who farted and when, right down to the two pieces of ass you almost got the entire time you were in the band.

While Kevin was writing in his journal the rest of the band gave it back to Lemmy in spades and he liked it. I walked up to him one day as he was holding court with a bunch of groupies telling some road stories. I said in a dead serious tone, "Yo, Lemmy. I got a great idea for some new Motorhead merchandising." I looked at him and said, "Stick-on Lemmy warts. Everyone in the crowd can go home looking like you." He basically laughed then told me to "Fuck off," in that oh so wonderful way the English do, middle finger included. If you think that was fucked up, just recently I saw him do an interview on TV and he was talking about cutting off his facial warts and auctioning them off on eBay to the highest bidder. So Lemmy, if you're reading this, I think I'm entitled to a small percentage of any proceeds derived from the sale of your warts, bro.

Here's a little advice for you opening bands: get in tight with the headliner's roadies. If they don't like you, you'll start finding your mic's smelling like they were up someone's ass and more than likely they probably were. Now don't get me wrong, the 'Mags never brownnosed anyone. Things just happened for us all the time because we had it like that. The thing that got us in even tighter with Motorhead and their roadies was when I got to put my cooking skills to good use. On tour, we were broke and really couldn't afford to go out to eat, so I improvised. We were playing these huge venues with these giant kitchens and what I did after a couple of shows was collect the small per diems from the guys in the Cro-Mags, go to the supermarket, get some groceries and throw down. One of Motorhead's roadies came in and caught a whiff of what I was making which I believe was a tofu stir-fry with spicy Schezuan sauce, pistachio risotto, a big old salad with a warm balsamic-vinaigrette dressing and hot French bread. He said he was vegetarian and asked if he could have some and naturally, I hooked him up. Turns out seven or eight guys on the Motorhead crew, including the guitar player were hardcore vegetarians and they were always complaining about how the food on tour sucked. Back in the '80s, when you put vegetarian meals on the tour rider (list of shit the band is provided by the show promoter) you always got two things: salad and pasta, with sauce from a can. This was also a time before tour catering was really up to snuff, complete with traveling chefs and shit like that. So, imagine eating that crummy food for three months straight.

Now I had the Motorhead roadies chipping in for groceries and every day during sound check I was in these arena kitchens cooking gourmet Ital for everyone. Someone even bought me an apron that said, "Grandma," and on several occasions I had to act like one and chase those fuckers out with a metal spoon because they were trying to steal food. After sound check we'd sit down like one big happy family and chow the fuck down, which brings people together. Every night at the dinner table was a comedy sketch, straight outta Monty Python complete with these crazy English fuckers. Lemmy came up to me one day and thanked me because he realized what an undertaking it was to do that every day. He knew that if your roadies ain't happy on tour you're fucked. Being a former roadie, I know nothing puts a smile on a roadie's face quicker than a quality meal.

Whatever we needed Motorhead and their roadies gave us. Guitar cables? No problem. Tuner's on the whack? No worries, they had an extra. Re-arrange the stage monitors for our set? Done. Outta beers? Have ours. No chicks? Shit, Lemmy ain't that stupid. We were on our own in that department. The other thing was we had a lot more stage production sound-wise than any opening band should have had. Motorhead was the loudest band on Earth and just to ensure that wouldn't ever be a problem because of a bad sound system, they traveled with their own. They had an eighteen-wheeler full of gear and the decibel level of that stage set up was tested and equaled that of a 747 blasting at full throttle. We played a smaller venue in West Virginia and Motorhead packed the entire fuckin' thing into this place from floor to ceiling. The entire club was nothing but sound gear. So when the 'Mags and Motorhead played, the ground shook for miles and our ears rang for days. Fuck, I think I'm still half-deaf from that gig.

Lemmy made sure everyone was cool with us and that included his band members, which we found out a few days into the tour. Our guitar player at the time, Doug Holland, went into Motorhead's dressing room and told their drummer they sounded great the night before. This guy was in Thin Lizzy back in the '70s and still had his perm and rock star attitude. He stood up with his pompous British attitude and said, "If you ever come in the headliner's dressing room again without being invited I will fuckin' rip off your arms and beat you with them. You got me? Now get the fuck out!" Doug came in and told me what happened and I wasn't having that shit, not from this fuckin' hired gun. One thing the 'Mags were notorious for, despite the internal problems, was sticking together. We were allowed to fight each other, be assholes and curse each other out, but if an outsider did it, look the fuck out. I mean, I didn't like Kevin, but on more than one occasion I had to fuck somebody up for messing with him, because that was the law on the road.

I walked into Motorhead's dressing room, got in his face and said, "Why don't you try to rip my arms off you fucking faggot and see what happens." Just then Lemmy walked in and asked what was going on. When I told him he walked up to his drummer, pointed in his face and said, "Don't you ever fucking disrespect these guys, again. They're not only our fans since day one, but they're our friends. I will fire your ass in a hot second if it ever happens again." The guy was Mr. Manners for the rest of the tour.

As for the shows, once we got to the venues it was great and night after night we tore it up. The problem for us was never the gigs; it was just getting there. The Kendik broke down no fewer than a dozen times going up and down the West Coast. We were getting ready to make the trek through the California desert to Texas and that's when I called CWV. I told him he had to get us a different vehicle because we would never make it. When I told him we'd end up broken down on the side of the highway, dying of thirst with vultures circling overhead like one of those scenes in an old western he just laughed and hung up the phone. My prediction came true as the carburetor finally gave out and we were left stranded. There we were, broken down in the desert, no water, no food and more importantly no weed, which is what I needed to calm down. I literally wanted to kill someone and I'll give you one guess who that person was. We sat on a desolate stretch of highway for at least three hours without a single car passing by. When one finally did I tried to flag him down, but he sped on by.

Another hour or so had passed before this hippie station wagon adorned with flowers painted on the side and two male, burnt-out flower people in their forties who somehow or another never heard the love-in was over, stopped. The best description I can give of these two individuals is to picture what Laurel and Hardy would have looked like had they been hippies. The only difference was the skinny one was the brains of the operation and the dumpy one was a burn out. The first words out of the skinny dude's mouth as he stood there pondering our desperate situation and copping this obvious attitude like he knew he had the upper hand was, "You guys got any drugs?"

What we were about to find out was these guys were only going to help us if we gave them drugs. If we didn't they were fully prepared to leave our asses out on the side of the road. When I asked, "What the hell happened to the peace and love, dude?" The skinny one said, "Fuck peace and love. Why do you think all those assholes are gone?" Wouldn't you know that out of all the cool hippies in the world I guess it was just Cro-Mags karma to find two who were total scumbags.

I knew something had to be done right away. Since the heat got to the rest of the fuckers' brains and they were just standing there dumbfounded, I decided it was time to take charge. I told them we were in a band and if they helped get us to the next concert we'd get them all the wine, women and drugs they could handle. They bought it hook, line and sinker, but the next problem became how to accomplish the task because they had no towlines and their vehicle was too beat-up to push us. That's when my Navy know-how kicked in (thanks Boats). I cut the seatbelts out of the Kendik and tied a square knot connecting the two of them. Then I put a bowline knot on their bumper and ours using the seatbelts. Roger put the Kendik in neutral and off we went.

The desert heat and the fact that the hippie's station wagon could only pull us at about ten miles an hour wasn't helping the situation. We were boiling and extremely agitated because it took three or four hours to reach the nearest town. When we finally arrived at the service station, they didn't have the part we needed, so off we went again. All I kept saying during the entire ordeal was I have to get some weed or I'm gonna flip the fuck out and kill somebody. My knots held up and after six or seven hours we finally reached Crockett County, Texas, which is midway between Houston and El Paso and about 100 miles north of the Texas/Mexican border. When we pulled into town, we were lucky enough to stop at a gas station that had the last carburetor for a 1971 Ford cargo van in stock.

We piled out of the vehicles and my first question to every son a bitch I saw in the street was, "Where the fuck can I buy some weed?" I just kept going from one person to the next like a madman, standing in their way and demanding they find me a joint. I asked mothers, fathers, daughters, shit, I think I might have even asked the local priest. Seeing me scrambling around, Harley warned me to chill out. Actually his exact words were, "Squidly, you don't know where you're at. Don't be fuckin' around down here. This is Texas, the cops don't play." The last thing I needed was comments from the peanut gallery and I told him so. He walked over this hill, across the highway to go to the supermarket and his last words were, I'm gonna come back here and all you assholes are gonna be in handcuffs." To which I responded, "Yeah right, dickhead." I was as streetwise as they came and no cop in a one-horse town was going to get the draw on me. To my surprise, minutes later I asked the mechanic at the station if he knew where he could get some herb. He said he had a friend who could get us some weed. So Doug, the hippies and I danced around the parking lot high-fiving each other.

Twenty minutes later as promised here comes this 6'5" American Indian dude with long hair named, Mike. He greets the mechanic, turns to us and says, "What do you guys need?" My reply, "I don't know…like a ten dollar bag." He laughs in my face, "Are you fucking joking?" With that Mike turns back to the gas station dude and tells him off about wasting his time. I knew our opportunity was slipping away and if I didn't do something fast, we were fucked. "Listen Big Mike. What I meant was a dime bag to start and if we like it when the rest of the guys get back we'll buy more." Mike said, "I'm a grower numb nuts, I don't sell less then a pound. Now if you guys had some drugs to trade that'd be another story." Doug blurted out, "We don't do…" and before he could say anymore I elbowed him. My days of beat acid, quick-on-your-feet-thinking kicked in, once again. "Doug" I said, "Remember that big bag of coke that guy gave you in L.A?" Doug was always a little slower than most. "What bag?" This time he caught another elbow to the ribs. "Oh yeah, yeah, umm…that bag of coke. Yeah, I uhh…still got that." Mike was elated. "You guys got coke?" Doug and I nodded and I said, "A lot of friggin' coke." Mike said we had a deal and literally jogged off down the one dirt road. Doug looked at me confused and said, "Squidly, I ain't got no coke, bro." I patted Doug on the back. "My boy, you are about to get an introduction to the wonderful world of Pseudo Products Incorporated."

As I stood on the side of the Kendik with the side doors open, pouring both full boxes of the baking soda Doug used to brush his teeth into the big zip-lock baggie, Doug and the hippies were bewildered. They begged me to fill them in and I did. The plan went like this. The deal had to go down right next to the Kendik and I'd have the side doors open. I'd take the bag of weed from Big Mike and give him the baggie full of baking soda. While he looked at it I'd turn around real quick, tap a bit of weed out of his bag and stash it in the van. Then once he noticed the coke was beat, I'd apologize, give him back his bag, minus a few joints, and we'd be puffin' away as soon as he fucked off back down the dirt road he came from. Doug and the hippies nodded in approval, very impressed with my keen sense of hustle.

We waited for what seemed like eternity, but in fact was only forty-five minutes, when Mike was spotted coming up the road. I took my position right next to the open van doors. He stopped in the middle of the road and waved me over. I looked at him like he was crazy and waved him over. He shook his head and waved me over, again. I shook my head and yelled, "Uhhh, Mike! It's just a hunch here, but I think it would be better if we didn't do this in the middle of the road!" He seemed a little nervous as he walked over and said, "Yeah? Well, I heard about you New Yorkers." I reminded him that he was bigger than all of us stacked one on top of each other, then I pulled out the bag of baking soda held it up and said, "Two ounces of pure Columbian flake, dude." His eyes lit up and he immediately lifted his shirt and pulled a pillow-sized bag of weed out from under it. "Holy fuckin' shit!" I blurted out. I realized I better calm down and said nonchalantly, "Wow, uhhh… must be a pound there, eh?" Mike's eyes were fixed on the coke. "Two pounds," he said. "Now gimme the coke." We made the switch. I turned around, took a fist full of weed out of the bag and stashed it.

Everything was going according to plan and a nice big smile came over my face as I thought about the look on Harley's face when he found out I had done the impossible…once again. On the road Harley always bet me that I couldn't find weed in some out of the way place. I always managed to prove him wrong, even though I knew his pea-brain was thinking, "I'll just use reverse psychology and tell Squidly there's no way he'll find weed in this town and knowing him he'll want to prove me wrong. He'll do all the work and I'll reap the reward." I knew he thought he was getting over, but for me it was about the challenge and this time was no different. I did the impossible. I found a grower in a town with a population of 67.

As I closed up the bag of weed and stood there with my back to him I waited for the complaint. Just to break the awkward moment of silence I said, "One of these jerk-offs in the band said I'm gonna end up in handcuffs." I continued on sarcastically, "You're not gonna try and snap the cuffs on me there now are ya Big Mike?" Just then I heard what sounded like the crackling of a walkie-talkie and Big Mike mumbled something. I turned around and he pulled out a shield on a chain from under his shirt and yelled, "Hold it right there – DEA!" Doug and the two hippies quickly walked away as Mike nervously fumbled for his cuffs that fell on the ground. I remember thinking he was just fucking with me and said smiling, "Yo, that's not even funny dude, don't fuck around." That's when he grabbed me and I realized the fucker was dead serious. Instinct took over and I swept his legs out and threw his big ass to the ground.

Just then dozens of cop cars filled that parking lot with lights and sirens blaring. The cops jumped out with M-16s, shotguns and various handguns pointed at us. They were shouting for us to get on the ground. I don't know how they do shit in Crockett County, Texas, but in New York City when a cop says get on the ground, you do what any New York hoodie would do. You break the 'Don't ever run asshole rule' and bolt. I took off out into the desert and when I got about fifty yards out, a tumbleweed rolled by me. I quickly realized there were no subways to duck into, no cars to hide under, no alleyways to run through and no fences to jump over. Simply put, I was fucked. I turned around with my hands up and walked back toward the arsenal of weapons that were pointed at me.

They made us lay with our faces in the dirt. Doug, Roger, Kevin and even the hippies were pissed at me. I told them not to worry that it was just a big misunderstanding and as soon as they realized it was just baking soda they'd have to let us go. They used zip ties to handcuff us together and then stood us up in one perp line, standing side by side. The skinny hippie started telling the cops that he didn't know anything about a drug deal. He claimed he and his boy were born-again Christians who were out doing the Lord's work and all they did was give us a tow. I told him to chill out and he yelled, "Don't talk to me you heathen!" Well, after the cops found a bag of magic mushrooms in their vehicle the cops told him to can the religious crap, 'cause they were goin' down too.

Of all places to look for weed we just happened to end up in one of the biggest smuggling towns near the Texas/Mexican border, which was under heavy police surveillance. As Mike walked over I thought, here's the moment I make this shit go away and make him look like a dickhead in the process. "Hey Mike," I said, "There's only one problem with your little bust scenario here…" I smiled and he got in my face. "Oh yeah, what's that tough guy?" he said. I smirked and answered, "I gave you baking soda. It's not real coke." I laughed and he hauled-off and punched me in the solar plexus. His punch knocked the wind out of me and doubled me over. He bent over and looked me in the eyes as I gasped for air. "That's for tripping me fuck-wad and by the way, it ain't no problem at all, you wanna know why?" "Why?" I said as I tried desperately to breath. Mike smiled, "Because just last month this town passed a law that says even if you sell fake contraband...they can still charge you with a crime." My reply, "Wow, lucky me," and he confirmed it with a "Yeah, good timing, fuck-nuts."

Well, after twenty minutes of us standing there guess who comes whistling fuckin' Dixie over the highway with his two bags of groceries? That's right Harley. Now, I just couldn't wait to see the expression on his face. As he reached the top of the hill he was looking down at the ground and for a second didn't notice the chaos. When he looked up, his jaw hung open, he dropped his groceries and I saw him mouth the words, "What the fuck?" He had that famous look on his face that resembled a confused chimp. I tried to lighten the moment with some humor. "Yo, Harley!" I said as I held up my right hand which was zip tied to Doug and my left which was cuffed to my religious hippie friend, "You were right, bro. We did end up in handcuffs!" His look quickly changed from confusion to anger. He used every curse word in his arsenal against me as the cops ran up the hill, grabbed him and added him to the rest of us 'Handcuffed Assholes.' I have to give it to Harley though...he did call it.

Because it was fake coke Mike was off the case. He said his goodbyes courtesy of his middle finger and handed us over to the local authorities. It was now a matter for the Crockett County courts to deal with us. Luckily I had someone else's I.D. on that tour. While I was in the paddy wagon I just kept whispering my pseudo name to the band so they didn't accidentally call me John. The only response out of Harley was, "Fuck you, fuck you, and fuck you again with a fuckin' wooly mammoth dick." Once we got to the police station that was an event in itself. When the cops found out we were from New York all they kept saying while they took our info was, "Bring me the next one and if this one tries to run shoot 'em in the back."

After they finished, it was time to put us in a holding cell. The jail guard walked us by the steel cell doors that didn't allow you to see who was inside. He stopped in front of one and the head jailer stopped him and said, "Nah, Bobbie Joe, put 'em in number eight." Bobbie Joe looked at him with this look of horror, swallowed and said, "Num.... number eight?" The head jailer confirmed it and told my handcuffed and shackled friends that they could thank me and my big mouth for it. They stared me down with daggers in their eyes as we walked to cell eight. As the jail guard reached for his keys he covered his nose and mouth with his shirt. He opened the door and a horrible stench filled the air. We looked in the cell and standing there were more than a dozen little Mexicans covered in shit. The manure covered Mexicans apparently snuck over the border and hid in a manure field a week before. To teach them a lesson the jailers weren't letting them bathe. Once they were released, they planned on deporting them covered in 100 percent good old U.S. of A. cow shit.

Eventually they let everyone in the Cro-Mags entourage go except for Doug and me. The next phase of this crap for the two of us was to deal with the kangaroo court in Crockett County. While we were sitting there in cuffs our lawyer proceeded to have an argument with the judge over who was supposed to bring the moonshine to a family shindig they planned for the weekend. Our lawyer and the judge were related and when I heard him call him Uncle Bob I turned to Doug and told him we were fucked. I was right because when Judge Bob read the charges he informed us that they carried a maximum penalty of up to five years in prison.

Doug just kept mumbling, "For fuckin' Arm and Hammer Baking Soda, you gotta be kidding me?" The judge looked over the bench at Roger with one of those one-eyed, crooked stares and a mouth full of chewing tobacco and said in Southern twang, "Bein' as it is a new law and all and the ink ain't even had a chance to dry yet...maybe we can uhhh...(clearing his throat)... work something out here." That working something out (according to CWV) turned out to be wiring $15,000 into that redneck judge's bank account. We never knew what the real amount of the bribe was. What we did know was that we were paying it back for a long time. According to CWV every few months the judge would hit him up for more money.

We got everyone together, piled in the Kendik and got the fuck outta Crockett County. As for the two hippies who made the mistake of getting involved with the 'Mags, they were charged with felony possession of a controlled dangerous substance. We drove like maniacs the entire day to make up for all the lost time and on October 24, we finally pulled into the Sunken Gardens Amphitheatre in San Antonio, Texas. We made it to the venue just in time to play and I gave everyone backstage a shortened rendition of our little adventure, which everyone got a kick out of. When I walked up the ramp towards the stage to start the night of chaos, I heard Lemmy say "Only the bloody fuckin' Cro-Mags."

Later on that tour, we played the Longhorn Ballroom in Dallas, the infamous club where the Sex Pistols were attacked in '78 by a bunch of rowdy redneck fans, the Cro-Mags shared the Motorhead bill with the late Wendy O. Williams of Plasmatics fame.

After that show we were flown back to NYC to be in Julia Phillips' movie, "The Beat." This was to be her big comeback movie and she talked about it in her '93 book, You'll Never Eat Lunch in This Town Again, which totally slammed the fake-ass, bullshit motherfuckers in Hollywood and told a lot of their deep, dark secrets. The industry bigwigs were so pissed when that book came out that she was immediately fired from the movie "Interview With A Vampire", which she was in the middle of producing.

I remembered feeling like such a rock star when Julia sent a stretch limo with the black, tinted windows to pick us up at the airport in New York. It was pouring rain and we were in the back of the limo blasting music, smoking huge spliffs and playing with the motorized glass partition between us and the driver, and fucking around with the intercom button. He was getting pissed and if he would have said, "Uhh…first time in a limo guys?" I would have said, "Uhh…fuck yeah, dude!" It was bumper-to-bumper traffic on the BQE. When we finally pulled up to the tollbooth at the Queens/Midtown Tunnel I could see that the poor guy inside was soaking wet and didn't look too happy. Since I was stoned and always up for a good laugh, I decided to fuck with him a bit. As we slowly pulled away, I rolled down the window halfway so he could see me. I lit up a huge spliff and blew a big puff of weed smoke in his face. I looked at him and said, "How's life treatin' ya?" and then rolled the window up. Everyone in the limo broke-up laughing and we looked back and saw the dude cursing and flipping me off. Maybe I was in a limo, but later that night it was back to a squat or someone's couch. So, in a lot of ways life was treating that soaking wet fucker a lot better than it was treating me.

The next morning I was on my way to The Ritz and I remember feeling a little bit of anxiety because I didn't know how the turnout was going to be. They only ran one little advertisement in the paper and this movie shoot was spread totally by word of mouth. I was wondering if any Cro-Mags fans would even show up at 10 a.m. on a weekday to represent. As I turned the corner onto 3rd Avenue and walked up toward 11th Street I saw the entire block was mobbed with Cro-Mags fans. I jumped up on the steps of The Ritz, looked over the Cro-Mags army and they all fell quiet as they waited for their orders. I didn't disappoint them. I yelled out, "I told these Hollywood fuckers that we were gonna show them what a real Cro-Mag show was all about. I wanna see you motherfuckers diving out of the balcony, off the sound system and each other.

Let's give them something they'll never fuckin' forget!" They went absolutely berserk and it gave me goose bumps as I walked into The Ritz.

I went upstairs and met with Julia and she showed us a table full of veggie food she ordered for us. We shared every bit of it with our crowd who were just as broke as we were. As we know, no army can do battle on an empty stomach. I informed the Cro-Mag army that they could also help themselves to the movie stars' beer, wine, food, girlfriends and anything else they wanted because how are you gonna stop a few hundred hungry Cro-Magnons that are demanding, "Me want food, me want drink." Answer: You Ain't Asshole. They took what they wanted, when they wanted it and nobody said shit because our posse and our bouncers were bigger and badder than any security the production crew had hired for their movie.

Julia informed me that we couldn't be called the Cro-Mags, but were going to be billed as the "Iron Skulls" in the movie. She told us that she couldn't use the music from Age of Quarrel for the movie soundtrack because the scumbags at Profile wanted too much money for the rights, so they recorded us live instead. I told her not to worry because she was about to see the illest shit, which obviously made her a little uneasy. I quickly put her mind at ease when I told her it would be a controlled chaos, orchestrated by the 'Mags.

The look on actor Kevin Dillon's face and the other talent was priceless when they saw the thugs filing in and realized they had to get shot in the mosh pit with them. Can you say Pampers? They definitely looked like they were about to shit their pants. I addressed the crowd again and told them to go easy on the actors because I promised Julia that they would go home in one piece, with all their teeth. I found out that Kevin's (Parris') brother, who shot footage during the entire tour for a video, was also going to be rolling tape that day. At that point I told the Cro-Mag cronies I really needed them to go off which made the actors even more nervous as they tried to imagine just exactly what "Going off" entailed. That footage we shot at The Ritz that afternoon became part of the "We Gotta Know" video.

After hours of setting up the lighting rigs, the sound gear and all the other shit involved on a movie set we heard the director say those two magic words, "Roll 'em," and all hell broke loose. Yeah, they got their footage, but not without a half dozen or so of our fans having to be taken away in ambulances, two of whom suffered broken necks and would spend the rest of their lives in wheelchairs. I heard one dove off the stage and hit the ground head on. The other was in the crowd and someone dove off the top of the sound system. The poor guy on the dance floor wasn't looking and he landed on him, snapping his neck. I still feel really badly that they got hurt at that shoot. The movie ended up having two major lawsuits against it and didn't have a theatrical release. It went straight to video. Not because of the lawsuits, but because it sucked. I saw "The Beat" and now I know why she had to have us in it, because our scenes were the most exciting moments in that piece of shit movie. Blame the writer.

As for Julia's big comeback, it never happened. She died of cancer on January 1, 2002 in West Hollywood, Calif., at age 57. I give her props because she stayed defiant against those Hollywood assholes all the way up to the end. She also never apologized for writing those things about Hollywood in her book, "You'll Never Eat Lunch in This Town Again." Now take notes all you posers because that's fuckin' punk.

We went back out on the road and finished the tour with Motorhead and when I got back to NYC it was back to the same old grind. I was broke and living with a friend over on Clinton Street on the LES. Since I had no money, it was back to being a bike messenger, but this time around it was really starting to fuck with me. We just played huge venues and won over crowds every night, did a movie and shot a video. Now I had to come back home, sleep on someone's floor and have cabbies spit at me and try to run me over on a daily basis. Something had to change. The Cro-Mags got booked to do some shows that winter and I decided to head down to Florida to stay with Crazy Cubano Dave, who lived just north of Miami. My plan was to take in some sun and relax before the tour started, but I should have known that hanging out with a wacko like him that wasn't going to be the case. I was also counting on the $1,000 check I got for having a few lines in Julia's movie. Since I had no bank account (for obvious reasons) I had to endorse it over to CWV who said he would put it in his account and when it cleared, he would give me the cash. Yeah right. That scumbag kept every penny and said he'd take it off the so-called debt with that Texas judge who we greased to let us off the drug charge.

I took some of the cash I saved from the bike messenger gig and flew down to Florida. Crazy Dave was living with his girlfriend and his crazier-than-shit brother Eddie in this ranch house. The very first night I'm there Eddie throws this party. Now, this isn't just any old party, it was a freebase party. He had a massive bag of coke that had to have weighed a quarter-pound and a dozen or so of his basehead friends were all around smoking it up. He was using the microwave to cook the powder into freebase. Now, back in New York, I had heard about people freebasing, but I never witnessed it first hand. He just kept cooking up these boulder-sized rocks of cocaine and smoking them. After some peer pressure by the entire party I decided to try a hit of this shit. Well, from the moment I put my mouth on the stem and took my first hit, I was hooked.

I've always had an addictive personality, especially when it came to any kind of intoxicants. There is no doubt in my mind that I inherited that trait from my alcoholic dad. See, I couldn't just smoke one joint. I had to roll up the entire bag and continuously smoke spliffs the size of your thumb until there was nothing left. Most weed smokers aren't like crackheads who'll beat your door down in the middle of the night in order to get high. Now keep in mind I said 'most' weed smokers. I was the type who would rappel off a fuckin' rooftop and into your window in the middle of the night and take your shit. A good friend of mine who sold weed almost suffered that exact fate. Allow me to elaborate.

Our modus operandi was always the same. We'd call him up and say we wanted to buy some smoke. Then after a couple of hours of smoking what must have been fifty bucks worth of his shit without paying, he'd get sick of us and say he had to go somewhere. When he asked us what we wanted we counted the loose change we found in his sofa and said, "Two dollars and eighty-seven cents worth please." He would shake his head, give us a bud and send us on our way after we hit him up for a pack of Club rolling papers. On this particular Friday afternoon he made the crucial mistake of informing me that he was going out of town for the weekend. What the hell was he thinking?

That night I had the rope, gloves and everything else required for my special ops mission. The only thing that saved him was the guy I was with (who asked to remain anonymous) chickened out at the last minute because people saw us on our way into the building. Luckily we scrapped the operation though, because our buddy never went out of town. I would have loved to have seen the look on his face when I came crashing through his bedroom window at two in the morning while he lay in bed with his girl. He'd be in shock and I'd have to be thinking quick on my feet as usual, "Uhhh...by any chance did I leave my lighter here this afternoon, dude?"

The point is from the moment I tried that freebase shit I was hooked. The problem was there was only one water pipe and too many base fiends, so I had to do what any coked-up, mesomorph in my position would do. I bogarted the pipe right out of their mouths, smoked their hits and told them to fuck off when they gave me dirty looks. When I freebased I felt indestructible, unstoppable and very violent. I was down to kick the shit out of the first fucker who complained about my etiquette, which obviously didn't sit too well with Eddie. He took his bag of coke, his rocks, his pipe and split with his friends.

Three days went by and Eddie had still not come near the house or called and Crazy Dave just figured he was still pissed off at me. One morning just before dawn I was sleeping in Eddie's room and I was in one of those half-awake, half-asleep, states of consciousness. I heard a car pull up and a car door open. The next thing I heard was a barrage of rounds being blasting from an AR-15 and hitting the walls in Eddie's bedroom. I couldn't even count the amount of shots I heard and when it was over the car raced off and I got up off the floor. Crazy Dave was yelling, "Is everybody alright?" to which we all answered, "Yes." When we walked around the house to survey the damage it was riddled with bullets. We were lucky because anyone who had been walking around would have been cut in half. I remember thinking that it was Eddie who was doing the shooting because he was just trying to scare me for being a dick at his party, but when round after round went into his walls, stereo and TV, I knew there was no way this dumb fucker was shooting up his own shit. My suspicions were correct as I later found out Eddie was in a world of shit with some pretty sick fuckin' individuals.

The local cops and police detectives arrived on the scene and started hammering us with questions, most of which related to selling and using drugs. Since the area we were in was known for drug dealing and drug related violence, the cops knew what was up. They knew all those AR-15 shots weren't a random act of violence, but an attempted hit. They just kept telling us how lucky we were to be alive and I was like, "Uhh, no shit assholes." It turns out that that very large bag of powder Eddie was using to cook up those three gram boulders was stolen from some Scarface-type, Cuban coke dealers in Miami. Two days after the drive-by three Cubans pulled up outside the house in a brand new Chevy Camaro Z-28. They jumped out and grabbed Crazy Dave. I walked outside and a very heated argument was taking place in Spanish. The only words I caught were Eddie's name and the word perico, which means coke. I never saw Crazy Dave so scared and not for himself, but for Eddie, because these guys were out to kill his ass. As I walked over to the car all three stared me down hard. I tried to lighten the mood a little by telling them I liked their style - shoot first and ask questions later, but they didn't find it amusing. The head honcho turned toward me, gave me a very sadistic look and got into his car with the other two guys and sped off.

Crazy Dave tipped Eddie off through some of his boys and when he found out about the shooting he split Florida. I felt bad about not being able to say goodbye to him. I really did want to thank him for being such a gracious host and letting me sleep in his bed, of all places. I cut my vacation short and made it back to New York in one piece for our headlining show at L'Amour in Brooklyn.

The gig was completely sold out and was amazing. In fact, it was one of the best Cro-Mags shows ever. The crowd sang along to every word and they went nuts. We tore shit up that night and in the dressing room after the gig people came up to me and said, "Did you fuckin' see James Hetfield in the mosh pit?" I hadn't, but sure enough two minutes later in walks Hetfield with Jason Newsted, who joined Metallica after their original bassist Cliff Burton was killed in a European tour bus accident in '86. They were blown away by the show and I was stoked to meet Hetfield because "Kill 'Em All", "Ride the Lightning" and "Master of Puppets" were three of my favorite metal albums of the '80s.

Later that year I read an interview with Hetfield and when the interviewer asked him what was one of the best shows he saw in '87 he said, "Hands down, the fuckin' Cro-Mags at L'Amour in New York City."

That winter we hit the road for the '87 tour, which ultimately was the beginning of the end for the Cro-Mags. Things between CWV and me got really heated when I discovered some of the scams this fucker was pulling to cheat us out of our money. When I tried to talk some sense into the band they just weren't listening. I found out later, CWV met with them behind my back and was trying to convince them (as he promised me he would) that they couldn't make it to the next level with me as the singer. He also convinced them to fire me. I guess CWV's divide and conquer method was working.

We had a string of shows booked including those with Motorhead, Megadeth, and Black Sabbath, who were touring on The Eternal Idol record. Every fucking night, people would come up to me and say that I was one of the best singers/front men they'd ever seen. Now, I'm not bringing this up to pat myself on the back. I'm merely doing it because it gives CWV's argument about me holding back the Cro-Mags' success about as much weight as George W. Bush's reasons for invading Iraq.

The tour was going great except that CWV hired us a tour manager who was a total douche bag, Jersey dude who lifted weights and came complete with a mullet. For some reason, this guy took a special interest in fucking with me and who do you suppose told him to do that? I informed him on several occasions that if he kept it up he would find out very soon that all the steroids in the world weren't gonna help his ass. He just laughed and said, "Anytime baby, bring the shit on any fuckin' time."

Our tour bus driver on that leg of shows was this English dude named Bronty. The rumor on him was that he snorted so much speed that Motorhead fired his ass. Now, if you know Lemmy's history with crank, that's quite an amazing feat. Bronty ate nothing but canned meat, stunk like shit, had brown teeth (worse than most English people) and if he told you he had turtleheads you better look the fuck out. The first time he ever used that term we were driving and he had this panicked look on his face. He immediately pulled the bus over and noticing the urgency I thought maybe something was wrong with the bus. I inquired and he replied, "The bus is fine I just got turtleheads, mate." He elaborated further after relieving himself on the side of the highway, because there's no shitting allowed on tour buses. I found out that turtleheads were the endearing term he used when you had to shit so bad that your turd was poking in and out of your ass like a turtle's head going in and out of its shell. He came back on the bus, looked at me and said in that deep, English accent, "Ahh... fresh as a daisy, mate." Needless to say, when he went to slap me five in approval, he got dissed.

As nasty as Bronty was, he was still cool. One thing that pissed me off was that some money was stolen out of his jacket late one night. Doug and I were the only people in the front of the bus that night and everyone blamed me. I swore I didn't take the money, but nobody believed me. Later on the tour, Doug admitted to me in his own underhanded, dope-fiend kind of way, that he in fact, was the guilty party.

On the last night of the tour came the final blow to the 'Mags. It was December 21 and we were playing a small indoor sports arena. Black Sabbath was supposed to play but canceled. So it was Motorhead, Girlschool, Cro-Mags and Finc. This was the first time in the history of the band we were going to actually come home with money following a tour. We were going to be paid at the end of the show and I was excited because I was going back to New York for

Christmas with money. I couldn't wait to get home because I had Christmas gifts for my mom and other relatives that I had bought on tour. I felt proud of my accomplishments and so did my mom because she knew what I endured to get to where I was. She loved telling the family and her friends that her son was a rock star and was out on tour. She lit up like a little girl when she talked about me and collected every single press clipping she could find on the Cro-Mags. She even made each one of my family members a VHS tape of the "We Gotta Know" video when it premiered on MTV.

The show went well and the crowd of 5,000 plus loved us. Unfortunately, at the end of the night CWV, Doug and Harley got in a play-fight, wrestling match and CWV dropped his wallet with the bands tour money inside. At first I thought he was bullshitting but as it turned out, he was telling the truth. Doug found the wallet and since I knew that, I was obviously on his case. Harley, who was planning to go see his family after the tour, immediately split the venue without even saying goodbye to me. I remember thinking that it was kind of weird since it was the holiday and we were boys.

Later that night while we were on the tour bus Petey told me something that blew me away. After the wrestling match Doug and Harley ran into the bathroom with CWV's wallet. They didn't realize Petey was in one of the toilet stalls taking a dump when he heard Doug say that it was the band's money and that maybe they should give it back. Harley's response was "Fuck them. I'm going on vacation. I need the money." That's right folks, my brother, the one who I looked out for year after year, traveled the country with, wrote songs with, the one I would risk my life for and give my last dollar to, ripped me off. I knew Doug was involved and I was roughing him up a bit on the bus, making him empty his pockets. I had no idea Harley was in on the scam, too. First, I was crushed and then I was fucking raging. Then it all made perfect sense. That's why the little bastard didn't say goodbye, because he was jetting off on vacation with our tour money.

That was THE FIRST BETRAYAL.

We landed at Newark Airport in New Jersey. It was there that the Jersey boy road manager made the mistake of mouthing off and calling me a thief for stealing the tour bus driver's money. I knocked the fucker off his feet with one punch and the Port Authority cops ran over and handcuffed me inside the airport. Luckily the dude didn't press any charges and instead of getting carted off to jail they made me leave my luggage and my Christmas presents at the airport, get into the van and split. I got back to NYC and was evicted from my place because I couldn't pay the rent. I was homeless that New Year's Eve and spent it alone. I remember being so pissed that night wondering how Harley could do that to me; he was supposed to be my boy. I mean, I could understand, why Doug did it. He was a drug addict, but Harley? I decided that my New Year's resolution was to quit the Cro-Mags. With everything this band stood for there was no way I could continue on with Harley. He didn't know what unfolded in terms of me finding out he was also guilty, and hearing how he was partying all over with our money infuriated me even more.

Harley eventually came back to NYC and I'll never forget the first time I saw him after he ripped me off. I was on 9th Street between First and Second Avenue and he came up with his pit bull and tried to apologize. I just kept saying, "How the fuck could you rip me off? I'm fuckin' homeless now. I hope you had fun." I told him I quit the band and then advised him to walk away for his own sake because just looking at him was pissing me off. The bottom line was apology not accepted. The scenario that had been unfolding in the last year was not a good one. As the Cro-Mags got more successful Harley's head swelled so big it could barely fit through the fuckin' door. Even Steve Jones of the Sex Pistols who was friends with Doug and came to our shows in L.A. commented by saying, "That fuckin' wanka Harley's startin' to believe his own bullshit, Dougie." When it was just Harley and I, he was cool, but as soon as we were in the public eye he turned into a real asshole and always felt the need to try and belittle or diss me. Fame fucks with some people and drives their egos out of control and Harley's one of those types. I guess that's how he was able to justify robbing our money. It was his world and we were just livin' in it.

In the weeks that followed, he begged me to sing on the follow up to Age of Quarrel, called Best Wishes and to do one last tour. I quit and I told him point blank I wanted nothing to do with him. CWV achieved his objective and not by his doing; I was stabbed in the back by my own band member, friend and brother. I would have gladly fought against CWV until I destroyed it, that was my nature, but when Harley pulled that shit I had enough. After I left the band CWV convinced Harley that he was the star, he was the one everyone came to see, and he could fill the front man position. Harley bought into it. He called in a good friend of ours, Douglas Crosby to help him write the lyrics on Best Wishes. He asked me if he could use the lyrics I wrote on "Crush the Demoniac" because we played that song for a while and people knew the words. I said yes, as long as he gave me the proper credit I deserved. He also pleaded with me to say that I left because of CWV and not because of what went down on that tour because it wouldn't look good if it got out in the press that he had ripped me off. I figured let bygones be bygones and agreed.

When Best Wishes was done and they hit the road, the momentum they had from headlining tours to doing interviews, etc., was from the years I fronted the band in support of Age of Quarrel. I put my shit on the line night after night doing flips off twenty-five-foot P.A. stacks into the crowd, while those fuckers made it seem like, "See, we got rid of John and look, we're blowing up." Yeah right, you fuckers blew up like swollen Pampers because you were all full of shit. They turned against me and talked a lot of trash. When the press started to roll in from the Best Wishes tour I started to read the stuff coming out of Harley's and the rest of their mouths. They said they fired me because I couldn't sing and I was a drug addict. They had a field day in the press at my expense and never once did they tell any interviewer the real story on why I quit. When you're having some problems be it drugs, or whatever, a real friend helps you out. Not Harley and the rest. They basically sold me down the river when they heard I was using a little coke. Never once did they try to talk to me about it or help me out with some words of advice, nothing. I accept full responsibility for my actions and I deserved the pain and suffering that came as a result, but you figured since I was in the band with these guys for so many years they would have been a little more compassionate. I mean what the fuck? I was there for them in their times of need. A little reciprocation on their part would have been much appreciated.

When the album came out, I got no credit for any lyrics and neither did Doug Crosby - everything was credited to Harley. Now I realized something else about this fucker - his word was absolute shit. I saw him in Central Park's sheep meadow later that spring and I cracked him one right in front of his skinhead cronies. What did mister big tough, big mouth Flanagan do? He ran to try and find a cop yelling, "You're going to jail for that shit, motherfucker. Don't forget you're AWOL!" I rode off on my bike, passed him and said that it would be a big mistake for him to go to the cops. When I got home later that day, there was a message on my answering machine from Harley saying that he filed a complaint and he would get an order of protection against me. He also said if I came near him I was going to jail.

My world really came crashing down after that. I felt alone and depressed and everything I worked so hard on for so many years was over in the blink of an eye. It was like part of me died. It was hard to hear anything about the 'Mags even though most of it was from fans saying how it wasn't the same without me, how Harley couldn't sing and I should get back in the band. I invested my entire life force into the Cro-Mags and Age of Quarrel. All the suffering in my life, all the pain, all I had been through everything I believed in and now, it was over. I think in any artistic endeavor no matter what medium, when the creator has a personal connection to it and puts the time in, the results stand the test of time. That's why the Age of Quarrel has gone down in the history of punk/hardcore as one of the most influential albums of the genre. There was real emotion flowing out of every groove on that record. The Cro-Mags were on the verge of knocking on the door to stardom. Fuck knocking! Cro-Mags don't knock. We break the fuckin' thing down. We were so close we could taste it, but the problem was we fell victim to the same traps that every other great, self-destructing band falls victim to. The sad part about the entire situation was, the 'Mags were supposed to stand for so much more.

base... how low can you go?

chapter 14

I sank further into depression and to make matters worse I moved in with Crazy "Cubano" Dave out in Williamsburg, Brooklyn. He was frequently using crack and coke and being in his company I eventually followed suit. I went from using recreationally to using more frequently. I also left my spiritual practice behind at a time when I was being tested and should have taken shelter of it. Things went downhill from there and in the moments that followed I realized something that still holds true, so many years later. Without music and spirituality in my life I get into trouble. Big trouble.

On one late spring evening, I crossed St. Mark's and Avenue A en route to Alcatraz, the local punk watering hole, when I heard a girl enthusiastically call out my name. I turned around to find the hottest, leggy blonde coming toward me wearing this one piece, black dress that fit her curves perfectly. Who was this goddess? As she got closer I realized it was a girl we will call "K," an L.A. girl who moved to New York some years back and took up with a friend of mine. She was really cool and I have to say, fine as all hell. We gave each other a deep hug and she looked amazing. She was shining from head to toe with positivity, which was a big change from the last time I saw her. In fact, she was the complete opposite of the woman who was depressed and in a dysfunctional relationship.

K and I talked for hours that night and she made me forget my problems I had with drugs and with the Cro-Mags. I felt the best I had in a long time and she said something so romantic it blew me away. She said she'd always loved me and came back to New York to try and find me. I thought that was so awesome because no one ever told me anything like that before. It was always me that was doing stuff like that. She gave me these lyrics she wrote for me and they were pretty deep, "I'm in love with you and you don't even notice me."

K had everything going for her in life and any guy would be lucky to have had her as a girlfriend. She had the looks, the brains, the personality and the devotion. She said the thing that attracted her to me the first time we met was the fact that I gave everything up and whole-heartedly devoted myself to God. At the time, I was a monk and she told me I looked beautiful with my saffron robes and shaved head. We spoke for hours and before we knew it, it was three in the morning. We were still gabbing when that awkward moment came. You know, the what do we do now moment. We knew we liked each other a hell of a lot and although there was serious sexual tension between us there was also a lot at risk if we hooked up. I said I wanted to take her to dinner, but that was also a little awkward, because her ex-boyfriend was still somewhat a friend of mine. I then thought, since this friend tried to pass his number to not just one, but two of my girlfriends, while I was going out with them, I figured it was fair game. What made it different was K and her ex-boyfriend had been separated for at least two years. With that I made dinner plans for the two of us. I realized something as I walked off after having given her a very soft kiss on the lips. I truly loved this girl just as much as she loved me.

I was prepared to spend my last forty bucks on our beautiful dinner at Vegetarian Paradise in Chinatown, but she wouldn't let me. She insisted on paying and afterward invited me up to an apartment she was housesitting for a friend on Fifth Avenue. It turned out the apartment belonged to Andy Williams the old crooner who had a hit with "Moon River." That night we had great sex and K was a sexual athlete. Afterward we cuddled completely naked in front of a big bay window that hung out over the building. We just lay there looking at each other and I remember thinking, "Shit, I could get used to this." The next night her millionaire dad who also owned a town house on the Upper East Side went out of town with his wife. We shacked up for the rest of the weekend and had wild sex all over his house, including the outside garden.

K's dad was a real player and she told me that as a kid she saw wild parties go down in the early-'70s at their California mansion. On a daily basis she witnessed orgies, drug use, wife swapping and all kinds of other decadent behavior. She divulged a deep, dark secret that a teacher at some rich private school molested her. A lot of people seem to think that just because kids grow up in rich families that their lives are all peaches and cream and free of drama. Well, after hearing some of K's stories and from the stories I've heard and read in the papers over the years from other rich people, I can tell you, that's not the case. In this day and age I believe most souls coming to this planet come with heavy past-life baggage, or karma. If they do take birth in a rich family, all that does is guarantee them that they're going to get the best psychiatric help and mood-altering prescription drugs money can buy. Other than that all bets are off as to how anyone, rich or poor, will turn out. K's mom re-married a big shot Hollywood producer who worked with Walt Disney, George Slaughter and other Tinseltown big shots. "D.H.," as we'll refer to him, even did the Statue of Liberty's 100th year anniversary celebration for former President Ronald Reagan's administration. This fucker D.H. ran in a lot of very rich and powerful circles and K's mom told her straight up that she was marrying him for one reason and one reason alone...cash. See, D.H. was gay as hell and in the closet deeper than Imelda Marcos's cheapest pair of shoes. In the '50s and '60s you never came out in Hollywood because they would blackball your ass. D.H. had kids with his ex-wife just to cover up his homosexuality as a lot of them did in the industry back then.

K stayed in NYC for a couple of months and during that time we fell head over heels in love. I remember feeling like my heart was being ripped away when she split. She left me her car to get around and promised she'd be back soon. The whole time I was with K we never did drugs or even thought about them. She mentioned the fact that she knew coke dealers in L.A. and it went in one ear and out the other. Or so I thought. Within weeks of her leaving she was sending me eight balls of coke via the U.S. Postal Service.

Even before the '87 tour I felt like the biggest hypocrite for sniffing a little here and there. After I did so, it was eating away at me spiritually. Now, I was beyond guilt because I was freebasing regularly. I dropped from a solid 165-pounds to a gaunt 130. I would run into people who I hadn't seen in a while and they would say, "Damn you lost a lot of weight. Are you alright?" I'd answer that I was just training a lot, lift up my shirt and say, "Look, you can see my six-pack" and they'd be like, "Yeah but, I can see your fuckin' spleen too bro."

It soon went from bad to worse as I took arms with Crazy Dave out in Williamsburg. I started smoking crack because the packages of coke from K stopped showing up. I sold all of my shit to the local crack dealers including a $2,000 Italian racing bicycle for two $10 vials of crack, which turned out to be soap chips. I wasn't your ordinary white boy crackhead though. If I was in Manhattan I copped from Pitt Street on the LES, which at the time was a pretty rough neighborhood. I remember this dude took my money to go cop what we referred to as "Jumbos" (larger vials) and he broke out on me. Now most white boys would say fuck it, take it as a loss and be glad that they didn't get shot or stabbed.

Well, this motherfucker took my last twenty bucks and I was determined to either get it back or let him know that he fucked up. I waited for his ass for almost two hours and sure enough he came back out to the exact spot to try and rip someone else off. I chased after him and he couldn't believe that a white boy had the balls to chase a Spanish brother through his projects. As he was running, he kept yelling in Spanish for his boys, but no one came for back up. Finally I caught him in the stairwell of one of the buildings and after calling me a crazy ass mother fuckin' white boy, he promptly returned my $20.

Before I got caught up in drugs I remember seeing the dumb-ass white drug addicts on the LES. I would laugh because I knew the scumbags they were dealing with were just going to rip them off. Me, I was a different breed. When I used, I was the hunter who went after the dealers. I strong-armed their bags of crack vials and ran or biked away. Crack was the poor man's freebase and since I was addicted I took a lot of risks to get my drugs. I would wake up, smoke all day, then by nightfall if I was broke, I would rip off some dealer for a few vials. Crazy Dave loved the fact that I was a crackhead because I had balls. Once again for me it was all about the challenge. Crazy Dave knew that I was either going to get cash to buy our crack, or I was going to turn into the freebase superhero, "The Notorious Crack Snatcher."

The bottom line was we were going to get high one way or another. Eventually with all addicts sooner or later you're bound hit the wall. That moment came when I had exhausted my financial resources, sold all my shit, owed everyone money and the Williamsburg and LES dealers put the word out about a "White boy, surfer-lookin' nigga with tattoos," who was ripping everyone off. I remember that day because by 9 p.m., I still hadn't smoked a single rock and I was ready to fuck someone up. We didn't have a phone in the place so I went out to use the pay phone under the J train. I wanted to call K in L.A. and try to get her to immediately wire me some money.

So I'm on the phone begging K to send me fifty bucks and she's telling me she can't do it until the morning. For a split second I thought, "Fuck it I'm selling her fuckin' car," but I quickly blocked that thought out of my head. Even though I was desperate to get high, I still wasn't at the point where I would burn the people I loved. You have to draw the line in the sand somewhere and for me that was it. What was weird though was it seemed she could read my mind because she asked, "By the way baby, how's my car?" Just fine darling, just fine. K didn't know how bad I was with the crack and I didn't let on because she was coming to stay with me in a few weeks. I thought if she knew she'd run for the hills. I told myself I would quit once she arrived in New York.

I was pissed at her because I was in need of that first hit of the day and she was going out to a club with her girlfriends. Where was your compassion K? Where was your humanity? Have you not a shred of decency woman? As the conversation almost became argumentative I noticed a figure lurking behind me concealing a knife in his hand. I let him approach me and acted like I didn't see him. When he got behind me I told K to hold on and I slammed him as hard as I could in the face with the receiver, which knocked him out cold. I went back to my pleading for money as if nothing happened. We ended our conversation with me having to deal with not getting any cash until the next day. I hung up the phone and looked down at my Spanish friend who was still out cold. I remembered being so pissed off at that point that I kicked him in the stomach. As I went through his empty pockets, it hit me. I'd never sell her car, but that don't mean I can't use it to get some shit.

Crazy and me smoked a big spliff as I sped over the Willie 'B' Bridge at 90 mph with no license, warrants in tow and evil intentions to inflict bodily harm on some poor fucker who got in my way. What was going through my mind at that precise moment? God how I love New York! It was a city of outlaws doing outlaw-type shit and getting away with it because the cops basically just didn't give a fuck.

We went over our simple plan a few times. Crazy knew these Colombians he dealt with on 18th Street and 8th Avenue who sold ounces and halves of flake. It was some of the purest shit around and being Cuban, Crazy spoke fluent Spanish, which was our in. All he had to do was lure one of them into the car under the pretense that we wanted an ounce. The guy would get in, we'd speed off and once we got a few blocks away he'd never know what him. That's because I'd given Crazy Dave a kiyoga, which was a martial arts baton made of steel. He was in the back seat and was going to crack the dude over the head with it when the time was right. The bottom line was we were getting an ounce and our Colombian friend was going to have one hell of a lumpy head in the morning.

We picked the guy up and I spoke what little Spanish I knew which was basically, "Como esta amigo?" He looked at me and smiled very uneasily and I could see in his eyes he could sense something was up. He fucked up royally by getting in the car with us. He handed me the ounce of blow and I stuffed it down my pants. I slowly drove down 18th Street toward 7th Avenue and gave the signal. "That's some good shit, bro," at which Crazy Dave was supposed to slam the guy with the baton before we threw his unconscious ass out of the car. Yeah, right. That's why they say in the military that all the strategic planning in the world never survives first contact with the enemy.

Crazy Dave lost his nuts and when I looked back at him I could see that he was scared shitless. This was the first time I had even been in some real shit with this dude and I realized that he was all talk. I grabbed the baton from him and the Colombian in the front passenger seat of K's brand new, five-speed Volkswagen Golf GT said, "Dame dinero," which means, "Gimme the money." I slammed on the brakes, looked over at him and said, "Get the fuck out of my car or I'm gonna fucking kill you." Wanna know what he did? He laughed. He thought I was joking. I took the kiyoga and slammed it into his temple which split his head wide open. The dude got the message loud and clear that I wasn't playing around.

I floored the accelerator and it revved high in first gear. I had one hand on the wheel and the other on his hand, which was going for the .357-caliber he had in a holster tucked under his jacket. I was screaming at Crazy Dave to open the guys' door and Dave just sat there frozen with fear. The guy was bleeding all over K's car and screaming in Spanish when Dave finally reached up and opened his door. I put my left foot on the gas and used my right to kick him out of the car at about 40 mph. He bounced off the pavement, rolled several times and dropped his gun. He then jumped up and screamed at us. I was laughing hysterically and Crazy Dave was still in shock mumbling, "Johnny you're crazy," over and over.

Driving back to the LES I called him every four-letter word in the book after which I appropriately added "Pussy-ass cock suckin' motherfucker." He almost got both of us shot and because of his cowardice Crazy Dave's official new nickname became, "Daisy Crave."

Just to spook Daisy Crave a little more before we went back to Williamsburg I pulled up to the dealers on Clinton and Houston Streets. One guy ran over and stuck his bag of crack vials inside my car. As we looked at one another time stood still for a split second because we recognized each other. I robbed him on my bike a week earlier for a few vials, but before he could pull his bag out of my car I reached in and pulled off with a bunch of vials. Daisy Crave covered his eyes as I drove the wrong way down Clinton Street toward Delancey at top speed. We hit a bump and were sent airborne. When I looked to my right, I saw a cop on the corner who was just staring at us in total disbelief. I raced onto the bridge, went home and freebased the hours away following a very action-packed, fun-filled evening.

K eventually came to New York for a couple of days and then took her car back to California with her. I think she could sense that something was definitely up with me because I wasn't the same warm and fuzzy person she met in front of the bar months earlier. After she split I hit an all-time low, taking solace in what had become my pillar of strength, crack cocaine. I roamed the streets of Brooklyn and the LES at all hours of the night to get drugs. I crawled around on my hands and knees looking for that crumb of crack rock that someone might have haphazardly dropped. I ripped off everything that wasn't bolted down and afterwards, I felt like shit about myself. How the fuck could I make it through everything in life thus far, gain so much knowledge and then end up like this? I cried myself to sleep every night swearing that in the morning I was quitting drugs cold turkey. I'd make it through the afternoon, but when those demonic urges struck I'd cave, thus starting the insane cycle all over again. I truly wanted to stop, but I honestly didn't know how. A month, or so, later I was given a choice by K who was now tired of the long-distance relationship. She gave me the ultimatum of moving out to California with her or stay in New York alone, in the dead of winter smoking the plaster chips I mistook for crack. Shit, New York State didn't raise no fool. I decided to pack my bags and go west.

I arrived in Los Angeles and K picked me up at LAX in her mom's convertible Mercedes. She was a typical sexy L.A. blonde driving a convertible with her hair blowing in the wind and wearing $300 Gucci sunglasses. It was so surreal, it was like a scene from a movie with this storyline: Beautiful, rich girl who's bored with the pretentious chumps in L.A. sends for her New York Bad Boy to shake up the town.

I remember a feeling of euphoria coming over me at that point. I thought, "This is it Johnny. It's all up hill from here and no more drugs. You're going to get a job and marry this girl. By God, K is going to make an honest man of you yet." We pulled up to her mom's mansion in Santa Monica on the Pacific Coast Highway. It was fuckin' huge. In less than 24 hours I went from living in a crack house in Williamsburg complete with crumbling walls and roaches, to the crème de la crème of high society living. It reminded me of my lateral move from the Valentis' to the McGowans'.

Her neighbor was a descendant of Charles William Post, as in the Post Cereal empire, and their daughter Nadine was K's friend. She didn't like me right from the start, for some reason I still can't recall. One thing I do remember as I walked through K's house to the backyard was that initial feeling of euphoria was gone. I quickly realized that L.A. might have nicer weather, more money and better-looking people compared to New York, but it also has a very seedy underbelly. Case in point, was the porn mag photoshoot that was wrapping up down by K's pool. To me, the entire scenario was a little weird. The girls, the blow, the champagne, the lights and the cameras bothered me. Any dude would have been singing, "I'm in heaven." Call me crazy, but I was disturbed by it. It seemed Babylon-like and that's when I realized I still had a minute spark of spirituality left in me. As minute and barely lit as it was, I needed to fan that spark and turn it back into a forest fire to kick the drugs and the bullshit I got involved with.

I looked around the house to find the bedroom we'd be sharing and that's when I was informed that we would not be living in these palatial digs. We were expected to get a place of our own. K's parents were away so it was cool to stay there a few days, but they definitely didn't want her with any crazy fucking New Yorkers after the hell they'd been through with her ex. Even after she dumped him and moved back to L.A. he would call the house in the middle of the night and threaten to kill them. She told me her parents would pay the first month's rent on her place but as soon as they found out she was dating me and not a preppy tennis instructor from Beverly Hills, she was going to get financially cut the fuck off.

She was prepared to do whatever it took because she truly loved me.

I got a job as a roofer and seven days into the gig I quit. On the eighth day K and I did a few lines of coke. That's when my trip on the West Coast took a turn for the worst. We were both fiending and bouncing around from hotel to hotel, friend's house to friend's house. Word soon got back to her family that she was with this dude from New York and together, we were doing massive amounts of coke. When you have the '80s L.A. jet-set crew bugging out on your cocaine intake you know your shits in over-drive. I don't know how many tens of thousands we spent, but what we would do is if a coke or weed dealer wanted a stereo, TV or whatever, we would buy it and then trade it for drugs. We maxed-out K's credit cards and when the bills started showing up at her parents house they flipped out and started looking for her. Of all the people, they called her ex-boyfriend to find out who the hell I was. He gladly filled them in saying, "He's a no-good, crackhead scumbag, thieving derelict and an ex-cult member. K is in great danger." Thanks bro.

After the credit cards accounts were maxed out and closed we focused our attention on writing bad checks. We passed forged checks worth thousands and thousands of dollars up and down the West Coast – from L.A. to Frisco. When the cashed checks started showing up against their parents' checking account, they finally hired a couple of top L.A. private investigators to find us. The problem for them was we moved underground to hide out in my punk rock circles, a place where the private investigators would never look. We stayed with dudes from the L.A. scene who remembered me from the Cro-Mags. When the P.I.'s came up with nothing they told K's mom, "These guys are good, real good." It wasn't that we were good; I just made sure we stayed away from K's friends and typical hangouts. See, back then punks and preppies were like oil and water. They never mixed and as long as we stayed clear of her uppity Santa Monica crew we were cool. I later heard that her family was so frustrated, K's real dad was seriously considering sending some bent-nose-fuckers from New York to do me bodily harm.

There was one drawback in hanging out and being a coke-fiend with the West Coast punk/hardcore scene people. I was supposed to be spiritual and word got around quickly that the singer from the Cro-Mags, Mr. Krsna Rocker himself, was a raging basehead. I even had my boy, "Pat the Skin," get me some coke one night. I remember him saying, "Dude, I thought you were into Krsna? Ain't this against the religion?" My reply, "Yeah it is, but I'm just taking some time off from God, bro. No biggie." We were still on the run and before we knew it there was only one check left. We cashed it in for a few hundred bucks and bought, what else, an eight ball of coke.

The problem with us as drug partners was that I based and she sniffed. This was horrible chemistry because I always finished my half first and then was out to get hers. I remember the day I hit rock bottom, which might sound ironic, but believe me there's always room at the bottom to sink deeper, especially if you're an addict. It was about 3 a.m. and we were staying in a flophouse crack motel in Compton, which ain't exactly the best neighborhood for whitey. As I sat there looking around the carpet for anything I might have dropped K was asleep. She was like a squirrel who always stashed some coke. This time it was under the mattress. After smoking what turned out to be plaster chips I decided, "You know what, who the hell is she to hold out on me? Fuck her."

I was about to cross that proverbial line in the sand and break the 'Honor Amongst Addicts' code. I went for it and she woke up screaming like a crazy person while punching and kicking at me. "Get the fuck out of here!" I tried to interrupt with a "But baby I..." She shut me down, "Fuck you, I'm sick of you coming after my shit when yours is done!" I never saw her get that angry, and drastic times called for drastic measures. I fell onto all fours and broke down in tears, "I need it, please just a little. If you love me you'll give me just a few crumbs...please." As I wept looking up at her from the dirty carpet she looked at my pathetic ass and said, "Look at you! Look at what you turned into. You're fucked up! You're starting to scare me. It's like you'd kill me for a rock."

I don't think I ever would have done that, but as I stared down at the dirty, stained carpet I thought K had a point. I became what I despised for so many years - a spineless drug addict. A couple of weeks earlier we were up in Frisco getting high and hanging out with some dudes I knew from the Fogtown Skate Shop and we were at their place watching the movie Hellraiser. That flick really affected me for two reasons. First because I saw it through the eyes of the Vedas and second, I felt God was showing me where I was heading.

According to the Vedas of India, Earth is a middle planetary system. There's mixed pleasure and pain on this planet and there is also knowledge contained here to elevate you to higher realms of consciousness, higher planetary systems and even spiritual planes. Now simultaneously on Earth there is knowledge and the opportunity according to our actions, for us to enter into hellish worlds where living entities, like the ones portrayed in Hellraiser, exist. It's up to us which world we want to live in after this life, which also applies to life on Earth. We can choose to live a positive and creative life, full of acts of kindness and love, or we can make our lives a living hell. I was choosing hell and I was finally starting to realize it, which was a step in the right direction.

I got up from that carpet, wiped off the African-American pubic hairs that were stuck to my knees and hands, washed up and opened a copy of the Bhagavad-Gita As It Is. I read all night until I passed out. In the morning we left Compton and I made a vow to never do coke again. That is, of course, right after I helped her sniff her little stash. Hey, I said I was making 'steps' in the right direction, not leaps and bounds.

Later that day I ran into this girl named Lisa, whom I had met a year prior on a Cro-Mag tour. She was the Red Hot Chili Peppers' merch girl and let us stay at her place as long as we wanted. Great, I thought, what a hook-up. We'll just stay here until we figure out what our next move is. The problem was K was jealous as hell and she kept saying that Lisa just wanted to fuck me. That may or may not have been true, but one thing is for certain, when I'm doing coke the only thing I used sex for was a workout so I could crash out after an all-nighter. That day we ran out of coke and switched to crank later that evening. As we sat there blasted on speed we hatched a plan in the wee hours of the morning to sell K's car. We would use the money to fly back to New York and get an apartment where we would get a clean start. Shit, I'd sniff to that.

The next morning we did the last bit of our crank and drove to some used car dealership. The fat, sweaty slime-ball fuck who was trying to rip us off fit every used car salesman cliché ever written. He was giving us a load of bullshit and refused to budge an inch from his offering price, which was $2,000 for a car that was at least worth $7,000. He could sense our desperation and that, combined with the fact that we were cranked out of our minds at 10 a.m., made him a tad suspicious. He took the title that was in K's mom's name and said he was going to ask his boss if he could do a little better on the price. He walked off towards a back office and after we waited for more than fifteen minutes my Spidey-senses were telling me something was up.

I told K that I was going to check him out and I walked towards the back. I stood outside his door and listened, "Don't worry ma'am. I have them in the waiting area. I'll just stall them until you get here with the police." This fucker called K's mom and she and 5-0 were in transit. I ran out and told K we had to go. At that moment the dealer walked out and said, "I got great news, my boss said I could offer you five-thousand for the car. I just have to do some paperwork and we'll get you two on your way with your money." He went back to his office and I told K the deal. She was so high, she was fuckin' delirious, "What are you talking about? You heard him, he's giving us five-thousand we're taking it." I grabbed her by the shoulders and shook her as she continued her rant. I reiterated that I heard him talking to her mother and that he was stalling us until the cops got there. She still didn't believe me and said I was just paranoid from all the coke. I walked into his office under the guise of asking him a question. He was on the phone with someone and I saw our title sitting there on his desk. We both looked down at it and he knew the gig was up. We grabbed for it at the same time, but I was faster than he was. He jumped up out of his chair and I threw him back over it, sending him to the floor. I bolted towards the front and grabbed K. We ran out and just as we got in her car, her mom pulled up with a police cruiser behind her. We took off and the chase was on. I didn't know any of the streets out there and we raced around with K yelling directions at me while I was doing 65 mph down side streets. We went up into the hills where Lisa lived and I finally lost them. I pulled into her driveway, put the car in park and let out a huge sigh of relief. K and I looked at each other spooked because we realized that the stakes had just gone way up. While Lisa was at work we came up with Plan B. K had a friend in Palm Springs, Calif., who owned a Mercedes dealership. She called him and he said he was interested in buying the car and would give us close to $7,000 for it. We were going to head out towards the desert the following day, until K came out of Lisa's bedroom with a fist full of cash. I said there's no way we can take Lisa's money and that I'd be burning a lot of bridges in the process. Lisa knew everyone in the L.A. music scene, but more importantly, I didn't want to rip someone off who helped me out. K was furious and now fully convinced that I liked this girl. She yelled how she burned all of her bridges by robbing her parents and if I won't rip off some bitch I barely knew, she was leaving me. I was facing a dilemma. Do I rob Lisa or have my girl and partner in crime bug-out and split on me? We decided to take the money and I left an IOU in its place. Lisa flipped the fuck out and told everyone, including the Chili Peppers, about how the singer from the Cro-Mags robbed her after she let me crash at her place. I still feel bad about it and since that time I've paid off all my other crack debts. Lisa if you're reading this, write me and I'll cash in that IOU for the money I took.

We drove out to Palm Springs and I was doing about 120 mph through the desert when I noticed the state police cruiser with its lights flashing in my rear view mirror. I knew I was probably going to jail and I nervously I pulled over to the side of the highway. As the trooper walked toward the driver's side with all the insanity we went through in the last week the thought of just getting out, knocking this fucker out and taking off did cross my mind. He stepped up to the vehicle with his big hat and Ray-Bans and asked for my license, registration and insurance card. Time stood still as I tried to figure out my options. If I told him I didn't have a license...I'd go to jail. If I jumped out to whip his ass and he pulled his gun...I'd probably get shot and then go to jail. If I pulled off they'd set up a roadblock, corner us and I'd go to jail. It seemed like the modern day Bonnie and Crackhead Clyde days of running from the law were over. He pulled off his sunglasses, put his hands on the door, leaned over and reiterated his point, "I said license, registration and insurance card, sir." I was just about to give up the gig when I looked on his left forearm and saw a sight from the heavens. "Hey Boats," I said, "When'd you make Shellback?" He was caught off-guard by the question and then he smiled, "Back in '58 and I beat up on the Pollywogs on that Tin-Can every year after."

See, the tattoo on his forearm was the Boatswain's Mate insignia along with the word "Shellback" and the letters DD-25, which meant he was a Boatswain's Mate (like myself) who crossed the equator on a destroyer bearing the hull Number 25. Once you cross the equator on a ship you're referred to as a Shellback and those who hadn't are called Pollywogs and catch hell from all the Shellbacks on board. Shellbacks stick together like a fraternity, so when I told him I Shell-backed in '80 (I didn't, that was when I got off the ship in P.R.), it wasn't a cop talking to a person who just drove almost 70 mph over the speed limit. At that point we were comrades. We talked for five minutes about Navy life and at the end he said, "Ah shit, I can't give no Shellback a ticket. You go on now. Just keep it under eighty, brother." K was absolutely fucking beside herself with laughter at how I handled the situation and as for me...I pulled off at the first gas station and changed my underwear.

We got to her friend's dealership and they caught up on old times for a few minutes, talked about school days, family members and all that bullshit and I kept giving her the 'let's go' signal. He said he was definitely interested in the car and as soon as he ran the VIN (Vehicle Identification Number) we'd be on our way with a check that we could cash at his local bank. He took the registration and off he went. He came back five minutes later looking like he just saw a ghost. He pulled us into his office, closed the door and said, "You guys better get out of here right away. When I checked the number the car came back reported stolen and there's a warrant for your arrests. K, for passing bad checks," and he pointed at me, "They've issued a warrant on you as well. They're saying you're a cult member and you kidnapped K." Her parents and the private investigators were making sure that if we tried to sell the car again, or got stopped by the police we'd get locked up.

We got the fuck out of there quickly and had one last ace card up our sleeves that would allow us to get back to the East Coast. We now were resorting to Plan 'C' as in cocaine, if you will. We were going to dump the car at K's dealer in L.A. giving him the title and the keys in exchange for two plane tickets, two half-ounces of blow and five hundred beans. Our new life in New York was officially going to start in less than 24 hours. I kept K isolated that night, making sure she didn't tell anyone what our plans were because her parents were on a mission to find us. Her Stepdad D.H. had the connections and the resources to shut down the entire fuckin' LAX Airport. We packed what little we had left into two bags and I put a half-ounce into the checked-in luggage. The other half-ounce was in my carry on bag, so I could blast out a toot here and there while we were airborne.

When we got to LAX, I was scanning every inch of airport space looking for anybody who might remotely look like they were onto us. We boarded the plane without incident, took off and gave each other a celebratory hug because we were home free. We were an hour or so into the flight and were both sober for the first time in a long time. K was sitting next to the window. I looked over at her as the sun lit up her face. As burnt as she was, she still looked really beautiful. I reached over and gently grabbed her hand. I hadn't touched her in such a tender way in a long time and she looked at me and smiled. I had the warmest feeling at that point, like it was all going to be okay from here on out. I told her that I loved her and she said she loved me, too. We made plans to sell the coke and get an apartment. We also talked about starting all over and going straight. Then I said, "Now you're sure you didn't tell anybody that we were flying into New York, right?" She hesitated. "Uhhh...not really," she said. I continued with my line of questioning,

"Whoa...whoa...whoa, what do you mean by not really?" Upon further questioning it turns out that she told her neighbor, Nadine, that we were flying to New York that morning. I yelled at her and said sarcastically that she should have given them our seat numbers while she was at it just to make it easier for them to catch us. I still believe that it was a cry for help from K because she knew damn well if she told Nadine she would tell her family.

I told K that our string of good luck was over and when we got to JFK the cops were going to be waiting for us. She was upset and started to cry. Now in a typical Hollywood love story my first words would be those of comfort as I looked in her eyes, "Don't worry, baby. It's you and me forever. Nothing can break us apart. No amount of time, no family, no cops, no Navy brig. Real love cannot be checked by anything in this world. One day I'll find you and we'll sail off into the sunset to some tropical island and live off love and mangos while we raise our kids." Then we'd embrace, kiss and say how much we loved each other. As police rushed the plane, pulling us apart we would reach for that last touch of our fingertips before we were hauled off to jail. But this wasn't a Hollywood love story it was the sick world of two sick and twisted cokeheads. As I looked at her sitting there crying the first words out of my mouth were, "We gotta sniff that whole fuckin' half-ounce in my knapsack before this plane lands!"

Every five minutes I'd run to the bathroom and sniff up boulder-sized rocks without even taking the time to chop them up. I had big chunks of coke caked all over my nose and my clothes were soaked because I was sweating like a madman. My heart was racing out of my chest and I had white foam all over my mouth like Mikey Debris, or a rabid dog. I ordered glass after glass of water and even yelled at the stewardess when she didn't immediately answer my seventeenth ring on that damn call button. I was freaking out and K was telling me to slow down, but I didn't want to hear it. I sniffed well over an eighth by myself and I was still running back to the bathroom for more. If someone was in there I banged on the door for them to hurry up and proceeded to frantically pace up and down the aisles while I waited.

After an hour or so of this, the other passengers started to nervously stare at me. The head stewardess came over to my seat and told me to calm down because I was making the other passengers uncomfortable. I watched them eating their meat and drinking. I was insulted. Who were they to judge, lest ye be judged themselves (or some shit like that). I stood up with my Bhagavad-Gita in hand and waved it around like a street corner preacher who just happened to be tweaked-out on almost a quarter-ounce of pure Peruvian white. "According to the Gita," I yelled. "If this plane crashes right now you meat-eating scumbags with your Salisbury steaks and ham and cheese croissants will have to come back in your next life as animals and be brutally hacked to death in slaughterhouses!" I immediately had no fewer then four stewardesses on me as I rambled on preaching my sermon. They said they were notifying the authorities in New York if I didn't sit down and shut up right away, which immediately got my attention. I sat down next to K who was totally freaked out and wouldn't even look at me. Her only words to me as she covered her face in embarrassment were, "You need serious fuckin' help, dude." Ya think?

As we approached our landing in New York I went over the game plan. She would walk off the plane first and I would conveniently blend in with the other passengers a few feet behind her. This way I could watch her and see if the coast is clear. If we did get separated we would meet at the Alcatraz on Avenue A later that night. I guess I thought meeting back where we first met was reminiscent of Casablanca where Humphrey Bogart was supposed to meet Ingrid Bergman at that train station as they fled Paris from the Nazis. I hoped our story turned out better, because as you may or may not recall, Bergman stood Bogey up.

The plane landed and K demanded I give her the last bit of the half-ounce, which I did. I was still extremely high when we taxied the runway and were towed to the gate. We got out of our seats and the moment of truth arrived. Fear consumed my entire body, gripping me like a champion wrestler. My legs went weak for a second as I watched the people at the front of the plane start to file off. Believe it or not, that fuckin' '70's O.J. Simpson commercial for Hertz Rental Cars, where he ran through the airport dodging people and jumping over chairs, flashed in my mind. I was ready to do the same if there was any heat waiting for us.

K was three or four passengers in front of me and as I made my way to the exit I put on a baseball cap and pulled it way down. We entered the corridor between the plane and the airport terminal and I looked ahead to see if I could spot anything. To my surprise it looked clear. Could it be that Nadine didn't say anything? K stepped out into the terminal and as she did I saw at least a half-dozen huge guys in raincoats with walkie-talkies come out of nowhere. They converged on K, grabbed her by the arms and busted her.

I hit the terminal and made an immediate left, merging into the middle of this family that was walking towards the baggage claim area. They looked at me like, "Who the hell are you?" I heard the guys in the raincoats yelling, "Where is he? Where is he?" I walked with my newfound family towards the stairs and ran down them as fast as I could. I was about to get in a cab when I remembered one very important detail; my luggage had a half-ounce of coke buried in it, which I sure as hell wasn't leaving for some baggage handler. I ran down the stairs and hid behind a pole near the baggage carousel. Standing there was a heavy metal kid with a Metallica shirt who was listening to some very loud speed metal on his Walkman. I tried to get his attention, but he didn't hear me. I threw a coin that hit him in the head. He was noticeably pissed and looked around for the person who threw it. He spotted me and I waved him over. He walked over then froze, staring at me. He pointed at me, smiled and yelled over his music, "Dude, aren't you John Joseph from the Cro-Mags?" I swear to you I nearly shit myself as I covered his mouth. This was no time for bullshitting and I told him to take off his headphones. When he did I explained that the cops were after me and I needed his help. I gave him $20 and an autograph on his boarding pass in exchange for picking up my bag. He said he would help me out and said, "Great show at the Beacon Theater with Anthrax."

I nonchalantly walked outside the terminal, headed over to a cabbie and said, "Lower East Side of Manhattan." As I was about to get in the cab a score of those raincoat fuckers yelled, "There he is!" and bolted toward me. I got in the cab and we pulled off blending in with the other cabs jostling to get onto the highway. I couldn't believe I got away. The ironic thing was that if I had just gotten into a cab and didn't retrieve my bag I would have been caught because the raincoat fuckers were waiting for me curbside. Never in their wildest dreams did they think I would have the balls to get my luggage. I don't think it was as much balls as it was my fiendish drug addict mentality, but whatever the case may be, I'd take it.

That night I went to meet K at Alcatraz and it was pouring rain. I waited for her and just like Bergman, she never showed. At about 9 p.m., the bartender Betsy told me I had a phone call from someone named K. When I grabbed the phone the first thing K told me was that I was lucky I got away because her dad and family had all kinds of law enforcement at the airport. I told her I loved her and I was getting off drugs (right after this half is gone anyway). She said they were locking her up at ACI Rehab on 57th Street and Tenth Avenue and if I stayed away from her, her family would drop the charges against me and call off the dogs. That's when her dad got on the phone. "Mr. McGowan, how are you?" I'm thinking, not good since he knows my last name. He went on, "You're good John, real good. I can't believe you got away. Anyway, you heard the deal, stay away from K or we'll come after you. End of story." I tried to tell him that I loved his daughter and he just laughed and hung up.

I walked out of the bar in a daze and went into Tompkins Square Park. It was raining so heavily that in a matter of minutes I was soaked. As I sat on a bench, I broke down crying. For the first time in my life, I felt like life was not worth living. Nothing I'd been through prior to crack ever made me think of wanting to die. In the past I always felt that whatever doesn't kill me makes me stronger, but I never experienced a demon like this before. Crack took my friends, my spirituality, my home, my possessions, my love...everything. I had no place to live and no money. I knew I had to eventually face everyone I burned in the last six months of my addiction, including my good friend and brother Jay Dubs, who I ripped off. I would spend a lot of time on my own in the months that followed and I needed it to do some serious soul-searching. I crawled up in a doorway on that rainy night and cried myself to sleep.

free your mind and the rest will follow

chapter 15

The week that followed was really tough. I was living in some filthy apartment with this homeboy crackhead on Avenue C. I was still using drugs even though I went back to work as a bike messenger. When I had deliveries uptown I would ride over to ACI and sit across the street on my bike hoping K would look out the window and see me. She never did and as I rode off each time, every turn of the pedals ripped away a piece of my heart because I knew I was never going to be with her again. I blew a great thing and I should have been the strong one and got us off drugs. Instead, I failed miserably and aided both of our addictions.

That weekend I went back to the Brooklyn Krsna temple for the Sunday Love Feast after months of hiatus. As soon as I walked in the temple room and looked at the deities (Their Lordships Sri Sri Radha Govinda), I broke down and started to sob uncontrollably. Some devotees heard the rumors about my drug use from Harley and others. When they saw me at the temple that night they knew I was there to finally come to terms with my addiction. They let me do my thing...cry and pray. I begged Krsna to take away my desire for this drug and help me get my life back together. I reached the point where my addiction scared the shit out of me because it was spinning out of control. As a kid I never had control over my life or the situations forced upon me. As a result I became a bit of a control freak later in life. This time my doing caused me to lose control. I lost all sense of reason and logic and I only lived for my next hit of crack.

I knew right then and there that I had reached a very serious turning point in my life. I had to choose where I wanted to go from that moment on. I knew what a life of addiction meant and how junkies suffered from years from abuse. Was that to be my fate? "Please, Krsna," I prayed. "From this moment on never let me have the desire to do cocaine, again." I begged and I pleaded. I didn't have a rich family to put me in a $3,000-a-week rehab and I sure as hell couldn't check myself into a hospital for detox; I was AWOL. I'd have to kick this demon myself and I knew I could only do it if God helped me. Later that night I asked the temple president if I could move in. I knew that if I didn't associate with God conscious people (other than the leaders most of the devotees were) and stay around the temple while I detoxed I would die. He agreed to let me stay under the conditions of being a full-time devotee and go on The Pick, or maintain a job and pay rent. I agreed and I tried The Pick at first, but it was useless. I was too burned out to deal with that hustle again, so I decided to bike messenger that spring. I paid the temple $100-a-week to live there, and let me tell all one thing...sincere prayer works. From that Sunday night on I never had the desire to touch crack again and I've haven't touched it since. Krsna knew in my heart of hearts that I truly was serious about becoming drug-free and He helped me put that dark period behind me.

Living at the temple was great because every morning and evening they had some type of spiritual program going on and I fully immersed myself in it. I worked as hard as hell each day as a messenger and a few nights a week I went into Central Park and did the 7 p.m. pack ride, which was basically a twenty-five mile bike race. When the end of the day came, I had no energy to even think about drugs, which was a good thing. Slowly, but surely, my soul and my mind healed from the chanting and sadhana (spiritual practice). My body healed, as well, as a result of a healthy vegetarian diet and all the running, cycling and calisthenics. I was feeling good, both inside and out, and from all my activities and martial arts training I got my weight back up to a solid 165.

It was the spring of '89 and the Cro-Mag line-up with Harley singing broke up because of certain individuals' out of control egos (namely Harley's and Kevin's). I heard through the grapevine that they acted like rock stars to everyone on the road and that just didn't sit well with our fan base, which were primarily punk and hardcore people. These guys thought they were going to be the next Metallica or some shit. The only problem was, Metallica's record went multi-platinum and the Cro-Mags second album went multi-cardboard. No one wanted to hear Harley do his patented 823 "Oh Yeahs!" on every song. His voice was compared by a lot to the Kool-Aid guy. You know the one, he's shaped like a jug of Kool-Aid and as he crashes through a brick wall he yells, "Kool-Aid...Oh Yeah!" I knew the break-up was inevitable. They may have made it appear like I was the problem and, I mean, I definitely contributed to the overall mess, but these guys were destined for destruction. It was just a matter of time before the band imploded and I think my boy, Mike Schnapp, was the one who told me to which I replied, "Shit...that didn't take long now, did it?"

I was still riding my bike and staying at the temple and one warm Friday night after work I road down to Avenue A and 7th Street. I hung out with a few of the old punk rock cronies like my Navy buddy Raybeez and a few others in front of a bar called King Tut's Wah Wah Hut. We hung out and reminisced about the old times and the characters that had come and gone from the punk/hardcore scene. As we stood around a brand-new convertible Mercedes pulled up with reggae music blasting while two chicks wearing way too much make-up were sitting up on the back of the car with their feet on the back seat. My first reaction was, "Look at these fuckin' Guidos."

Just then the car parked right in front of us, the driver's door opened and standing there in a full-length fur (it was 75 degrees mind you), an Armani suit, expensive shoes, diamond necklace and a Rolex, was none other than Kontra 'The Anarchist'. Fuck double takes! I did a fuckin' quadruple take. I couldn't believe how tacky this motherfucker looked. He rolled up and with that thick-as-thieves Russian accent shouted, "Yo, Johnny. What's up money grip, we're in da house!" I replied, "What's up? You tell me what's up. The last time I saw you you had a big anarchy symbol on your ripped-up jacket, you were listening to Crass and hadn't showered in three days." He commented, "The good life brother, the good life." The good life meant he went down to Wall Street and did very well for himself milking people out of their life savings in a boiler room operation with a bunch of other crooked Russian mob-types. These guys made millions in the late-'80s and early-'90s on bogus pump and dump penny stocks.

Kontra told me riding a bike for work was getting paid from the neck down. He got paid from the neck up. He was so arrogant about his money it was sickening. We were driving around one day and a construction worker driving a van cut him off in traffic. Kontra yelled, "Yo neck down - watch where the fuck you're going. If you hit this car it'll take you a lifetime to pay it off!" He bragged about owning his own company and that he could give me a job, so I could make some quick cash and get an apartment. It sounded like a good idea and I took him up on his offer, still unaware that his gig was just a scam. He told me to show up first thing Monday morning in a suit and I could start right away. We hung out for a while and then he got in his Mercedes with his two gold digger bitches and pulled off.

I was psyched all weekend as I thought about the possibilities of making thousands of dollars and getting myself situated in an apartment again. Kontra made the gig sound so easy, "Candy from a baby, Johnny. Candy from a baby." I figured what the fuck, I've been selling shit in one-way or another my entire life. How hard could this be? One of the great things that came as a result of living the life I had led was there were new adventures at every turn and rarely ever a dull moment. Everything was unpredictable and nothing was scripted. In the beginning of this Wall Street thing I figured hey, here's another chance to add to my résumé. The night before I was to start my job I had no suit, shoes or tie. Just when I thought I would miss my first day of work, a devotee came through on the clothing tip.

Do you remember that scene in Wall Street where Michael Douglas' character takes Charlie Sheen's character out to buy clothes and they get the most expensive hand-tailored suits money could buy? Well, this was the complete polar opposite. My wardrobe for Wall Street was an old tuxedo with ruffled white shirt, bowtie, slacks and a jacket with tails. When it came to footwear forget Armani or Giraudon. I had a cheap pair of penny loafers, size 13, even though my shoe size was 9.

Monday morning came and I got to the Nevins Street train station in Brooklyn and even the brothers were snapping on my ass. It was summer and the tux I borrowed was out of season. I was sweating like hell and everything I was wearing was ill fitted from head to toe. I used duct tape to tailor the suit to my body and had to stuff wadded up newspaper in the front of the shoes. I looked like a reject from a bad, white trash Jersey wedding, but I took it in stride. I knew just as I did when I was selling beat acid, or hustling quarters outside church while I lived at the Valentis', I was in a jam and that meant a brotha had to do what a brotha had to do.

When I walked in the boiler room the entire office full of cold-callers and brokers in expensive suits were yelling into their phones and pitching. When they laid eyes on me they all fell completely silent before the entire office erupted in laughter. This one fat fucker yelled, "Hey kid where's the fuckin' wedding?" Which obviously produced even more laughs. That's when Kontra came out of his office and cracked up so hard he had tears running down his face. After a few minutes he calmed down and escorted me to his office.

Kontra sat me down, lit up a spliff and gave me the run-down on the job situation. I would get the clients on the phone, pitch the stock and he would close the sale, of which I would get a percentage. I figured this was no problem since I was a salesman by nature. Up until this point, all my hustles had been face to face. Now I was just a voice on the phone, a voice these fuckers could just hang up on, and they did. Every person I called, at least three hundred a day, hung up on me and many had some choice four-letter words about never calling them back. My rejection percentage was a whopping 100 percent. I was completely crushed.

The other thing that made my time on Wall Street even worse was my fat friend fucked with me non-stop about the tuxedo I wore every day for three weeks straight. Sure it was stained, sure it was too big, sure it smelled like a homeless person's pair of dirty draws and was way out of fashion, but he didn't have to remind every day by snapping on me, or by humming, "Here comes the bride," and constantly referring to me as the "Piker (amateur) in the tux." I really wanted to punch this fucker out, but he was one of the partners in the company and if I did it meant no money, no apartment and no nothing.

As for the rest of the fuckers at the office they were by no means saints. This office was out of control and the bullshit never stopped. These guys got on the phone and tried to convince the poor suckers on the other end that their stock tips were guaranteed moneymakers, and they were, just not for the clients. One thing that really cracked me up was the handful of rabbis that worked there. They dressed in the whole religious garb and would be pitching away and lying through their fucking teeth. At times they would just stop and hang up, because it was time for prayer. They would break out their prayer paraphernalia and start praying in unison. When they finished they'd recklessly throw the prayer books back in their drawers, pick up the phone and continued guilt tripping their Jewish clients again about how they needed to do their mitzvahs and they should buy some stock.

By the end of my third week I hadn't opened a single account and I was completely broke. I figured, shit, at least being a messenger I had a steady paycheck and I stayed in tremendous shape. Plus, I was out doors all day looking at the hot New York women while I worked. I'd had enough of my Wall Street dream and told Kontra I had to quit. I felt a little pissed-off because I was giving up on the endeavor without conquering it, but it was okay. I knew cold calling over the phone just wasn't for me.

When I left the office and the elevator doors opened in the lobby, guess who was waiting there with his buddies and continued to talk trash about my wardrobe? You got it, fat boy. I calmly walked off the elevator, slammed him up against the wall by his throat, got in his face and said, "Bad news motherfucker. I just quit." I punched him as hard as I could in his stomach and he doubled over puking up his expensive lunch all over his designer suit. I walked toward the revolving doors to exit the building and the guy at the newsstand gave me a high-five and said, "It's about time somebody did that to that prick." I left the building smiling and feeling a whole lot better about quitting. I was a fish out of water in that office and when my feet hit the NYC concrete a surge of energy came over me. This was my stomping ground. I ruled out here. I knew fuckers like that fat asshole could never survive even a week of what I had endured year after year. I looked north, took off the tux jacket and shirt and made my way back to the LES.

One good thing did come out of the Wall Street thing. I got my brother E a job with Kontra and he was a natural. He was no longer E Dog, the two-bit scammer from the LES who would vic your weed, hustle you in a game of pool for your last ten bucks, or use chicks for a free place to live. His new persona was brokering extraordinaire Gene McGowan. G.M. was smart as hell and knew the rap. He aced the Series 7, the Series 63 and Branch Manager's tests on his first try, scoring higher than anyone else in the office. Shortly after arriving on "The Street" as he called it, while he was waiting for his license, he opened accounts by the dozens under Kontra's name. G.M. loved the lifestyle and everything that came with it: the suits, the cars, the dinners and especially the loot, which he had an abundance of. I was glad to be outta there and it seemed like it was just in time because shortly after I quit Kontra went on a major crack binge, spending thousands of dollars a week. I knew there was no way I would have been able to resist the urges if I was there.

E was living with Kontra at the time and what he told me was pretty funny. Kontra lived in a luxury building down by Wall Street and he scared the shit out of all the straight-laced fuckers who lived in his building. When he smoked crack and was out of his mind, they got a glimpse of the old punk rock Kontra. He carved a huge 666 in the lobby wall, threw his stereo out of his 15th floor apartment window and had black and Spanish thug-ass lookin' crack dealers from the 'hood coming and going at all hours of the night. E told me that one night Kontra locked himself in his bedroom for three days while he went on a crack smoking bender. He said that all he heard was shit being smashed to pieces and this horrible moaning and crying. On the morning of the fourth day Kontra pops out of his room all bright-eyed and bushy-tailed and said, "Yo money-grip… let's go get some wheatgrass juice!" E was like, "Wheatgrass juice? Motherfucker your ass don't need wheatgrass juice, you need a fuckin' straightjacket and a bottle of Percocets."

Kontra would disappear from the office for a week at a pop and E would have to search a West Side crack house near the meatpacking district in order to find him. The prostitutes, pimps and dealers down there knew Kontra as "Mister Mercedes" because he was like the "Pied Piper" of crackheads. He would treat everyone to vials of crack so they wouldn't rob his ass. On one occasion Kontra invited a couple of his "Wall Street Whales" (big clients) from out of town and then he went missing for days, only to be on another crack bender. By the time they showed up, as usual, E had to hold down the fort and chaperone the Texas millionaires around the city in Kontra's absence. One morning they said to him, "You know it was the strangest thing, last night. We were on our way to the theatre district for dinner and a play and as we were stopped at a light on the West Side Highway. A dirty, homeless guy who looked just like James (Kontra) walked by us with these two African-American drug-addict looking fellas. We swore it was James, but we knew there was no way on Earth he'd look like that or be involved with the riff-raff this guy was with." Once again had these Texans, who lost millions to Kontra, only read my writing teacher Robert McKee's chapter on true character they'd understand that it wasn't a look-alike, but the real thing.

As I walked around the LES in my tux pants and oversized shoes en route to Flash Courier Service to get my old job back, I ran into a friend who happened to be working for "Pope of Pot." In the '80s, the Pope of Pot operated a massive well-known weed delivery service in NYC.

The Pope was the same motherfucker who ran the "Church of the Realized Fantasy," who passed out joints and weed as part of a ceremonial ritual in Central

Park's sheep meadow. Now, the Pope of Pot had a toll-free number for those who wanted to buy weed: 1-800-WANT-POT. My friend told me one of the bike couriers got fired for tapping the bags and he would put in a good word for me if I was serious about the job. Within two days I moved out of the temple and was delivering weed on my bike. When a potential customer called the 1-800 number I would show up at their door an hour later with the best hydroponic herb money could buy. When I was working I road a $3,000 Italian racing bike and always wore the cycling shorts, a racing jersey and shoes, so it looked like I was a serious cyclist out on a ride. I also carried a small backpack, so I never drew any attention to myself.

The Pope's illegal operation was impressive. He had twenty or so riders and yeah, we all did well. But the Pope did extremely well. I would make $10 for each bag I delivered and I was doing roughly 70 to 80 bags a day. That meant on an average day he got about $3,000 just from what I delivered. Now multiply that by twenty riders, add in the fact that he bought directly from growers and paid maybe $3,000 a pound, and you could see how his numbers start to add up.

When a potential customer called the 1-800 number, the calls would go to a dispatch room that ironically was located directly across the street from The Tombs on Centre Street. The place where we picked up the weed and dropped off the dough was inside this comic book store on Hudson Street in lower Manhattan. Although the Pope was a shrewd businessman, he was a nasty, old gay fucker that had psoriasis all over his body. He would sit in his office reading the latest issue of Honcho (gay porn mag) and eat steak tartar that was freshly cut from the distributors in the meatpacking district. I would walk in and he would look directly at my crotch and say, "Looking good in those bike shorts, toots." Now, ordinarily a comment like that would get you knocked the fuck out, but I put up with his queer remarks day after day because of the money I was raking in. The main dispatcher of the entire operation was a big Cro-Mags fan and he made sure I did my quota every day.

The money was rolling in and by my second week I saved enough to get a studio apartment at 195 Stanton Street where an up and coming actor, John Leguizamo, also lived. I moved into my ground floor apartment with my girlfriend Mystelle. She was from Colorado and she and her mother were both concerned about the neighborhood. Back then both Stanton and Ridge Streets were still a real fuckin' zoo. The Pitt Street projects were a block away and that entire area was infested with crack dealers, crackheads and all around shady fuckers. The rule would be that Mystelle was never allowed to walk home alone after dark and I assured her and her mom not to worry because the 'hood was changing. As Mystelle and I laid down that first night and began to make love in our new apartment, we heard sirens speeding toward us from the back window. Tires screeched to a halt and cops yelled, "Freeze motherfucker! Drop the gun!" That was followed by a barrage of gunfire and bullets bouncing off the wall next to our window. When I looked outside towards the Seward Park School playground there was a guy shot to death with a gun lying nearby. Shortly after that, Mystelle moved to the West Side.

In 1990 I started to train for triathlons and worked out religiously with weights at a small gym on East Sixth Street called Gladiators (RIP). At the time it was one of the oldest gyms in Manhattan and the thing I liked about it was all of the colorful characters who worked-out there. Ninety-nine percent of them were either Puerto Rican or Dominican and this led to many funny situations because of the ongoing machismo shit that takes place between the two ethnic groups. Point being, Dominicans swear they're the ladies' men and the Boriquas ain't letting them get away with that shit, which always leads to arguments. Even from the outside of this place the mood is set because of the hysterical, cartoonish-looking paintings of bodybuilders on the windows.

Gladiators was like a fuckin' comedy hour. The owner, Victor made all the equipment right there in the basement of the gym while you were training! The air was constantly filled with either the smell of burning metal from welding and grinding, or spray paint fumes from spraying everything gold, his trademark color. If he was working and you were on the treadmill in the basement you were guaranteed to walk out with a good buzz free of charge. One time, I remember getting so dizzy that I almost fell off the fucking thing. It didn't help that the machine was from the '70's and would speed up from 3 to 10 mph on its own.

It even smelled like a real gym. No potpourri diffusers here guys and gals, just good old-fashioned B.O., ass, an occasional dead rat and sweat all over everything because no one ever wiped down the equipment. As Arnold Schwarzenegger would say, "That's for girlie men." People would come in dirty from their day jobs and sweat all over everything. If you were lucky, the manager wiped the shit down once a week. Victor didn't discriminate either; he even let the homeless train and shower all for the amazing price of $5. Shit, that's a better deal than the YMCA and they knew it. The machines Victor built… let's just say geometry wasn't his best subject.

People would walk in with equipment catalogs from Weider or Cybex, give it to Victor and say, "Can you make me that chest machine Victor?" He would take one look at the photo and say in his heavy accent, "No problem, mang. Jew you got it." Nothing was measured properly and the equipment he made wasn't balanced. You could look at your form and see that you were pushing or pulling much more with one side than the other. Now factor that in with the warped floor in certain sections of the gym and you felt like you were on an old set from Batman. That would explain why certain muscles on one side of my body were getting bigger and stronger than the other side. After ten years of working out at Gladiators my alignment was so off that I'm still trying to correct all that shit through yoga.

Besides the equipment Victor built, there was also an assortment of outdated antique machines from the late-'60s that he bought when old-school gyms upgraded their stuff. So when it came to working out, the rule at Gladiators was, "Don't forget your can of WD-40, mang." One thing I immediately noticed when I worked out at legitimate gyms, like Crunch, was that lifting 50-pounds on a Gladiators' machine was the equivalent of lifting 100 anywhere else. This was due to the fact you had to add in the age and rust factor of the equipment at Victor's place. Even Jerry Seinfeld was able to see the comic possibilities there and included it in a '97 episode of Seinfeld called "The Blood." During this one particular scene Jerry walked in, looked around at the dirty red floor (the paint came off on your hands when you did push-ups), the old gold equipment and the outdated and yellowed 8x10 photos of Victor's friends on the walls and said, "Jesus, is this a health club or a fitness museum?" It's obviously both, Jerry.

And let's not forget the best part off all…the members. These body builders smoked weed between sets and drank 'til they dropped at their Friday night salsa workout parties. During these events they danced with each other on the sidewalk, believed in the Chupacabra (goat sucker) demon in Puerto Rico and ate the worst fried food imaginable, but could still out-train most fuckers in any gym. Some of these guys were pushing 60 and still had solid 250-pound bench presses. There was Supa, who swore by fried ALPO burgers (which he cooked on a barbecue out back and they smelled like shit) and steroids to get 'big' as he called it. He would say, "Mira, it's the chemicals in the dog meat mixed with the 'roids, that's the secret. See but they don't know Johnny. They don't know." Another member, Crazy Ray (RIP), would always train with his dick hanging out. It was for that and many other reasons, why hardly any women ever worked-out there. Last but not least, I have to mention my trainer and favorite member, "Blackout Pete," who was a tunnel rat in Vietnam and happened to be outta his fuckin' mind. Blackout looked like The Incredible Hulk with bifocals and would get in your face while you were on your 39th rep (he emphasized extremely high reps) and scream in a thick accent, "Jew gotta black out! Don't feel the pain, mang! Don't look around, mang! Jew gotta get in that tunnel in your mind and black out!" Can you say post-traumatic stress disorder? I swear Hollywood should come calling because I'd write them a pilot for the funniest sitcom they've ever seen.

I think if people trained around guys like them they would have no problem staying with their regimens based solely on sheer entertainment value. I know I did. There were many days I was feeling down about something or other, went to workout there and came home feeling like a million bucks. They were family, and you had to love these guys. Why? Because they were real. I was pretty much the only Caucasian member back then and they embraced me, lovingly referring to me simply as "Whiteboy John." I respect them all because they stayed with their training over the years while a lot of their homies got caught up in crime and drugs during the '70s and '80s, went to jail or died. Victor's got a heart of gold and has always let the guys owe him for memberships because he knows working out is all they have. Victor's good-hearted nature was one of the main reasons Gladiators on 6th Street closed. Nowadays, if you head down to the new Gladiators on Colombia Street in Manhattan, just tell them Whiteboy John sent you and I guarantee, you'll be good to go. Shit…Supa might even make you an ALPO burger.

The spring of '91 rolled around and everything was going great. I was drug-free and I was in phenomenal shape. My band at the time, Both Worlds, opened for the Red Hot Chili Peppers during their Mother's Milk tour and thus squashed the beef with Flea and Anthony Kiedis over stealing Lisa's money. Around that time I got a tip from my boy at the Pope's operation that he was probably going to get busted soon. He was flaunting his shit in the media and begging the cops to arrest him so he could fight the marijuana laws. Shit, if you want to be an activist asshole, walk into the precinct with ten pounds and get yourself busted, don't jeopardize everyone else's gig. I quit and sure enough he was put in jail a week later where he later died of cancer. It was at that point that the SECOND BETRAYAL BEGAN.

the final **evolution**

chapter 16

A mutual friend of Harley and mine, who worked with Howard Stern at K-Rock radio in NYC found me downtown and talked to me about possibly reforming the Cro-Mags. At first I wasn't interested, but as I got repeated calls from him I began to consider the possibility of reuniting the band. Then Harley called and said that the tour was already set up, so I thought what the hell. I would also make some pretty good money, so I figured it would be a paid vacation. I signed on and we started rehearsing.

For me, music was never about the money. At the time, I had an apartment and my own small business that paid the rent. If I did the tour I would have to give up the company, so it was obviously a concern of mine. I was promised $100 a show and since there was forty shows booked that would definitely take care of the bills. Harley was talking about a label called Century Media who was very interested in putting out a Cro-Mags album providing we could get most of the original line-up back together. I initially got Doug Holland on board and Mackie (who wisely backed out after not wanting to deal with Harley) to sign on for the recording. After all this time, a few pieces were in place and it started to look like the band was going to make a come back. I quit my gig, packed my bags and boarded a flight.

When we landed I was sick as dog from the vegetarian curry I ate on the plane. My stomach was killing me and as soon as we exited the plane I knew something else was wrong. We stayed at this one dude's house; myself, the drummer, the guitarist (I got a story about them two for you guys later) and Bleu the bad-ass who was our one-man security detail. Staying at the tour manager's house was Harley and his girl. Hmmm. We didn't see them at all for the first few days we were there until it was time to rehearse. I had a meeting and told the drummer and guitarist we better keep an eye on Harley because he was a shifty fuck when it came to money, which they agreed.

The first few shows were practically sold-out and packed to the rafters with thousands of kids each night and the two promoters were a little discombobulated. Why? Well, they expected to see gnarly-looking tattooed fuckers and sure they may have gotten that from Harley and me, but the guitarist and the drummer... I'll let you fill in the blanks on those two. The guitarist wore pre-ripped jeans, those gay rocker belts with the little silver medallions on them and a Cro-Mags shirt with cut off sleeves. He walked around in the parking lot right before the doors opened and strolled down the line of fans with his guitar around his neck. He then announced he was the guitarist for the 'Mags while he flexed his muscles in the girls' faces and asked them what their astrological sign was. Most replied, "Stop Sign, Poser."

On stage he was even worse. He played leads in between his legs, flexed and walked over and humped his Marshall amplifiers, making love to it like Jimi Hendrix did in the '60s. What he didn't realize was Jimi had two roadies behind his amps holding them up, so when our guitarist went humping away the entire stack fell over and caused a ten-minute show delay. The punk and hardcore kids could not believe it and neither could I. I swore I'd kick him right off the stage in the middle of the next in-between-the-legs-lead if he didn't stop those idiotic metal antics.

As for the drummer, who was the sloppiest Lenny White wannabe I ever saw in my life, he played rolls on top of rolls and then threw another one on top of that just for good measure. He fucked up almost every song with his over-playing and offstage he constantly asked the promoters about the money. He made no secret that he was Jewish and proud of it and with the stereotypes that exist about Jewish people being greedy...well. His tour mantra became, "Where's the money? What's up with the money? Can we get some money? How come I haven't seen any money? The money, the money, the money...Oy fuckin' vey... where the hell are my sheckles?" Now I understand his concerns after the meeting we had about Harley, but shit, dude, play it off a little. I mean, I was an original member and even I wasn't asking about the money as much as he was.

I'll never forget, after one of the first few shows into the tour when the promoter's German girlfriend, Uta, walked on the tour bus looking completely bewildered. Uta looked, dressed and talked like a cross between Ilsa, She-Wolf of the SS and the chick Fabruka from the movie Young Frankenstein. Oddly enough her boyfriend, Marc, looked just like Frankenstein and that's what we called him. Uta sported the largest set of breasts in punk rock and her pet name, which I always said in the worst fake German accent you've ever heard was, "Uta Von Sluta with da Hootahs!"

Uta V.S.W.D.H. came to the back of the bus, looked at me and Harley and said in her ultra-thick German accent, "John…Harley…vhat is up vit za vinger (as in the poser metal band Winger) dude and za Jew?" I looked at her in a state of shock that almost produced laughter and responded, "Yo, that shit you guys did in WW II wasn't that long ago. I think you should chill with that." Honestly, I knew what she meant. This shit wasn't the Cro-Mags, it was a very bad cover band and it bugged them out. They expected an all-out hardcore assault and what they got were bad heavy metal stage antics and lousy over-playing. The sick thing was I would come to find out almost a year later, from his own girlfriend, that Harley threw this thing together for one reason and one reason alone, and it wasn't the love of music.

At the beginning of the tour Harley tried to test the waters to see if I was down to jerk these guys. He pulled me aside one day and gave me this speech about how we were the Cro-Mags and how people were paying to see us and so on and so forth. My feelings were and still are; if you risked life and limb by touring, if you get in that van or bus, you deserve an equal cut of everything, regardless of how long you were in the band. My record speaks for itself, because I have always been fair and honest. Then ask people who played in Harley's line-up and make sure you have a few hours to hear all their gripes. Even when he and Kevin got back together, Kevin quit because of Harley's crooked nature.

Anyway what happened was Harley's girlfriend (who did have health issues but was pretending to be sick this time) flew home first class some twenty odd shows into the tour which the band, not Harley, paid for. I mean, how sick could she have been when Doug Holland saw her the very night she landed hanging out on the

LES partying it up? On the tour, the three of us never received any money other than the $10 per diems for food while Harley was getting hit off with hundreds to buy hash, vintage records, clothes, nice meals for him and his girl and basically whatever he fancied. Watching his spending habits I constantly asked the tour promoter as to whether or not the band's money was cool. He said we were going to get the salary we were promised, $100 a show. As a matter of fact, his answer time and time again, even at the last show was…a definitive YES.

We finished the tour and drove by the airport to fly out the next morning. That night I took a shower and then wanted to settle up the finances for the tour. I was informed that we would do it the next day. Oh yeah, we did it the next day all right…one hour before we were driven to the airport to get on our flight. Harley and the promoter took me out to the parking lot and said, "The tour lost money. Here's your pay." It was $700, a far cry from the $4,000 I was promised. I flipped-out and called both of them rip-off artists. How could every gig be packed and we lose money? It didn't logically add up.

Everyone came back off the tour broke except Harley. He bought all the latest stereo equipment, a camcorder and massive amounts of weed, but he wasn't done yet. He strung us along with the promise of being on salary from the Century Media deal. At that point I had no choice. I gave up my company and the only other way I could make money was going back to being a messenger, which I wasn't up for. Soon after that tour we headed up to Normandy Sound in Warren, Rhode Island to make a record and the Alpha-Omega sessions were another fiasco. Harley acted like an asshole and a dictator in the studio saying repeatedly that this was all because of him and if we didn't like it we could fuck off and quit. Century Media said we would only get the deal if I sung and some other original Cro-Mags were involved. Mackie was out, but Doug was on board (notice he's flipping Harley off on the album photo). The label made a very crucial mistake by putting Harley in charge of not only the project but the finances as well. He very conveniently put his aunt in place as the band's accountant.

Harley acted strangely up at the studio in Rhode Island constantly walking around in a robe like Hugh Heffner with a pipe, smoking weed 24/7. Every day I ran eight miles, did an hour of vocal exercises and cooked for everyone. Shit got really weird when he started talking all kinds of crap about starting his own religion and having hardcore kids go out and collect money for us while we fucked their girls. "John," he said, "even the guys on the scene who are into Krsna say we're like demigods." (Just look on the Harley's War record and you'll see for yourself; he refers to himself as the "Reverend" Harley Francis Flanagan). My reaction to all his Charlie Manson wannabe rhetoric, "Uh dude that's called a cult and having just got out of one, I ain't interested."

Harley was so obsessed with Manson, he wanted to put a track by Lynette "Squeaky" Fromme on the record, but we shot that shit down really quickly. We had an epiphany during the making of this record...we never knew we had the Golden Avatar in the band. It turns out Harley informed our guitar player that he was the Golden Avatar, the incarnation of a God for this age and was sent here to save all mankind. When he told me Harley said that I was in stitches because he said Harley got up next to him and kind of whispered it in his ear. When he told me the story he was like, "Dude, Harley's breath and B.O. was so bad all I could think was man, you ain't no Golden Avatar, you're more like the moldin' avatar." Harley hooked up with a dude that practiced black magic and he thought he had everything and everyone under his control. That was his mistake.

The recording of that album was a nightmare for many reasons. I still have bad dreams about walking in on the owner Phil 'The Admiral' while he was in the bathroom. Why? Well that comes back to why he's called the Admiral in the first place. Phil could not have a bowel movement unless he had an enema – a Fleet brand enema. He was appropriately nicknamed the "Admiral of The Fleet," then just "The Admiral." One morning at about 3 a.m., after working on music all night I walked in the bathroom and saw this fucker bent over with his enema tube up his hairy, pimply ass. I screamed in horror and took off running because the sight was scarier than The Exorcist, Friday the 13th and The Shining all combined.

Then came the other part of the nightmarish equation: Harley as a producer. Although he claims he produced that record, he didn't. Tom Soares from Normandy Sound did. All Harley did was smoke massive amounts of weed and pop into the engineer booth every now and then to fuck up Tom's sounds. He acted like a dictator while everyone was doing their tracks, even yelling orders into our headphones. That doesn't exactly encourage anyone to perform better. That's why the running joke became that he 'RE-DUCED' Alpha-Omega. Harley had me record my vocals first, mimicked all my vocal tracks so no one could tell who was singing on what song and it was for a very good reason.

The first thing that raised the flag of suspicion financially was that, according to Harley, the band had to give up 80 percent of our publishing money to cancer research. I was like "Dude, I appreciate the fact that you're such a kind-hearted philanthropist, but I'll pick my own charity, thank you very fucking much." The rest of the band agreed, having witnessed firsthand Harley's accounting practices on the tour. That's when we got into an argument because he claimed he wrote all the lyrics and that was just total bullshit. He had me write three different sets of lyrics to each song on Alpha-Omega (except "Victims" and "The Paths of Perfection") and then we mixed and matched them together to the music. The second thing was when the recording was done he demanded that no one be allowed in to mix but him and that if we argued about it he would shit-can the whole record. Like I said, he was planning to mix our vocals so closely that you couldn't tell the difference because he knew I was about to quit. Why? Just the fact that when the album was done and I informed him we wanted to buy the band's equipment with the $15,000 that was allocated by Century Media for that purpose. Harley and his aunt then told me that the money was spent on band expenses. When I heard that, the shit hit the fan. That's why he doubled the vocal tracks; he knew when I found out the money was gone I would quit. When the album did come out it wouldn't matter because he could tour and it would sound just like the album even if I wasn't there.

He claimed it was because my singing sucked, but that wasn't the case. I ran and did my daily vocal training while he constantly smoked weed. When he finally sang his voice was blown out after only one song. He even vomited in the vocal booth after hyperventilating. I had to come in and give him some vocal exercises so he could make it through his sessions. As to the legitimacy of what you've just read, don't just take my word for it. If you have any doubts, you could contact Century Media or the rest of the band members who could confirm everything I've said. As a footnote - all the music on the album that Harley claimed he wrote; that wasn't his either. He stole it from Kevin by pulling out old rehearsal tapes. When Kevin heard that we were releasing that stuff he threatened to sue. When Harley got wind of it he tried to pull a Charles Manson by telling me to climb in Kevin's window, steal all the Cro-Mags videotapes he compiled over the years and then inject him with tainted blood taken from a friend of his who was dying of AIDS. The bottom line was we never toured to support Alpha-Omega. The band broke up and soon after Harley would deliver his THIRD AND FINAL BETRAYAL, but this time he had a little help.

A year or so passed and I was in the process of putting together a new band. There was already label interest, so I contacted Century Media to get an artist release form. They told me point blank, "Harley signed each of you guys as individual artists and because we spent a large amount of money and never recouped a dime we're not releasing you." So here's the deal they gave me... finish the tracks from the Alpha-Omega sessions, tour the states so we can sell some records and we'll release you. That's what started me doing the band without Harley. He was off in California spending our money and shooting heroin while we were all broke and had no music happening because he signed our lives away. Fuck that! The album was called Near Death Experience and although Harley still claims to this day he didn't play on it, every bass note was his. The only thing I added to it was vocals. If you don't believe me, ask A.J. Novello (Leeway and Both Worlds) who did the guitar over-dubs on the record. I didn't like the music on that record. It was wack metal crap. But, like I said before... a brotha's gotta do, what a brotha's gotta do.

Shortly after I got back from the U.S. tour the phone calls started. Two, three, four in the morning. A junked-out Harley was on the line threatening that if I didn't stop using the name Cro-Mags and playing the music (which I co-wrote by the way) that he was going to rat me out for everything - being AWOL, selling weed, as well as a host of other shit. His exact words were, "Motherfucker, if you don't stop stealing my band you're gonna be locked up for so long you'll be fifty by the time you get out." I told him that wouldn't be a wise thing to do and I continued to tour despite his many threats.

In '95 Harley came back to New York and the first time I saw him he was playing drums with Murphy's Law during their St. Patrick's Day show. I was on stage while they played and he didn't say anything, but just kept shooting me this shit-eating grin all night. The next day, my pager went off while I was working on a construction job site. When I called the number back the voice on the other end of the line said, "Detective Negron, Ninth Precinct," which caught me totally off guard. I said, "Yeah... uhh... somebody paged me." His reply, "Is this John J. McGowan?" My heart skipped a beat, blood rushed to my head and I remembered leaning against the wall I just painted. No one ever used my real name. I went by John Joseph and now I had a detective calling me McGowan. I told him that it was and he said, "Do you know a Harley Flanagan and a Kevin "Parris" Mitchell Mayhew?" Again, I said, "Yes." He told me that they pressed charges on me and I needed to come down to the 9th Precinct and straighten everything out. I realized what was up; the anger kicked in and I distinctly remembered mumbling, "Those motherfuckers," into the phone. Then I said, "Listen detective, I know you know I'm AWOL so I'm going to the Navy to deal with that and then I'll be back to answer these bullshit charges." See if you turn yourself in the penalty is much less severe than if you get arrested and then the cops turn you over to the Navy. I hung up on the detective and slowly put the pieces together. Here's what went down.

Harley and Parris wanted to get the Cro-Mags back together, but the problem was I was touring as the 'Mags. They figured they had to get me out of the way and what better way to do that then to have me incarcerated? They went to the cops and made up a bunch of shit knowing that when they ran my name the warrants would come up. They gave the cops my beeper number, a photo of me from Age of Quarrel and told them I lived at 78 Second Avenue. Harley kept his word about ratting me out for everything. I'll tell you how I found that out a little later, but for now the race was on. I had to get out of town quickly. I was staying with E, so I called him and told him what was going on, but it seemed he already knew because 5-0 was at the apartment. E told me that there were no fewer then four detectives in the hallway and more downstairs because, conveniently for them, the 9th Precinct was right around the corner. After the cops left E threw together a bag of my clothes and I made plans to split New York.

Over the years, I'd had so many close calls with the cops and had gotten away, but ironically it took my two ex-band members to turn me in. The first thing I did was launch a press campaign against those scumbags. I called everyone to tell them that Harley and Parris had ratted me out. I thought, I might go down, but I'm letting everyone know the hows and the whys. After making about a hundred and fifty or so phone calls, I split to D.C. to stay with friends and figure out what to do next. That's when the New York hardcore scene saved the day. I needed a military attorney and a good one. The ironic thing was Harley's aunt, the 'accountant' (and I use the term loosely) at the helm for the Century Media deal, gave me this Navy commander's name a few years back just to see what he could do with my case. I still had his number so I called him from D.C. and he said he wanted $3,000 to handle it. That was a big problem because I was broke. So a bunch of bands threw together a benefit at Coney Island High and my hardcore family helped raise the money for my legal fees. The lawyer wanted payment pronto and the gig was a month away. My friend and tattoo artist Chris Garver (from the show Miami Ink) agreed to fork out the money providing he got paid back after the show.

I spent a month in D.C. and finally D-day came. I got in the commander's car and he was in full uniform, which looked impressive. We drove down to Norfolk Naval Station and just pulling through the main gate on Hampton Boulevard brought back a lot of memories. We walked into Nimitz Hall where they process all AWOLs and my lawyer announced, "This is seaman recruit McGowan. He's been AWOL for fifteen years." Every fuckin' pen in the place dropped and the sailors just looked up in shock. I believe they said I had the second longest AWOL status in Norfolk Naval history. After a few minutes of them arguing about who was going to get to do the mountain of paperwork on me I was taken into custody. My defense was to be that I was a conscientious objector and I spent years living as a Hare Krsna monk. My lawyer split but promised that he would do his best to expedite my case through the military channels that usually dragged their feet in these kinds of cases. "Be prepared to spend at least sixth months in Norfolk, McGowan," he said.

The first day I woke up at 4 a.m. and began chanting loudly up and down the isles of the dorm-like set up, which didn't sit too well with the other sailors. I remember waking up and thinking I was in a bad dream, but it was no dream, it was reality. As it turned out, my lawyer proved to have major legal juice. Within a few days I saw a judge and they decided not to court-martial me, which was very cool because that would have meant time in a military prison. I was getting an OTH (Other Than Honorable) discharge and I was sent back to Nimitz Hall for the two-month wait for the paperwork to come from Bupers in (Bureau of Personnel) in Washington, D.C.

More good fortune came my way. While I was under restrictions in Nimitz Hall and had to be head-counted every hour on the hour one sailor kept looking at me and finally said, "Dude, you look familiar. Where do I know you from?" I never saw this fucker before in my life. Then he said, "Holy shit, man. You're the singer for the Cro-Mags!" This guy was into hardcore music and before I knew it the entire population of punk and hardcore fuckers on that base knew I was there. Even the chief who ran the wing had a son who knew the band and he gave his dad a Cro-Mags album for me to sign, which gave me carte blanche. The chief brought me food from the health food store, he let me make free phone calls and I never had to muster for head counts. E and my bros from New York's Fun City Tattoos

- Jonathan Shaw, Chris Garver, Snake-Eyes and Big Dan New York - sent me several boxes of health food as well as some money. I was like, "Shit, I'm living better being locked up down here than I was in New York."

Within two weeks I had an I.D. card and was able to leave the base. Guess where I went first? You got it, NYC. My friend Kim bought me a plane ticket and that weekend I was on Avenue A. Guess who I saw? Kevin, and he was rather stunned when I tapped him on the shoulder in Ray's Candy Store. Actually he looked like he shit his pants and I said, "Looks like your little plan failed asshole." He stuttered, "Uhh...that's great." I looked him dead in his eyes with all the bad intent I could muster up and said, "No, what's great is now you two pieces of shit are gonna have to watch your backs every minute of the fuckin' day." I found out later he ran and called the cops telling them that I was back in New York.

Back in Norfolk things couldn't have been better. I saw a lot of the old crew from the early-'80s, including Vic Demise and a bunch of the others. I jumped out the window one night with my Squid posse after hours and we borrowed (okay... stole), this sailor's car and drove up to D.C. to see the Bad Brains. I took them to see Danzig and Korn at The Boathouse in Norfolk and we had backstage passes, which impressed the shit out of them. Spin magazine flew down to interview me and an interview also came out in the tattoo rag, International Tattoo. I did countless other interviews over the phone, letting the music world know what really had happened with the Cro-Mags. Everything Harley and Parris tried to do had backfired. Finally after three months I was discharged from the United States Navy and I headed back to New York.

I walked into the 9th Precinct and was immediately put in handcuffs. As for the charges, they were ridiculous. Harley said I called his grandmother and threatened to kill her and Kevin claimed I menaced him. They knew their cases would eventually be dropped, but what they also knew, and the reason they did it in the first place, was by having the cops check me out the military would come after me. Detective Negron handled my case with Kevin and another detective handled my case with Harley. This detective was actually really cool and he was impressed by my tattoo work. It turns out that he had been tattooed by my good friend, Jonathan Shaw. We shot-the-shit for a while and that's when he told me "I can't believe you were in a band with that guy Flanagan. He's a real prick. He came in here telling me everything under the sun about you and I had to tell him that I was only concerned about this case." He showed me Harley's statement in the police report and the Age of Quarrel album photo they gave to the cops to identify me. Harley made good on all those early morning calls to my house and in the months that followed he never showed his face anywhere downtown.

It was two years before he came around again. When he did I got a phone call at 2 a.m., that he was in CBGB's. I got dressed, walked over and knocked his ass out. He called it a sucker punch, and in all honesty, he was right, it was. My philosophy is this: if you try to have someone locked up for years … watch your back. I mean, after all, wasn't catching me off-guard by going to the cops just a different kind of sucker punch?

Kevin had me arrested on two other occasions so he could keep orders of protection against me. He even walked into my gym, Gladiators, where he never worked-out before. While I trained, he sat right across from me giving me dirty looks and talking shit. He challenged me to a fight and when I stepped outside he ran to the precinct and had me arrested for violating the order of protection he filed against me. He cost me lawyer fees, time in The Tombs and countless hours of community service, but it was my fault. He knew I had a bad temper and he used it to his advantage.

I've moved on and left the anger in the past because this book is about evolution and growth. The reason I went on in such detail about this whole thing is because of the lies and deceit that's been generated over the years by Harley and Parris on the Internet and in countless interviews. They even had the audacity to claim that I made all of this up. For years Parris and Harley have beaten a dead horse and ran their mouths claiming that I contributed basically nothing to the Age of Quarrel, which in fact, is a blatant lie. Just to clear the air for the Cro-Mags fans and to set the record straight once and for all, I wrote the following songs in their entirety without any influence from Harley and Parris. They include the tracks, "We Gotta Know," "Show You No Mercy," "Malfunction," "Seekers of the Truth," "It's the Limit," "By Myself," "Face the Facts," "Do Unto Others," and "Signs of the Times." I also wrote the chorus of "Hard Times," which amounts to ten out of the fifteen tracks on Age of Quarrel. Perhaps the reason Harley and Parris claimed I contributed nothing is due to the fact they illegally stole my publishing rights for the songs on the record, which I didn't get paid for.

So once and for all you got to hear the real story about what happened. Both of their names are on the police reports and when it comes to Kevin, I can understand, because he's always been a chump, but Mr. Punk Rock Harley Flanagan? Well, ratting people out to the cops ain't too punk, now is it?

I have to admit; I've always been a person to hold grudges. Some I've had for more than thirty years only because I've yet to confront certain individuals on the crap they did to me. I know that isn't a healthy way to go about life and I need to grow in that regard. In 2002 some of my close friends suggested I squash the beef with Harley and for my own personal growth forgive him for all the bullshit he's done and move on spiritually. At that point I was writing my film and writing about my childhood, which was a heavy thing for me, much heavier than I ever anticipated. Since I was trying to take steps in the healing process I knew forgiveness was the first step. In an effort to keep moving in the right direction I figured, what the hell, why not let it go and squash the beef with Harley? Well, for some strange reason that cat and I seem to have this vibe floating around because right around that time I got a call from him. I apologized for slugging him in the lobby of Manhattan's Electric Lady Studios and his exact words were, "I deserved it, bro." No Doubt.

That's the Cro-Mags saga in a nutshell and whatever you take away from it is up to you because there's no need to slant the story. I just presented the facts and the chain of events that led to the internal combustion and final destruction of the band. I guess when you have so many volatile personalities in one band chaos is inevitable. I was recently interviewed and asked how I felt about being one of the main influences in hardcore and punk. My answer was this: I don't give two shits about the fact that people got tattoos, played a certain kind of music, or dressed a certain way because of me. Over the years, what's been validating is when people come up to me and say, "Thanks. The message behind the lyrics on Age of Quarrel saved my life." At the end of the day, or the end of your life for that matter, all that really counts is how we led this life. Were we selfish or were we compassionate towards others? I can't even count the number of letters I got from people telling me that they were close to committing suicide, but when they heard "Malfunction" or "Seekers of the Truth" they knew someone else was struggling and if we could fight through it, so could they. That's the gift the Cro-Mags had to offer the world… an alternative, an answer, and the only reason we had that was because of Srila Prabhupada and the message of the Vedas. If we didn't we were just like every other knucklehead band singing about chicks, drugs, or how tough we are. Yeah, sure, we weren't the purest messengers, but then again, who could have imagined in their wildest dreams that some street hooligan musicians would get access to the Vedic blueprint on how to escape this material world and in our own warped way, inject that into our music. The bottom line is…I like to think that can never be contaminated no matter how big a bunch of screw-ups we were.

Lately, I find myself at one of the most positive places I've ever been in my life. Besides writing this book, which has been a real journey, I have a new band, Bloodclot and also have several screenplays and other books in the works. My spiritual practice, emotional state and training regimen are aligned perfectly and life finally seems to be balanced as all work in harmony with each other. Writing this book has definitely helped me exorcise a lot of the demons from my past, but it hasn't been the book alone that got me to where I am. It was good friends that did the trick for me; friends that were there when I needed them and friends that gave me the right advice.

I ate dinner at Vegetarian Paradise one night right before I finished this book and the fortune inside my fortune cookie said, "Depart not from the path and the relations fate has assigned you." I took it as one more confirmation that I'm finally in the right place. Besides friends pushing me through my uphill battles, there were four major events, all happening in close proximity to one another, all in their own way; meant to teach me a lesson. Each brought me to the level of sobriety, spiritual consciousness and appreciation for life I find myself at today. I honestly feel that God puts every test in front of us to make us grow. If He didn't, we'd become stagnant and complacent in our spiritual development.

Looking back, I see that each of these four events made me realize just how valuable life really is and that I shouldn't waste a single second of a day dwelling in negativity, but rather always act in a positive way toward others and help anyone who crosses my path. That in turn would make me a better person because this world won't change because of some governmental policy or United Nations resolution. It can only change if each individual one of us grows, one soul at a time.

As I made plans after Christmas of '99 with my girlfriend for the New Year's millennium celebration the phone rang in my Brooklyn apartment. I picked it up and the voice on the other end said, "Hi, John. This is your father." I stood there stunned. I remember thinking I'd always know exactly what to say when this day arrived. I thought, "I'd give that fucker a piece of my mind, just wait." The truth was I couldn't. I was speechless and for anyone who knows me, that doesn't usually happen. My reply after a brief pause was a straight up, "Fuck you," before I hung up. Not very witty but hey, it got the point across. Now I don't know if all the Y2K doomsday predictions finally gave the prick an ounce of conscience, or there was some curiosity on his part to see how I turned out. Whatever the case may be I had no desire to see him or talk to him. I do however want to thank him publicly for being an asshole, because had it not been for him, I might have led some boring, run-of-the-mill life. So let's make it official...Thanks Dad! Adversity builds character and one thing I got from all the shit I went through as a result of you being a schmuck is a bit of character.

My brothers E and Frank got similar phone calls and they decided to meet with him. E had met someone in Astoria who knew our dad and knew where he was, so E gave him his number (and then mine, thanks a lot bro) and the guy passed it on. As it turns out my dad is still a scammer and a scrapper. He had kids with another woman and I have a half-sister, who by the way ended up staying with Frank. After she binged-out on coke with him for a week, she robbed Frank's remaining blow, money and jewelry. She split in the middle of the night and has not been heard from since. Don't you just love family?

After I hung up I thought it would be easy to forget the entire thing, but what happened in the weeks and months that followed made me angry and confused. First I thought, "Fuck him I don't need him at this point." Then as I let it sink in I became angry. If he really wanted to try and make amends with me why did he give up after just one phone call? I remember calling girls a half a dozen times to finally get them to go out with my ass. Doesn't he owe me more than one call? At first I shrugged it off in typical tough guy, "nothing can get to me, fuck you" fashion. As time passed and I reminisced about all the suffering I went through as a result of him, it opened up a lot of wounds that I thought had healed.

The truth was they hadn't, they just became nasty scars. Scars of abandonment, inadequacy, unimportance, the feeling of being unwanted and that no one loved or cared about me. Not to mention reminiscing over all the shit that was done to me as a kid. The scars were now open and they were oozing. I became angry at the sense of unimportance my existence meant to him and unfortunately that anger ended up being directed at those around me, those I cared about. When you break a bone and don't have it set properly the doctor has to re-break the bone to fix it. Well, my wounds had not healed and for some reason I was being forced to deal with them. My mom went through a messy divorce with this asshole named George and he basically scammed her out of the house they bought and fixed up together. He amassed huge gambling debts and took out homeowner's loans without her knowledge. She walked away with nothing and no place to live. After staying in an apartment where the woman landlord was a total bitch to her, I got her a nice place in Astoria and footed the bill. Yeah, deep down inside I still had some resentment toward her for everything. I knew it wasn't the right thing to do because I swore way back when I saw those old lonely people at Martin's Corner that I would never let my mom be like that. Several months later she dropped a bombshell on me...her old boyfriend Carl was back in her life and, wait it gets even better, he was going to move into the apartment I was paying for.

This was the same Carl who dated her in the late-'60s and '70s, who knew we were being abused at the Valentis' and still gave my mom the ultimatum... them or me. My mom always picked the wrong guys. From my father who probably would have eventually killed her, to her husband George who ripped her off and was fucking someone else behind her back, to Carl. To hear he was back in the picture was like a knife twisting in my gut and I expressed that to her with some choice four letter expletives. But the fact was I wanted my mom to be happy and so I went along with it. She was lonely and depressed and if that's what she wanted, I had to accept it unconditionally.

Soon after they got back together I sent them on an all-expense paid trip to Vegas. My mom was and still is a hopeless romantic and always told me about how her dream was to meet a nice fella and go to Vegas with him to see the shows. She didn't even care about the gambling. I mean, sure, she played a few slots, but she came from a romantic and glamorous period and Vegas represented that to her. She loved Carl no matter what he did in the past; cheated, was an asshole, forced her to abort their child and kept her away from her kids. None of that mattered and I believe spiritually he came back into our lives so that we learned something and the reason was a few months later he announced he had cancer.

Carl was always a mean, tough son of a bitch and hated just about everything and everyone except for his small circle of friends. He was from the old-school, the Frank Sinatra clan and I think he drove Ol' Blue Eyes around in his limo on more than one occasion. Carl loved Sinatra. In fact, he fuckin' worshiped the guy like a demigod. Carl talked the tough talk, but he could walk the walk, too. When he first took interest in my mom after we were in foster care, my dad came around and Carl kicked his ass and made several threats about what would happen to him if he bothered her again. Well, my dad took them seriously and was never heard from again. Carl reminded me of the Archie Bunker character from All in the Family at full throttle and nothing got to him. He was fearless, but cancer and the thought of dying scared the living shit out of him.

The prognosis was not good because the cancer spread throughout his body and the chemo wasn't working. I could see my mom wanted to break down on more than one occasion, but she couldn't. She had to be strong. To see someone you love disintegrate before your eyes and wither away is not easy. She chose not to put him in some hospital or hospice either. She cared for him the entire time driving him around to all the hospitals and it eventually took its toll on her.

Through it all Carl was changing and he was becoming a different person. That summer he would come and sit on my stoop with my mom and we would just talk about life. I could see he was in terrible pain and getting worse, but he never complained or spoke about his condition. He didn't have to because the outcome was inevitable. I saw this bitter, tough guy with tears in his eyes, and not because he felt sorry for himself. I believe it was because he was dying and his own family wasn't there for him. Here was a woman he left almost thirty years earlier and the kids that he didn't want around, who helped him during his time of need.

During his last days I brought him holy water from the Ganges River, sacred flowers from the temple and put a tape player in his room that played spiritual music around the clock. Carl died a few weeks before 9/11 and he left his body listening to the Hare Krsna Maha-Mantra, which according to the Vedic literatures meant he automatically got a higher birth in his next life. That experience taught me one very important lesson: it's never too late for someone to change. When they do you have to be ready to forgive because when all was said and done with Carl, underneath that tough guy exterior, there was a kind soul waiting to come out and it did. That was his TRUE CHARACTER.

By the time summer of 2001 rolled around my brother Frank was whacked out on coke and drinking heavily. He had abandoned his two teenage sons for half their lives. That's when I got the phone call that his girlfriend and mother of his six-year-old daughter stabbed Frank right in front of their child. When Frank left the house after an argument she ran up behind him and plunged a knife deep into him, missing vital organs by centimeters. The cops wanted to charge her for attempted murder, but Frank eventually dropped the charges for the sake of their daughter. Now, sure, Frank was a fuck up, but I also happen to know the girl he was with was a complete psycho and was the cause of a lot of the trouble in their relationship. Some years back Frank stayed with me while they were homeless and she had to go back to live with her mother, with the child. She wasn't happy about this so she kept leaving him messages on my machine, which typically went like this, "Frank did you find an apartment? Frank I need money to move out of here. Frank you're a loser. Frank! Frank! Frank!" One day I came home to this message: "Frank I'm sick of your shit. I hate living here. If you don't get me an apartment I will... I am... going back to whipping ass and giving enemas!" And she meant it, too. She used to be a dominatrix who shit and pissed on people and did all kinds of other weird shit for money. Well for me that did it. I was officially pissed. No pun intended. I called her mom's house and I left that whipping ass and enema message on her mom's machine fifteen times in a row. It turned out momma-dukes had no idea what her sweet little daughter was up to. It seems that the whip her daughter claimed was for her horseback riding classes wasn't, and all those enema boxes in her room weren't there because she had irritable bowel syndrome

On September 9, 2001 I got a call from the lady who was letting Frank sleep in the dirty attic of her house. She said point blank, "If you don't do something with Frank he's going to be dead soon." Frank always had a good heart. He was a great guy, but he took what happened to us as kids the hardest. He was the youngest of the three and the most vulnerable and didn't know how to deal with all the pain he suffered. As a result, he did what most victims of child abuse do...never tell anyone and destroy themselves self-medicating with the help of drugs and alcohol.

The next day I showed up at Frank's job on Staten Island to conduct my intervention. He was dirty, tired, extremely thin and very surprised to see me. I told him I booked him a plane ticket to Puerto Rico for the following day. I promised that if he put up an argument I was going to kick his ass, drag him onto the Staten Island Ferry and bring him back to my house. On the ferry ride over to Lower Manhattan he just kept thanking me for my gesture. I knew he meant it because he was crying and in the worst shape I'd ever seen him in.

On Sept. 11, Frank was scheduled to fly out of New York, but after the second plane hit the Twin Towers I knew that wasn't going to happen. We witnessed the rest of the day's events from my rooftop and every roof on the LES was packed with spectators. It was so surreal. I couldn't believe it was happening. I remember seeing millions of tiny glass particles from the windows and façade of the building reflecting in the sunlight as they fell to Earth. It was mesmerizing, like the jewel on the head of a serpent, because I knew what it meant. The world would never be the same. We saw people jumping to their deaths and when the first tower fell thousands lost their lives. I also heard the collective scream for blocks. When I looked through the dust cloud I thought maybe just the top fell off, but when the smoke cleared all I kept saying was, "Holy, shit. It's fuckin' gone."

Then the second tower fell and we also heard the Pentagon had been hit. As a footnote on how burnt Frank was, when the first tower fell he saw someone on an adjacent rooftop that worked in a bar in St. Thomas. Frank runs over to the guy like he's at a rooftop party and yells, "Hey Dude! What's up bro? Yo, John. This dude made the best margaritas on the whole island." Then he started introducing everyone and I'm like, "Frank shut the fuck up, thousands of people just died!"

I sat glued to the TV in the days that followed crying as people held up pictures of their loved-ones begging for someone to call who might have information as to their whereabouts. The smells of Ground Zero crept up the West Side Highway and made their way through my living room window. I can honestly say that after 9/11 my life was changed forever. The days that followed really showed what a lot of people were made of. There was no middle ground it seemed; you either went one way or the other. On one side you had people helping down at Ground Zero, or at hospitals, or wherever they could in order to keep hope alive. Others appreciated life and family and even got more spiritual (it's a fact, after 9/11 he churches, synagogues, temples and yoga centers in NYC were packed). Then on the flipside there were a lot of people who I personally saw relapse into drug and alcohol consumption and unfortunately, after returning from Puerto Rico a month later, Frank was one of them.

For me the events of that day were a wake-up call to humanity as a whole. In New York everyone got real spiritual for a minute and people acted kindly toward each other. I went to Union Square Park with some devotees, sat down on a blanket and chanted for hours. People joined in by the dozens and if anything positive can come out of such an atrocious act, let it be that we all strive to be better human beings, filled with the compassion I saw in the days after 9/11. Then at least those 3,000 plus victims who lost their lives that day didn't do so in vain and we can honor their sacrifice in some way.

Shortly after my fortieth birthday things got pretty bad between my mom and me. Not only was I writing this book, I was also writing a movie and I based the lead character's childhood on a lot of the stuff I went through. So naturally getting that call from my dad and actually re-living all the shit as I wrote about it was heavy. It was like a cloud of explosive fumes that just needed a small spark to ignite and it came one day on a phone call with my mom. We were arguing because she owed me a bit of money. I was dead broke and about to lose my apartment. I needed her to pay it back, but she didn't have it. Over the years I held a lot of resentment in my heart toward her because I honestly felt she could have done more for us when we were kids. Anger poured out of me and I yelled, "You never loved me. Otherwise you would have taken us out of that home. You loved E, he was the one you cared about. You got rid of me and Frank." My mother begged me to stop saying the hurtful things I was saying, but I couldn't. I had to get it out and so I continued on saying some pretty horrible things I never said before. Finally she broke down sobbing, "I never planned to have you. Your father beat and raped me!" I was stunned and fell silent. She went on, "Everyone said I should get an abortion, but I couldn't. You were my child. I was a kid and I was scared. He did the same thing again and then I had your younger brother Frank. Gene was the only child I was prepared to have, but I loved all three of you just the same. It killed me to have to give you guys up." I was silent as she sat on the other end sobbing. I began to cry, too.

It took my mom forty years to tell me, through her tears, that my father, the welterweight fighter, stumbled drunk to her house, right around New Year's 1962, and brutally raped her. Now it all made sense. Now I know why she had to give us up. Now I knew I had to forgive her for leaving us at the Valentis'. When I was twenty I didn't know my ass from my elbow. By the time she was twenty she had three young boys, no way to support us and was being beaten-up constantly by my dad. That was a huge turning point in our relationship and since then we've been closer than ever. What separated us for so many years now made us closer. I finally got to hear her side of it and now I realized what she went through. I've gained a new respect and love for her and I truly believe she's one of the strongest people I know. As bad as the circumstances may have been for me, in comparison to what she's been through, they were nothing. She had to give up her babies.

In a lot of ways my mom telling me her secret was the final thing that made my healing complete. Going through each of these things, whether it was learning about my conception, or having to reflect upon my childhood as a result of my father surfacing, or watching someone die and learning to forgive, or 9/11… each forced me to look inside myself and do a serious gut check. Each gave me that push I needed to get up that hill.

After more than a decade of writing down thoughts and memories that filled dozens of notebooks, I began writing this book at the urging of my screenplay writing partner and good friend Priscilla Sommer who kept saying, "Your stories are crazy dude. Get them shits out." Well, it started with one sentence, "The last memory I have of my father was the night he kicked down our door and beat my mom…" The story poured onto the pages from there and almost six years later, here it is. There's no doubt I entered this world into some pretty tough circumstances. When I wrote about the orphanages, foster homes, bread bags, beatings, dog biscuits, street hustles, police chases, lock-ups, Navy adventures, cult scams, crazy tours and betrayals, I thought, "Through all the crap I'd been through in my life it seemed Krsna always protected me, always gave me another chance to do the right thing." I believe karma from my past life put me in some pretty hellish situations in the beginning of this one, having grown up with no family; but music and spirituality came as a blessing from God and has taken me all over the world. I've been to Malaysia, Japan, Singapore, Australia, Europe, Hawaii and Puerto Rico and I am also planning an upcoming spiritual journey to the holy land of India.

I can't even begin to tell you the feelings I've had inside over the years, as I got up at sunrise wherever I was on the planet and did my morning rituals… chanting meditation and a nice long run to see the local culture. My life has always been about turning adversity and negative situations into positive ones. My motivation to write this book wasn't to make people feel sorry for me, or pat myself on the back for any of my accomplishments, but to connect to everyone out there who struggles day-to-day with life and its hurdles. If I can make it through the adversity anyone can. When we strip away all the intellectual, mental, as well as physical aspects that make up our gross and subtle bodies and go beyond them to our real self, the spiritual spark, we're all made of the same thing and we all have the potential for unlimited greatness. Statistically I probably was doomed to fail just as so many predicted, but my spirituality pulled me back from the brink of disaster each time. That was especially true when the con artists who hijacked the Hare Krsna Movement sidetracked that spirituality.

I've always searched for unconditional love, as we all do, and what we find on our search as we invest our love usually amounts to one disappointment after another. As human beings we have the tendency to make mistakes, which everyone has. The biggest mistake we can make in this world is to invest our love and not have it reciprocated. I've made that mistake over and over again and so now I choose to invest my love in those I know I can trust. The thing about mistakes is they're tests and if we're willing to pick ourselves up after each failure there's always another shot. I've had my ups and downs, highs and lows. That's what life's about. That's why in yoga they teach you to go beyond dualities; there is no good, there is no bad, there's just the goal. That goal is to get out of this material world and go back home to Godhead.

We have to fight the right fight against ignorance. I think the Cro-Mags lyrics to the song "Life of my Own" said it best: "You come into this world with nothing except yourself...you leave this world with nothing except yourself," and whatever advancement you've made spiritually.

Even if one person is helped by what's contained in the pages of this book, it was a success. I believe so strongly in what Srila Prabhupada's teachings on Bhakti-Yoga have personally done for me that I'm willing to send that knowledge to you for free. Just shoot me an e-mail to the address at the back of this book and I'll send it out right away.

I honestly feel the world's religions as a whole have failed humanity because of their dogmatic, sectarian views that their God is the only God and their way the only way. Real spirituality is not like that, and as you search on your path in life you'll see what I mean. Knowledge is power and when we get that power we must apply it practically to our lives; as Srila Prabhupada himself always said, "We don't want armchair philosophers." What he did want was spiritual warriors who take action and that's why if I have one message to give, let it be the code by which the true warrior lives: NEVER GIVE UP.

Srila Prabhupada built a house for the whole world to live in and the front door is always wide open for all to enter. From the inciting incident of this story the balance of my life has been disrupted, and I've struggled through so many phases to restore it. Balance for me is family, and now that I've entered this house of love, I've gained a loving, universal family, and that love is unconditional.

BALANCE RESTORED. Peace and Hare Krsna.

credits

Edited by John Z
Project advisor Stephanie Swane
Art direction and design by Todd Irwin
for The Irwin Slater Organization
Cover photography Forest Barber
Graphic design by Tara Keleher and Seungwon Lee
Additional editing by Stephanie Swane and Erin Fierst
Proofing Steve Marlowe

acknowledgements

Mom, "E" McGowan, Frank McGowan Sr. and Jr., Sean McGowan, Blaise, Todd "Meato" Irwin, Paul Slater, Brahma & Mother Vani, Stephanie Swane, Megan La Framboise ♡, Jon Z, Priscilla Sommer, The IRM Devotees, Sacha Jenkins, Scott Roberts, Jen Irwin, Bliss, Lego, Mike Rappaport, Lars and Tim (Rancid), Bad Brains, Lemme & Motorhead, Steve Marcus, Bleu L., Brian Callen & Vicki Morgan Spurlock, Billy "Straight Edge" Cox, AJ Novello, Joe Hardcore, Johnny Pain and the FSU Crew (thanks for fighting the good fight), Ricky Powell, Max Wilker, Jinx-Proof Running Crew, Pieter Coolen, Danny Ilchuk, Mackie, Patty Jenkins (my inspiration), Mr. Robert McKee, Dan Edge & the Montreal crew, Gee-Bee, Adam Y. (Beasties), Paget, Madball, Pete Abordi, Graham (Aussie Crew), Doug Crosby, Tim Borer, Nos (Hawaii) Grant, Jamey Jasta, Keene (Team), Bloodclot, Cousin Joe, Jan (Germany), Jay Dublee, Mark Pollack, Brooklyn, Ezec, Sam Sheridan, Chris (Skid), Gary Hanna, Loki & crew, Peter Nussabaum, Jack Marshall, Chris Garver, Snake Eyes, Dito, Moby, Dirty Dan, 40oz Frankie, Al (Dropkicks) and all those who fight for truth, no matter the cost.

For free literature on Yoga and Meditation
you can email John at johnjoseph@punkhouse.org